Religion
and the Law
in America

RELIGION AND THE LAW IN AMERICA

An Encyclopedia of Personal Belief and Public Policy

VOLUME 1

Scott A. Merriman

A B C ☰ C L I O

Santa Barbara, California   Denver, Colorado   Oxford, England

Library of Congress Cataloging-in-Publication Data
Merriman, Scott A.
Religion and the law in America : an encyclopedia of personal belief and public policy / Scott A. Merriman.
　　p.　cm.
　Includes bibliographical references and index.
　978-1-85109-863-7 (hardcopy : alk. paper) — 978-1-85109-864-4 (ebook)
　　1. Freedom of religion—United States—Encyclopedias.　2. Religion and law—United States—Encyclopedias.　3. Church and state—United States—Encyclopedias.　4. Religion and law—United States—Cases.　I. Title.

　KF4783.A68M47 2007
　342.7308'5203—dc22

　　　　　　　　　　　　2007002579

11　10　09　08　07　　　1　2　3　4　5　6　7　8　9　10

Production Editor: Vicki Moran
Editorial Assistant: Sara Springer
Production Manager: Don Schmidt
Media Editor: J. R. Withers
Media Resources Coordinator: Ellen Brenna Dougherty
Media Resources Manager: Caroline Price
File Manager: Paula Gerard

ABC-CLIO, Inc.
130 Cremona Drive, P.O. Box 1911
Santa Barbara, California 93116-1911

This book is also available on the World Wide Web as an ebook. Visit http://www.abc-clio.com for details.

This book is printed on acid-free paper ∞

Manufactured in the United States of America

To my mentors who have been teachers,
inspirers, believers, prophets, and friends;
to my wife, Jessie, who has been all of those
and more; and to my daughter, Caroline,
who makes me laugh and smile.

CONTENTS

VOLUME 2

INTRODUCTION

Freedom of religion is probably the freedom that Americans hold the dearest, at least publicly. However, the limits of that freedom, and the limits of the corresponding First Amendment clause against a governmental establishment of religion, are very murky, especially when the freedom of one individual's religion begins to clash with the prohibition against the government's establishment. This encyclopedia identifies some of the boundaries of those freedoms, seeks to explain the overall development of the freedom of religion, and highlights some of the important judicial decisions that have shaped it. The encyclopedia discusses the interaction between religion and the law in America; it does not aim to give legal advice.

Before we look at the history of freedom of religion in America, a short explanation is in order about the workings of the U.S. court system and how cases come before the U.S. Supreme Court. The Supreme Court is generally seen as the top court in America—and it is, for America, especially in the area of religion. However, in many matters, the U.S. Supreme Court is mostly irrelevant as one can take a case to that court only if the federal Constitution is in some way involved. Thus, if the matter involves a state law and no provision of the U.S. Constitution is implicated, the case must end at the highest level of state courts and often does not even get there. If only the state constitution or a state law is involved, the case would probably begin in the lowest state court, and if an acquittal occurred (assuming it was a criminal case) the matter would end there. If a conviction occurred, or if a civil case was decided under a civil law (civil law is concerned with personal rights, such as contracts), then whoever lost could appeal it; if the person did not

appeal, the matter would end. Many cases end just like that. Above the lower court is an appeals court (even though each state's court system has different names for each level), and there can be more than one level of appeals courts. The loser there can again appeal, and the state's highest court often has choice, or what is called discretionary authority, to decide whether to hear the appeals. After the highest level of the state court, if there is a federal constitutional issue involved, like the First Amendment for issues of religion, the case can be appealed to the U.S. Supreme Court. The federal court system hears all cases under federal law, whether civil or criminal law, and also can hear cases involving federal issues that began in state court. Cases start at the district court level; there are ninety-four district courts, with most handling the cases that arise in a certain geographical district. The loser (except in the case of an acquittal with a criminal trial) can always appeal the verdict from the district court to a circuit court of appeals. There are thirteen circuit courts of appeals in the United States, and all but one have geographical jurisdictions (the last handles almost all cases dealing with patents, trademarks, and trade, among others, from across the nation). The circuit courts of appeals generally must hear the cases brought before them, and appeals can be taken from these courts to the U.S. Supreme Court. The U.S. Supreme Court, however, has discretion in deciding what cases it hears, and at least four Supreme Court justices must vote to hear a case before it will be heard. The Supreme Court also hears relatively few cases—only around one hundred cases a year in recent years.

The American colonies were founded for many different reasons, and as many different desires led people to come to this country;

only one of these was religion. Thus, the often cherished idea that people came to America solely for religious freedom is clearly not true. However, it is also true, obviously, that religion did motivate some. Many of the early colonies had established churches, as religious freedom meant, to many early colonial leaders, freedom to practice the religion of the colony's founders, not freedom to practice any religion (and certainly not the freedom to be without a religion). Many pitched ideological battles were fought over religion in the early colonies, and a few—most notably Rhode Island and Pennsylvania—expressly granted toleration to all religions. By the time of the American Revolution, official churches had been removed in several colonies, and the trend was clearly to slowly move away from an official church.

The American Revolution itself did little to change religion, but the colonies all had to create their own constitutions once independence had been declared, and this process led some to formally remove the state-supported church or to alter its status. The national government created during the American Revolution also did little with religion, but this was in large part because the Articles of Confederation gave the federal government little power in any area. When the time came to change the articles, the result was our current Constitution (even though it has been amended several times since). The new Constitution gave much more power to the central government, enough that some people became nervous, fearing that a tyrannical government would emerge and that all the people's rights would disappear. This fear was not sufficient to stop the Constitution's adoption, but it was pervasive enough that several states called for the national government to adopt a bill of rights that would spell out the limits on the federal government. The first Congress undertook this assignment, and James Madison was the leading figure in the discussions. He took the states' suggestions and drafted a number of dif-

ferent amendments; after discussion in the Congress, twelve were formulated and passed on to the states for ratification. The states passed all but the first two of those, and the resulting ten amendments became what we today know as the Bill of Rights. The First Amendment reads, "Congress shall make no law respecting an establishment of religion, or prohibiting the free exercise thereof; or abridging the freedom of speech, or of the press, or the right of the people peaceably to assemble, and to petition the government for a redress of grievances." Thus, the First Amendment contains two parts, both a prohibition against the government's establishment of a religion and the prohibition against the government's interference with someone's freedom of religion. The first part has frequently been called the establishment clause and the second part the free exercise clause, and neither is, obviously, self-defining.

Even though there is ambiguity about the First Amendment's precise boundaries in the area of religion, the First Amendment seldom came before the Supreme Court in the first one and a half centuries after the amendment's passage. This was largely due to two factors. The first was that the First Amendment was held to apply only to federal actions. Thus, if a state acted in a way that might be viewed as infringing a person's freedom of religion or as establishing a religion, the First Amendment did not come into consideration. If a state constitution had provisions similar to those of the First Amendment, the state's law might still be unconstitutional, but it would be so because it violated the state constitution, not the federal one. The reason was because the Supreme Court in 1833 ruled that the Bill of Rights limited only the federal government and did not limit the state governments. The second is that the states were the most likely bodies, particularly at the time, to pass laws in the area of religion. The federal government did not concern itself much with education or personal conduct in the states, and those are the areas where most questions of religion arise today. Thus, it is not surprising that few cases involving religion made it to the Supreme Court.

In the few that did, federal power was generally upheld at the expense of religion. In the last half of the nineteenth century, the federal government did pass laws that regulated conduct in the federal territories, and some of these involved religion. The best-known law was one banning polygamy (or being married to multiple women at the same time), which was passed in 1862. The law was aimed at the Mormon Church in the Utah territory, as it sanctioned multiple marriages among its church leaders. Congress passed a series of laws directed against that practice, eventually removing the vote from anyone who publicly supported the practice and revoking the charter of the Mormon Church. The Supreme Court, starting in 1879 and running through the 1890s, decided several cases that upheld the right of the federal government to pass such laws, holding that churches advocating illegal acts were not protected by the freedom of religion clause and that illegal practices, even when based in religion, were still illegal. Those decisions have not been overturned and are still binding precedents today.

The First Amendment's religion clauses increased in both importance and frequency of use in court cases starting in 1925. In that year, the Supreme Court held that the Fourteenth Amendment extended the reach of the First Amendment. The Fourteenth Amendment had been passed after the Civil War to protect the rights of the former slaves, and it held that state governments could not, among other things, infringe upon anyone's right of liberty without due process of law. The Supreme Court in 1925 held that liberty included some of the items that many Americans hold dear, and the Court specifically mentioned the freedom of the press and the freedom of speech contained in the First Amendment. This meant that state actions that infringed upon our liberties, not just federal actions, might be held unconstitutional under the First Amendment. The Supreme Court did not give any reason for deciding to interpret the Fourteenth Amendment in this way, nor did they give a reason for not including the freedom of religion, but the case in question involved freedom of speech and the press, and that probably was why these were the only two freedoms mentioned. It is also clear that the liberty mentioned in the Fourteenth Amendment is not self-defining, and so the Supreme Court was right to define it, regardless of one's opinion on whether the First Amendment is part of that liberty. In 1940, the Supreme Court took the next step in applying the First Amendment against the states and held that the liberty of the Fourteenth Amendment which limited the states included the freedom of religion. Thus, states could no longer infringe upon the free exercise of religion, and in 1947 the Supreme Court completed the process by adding that states could not create an establishment of religion either. In twenty-two short years, the Court moved the religion clauses of the First Amendment from being relevant only in federal actions to applying in all state actions. This process greatly expanded the scope of the First Amendment and protected more of our freedom of religion and limited the government much more in what it could do in terms of establishing a religion. Since 1947, there has not been much serious reconsideration of reversing these decisions and thus applying the First Amendment only to the federal government again.

Instead, for the last half century, the Supreme Court has been forced to consider a wide range of government actions, on both the state and federal levels, which people have considered as either creating an establishment of religion or interfering with a person's freedom of religion. The general trend of the courts, over the long term, has been to increase the protections and to decrease government power, but that trend has become less pronounced in recent years. The first Court to consider issues in this area was the Stone

Court, which examined state provisions ordering students to say the Pledge of Allegiance and state restrictions on religious canvassing. (Supreme Courts are frequently described by the name of the chief justice at the time, and thus the Stone Court was the Court led by Harlan Stone. The current Court would be thus described as the Roberts Court.) In the first cases, several Jehovah's Witnesses objected to states' requirements that they recite the Pledge of Allegiance. The Jehovah's Witnesses believed that swearing an oath to a flag was worshiping a graven image, and that worship had been banned by the Bible. Thus, being forced to state the pledge was a violation of their free exercise of religion. The Supreme Court at first upheld the states' requirement that students recite the pledge, but three years later (in 1943) the Court reversed itself and held that the free exercise of religion portion of the Constitution prohibited states from ordering students to recite the pledge. The Stone Court also considered a case dealing with a conviction of a Jehovah's Witness as he had gone through a town trying to convince people to join his religion. The man had been orderly, but his religious message had been opposed and so the Jehovah's Witness had been convicted of a "breach of the peace," or what most people today might describe as disorderly conduct. As the only reason for his conviction had been opposition to his religion, the Supreme Court overturned his conviction, stating that religious conduct, if it was legal, was protected by the First Amendment. This expanded the free exercise of religion portion of the First Amendment to include some religious acts as well as religious beliefs.

The next Court, the Vinson Court, continued to deal with religion cases. Most of their major cases addressed "released-time" programs, which allowed students to be released from their public school classrooms to attend religion classes. The Supreme Court first struck down a program permitting students to be released to attend classes in their own schools, as

they held that the government was establishing a religion; but a few years later, the Court allowed a program that released students to attend programs at sites off the school grounds. This was believed to be a reasonable accommodation of religion that did not rise to the level of being an establishment of religion. The Supreme Court also upheld a program that reimbursed parents for the cost of transportation to religious schools, holding that this program was neutral in the area of religion; it did not favor religious schools over public schools as transportation was being provided to both.

The Warren Court, much to the consternation of many conservatives, considered several freedom of religion cases in its later years and provoked much controversy. In 1962, the Court considered a case involving mandatory Bible reading and reciting of the Lord's Prayer to open each school day. The Court struck down this program as an establishment of religion, as it put the force of the state behind the Christian religion. The next year, the Court considered a state-mandated prayer from New York and struck down this program as well, once again holding it to be an establishment of religion. These two decisions sparked a firestorm of protest. People saw this as taking God out of the public schools, and many saw communism as the driving force for the decision. One of the main differences between the United States and the USSR, America's opponent in the Cold War, was the importance of Christianity in the United States (the USSR was atheist), and this decision seemed to undermine that difference. The Warren Court also entered the area of evolution in the public schools for the first time, striking down an Arkansas law that banned the teaching of evolution. The Court held that the only purpose of this law was to protect the Christian religion and such a law was an unconstitutional establishment of religion. The Warren Court returned to an area associated with religion in 1967, that of marriage. Marriage is, for many people, both a religious and a civil issue, even though the state considers it only in the civil context. Some states in the South had banned marriages between people of different races and the Supreme Court struck down this ban, holding it to be a violation of people's privacy to tell them that they could not marry someone of a different race. The Supreme Court also, although it was not as controversial as the other decisions, held that a state cannot impose a substantial burden upon someone's free exercise of religion unless there is a compelling interest behind that burden. This greatly increased the free exercise of religion.

After the Warren Court came the Burger Court, which many expected to roll back the Warren Court's decisions in many areas, including that of religion. However, the Burger Court mostly maintained things the way they were rather than advancing or rolling back the decisions of previous courts. In 1971, the Supreme Court set up a test for determining the constitutionality of any given government regulation. The Court held that regulations had to have a secular purpose, had to have a primary effect of neither enhancing nor hurting religion, and had to avoid an excessive entanglement of the state and religion. That test, although often challenged, still in many ways remains the basis of the tests used today. In 1972, the Supreme Court entered an area that has become even more charged with religion than it was then, that of abortion. In *Roe* v. *Wade,* the Court held that laws preventing abortion, especially in the first trimester of pregnancy, must generally yield to a woman's privacy interest. The Burger Court continued the Warren Court's trend in the general area of religion, holding that a state could not order Amish children to attend school past the eighth grade as this would damage the Amish religion, thus again upholding the free exercise of religion versus governmental attempts to regulate general conduct. The Supreme Court also continued to be active in the area of governmental aid to private schools, mostly striking down any direct aid and being very restrictive in what type of general aid was

allowed that also went to private religious schools. The Court also forbade private schools from receiving government aid on school grounds. Thus, programs that aided students in private schools might be legal off school grounds, such as remedial tutoring, but not on school grounds. In 1980, the Supreme Court dealt with the issue of posting the Ten Commandments in schools, holding that the state could not order their display as this was an establishment of religion. In 1983, though, the Supreme Court did allow tax deductions for parental expenses for education, even though most of the deductions taken were for expenses at religious schools. The Burger Court in 1985 dealt with another major issue of religion and the law in the form of a moment of silence. Arkansas had passed a law allowing a moment of silence for "meditation or prayer" and the Court held that the mention of prayer made this unconstitutional as the state was telling you how to spend your moment of silence.

The Rehnquist Court, lasting from 1986 to 2005, dealt with a plethora of cases dealing with religious issues and issues associated with religion. In 1987, evolution again entered the Supreme Court, as the Court struck down a Louisiana law mandating that evolution and creation science be given equal amounts of time in the classroom. Proponents of creation science argued that there was scientific evidence to back up a literal reading of the book of Genesis, and the Court held that the ordering of this scientific idea along with evolution amounted to an establishment of religion. In 1990, the Supreme Court returned to the issue of the general regulation of conduct in areas associated with religion, holding that the state could regulate conduct if it had a general reason to do so, and did not need a compelling state interest; so the Court upheld an Oregon law banning peyote use, which conflicted with the religion of some Native Americans. The Supreme Court in 1992 dealt with school prayer, holding that school prayer at graduations, even when it was nondenominational, was still unconstitutional as it amounted to government promotion of religion. In 1997, the Court struck down a congressional law aimed at overturning the 1990 decision and thus forcing states and Congress to have a compelling state interest to regulate religion-related conduct. The Court also reversed an earlier court decision, and held that private schools could receive aid on their grounds, as long as the aid was of a secular nature.

The new decade did not bring an end to religious cases or controversial ones in the Supreme Court. In 2002, the Court upheld an Ohio law allowing the use of vouchers in the schools. Vouchers allowed parents to choose whether their students attended private school or public school, under certain circumstances, and if private school was chosen the state would pay for part of the cost. Many private schools are, of course, religious, and so this program, in one side's view, seemed to allow the state to subsidize religion, and in the other, it allowed school choice and better schools. The Supreme Court allowed the program, holding that the state was not establishing religion as the parents' choice, not the state, was directing the money into the religious schools. In 2003, the Court turned to an area that is tinged with religion—homosexual rights. The Court struck down a Texas law that penalized only homosexual sodomy. The Court did not consider religion, even though religion is the basis of many people's opposition to giving any rights to homosexuals or their conduct. In 2004, the Pledge of Allegiance returned to the Supreme Court, as a parent protested his child being forced to say the pledge; the parent claimed that as the pledge, in its current incarnation, contained the words "under God," this constituted an establishment of religion. The Supreme Court avoided the issue, holding that the parent did not have custody of his child and so did not have the right to sue. In 2005, the Court decided that under certain circumstances, the Ten Commandments may be posted in public places. A Texas display was allowed to remain, as it had existed for forty years without challenge, whereas a Kentucky display was struck down, largely because it was challenged very soon after it was erected. Thus, the Supreme Court, through the end of Rehnquist's tenure as chief justice, remained embroiled in the area of religion and the law.

The Roberts Court will, undoubtedly, also be involved in the area of religion and the law, even though it has not heard that many major cases. One of the few to have come before the Court involved a congressional law attempting to protect the rights of churches and prisoners, holding that prisons that get state funding and churches involved in interstate commerce (meaning nearly all churches and all prisons) could not have their rights restricted unless the government had a compelling state interest. This differs from the law struck down in 1997 as the connection with governmental funding and the commerce issue gives Congress authority, which the Court said they lacked with the previous law. This law was upheld when the Supreme Court considered it in 2006, thus increasing protection for religion for certain individuals and groups.

Even though one cannot predict the decisions of the Court on future issues, it is safe to predict which issues will definitely arise again. Those issues include evolution, the Pledge of Allegiance, prayer in public schools, and school funding. Evolution seems destined to appear again, as new policies have been developed to once more remove evolution from the public schools. In 2005, a district court struck down a Pennsylvania school district's attempt to mandate that the school mention intelligent design. This idea holds that the world is so complicated in some of its parts that there must have been an intelligence involved. The idea was struck down as an establishment of religion. Thus, religion is here to stay as an issue in the courts.

Besides the U.S. Supreme Court, another factor in religion and the law is the executive and legislative branches of the system. While the court system is legally the one responsible for interpreting the U.S. Constitution, the executive and legislative branches are still involved. The executive branch is connected as the arm of government that enforces Supreme Court decisions. The 1954 *Brown* decision banning school segregation was slow to be implemented in large part because presidents Eisenhower and Kennedy were not interested in enforcing it. In the legislative branch, as mentioned previously, on a number of occasions Congress has tried to pass legislation overturning the decisions of the Supreme Court. While the Court has looked with displeasure on most direct efforts, some of these have still been successful. Recent congressional moves to increase the legal protections for prisoners and churches succeeded. The Court is always very careful to make sure that congressional legislation, especially any that attempts to overturn or limit Court decisions, has a firm constitutional basis. Congress is also the origin of attempts to pass constitutional amendments aimed at overturning Court decisions. In every session of Congress, bills are introduced to pass constitutional amendments aimed at allowing school prayer and banning abortion, just to name the two most popular. These efforts, though, seldom reach a vote on the floor of the Senate or the House of Representatives, and since such bills almost always fail to be considered, they may be introduced simply to placate the voting public.

Congress has also passed legislation that has reshaped the interaction of religion and the law. For instance, Congress passed Title VII of the Civil Rights Act of 1964—legislation banning most instances of religious-based discrimination in the workforce. This effort was not in response to any specific Supreme Court decision but was aimed at ending discrimination (the same act also banned discrimination on the basis of race in employment), and the Supreme Court upheld the legislation. Thus, Congress can and often does act to protect people in the area of religion and can also act, sometimes successfully, in protesting Supreme Court decisions.

The public is also involved in the interaction between religion and the law, even though (obviously) there is not any direct public vote on Supreme Court cases or nominees. For instance, there was long (and still is, in many people's estimation) a bias against Catholic candidates for public office, and in the 1800s there was often a bias against Catholic immigrants. A whole political party, the Know-Nothing or American Party, was formed to push for anti-immigrant legislation. The fear was that Catholic immigrants would remain loyal to the pope and could not be trusted to become good Americans. Catholics also wanted a different version of the Bible used in the public schools; they favored the Douay version rather than the King James translation preferred by Protestants, and this difference in opinion created tension. Riots broke out in many cities in the 1840s over the issue and tensions remained even after the riots had ended. Throughout the nineteenth and early twentieth centuries, Catholic candidates for president did not fare well in seeking their parties' nomination, as the first Catholic presidential candidate did not win nomination until 1928. Even then, a full eighty years after the Bible riots, many feared that if Al Smith, Democratic nominee in that campaign, was elected, the pope would be in control of America. It is difficult to assess the number of votes this controversy cost Smith, as the battle over the Catholic issue pushed many Catholics, who might have stayed home otherwise or voted for the Republican candidate, to come out and vote for Smith; but the level of hostility caused by the issue demonstrates that religion played a role in politics throughout the period. Religion next played a major role in presidential elections in 1960, when John F. Kennedy battled Richard Nixon. Kennedy tackled the issue head-on and managed to blunt its impact, but many at the time (and later) believed that a significant number of votes, both for and against Kennedy, were moved by the religion issue. Even in 2004 some put forth religion as an issue with John Kerry. The complaint against Kerry, however, was not that he was too Catholic or that the pope would have too much power, as was the charge with Kennedy and Smith; rather, Kerry was accused of not being Catholic enough as he did not share the pope's views on abortion. A final area where religion shapes the law is in many people's attitudes—most prominently, the subject of abortion. Many people's decisions on the abortion debate/maelstrom (or mud-throwing contest if you prefer) are based in their religion. Thus, religion continues to influence politics and public attitudes, both of which in turn shape the law.

Battles over religion and politics are often said to produce much heat and little light, and when the two are combined, that cliché might be expected to be squared. Many people hold their religion dear, and when one considers the subject, this attitude is quite understandable. Religion for many tells them who they are and what they believe, and religion (oddly enough, along with politics) is often the most important mutable characteristic of an individual's personality. Sex and race are not characteristics that people choose, so religion and political affiliation often become the most important markers of who a person decides to be. Thus, the laws that shape religion, and how religion is implemented, are vitally important. The same has been true of law and religion throughout American history. America has become more tolerant over the years, and the colonies also became more tolerant as they moved toward what became the United States, but that does not mean that this toleration was easily gained or granted. The current wide scope of the First Amendment did not just occur the day after that amendment was passed; it has developed slowly over the nation's history.

Another ongoing tension arises between the establishment clause of the First Amendment, which holds that government cannot establish a religion, and the free exercise clause, which says that people should be free to worship as they choose. However, those in political power often feel justified by their religion (and within their free exercise rights) to use that political power in the area of religion (or morality in their minds), and this, of course, conflicts with others' free exercise rights and their rights to have a government free of religious entanglement. The First Amendment is simple in its concept: government cannot establish a religion and must allow people to worship freely—but the devil comes in the details, and the exact contours of that amendment are forever changing. To make a complex situation more difficult, of course, religion is very important to many Americans, and to many of the rest, the right to be left alone to practice no religion is equally important. Thus, religion and the law will always intersect, but this interaction must be considered with thoughtfulness as it represents a vital balance in the freedoms so essential to the nation.

ACKNOWLEDGMENTS

I would be truly amiss if I did not thank my friends who have shepherded me along and provided me with laughs and companionship. These include Dennis Trinkle, Paul Wexler, Elizabeth Hill, Fred "Bud" Burkhardt, Linda Ruggles, and David Staley, among many others. I would also like to thank my family, including my parents and sisters.

I would like to thank the history department and my students at the University of Kentucky, particularly Dr. Robert Ireland and Dr. Robert Olson. These two professors have given me numerous opportunities to expand my learning, and my students constantly make me reconsider my ideas, and remind me why I became a historian with their interests and questions.

I would also like to thank all those who took the time to answer my questions throughout this project. This includes all the librarians, scholars, and religious figures I contacted during the course of the work. Without their help this project would have been much more difficult.

I would like to especially thank the Church of Jesus Christ of Latter-day Saints headquarters in Salt Lake City, Utah, as a number of people there took the time to discuss several issues with me at length and to return my long-distance calls.

Though it feels peculiar to express gratitude to someone dead for nearly two centuries, I would like to thank James Madison. Without his work adding the freedom of religion to the Bill of Rights, our religious freedom would not be nearly as expansive as it is today. Similarly, the Taft Court needs to be thanked for its decision in *Gitlow* v. *New York,* which began the process that broadened the freedom of (and from) religion to include the states.

The editorial team at ABC-CLIO has been stellar throughout the project. My thanks go out especially to Steven Danver, lead acquisitions editor, and to Alex Mikaberidze, submissions editor. Their input and feedback helped me immeasurably in the preparation of this manuscript. I would also like to thank copyeditor Patterson Lamb, senior production editor Vicki Moran, and media editor Ellen Rasmussen. Their careful and meticulous editing and research, along with their patience, have greatly improved this encyclopedia.

However, any faults that remain in this work are my responsibility alone.

This volume is dedicated to my mentors, who have pushed me to be better while still believing in me, who have given me encouragement and have shown me by example how to be a true scholar. True mentorship is knowing how to encourage, support, and push all at the same time, and many people have filled this role in my life. This volume is also dedicated to my wife, Jessie, who has been my most important supporter, and to my daughter, Caroline.

TIMELINE

1215 The Magna Carta is issued by King James; this document set forth the rights of Englishmen, particularly the lords, and is seen as the first written set of rights in Western civilization.

1607 Jamestown is founded, with a focus more economic than religious. Virginia, principally economic in its founding, is somewhat less influenced by religion and so is more favorable than Massachusetts toward separation of church and state.

1620 Plymouth Colony is founded by the Pilgrims, who wanted to separate from the church of England and avoid its influence.

1630 Puritan migration from England. John Winthrop issues his "City on a Hill" sermon setting up Massachusetts as a model to encourage the rest of the world, particularly England, to behave better (and thus become Puritan).

1633 Maryland is established as a haven for Catholics, but it also accepts Protestants.

1635 Roger Williams is forced out of the Massachusetts Bay Colony, eventually settling in what will become Rhode Island. Rhode Island is the first colony to grant religious toleration.

1637 Anne Hutchinson is banned from Massachusetts Bay Colony.

1649 Toleration Act is passed in Maryland, allowing religious toleration for Catholics and Protestants. This act is in effect for only five years, as in 1654 Maryland passes laws removing religious freedom from Catholics.

1681 Pennsylvania is formed as a religious haven for Quakers and others. In 1682, Pennsylvania announces its governing laws, including religious toleration for all. Pennsylvania is the second colony, after Rhode Island, to grant religious toleration.

1689 The English Parliament passes the Act of Toleration as part of the Glorious Revolution, which grants toleration to all Protestant sects, but only Protestants.

1692 Salem Witch Trials. This is one of the most noted instances in which the church and state worked together, with about 300 people accused of being witches, 100 being jailed, 20 being executed, and 1 being pressed to death by stones during an investigation.

1720–1740 First Great Awakening. This is a period of great religious fervor and results in several new religious denominations in the colonies.

1776 U.S. Declaration of Independence.

1782   Jefferson writes the Virginia Bill for Establishing Religious Freedom. It allows religious freedom to all, ends payments by the state to an established church, and does not allow government penalties for religious infringements. It is not passed until 1786.

1786   Virginia passes the Bill for Establishing Religious Liberty. James Madison is largely behind this passage, as Jefferson is in France.

1787   Constitutional Convention meets and writes the Constitution.

1789   In response to state requests, twelve amendments are passed by Congress and sent on to the states for ratification.

1791   Amendments Three through Twelve are adopted by the states, becoming our First through Tenth Amendments (the Bill of Rights). Amendment Three, which becomes Amendment One, or the First Amendment, contains the following language: "Congress shall make no law respecting an establishment of religion nor prohibiting the free exercise thereof. . . ."

1800–1840   Second Great Awakening. This is a series of religious revivals that generates both new Christian denominations, including Mormonism, and a new interest in reform, leading to abolitionism and temperance. The connection between religion and reform of others' personal lives will remain a dominant theme in the nation. The abolitionist movement continues past the Great Awakening, and it, along with some of the works generated under its influence, like Harriet Beecher Stowe's *Uncle Tom's Cabin,* helps move the nation toward the Civil War in 1860 and the eventual end of slavery in 1865.

1802   Thomas Jefferson, president at the time, writes a letter that contains the phrase "wall of separation between church and state." This phrase is seen by many as what Jefferson and Madison believed the First Amendment to be, an act completely severing church from state. However, this interpretation of what the First Amendment means is opposed, not surprisingly, by others, largely those who want to allow the interaction of church and state.

1810   Congress passes a law calling for mail delivery to occur and postal offices to be open on Sundays, leaving them open seven days a week. Opposition from those who want Sunday to be a holy day of rest finally ends Sunday mail delivery in 1830, except for a few towns like Loma Linda, California, where Saturday is the day mail is not delivered due to the large percentage of Saturday Sabbath observers, and Sunday mail delivery continues.

1833   Bill of Rights is held to apply only to the federal government; Massachusetts, the last state to maintain a tax-supported church, formally disestablishes its Congregational Church.

1840–1860   This period sees a surge of anti-immigrant sentiment, particularly in response to the arrival of millions of Roman Catholics from Ireland, who face opposition both for being Irish and for being Catholic. A political party forms in the time period—the American, or Know-Nothing, Party. Though the party is ultimately unsuccessful, tension over immigration continues. Disputes over which Bible to use in the schools (Catholics favor the Douay Bible and the Protestants favor the King James Bible) lead to rioting in several cities.

1843   Most members of the Mormon Church leave Illinois and head out to the Utah territory, arriving there in 1847.

1859   Charles Darwin publishes his *Origin of Species,* which, as articulated largely in his 1871 book *The Descent of Man,* postulates that man evolved from other species. This view is eventually taken by many to challenge the biblical account and in time it leads to a great controversy over the amount of evolution that should be taught in the schools.

1862   The Morrill Act, mostly aimed against Mormons, is passed, allowing the federal government to begin prosecuting bigamy in the federal territories.

1868   The Fourteenth Amendment is passed, guaranteeing that "no state shall make or enforce any law which shall abridge the privileges and immunities of citizens of the United States; nor shall any State deprive any person of life, liberty or property, without due process of law; nor

deny to any person within its jurisdiction the equal protection of the laws."

1879   *Reynolds* v. *United States,* decided by the Supreme Court, upholds a conviction under a federal anti-polygamy law, creating a distinction between religious belief (always protected) and action based in religion (sometimes protected).

1890   U.S. Supreme Court upholds seizure of Mormon Church property under an act allowing the seizure of property belonging to any organization that supports polygamy. Mormon Church renounces polygamy the same year.

1899   The Supreme Court finds that the government can provide funds for a hospital operated in Washington, D.C., under the direction of nuns.

1907   Kansas mandates a flag salute in the public schools.

1910   The Illinois Supreme Court forbids Bible reading in the public schools because the King James Bible discriminates against Catholic children. Catholic children had been allowed to be excused, but the court held that this exclusion also stigmatized the children and so was not allowable. Most other states, though, do not follow this ruling.

1916   Woodrow Wilson appoints Louis Brandeis as the first Jewish Supreme Court justice. Brandeis faces opposition due to his religion and his progressive views, but is eventually confirmed.

1919   The Eighteenth Amendment, prohibiting manufacture and possession of alcohol, is ratified, going into effect in 1920. It is repealed, but not until 1933.

1925   Scopes "Monkey" Trial occurs in Dayton, Tennessee, where a high school teacher deliberately violates a law banning the teaching of evolution; he is tried for that violation in a highly politicized courtroom event. He is found guilty and fined $100, but the fine is overturned on a technicality. The Supreme Court, in *Gitlow* v. *New York,* in the same year, extends the protections of portions of the Bill of Rights, including the freedom of speech, against state, as well as federal government, actions.

1928   Al Smith of New York, nominated by the Democratic Party, is the first Roman Catholic to be nominated for president by a major political party.

1940   In *Cantwell* v. *Connecticut,* the Supreme Court holds that the Bill of Rights extends the religion clauses of the First Amendment against the states and uses this holding to overturn the conviction of a Jehovah's Witness on a charge of breach of the peace. The same year, the Supreme Court upholds the expulsion from school of two Jehovah's Witnesses for their failure to salute the American flag in *Minersville* v. *Gobitis.*

1943   The Supreme Court strikes down a Pennsylvania ordinance requiring licensing of door-to-door solicitors as it violates the free exercise of religion, specifically for the suing group, Jehovah's Witnesses. The Supreme Court in the same year, in *West Virginia* v. *Barnette,* reverses its *Gobitis* decision and strikes down a West Virginia law, ruling that the state cannot force students to salute the flag, as doing so creates an establishment of religion.

1945   The United States is on the winning side of World War II, but tension soon breaks out between America and its wartime ally the USSR, starting the Cold War. One main difference between the two countries, particularly in the minds of Americans, is the atheist nature of the USSR and the Christian nature of the United States, and thus many people push the nation to demonstrate national Christianity more openly.

1947   The Supreme Court, in the *Everson* case, first rules in the area of education and religion in terms of a state program, holding that the state could reimburse parents for the cost of transportation of students to a private religious school.

1948   The Supreme Court first rules on the question of religious education in the public schools, disallowing a program in Illinois (the *McCollum* case) where religious education is taking place on public school grounds.

1952   Varying from their 1948 ruling, the Supreme Court in *Zorach* approves a program of religious education that takes place off school grounds.

1954–1956 Due in large part to Cold War–era pressures, the United States adopts "In God We Trust" as a national motto and adds the words "under God" to the Pledge of Allegiance.

1960 John F. Kennedy becomes the first Catholic to win a U.S. presidential election.

1961 The Supreme Court upholds a blue law, in *McGowan,* allowing states to set aside Sunday as a day of rest. The Supreme Court holds that while the original purpose may have been religious, there are now secular (nonreligious) reasons supporting the practice.

1962 The Supreme Court, in *Engel* v. *Vitale,* rules that state-created prayer in public school is unconstitutional.

1963 In the *Abbington Township* case, the Supreme Court rules that Bible reading is unconstitutional in public schools. The Court also rules there that a balancing test must be used to determine whether rules that infringe on religious practices are constitutional, with the rules being constitutional only if the infringement caused by the rule is needed to advance a compelling state interest. It should be noted that the law itself may still stand, but that all who bring legitimate religious objections to its application would be exempted. This decision, along with *Engel,* creates a firestorm of opposition with many people labeling the Supreme Court "atheistic" or "godless" or calling for

the impeachment of the justices (or all of the above). The Supreme Court, in *Sherbert* v. *Verner,* states that a Seventh-Day Adventist who refused to work on her day of religious observance, Saturday, cannot be denied unemployment compensation.

1964 Congress passes Title VII of the 1964 Civil Rights Act forbidding religious discrimination. The larger bill is aimed at prohibiting discrimination on the basis of race. Note that religious belief and practice are protected outside the workplace, but only religious belief is protected inside it, generally. Religious practices in the workplace need to be accommodated, a later amendment states, only if an employer can do so without undue hardship. Religious organizations are still allowed to discriminate when religion is part of a true job prerequisite (a bona fide occupational qualification, in the words of the act) and religious entities are still allowed to control their own hiring and firing.

1968 The Indian Bill of Rights extends the Bill of Rights to Native Americans but exempts tribes from the establishment part of the First Amendment. This means that tribes can establish religions if they choose. Traditionally many tribes mixed religion and government, and the Indian Bill of Rights allows them to continue doing this.

1970 The Supreme Court, in *Walz,* upholds tax exemptions for churches, stating that the practice is supported by history and public policy. Note that tax exemptions need to be given to all bona fide churches in order for such a policy to be legal. Tax exemptions could not legally be given to Christian churches but denied to Jewish synagogues, for example.

1971 The Supreme Court, in *Lemon* v. *Kurtzman,* creates the *Lemon* test, a three-part test for determining whether a law in the area of religion is constitutional: a law must have a secular purpose, must neither advance nor retard religion as its primary effect, and must not create an excessive entanglement for the government with religion.

1972 The Supreme Court, in *Yoder,* allows Amish families to remove their children from public high schools.

1973 The Supreme Court, in *Roe* v. *Wade,* strikes down a law restricting an abortion and recognizes, for the first time, a nationwide right to abortion under certain circumstances. This decision touches off much widespread protest, including religious-based protests.

1978 Congress passes the American Indian Religious Freedom Act, which professes to force the federal government to respect the religious rights of Native Americans but really does little. The Supreme Court ignores it for the most part and slights it when it does recognize it, and Congress also does not take strong steps to force increased rights for Native Americans.

1980 Ronald Reagan is elected president. He is greatly supported by the Moral Majority, founded by Jerry Falwell, a Baptist preacher and college president from Virginia, and their fund-raising efforts. The Moral Majority aims, among other things, to reintroduce prayer into public schools and to overturn *Roe* v. *Wade.* Reagan promises to appoint judges who agree with his views on these issues. The Supreme Court, in *Stone* v. *Graham,* orders the removal of the Ten Commandments from public school classrooms.

1981 Reagan appoints Sandra Day O'Connor to the Supreme Court, the first woman to so serve. While it is generally assumed that O'Connor agrees with Reagan's views, she eventually moves toward the center on the abortion issue, voting to uphold a woman's right to an abortion even while allowing the state to impose more restrictions on them.

1982 Reagan makes good on his campaign promise to support an amendment allowing prayer in public schools. However, the amendment fails.

1983 *Mueller* v. *Allen* allows tax deductions for expenses in both public and private schools (but private school parents are the ones who use them the most). This is the first decision upholding such a tax code provision.

1984 Congress passes the Equal Access Act. This act orders schools to allow equal access (hence the title of the act) to all groups of students who wish to meet, and thus schools are no longer able to ban student groups purely on religious grounds.

1985 The Supreme Court, in *Wallace* v. *Jaffree,* overturns an Alabama statute that had permitted a moment of silence for prayer in schools.

1987 The Supreme Court holds that the secretary of defense can force an Orthodox Jew to remove his yarmulke if that Jew is in the military in *Goldman* v. *Weinberger.* In *Edwards* v. *Aguillard,* the court strikes down a Louisiana law requiring evolution and creation science to be taught equally, if either is taught at all.

1988 Congress passes legislation ordering the secretary of defense not to follow the *Goldman* decision and to allow some religious exceptions to military dress codes, within reason.

1990 In *Employment Division* v. *Smith,* the Supreme Court reverses the decision of *Sherbert* v. *Verner* (1963) and holds that only a rational relationship is needed between a state interest and a law before the state can burden the free exercise of religion if the law is neutral in terms of religion.

1992 In *Lee* v. *Weisman,* the Supreme Court rules that prayer at a public school graduation is unconstitutional, even when the prayer is nondenominational, if it is done at the behest of the school authorities.

1993 Congress passes the Religious Freedom Restoration Act (RFRA), which is aimed at reversing *Employment Division* v. *Smith* and restoring the compelling state interest test.

1997 The Supreme Court, in *Boerne* v. *Flores,* overturns the Religious Freedom Restoration Act when it is applied against the states, ruling that Congress had gone beyond the powers granted to it by the Constitution in reinstating the compelling interest test. The compelling government interest test of the Religious Freedom Restoration Act, however, is still considered a restraint against the federal government, as Congress can almost always legislate for the federal government but cannot create new rights while claiming to protect old ones, as the Supreme Court saw Congress doing here.

1998 Congress attempts to pass the Religious Freedom Amendment, which does not go back to the Religious Freedom Restoration Act, as some might expect, but instead goes back against *Lee* v. *Weisman* and against *Engel* v. *Vitale,* in many respects. It attempts to allow voluntary school prayer and prayer at graduations as well as the posting of the Ten Commandments on school grounds and the printing of "In God We Trust" on our currency. It should be noted that the last instance had been already upheld by the Supreme Court. It fails by two votes in the House of Representatives and so is not sent on to the Senate.

2000   Joe Lieberman, vice-presidential candidate on the Democratic ticket, is the first Jewish vice-presidential candidate. Congress considers using a Catholic priest as its chaplain, but the move is opposed, as some see the priest as unavailable to help families due to his celibacy, while others oppose his appearing as the U.S. chaplain in clerical vestments. Congress uses a Protestant clergyman instead, as it always has. Congress also passes the Religious Land Use and Institutionalized Persons Act (RLUIPA), which aims to give more protection to religious organizations in their land use and to people who are in prison. It requires that the state and federal government demonstrate a compelling interest before imposing a substantial burden upon these two groups.

2002   The Supreme Court, in *Zelman,* approves Ohio's program of school vouchers, where the parents choose which schools their child attends (and which school receives money from the state through a voucher) even though most of the schools chosen have a religious affiliation and thus a large amount of funding is channeled to religious schools. The parental choice, in the eyes of the Court, keeps this from being an endorsement of religion by the government.

2003   The Supreme Court, in *Lawrence and Garner,* strikes down a Texas law criminalizing private homosexual sodomy because it violates the constitutional right to privacy. Those on the Court opposed to this decision cite as one of their reasons the belief that this decision will lead to same-sex marriages.

2004   John Kerry is the third Catholic presidential nominee. Kerry fails, but unlike the situation in 1960, opposition to him in the area of faith does not come from those who feel that he follows (and would follow as president) too strict an adherence to his religion, but from those who feel that he follows it too loosely, particularly in the area of abortion; Kerry is pro-choice, putting him at odds with the official church doctrine. The Supreme Court, in *Newdow,* rules that a California parent who sued, on behalf of his daughter, against the phrase "under God" in the Pledge of Allegiance, did not have standing to sue. As Newdow did not have custody of his daughter, the Court ruled he could not sue for her.

2005   President George W. Bush, in August, suggests that intelligent design and evolution should be taught equally in the classroom. Some suggest that this move is to boost his ratings with the social conservatives. In December, the case *Kitzmiller* v. *Dover Area School District* is decided by the District Court for the Middle District of Pennsylvania. It declares unconstitutional Dover's policy of requiring teachers to read a disclaimer noting that evolution is only a theory and suggesting an alternative textbook based on intelligent design. The Supreme Court also rules, in *Cutter,* that the RLUIPA, adopted in 2000, is constitutional.

2006   The Supreme Court, in *UDV,* rules that the RFRA is constitutional in requiring the federal government to prove a compelling interest before it can ban a drug used in a religious ceremony. This, in many ways, is seen as a move back toward reversing (or at least limiting) *Employment Division,* which allowed the government to penalize use of peyote, another drug used in religious ceremonies.

Essays

Church-State Relations

Government has had a shaping influence on the scope of organized religion in this country, at the federal, state, and local levels. Similarly, organized religions have had some subtle and not-so-subtle influences on the U.S. government. This might seem to clash with the idea of freedom of religion, and, indeed, sometimes it has done so, but the relationship between church and state is much more complicated than it might seem to be at a brief glance. Church efforts to shape government affairs and government attempts to influence church positions can be examined in legal cases. A brief study of the issues arising when an organized religion is restricted by government practice will help illustrate how difficult it can sometimes be to separate church from state and vice versa. Some cases deal with individuals, but the decisions arising from those cases affect an entire religion. (Discussions of individual freedoms of religion and direct attempts by the state to establish religion appear elsewhere in this encyclopedia.)

The state has had a shaping influence on many areas of church policy. Despite the beliefs of some, the state is allowed to generally regulate the nonreligious behavior of churches, especially when that behavior is pretty much fully separate from religion. Thus, if a religious organization operates a day care program in its building, the program is still subject to the same safety and health regulations that any other day care program would be. The same is true for the regulations of the workers, except in the area of religion, or where religion affects the worker. For instance, churches are not allowed to discriminate on the basis of sex except when the discrimination is shown to stem from direct religious belief.

The Seventh-Day Adventists were allowed, in a lawsuit decided in 1985, to discriminate against women and not hire a woman minister because they had a preexisting specific and clear doctrine that they did not hire women as ministers. In another case, though, the Seventh-Day Adventists were not allowed to discriminate on the basis of sex in their general hiring practices, as there was no specific doctrine that the church could point to that justified their action. (As a matter of fact, the church claimed not to discriminate against women generally.) Religious organizations are allowed a lot more leeway in the hiring and firing of ministers than in the hiring of other employees, as the ministers are directly involved with religion in a way that other employees are not.

Churches, and even church-run organizations, are allowed to stipulate that general employees be members of a specific religion or that they observe the church's standards, or both, and those qualifications have been upheld. However, discrimination outside of those religious qualifications is not allowed. For example, a religious school was allowed to fire a person for divorcing and then remarrying without having the first marriage annulled, as Catholic doctrine required, because the teacher was previously informed of this in the handbook containing the code of conduct. However, a church was not allowed to use religion as a defense against an age discrimination suit because it had no religious doctrine dictating age discrimination.

Religious discrimination is also permitted when the religious qualification is an important part of the job, or, in the words of the law, a "bona fide occupational qualification." Even groups that are not traditionally thought of as being a religion are allowed to discriminate on the basis of religion. Loyola University, a college that is affiliated with the Jesuits, was not defined to be a religion but was allowed to have a religious qualification for hiring professors in some departments, as the school wanted to keep its Jesuit orientation. One way to do this, and a legitimate way in the eyes of the courts, was to require the hiring of Jesuits in some departments.

However, just because some organizations or companies think of themselves as religions, the courts are not required to consider them as such. A company that believed itself to be religious required church service attendance from its employees. But it learned it was not allowed to fire people for not attending those services. Just having religious people run a company does not make that company a religion. Similarly, a children's home believed itself to be religiously affiliated but it did not require church services or require children to have a Bible. The children's home was allowed to fire its director and hire a minister (of the same religion) in his place because the decision was determined to have been based on an educational requirement. However, the home would not have been allowed to discriminate based on the actual religion practiced by its director. These two cases show that companies must be directly controlled by a church, or at least have a strong affiliation with one, and act in ways to reinforce that affiliation to be able to discriminate on the basis of religion. Generally, all other discrimination will be open to scrutiny, even though it may turn out to be justifiable if the church or company can support it with specific church doctrine.

Another item to examine is what generally applicable regulations, outside of employment, are allowed to be applied to religions, either in the area of their worship or in their general practices. First, most such generally applicable regulations do still apply to religions. This is especially true when the laws only incidentally burden the practice of religion. An evangelist protested California's tax law, which required

his church to pay sales taxes on all items sold during a revival that occurred in California. The Supreme Court held that this tax could be applied to the items sold as long as the tax was not aimed, either on its face or in how it was written, at religions in general or this type of religion in particular. As the issue occurring here was the regular sales tax being applied to the pamphlets sold by the church, collecting the tax was allowed. Laws that incidentally burden religion, similar to those that incidentally benefit religion, are both permitted as the first is not a ban on the freedom of religion nor is the second an establishment of religion. This rule has generally held true for the last seventy years, ever since the First Amendment was applied against the states in the area of religion.

Laws that have a substantial effect on religion but are general in nature, have a more checkered response from the courts. In the 1960s, in *Sherbert* v. *Verner,* the Supreme Court dealt with an employee who had first been fired for refusing to work on her religious Sabbath (Saturday in this case) and then was denied unemployment benefits on the basis of what was considered an unwillingness to work. The system considered her refusal to work on Saturdays to mean that she was unwilling to work at all, but the Supreme Court held that the policy infringed upon the employee's freedom of religion and so was illegal. The Court held that a "compelling state interest" was needed to justify regulations that impacted religion through their effect. This was a pretty high burden to meet, and while fewer regulations could do so, some were still allowed. For instance, a state law requiring certain businesses to close on Sundays was upheld, as a regulated day of rest was deemed a compelling state interest. Past laws regulating public conduct were also cited as being able to meet this test, including a law banning polygamy, which was upheld as part of the state's police power.

In 1990, the Supreme Court reversed *Sherbert* in *Employment Division* v. *Smith.* Similar to the facts in *Sherbert,* unemployment benefits were once again involved. In this case, two Native Americans had used peyote in a religious ceremony and then were fired from their jobs at a drug treatment facility. The state then denied them unemployment benefits, as they had been fired for misconduct. Those suing argued that this regulation basically banned their religion, as a part of their religion required them to use peyote. The Supreme Court held that the regulation and denial of benefits was admissible and fashioned a new rule for testing the constitutionality of laws that impact religion. The Court first commented, "We have never held that an individual's religious beliefs excuse him from compliance with an otherwise valid law prohibiting conduct that the State is free to regulate" (494 U.S. 872: 878–879). The Court also refused to order that an exception to the drug laws be allowed for religious drug use. Thus, laws only had to be general and justified, and they could burden religion.

Laws that are not general, however, are still very much suspect. When it can be proven, either through the way the law is written or the way the law is applied, that the law is targeting a certain religion, then the law will probably be struck down. This is not always the case, however, and the courts do not have to admit this. For instance, the regulation just noted banning polygamy was passed to restrain the Mormon Church. However, rather than examining it as a law targeted at one religion, all of the courts looked to see whether polygamy was an evil, and as it was held to be such, it was allowed to be banned.

Recent courts have often been a bit more suspicious of legislation and have often struck down laws that seemed to be aimed at only one group. In one of the more recent attempts, the city of Hialeah regulated the Church of the Lukumi Babalu Aye out of existence. That church practiced the Santeria religion, which originated in Cuba and moved to the United States and includes animal sacrifice in some of its rituals. The city claimed not to be trying to ban the religion but to be regulating the killing of animals, citing a number of interests, including protecting health in general, preventing animal cruelty, and protecting children (who might have been harmed by watching the sacrifices). The Supreme Court, however, did not accept this justification. They first articulated the standard for laws that were not neutral and not general, and that standard was that laws "must be justified by a compelling governmental interest, and must be narrowly tailored to advance that interest" (508 U.S. 520: 531–532). This standard, of course, is very close to that of the *Sherbert* case. The Court then found that the law was targeted against the Santeria religion, as, for instance, it allowed the killing of animals for food purposes, but did not allow it for animal sacrifices. The Court also found that the laws were not narrowly tailored and that the city had not been as vigilant about going after other practices that affected the same claimed interests. Thus, if the city was not really interested in protecting these interests, there was no reason for it to pass those laws except to ban the Santeria religion, which clearly was unacceptable under the First Amendment.

The Supreme Court has also struck down legislation that appears to be neutral but really uses the parameters of the majority to suppress the minority, particularly in religion. A prime case of this is in *Cantwell* v. *Connecticut,* decided in 1940. There, a Jehovah's Witness was going door to door and asking to play a record. Upon playing the record, which contained an attack on the Roman Catholic Church, Jesse Cantwell (and his brother and father) were all arrested for failure to register their intent to canvass door to door and for "breach of the peace." The registration statute was struck down as it created a prior restraint upon the religious freedom of the three, and the Supreme Court weighed the interest in religious freedom versus the interest of the public to keep peace. The Court did not deny that the public has an interest in keeping the peace but pointed out that no riot had erupted and that Cantwell would have moved on if he had been asked to do so. Thus, the

Court held that the hearers could not shut off discussion of ideas they found offensive as that would mean that only the majority would be heard, and this idea of the majority having an absolute veto violated the First Amendment's right to freedom of religion. This is an example of a case that dealt with an individual but affected an entire religion. One duty of Jehovah's Witnesses is to witness, and if the Cantwells' convictions had been upheld, others in that religion would have had a more difficult time protecting their right to practice their religion.

The Jehovah's Witnesses came before the Court several times in the 1930s and 1940s in precedent-setting cases. Two cases came from Alabama in the early 1940s, and the first case upheld the conviction of Jehovah's Witnesses for canvassing without a license. The Witnesses would have been required to pay for a license as the state argued that their practice was similar to a door-to door business, and both should be regulated. It was a narrow decision, and the case was heard for re-argument the next year. After the new set of arguments, the convictions were overturned. In the mind of Justice Douglas, writing for the Court in the second case, the state was never allowed to tax ideas in advance. Taxes after the fact, like sales and income, might be allowed, but never prior taxes. He wrote, "Plainly a community may not suppress, or the state tax, the dissemination of views because they are unpopular, annoying or distasteful. If that device were ever sanctioned, there would have been forged a ready instrument for the suppression of the faith which any minority cherishes but which does not happen to be in favor. That would be a complete repudiation of the philosophy of the Bill of Rights" (319 U.S. 105: 116). Thus, religious licensing taxes were not allowed after the early 1940s, and neither were arrests merely because what was heard disturbed the person hearing it, when that was not the purpose of the person undertaking the religious message.

Jehovah's Witnesses were also the subjects of the cases *Lovell* v. *Griffin* (1938) and *Marsh* v. *Alabama* (1946). In *Lovell,* the Court held that distributing literature was part of the freedom of the press and that a state ordinance was censorship when it required that everyone distributing literature first apply to the city council for permission; this kind of censorship was banned under the First Amendment. *Lovell* did not directly consider the religious nature of the publication, preferring to deal with the freedom of the press, and the legal background of freedom of the press had been more defined at that point, but the case was still an important landmark for the freedom of religion. In *Marsh,* the Court considered a company town that had posted a notice not allowing any distribution of literature without written permission. The company town had claimed that they were a private company and so were not covered under decisions such as that announced in *Lovell.* The Court, however, weighed the corporation's property interest versus the right of the people to be informed and the right of the Witnesses to practice their religion and held that the First Amendment guarantees must triumph.

The Jehovah's Witnesses are not the only ones who have had potential restrictions on their recruiting/proselytizing considered by the courts. Among the other groups are the Jews for Jesus and the Hare Krishnas. The Jews for Jesus had been passing out literature and asking for contributions in the Los Angeles International Airport. In order to curtail these activities, the airport commissioners passed a simple ban on "all First Amendment activities" in the airport. The Supreme Court struck down this ban as being overbroad. With First Amendment activities, a significant government interest must justify restrictions and the restrictions need to be narrowly drawn, but the ban here was so broad that nothing could have justified it. The Hare Krishnas consider it part of their religious duty to ask for contributions and to pass out literature, and thus often congregate in airports and at other public events. One airport banned both solicitation and literature distribution from the Hare Krishnas, and the Supreme Court upheld the solicitation ban, but struck down the ban on literature distribution. The reason for the split was that one justice in the middle felt that there was enough of a concern about fraud to justify the restriction on solicitation, but the fraud vanished when only literature distribution was considered. A second justice felt that this was a public area and so should be open to discussion of issues, but could be restricted in the area of solicitation of funds. It should be noted that four justices did feel that both bans were acceptable, as concerns over litter and congestion were enough to allow both bans. In another case, a fair adopted a regulation requiring the Hare Krishnas to stay in one place and the Supreme Court found this to be allowable as the minimal restriction on the First Amendment rights of the Hare Krishnas was acceptable when balanced against the fraud concerns of the state (and other concerns). Thus, limitations on the freedom of religion are allowable, as well as even more strict limitations on solicitation as part of the freedom of religion, but no total bans are allowed, which says that the state can limit religion more closely when religion steps outside of the traditional church and into the public sphere.

Religious groups have also tried to influence the state and encourage it to pass legislation. The efforts discussed here generally regard those individuals and groups who pushed for legislation on behalf of a specific religious faction rather than those religious individuals who pushed for legislation on their own. One particular movement that saw the influence of religion was the move toward the addition of the phrase "under God" in the Pledge of Allegiance in the 1950s. The Pledge of Allegiance, in a slightly altered form, was originally written in the late 1890s and was adopted in 1942 as the national flag salute. In the 1950s, the Cold War was in full swing, and some argued that the pledge could be said equally for the United States and the USSR by just changing the

name of the nation, and so those people argued for language identifying the United States as different from the USSR, focusing on the religious element of this country. Among those groups were the Knights of Columbus, a fraternal group that had been formed to give Catholics a fraternal organization to join (many of the existing fraternal groups limited membership, either officially or unofficially, to Protestants). Individuals were also important in pushing this change through, one of whom was the Reverend Dr. George M. Docherty, a Presbyterian minister from Washington, D.C.

Religiously oriented groups were also behind part of a more recent controversy (at least more recent in terms of when it reached the Supreme Court). In the 1960s, the Fraternal Order of Eagles set up on the statehouse grounds in Texas, as they did in other places in a variety of states, a large monument displaying the Ten Commandments. The Eagles believed that by stating the Ten Commandments they would be fighting juvenile delinquency and other things they believed to be running rampant in the 1950s. The Fraternal Order of Eagles required belief in a supreme being before allowing membership to an individual, and their belief that a Christian lifestyle was the best way to fight that delinquency left little doubt as to which supreme being they favored. This monument was not challenged until 2001 (and the challenge was struck down), but it does clearly demonstrate that throughout the 1950s and 1960s, religiously oriented groups were trying to shape public legislation and public monuments to favor religion.

In the 1970s and 1980s, religious groups took a more direct approach to shaping the state. The Moral Majority, led by Southern Baptist minister Jerry Falwell, was formed to funnel support to conservative political candidates. This group was a strong supporter of Ronald Reagan and argued for a variety of conservative laws. The "pro-life" movement, which sprang up after the *Roe* v. *Wade* decision, was led in part by many conservative Protestant

*Evangelist Jerry Falwell, founder of the "Moral Majority,"
greets GOP presidential candidate Ronald Reagan as he
arrives to address the National Religious Broadcasters in
Lynchburg, Virginia, on October 3, 1980. (Bettmann/
Corbis)*

clearly demonstrates, regardless of what future politicians, courts, and populaces determine, that the church has not been wholly free from state regulation, even while the state has given it more leeway than other similarly situated organizations, and that the church has also attempted, with a modicum of success, to influence the state. Thus, pundits, who, when asked what they thought about the separation of church and state, simply responded "it would be a good idea," still clearly have a point.

Freedom of Religion

The freedom of religion is one of the most treasured individual freedoms in American history and is, in many people's minds, the reason large groups of immigrants came to America. However, freedom of religion is not self-defining, and many Supreme Court cases have therefore examined exactly what limits may be placed on the freedom of religion. The focus here is on individual freedom of religion rather than freedom from government establishment of religion or the government's legal interactions with churches, though the discussion brushes on both of those topics. Those topics are covered elsewhere in this volume.

Freedom of religion, particularly for the individual, was not part of early American history. Many of the early colonies had state-established churches. It is true that many groups left England, particularly the Pilgrims, because they faced harassment for their religious choices. But those groups did not necessarily want, in turn, to give others religious choices. They merely wished to have the freedom to establish their own religion. Many of those established churches were aided by state-collected taxes. Eventually some colonies moved to a policy of allowing individuals to choose which churches their taxes supported, but people were still forced to support an individual church. Some might have considered this freedom of religion, since the choice of churches was available; however, many felt it was not freedom at all, as not

ministers and drew from conservative Protestants and Roman Catholics. In the early 1980s, when AIDS was first discovered, many conservatives argued that this was "God's wrath" on homosexuals for their behavior, and this view was the main reason that the Reagan administration took so long to fund AIDS research. Indeed, it is generally accepted that Reagan changed his opinion only when Rock Hudson, a Hollywood leading man in Reagan's era, was publicly revealed to have AIDS. Falwell, in the early 2000s, supported President Bush's programs that provided funds to churches and other groups to provide social services, in the effort called Faith-Based Initiatives (later also called Faith-Based and Community Initiatives). The idea was that churches were good avenues for providing social services.

Separation of church and state is often debated in America, particularly in terms of exactly what degree of separation is supposed to exist between the two. American legal history supporting any church was not an option. For much of American history, many people did not think that freedom of religion included freedom not to have a religion, and a significant percentage of people today still hold that view. However, situations in which the freedom of religion included the freedom to choose no religion were (and generally are) considered freedom of religion cases by the Supreme Court, and the whole spectrum of religious choice needs to be available in order to have true understanding of freedom of religion in this country today.

In early American history, few legal cases arose purely from individuals seeking freedom of religion. Some did try to have the state reduce or abolish support for a government-approved religion, but those campaigns against established state-chosen and supported churches are more freedom from an establishment of religion than freedom of religion. Those who believed that a state was not treating a religion fairly often just went elsewhere or suffered in silence. The Supreme Court also did not consider many cases dealing with the freedom of religion in the early years, as the First Amendment was held to deal only with federal laws, while most laws were (and are) passed at the state level. The federal government generally dealt, especially in the country's early history, only with the federal territories. It was not until the early twentieth century that the First Amendment was extended to also regulate the laws of states, in *Gitlow* v. *New York*.

Shortly before that, the Supreme Court heard the first major cases focused on freedom of religion. These were a series of cases dealing with polygamy in Utah. The Latter-day Saints, after their founding, relocated to Utah in response to fierce opposition to their religion. Mormon doctrine included polygamy, and it was a relatively prevalent practice, particularly among the leaders. Brigham Young, longtime leader of the Mormons, had twenty-seven acknowledged wives. The U.S. government fiercely opposed polygamy, in part because of

the moral and political issues involved. Congress, acting for the territories, quickly banned polygamy, and then, when that did not seem effective, added an act disenfranchising anyone who believed in polygamy. In 1887, Congress completed the anti-Mormon and anti-polygamy legislation by revoking the church's charter and seizing its property.

The Supreme Court first heard a case dealing with polygamy in 1879 in *Reynolds* v. *United States.* There the secretary of the Mormon Church was convicted of polygamy, and the Court held that claims of a free exercise of religion could not stand against bans on illegal actions. While belief was held not to be regulated (at this time), actions that ran contrary to society were not allowed, as the Supreme Court believed that allowing religion to excuse illegal actions would create anarchy. In 1890, the Supreme Court heard a case dealing with someone disenfranchised for believing in polygamy, and held that polygamy was enough of a crime that advocating it was also allowed to be a crime. The final case, also in 1890, tested the 1887 law disenfranchising the church and also upheld that, but examined the contracts issue rather than religion. Even though the Supreme Court had previously held contracts to be generally unable to be voided, the Court here held that corporations that did illegal deeds, like polygamy, or advocated them, could be dissolved. The Mormon Church later disowned the practice of polygamy and was allowed to reestablish itself as a religion, and in 1894 Congress gave back its remaining funds.

The Supreme Court did not return to the freedom of religion until 1940, well after the First Amendment had been held to apply against the states in *Gitlow* v. *New York,* which was decided in 1925. In 1940 the case of *Cantwell* v. *Connecticut* tested the constitutionality of a breach of the peace statute that had been applied against Jesse Cantwell, a Jehovah's Witness. Cantwell had been traveling through New Haven, Connecticut, playing a record that attacked the Catholic Church among other

Walter Gobitis and his children William and Lillian at the U.S. District Court in Philadelphia, Pennsylvania, on February 16, 1938. The children testified that saluting the American flag violated their religious principles as members of the sect known as Jehovah's Witnesses. (Bettmann/Corbis)

things as a way to promote the Jehovah's Witnesses. Even though he offered to move along, he was arrested. The Supreme Court struck down the statute as infringing upon Cantwell's free exercise of religion and thus formally extended the protection of the First Amendment against state laws.

The next major Supreme Court case that focused on freedom of religion was *Minersville v. Gobitis* in the same year as *Cantwell,* which examined the right of Jehovah's Witnesses not to salute the flag. By this time, Jehovah's Witnesses considered flag salutes to be the worship of a graven image, which is strictly prohibited in that religion. Thus, the mandatory flag salute existing at the time violated their religion.

Many Witnesses refused to salute the flag and, before 1939, it was not often a legal matter. After 1939, though, war was brewing in Europe and many states moved to force patriotism in their citizens; one way to do this was a mandatory daily flag salute and saying of the Pledge of Allegiance. When the Witnesses refused, they were considered un-American. Thus the chances for controversy and the stakes were raised by the coming of war in Europe. However, the actual first Supreme Court case on the topic had started before 1939, when, in 1938, Lillian and William Gobitis had been suspended for refusal to salute the flag. Two lower courts ordered that they be allowed to attend school and held in their favor. In 1940 their case reached the Supreme Court, which reversed the two lower courts, holding that the state could force Witnesses to salute the flag. The opinion reverberated with war overtones, holding that states were able to force their citizens into patriotic exercises. Many Witnesses still refused and they were treated very poorly by their communities. In part due to this reaction, and in part perhaps due to the improving war results throughout 1942 and 1943, and in part due to a rethinking of the law, the Supreme Court reversed itself in 1943 and held in favor of another set of Witnesses in *West Virginia* v. *Barnette*. This decision was celebrated by the law reviews and periodicals that had condemned the *Gobitis* decision, but it also received a negative review from those who had been attacking the Witnesses, both verbally and otherwise.

After the *Barnette* case, the Witnesses were generally left alone on the flag salute issue, even though they continued to have difficulty with the law in the area of their door-to-door religious activity. Part of the doctrine of the Jehovah's Witnesses (and hence their name) is that they should travel and spread the word of their beliefs. While many religions are willing to discuss their beliefs and advocate them, the Witnesses are some of the most forward, particularly in the area of reaching out, as they literally witness door to door. This has caused quite a few prosecutions. The Witnesses were first arrested for a breach of the peace in the *Cantwell* case noted above. The Witnesses were next arrested for refusal to register, as many towns had ordinances that one could not go door to door without a permit and/or without registering, and many Witnesses either refused to register or to pay for a permit. A series of cases, starting in the 1940s, held that communities could not force Witnesses to pay licensing taxes or to register, or to get prior approval of their witnessing and materials, as all of these were infringements on their freedom of religion; in the case of the approval of materials, the laws were also infringements on

their freedom of the press. Freedom of speech also sometimes entered into the equation. These cases have not gone away, as in 2002 the Supreme Court again heard a case concerning an Ohio village ordinance that required registration, striking the ordinance on an 8–1 vote (*Watchtower Bible and Tract Society of New York* v. *Village of Stratton,* 536 U.S. 150).

After the Jehovah's Witnesses cases in the 1940s, the next time the Supreme Court ruled on items it considered related to the freedom of religion was dealing with religious observances. The first case the Court considered concerned the so-called "blue laws" that required certain businesses to close on Sundays, or required certain things not to be sold on Sundays. These were challenged in the instance of Sunday closings as a restriction on the free exercise of religion by Orthodox Jews who argued that these laws required them to close twice, once on Saturday to observe their religious holiday, and then on Sunday. The Supreme Court upheld these laws, saying they had moved from religious to secular regulations, as the purpose was a mandated day of rest, and that regulations neutrally drawn that infringed upon one religion more than another were still valid. A different result about Sabbath observances was reached in 1963 in *Sherbert* v. *Verner.* That case considered the situation of a Seventh-Day Adventist who refused to work on Saturdays, as that was her day of religious observance. For this refusal, she was fired from her job and then denied unemployment compensation, as the state allowed such compensation only if one was willing to work and was looking for work, and the state defined her refusal to work on Saturdays as not being willing to work. The Warren Court overturned the state's decision, holding that it was a restriction on the woman's freedom of religion to require her to work on her Sabbath. Restrictions on the freedom of religion were still allowed, but only if the state could demonstrate a compelling state interest that was served by the regulation. The Court found none, and differentiated that from the Sunday closing laws in holding that providing a day off each week, and ordering Sunday to be that day, was both a compelling state interest and the only way to reach that goal. Thus, by the end of the 1960s, Sunday closing laws were upheld while a state could not order those who observed their religious Sabbath on Saturdays to work.

The Burger Court, which followed the Warren Court, considered once again the reach of the free exercise of religion, but this time in the context of secondary education, in *Wisconsin v. Yoder*. While the Burger Court is generally considered to be more conservative than the Warren Court, here the Burger Court reaffirmed the holding in *Sherbert* that a compelling government interest is required to restrict the free exercise of religion. In this case, the state of Wisconsin had passed a compulsory education law requiring students to attend high school until graduation or age sixteen. The Amish did not object to having their children attend the first eight years of schooling, but felt that high school would threaten their lifestyle, as the ideas taught there clashed with their Amish values. The Supreme Court agreed with the Amish and did not find that Wisconsin had advanced a compelling state interest in the case. Subsequent plaintiffs, particularly those who were not as appealing as the Amish to the Court, did not have as much success under the free exercise of religion clause, but *Sherbert* was not overruled—just ignored or limited. For example, a Jewish air force psychiatrist wished to wear his yarmulke. He did so for five years without incident, but then was reported after testifying in his yarmulke in a court case, and it is suggested that the report may have been retaliation for the testimony. Regardless, the psychiatrist had his career ended and so he sued. The Supreme Court upheld the military dismissal, not wanting to challenge the military and also arguing that all neutrally written laws (like the military clothing regulation here) should be upheld. It should be noted that Congress ordered the secretary of defense to change the regulation the following year.

The Supreme Court's major response to *Sherbert* came in 1990 in *Employment Division v. Smith*. That case concerned two Native Americans who had taken peyote as part of a religious ceremony and then been fired from their jobs as drug counselors. They then were further denied unemployment compensation as their firings were caused by what the state considered misconduct related to their jobs, a circumstance that did not allow unemployment compensation. The Supreme Court upheld the denial of unemployment benefits, holding that neutrally written laws that were justified by a government interest are constitutional, unless the free exercise claims in the area of actions were combined with other interests, such as free speech or freedom of the press or parental rights. Thus, the free exercise clause was made less important than the other parts of the First Amendment. Many people were outraged by this case, not so much because it hurt Native American religion (the Native Americans have been, unfortunately, regularly on the losing end of decisions, especially in the area of religion, for most of the twentieth century), but because it threatened other religions. If Native Americans could be penalized for using peyote, could Jews be penalized for wearing yarmulkes or Catholics for wearing crosses? Some might say that the behavior was different, but all are parts of the free exercise of religion in the area of actions. Congress passed the Religious Freedom Restoration Act (RFRA) in 1993 to try to restore *Sherbert* and the compelling interest test.

The Supreme Court, however, relatively soon acted to strike down this act in *City of Boerne v. Flores*. There, a Catholic church had wished to expand its facilities, but the city had denied its application for a housing permit. The church sued, claiming that the city lacked a compelling state interest. The Supreme Court in 1997 agreed with the city, striking down the RFRA requirements in that case. The reason given was that Congress had used its enforcement powers under the Fourteenth Amendment to pass this law, saying that they were enforcing the people's religious rights. However, the Supreme Court held that they were reinterpreting the rights, not enforcing the existing rights. Enforcement was still within the bounds of Congress, but interpretation, and what was protected and with what standard, was the Supreme Court's province. Unlike the original *Smith* decision, which was a 5–4 decision, this decision was unanimous in holding that Congress had gone too far—although the Supreme Court was still divided over whether the compelling state interest standard or the *Smith* standard should hold. Thus, even those who dissented in Smith agreed that the RFRA was wrong.

Since *Boerne,* Congress has continued to try to reverse *Smith,* at least in the area of zoning. In 2000, Congress passed the Religious Land Use and Institutionalized Persons Act (RLUIPA). In the area of zoning, it holds that states cannot burden the free exercise of religion without a compelling interest, and even with such an interest the state must use the "least restrictive means" available. It holds that prisoners and others who are institutionalized (like those in nursing homes) have the right to the free exercise of religion. This differs from the RFRA in that it does not increase (at least arguably) the religious rights of people but just makes it more difficult for a state to infringe on them. Congress also limited the legislation to prisons that receive federal dollars and churches connected to interstate commerce, both of which areas give Congress more power to legislate.

The courts have generally upheld RLUIPA. In 2005 and 2006, the Supreme Court upheld the RLUIPA and the RFRA. In 2005, the Supreme Court held that prison officials can be forced to accommodate the religious rights of prisoners. The Court added that safety was still a consideration, but that prison officials could not summarily dismiss the religious rights of prisoners, particularly those of prisoners who belonged to faiths with few adherents. Among those suing in the 2005 case were a Satan worshiper and a witch. The Court held that this law did not promote religion but merely leveled the

playing field. In 2006, under the RFRA, the Supreme Court ruled that the federal government could not prevent a church from using an otherwise illegal drug in its ceremonies. The drug in question was DMT (diemethyltryptamine), used in a tea drunk by adherents of the Union of the Plants (or UDV after its Spanish name Uniao Do Vegetal) religion. The Court held that the federal government had not proven the compelling interest necessary to ban DMT from the ceremonies. It should be noted that this case concerned only a preliminary injunction, which is harder to obtain than a trial verdict—the federal government still had the right, if it chose to, to return to court and try the case under the normal channels, but the federal government could not receive that preliminary injunction to prevent the UDV from using the DMT until trial. Thus, even though the RFRA does not apply to the states, it has been upheld as applying against the federal government and the RLUIPA has been upheld as applying against the states.

One final area in which government regulation intersects with freedom of religion is that of blood transfusions. Some religions, most notably the Jehovah's Witnesses, do not believe in blood transfusions, and some of these religions do not believe in certain kinds of modern medicine. Generally, when there is an adult involved and no other party's interests are at stake, the adult will be allowed to refuse treatment, including refusing blood transfusions. However, when a child's health is at issue, or when a child's interests become involved, the state then takes a more active role.

States have repeatedly intervened to force medical treatment of children including forcing blood transfusions, and the courts have generally sided with the state, holding that a parent's freedom of religion does not extend to being allowed to put the child's life at risk. One of the leading cases on this issue is *Application of the President and Director of Georgetown College* (1964), when a woman at the Georgetown University Hospital who was the mother of a seven-month-old child wished to refuse a transfusion. To protect the interests of the child, the court ordered the transfusion. In 1991, a Massachusetts court had to decide whether to order a woman to accept blood transfusions in the future, as she had recovered once without the need for a blood transfusion but probably would need one in the future, so the hospital wanted an order allowing future transfusions. The woman, a Jehovah's Witness, had a young child, but there were also others in the family who could care for the child (the father worked so much that he was not able to be considered as a caregiver), and the court found for the woman, as the child would not have been abandoned, and they found that her interest in being able to reject medical treatment outweighed that of the child. The court here looked at it as a case of being able to reject medical treatment, not as a case of the freedom of religion.

Courts have also found, though, that those parents who do not seek medical treatment for their children due to their own religion, are still liable for any harm, including death, that might befall the child from their decisions. Thus, freedom of religion is a factor, but only one to be balanced off against other interests, in rejecting medical treatment for oneself if one has a child, or in rejecting medical treatment for one's children.

The free exercise clause has not ceased to be controversial, even with the movement by the *Smith* decision in decreasing protection for that right. Cases filed relatively recently have ranged from the religious rights of prisoners to when high school sports tournaments may be played. In the latter area, some groups of Saturday Sabbath observers have sued sports tournaments, holding that the placement of the sports tournaments finals on Saturdays forces them to choose between their religion and their sports.

New areas are continuing to emerge in the discussion over the free exercise of religion, and the old areas are not going away either. With the

first cases testing the Jehovah's Witnesses' right to go door to door now being over sixty-five years old, one would expect the issue to be settled (especially as nearly every significant court case has upheld that right). However, villages still try to pass legislation to restrict door-to-door solicitation, and the Jehovah's Witnesses are still going to court over that legislation. The last significant Supreme Court case on the issue was in 2002 with *Watchtower* v. *Stratton,* when the Supreme Court struck down an Ohio village's regulation requiring prior registration of those people traveling door to door for any religious or commercial purpose.

America is a democracy, so many laws reflect what the majority of the people desire. However, a majority is far from an entirety, and some people's opposition to a given law may very well be based in religion, particularly when control of one's body or control of one's most personal behavior is at issue. In the early years of American history, few laws were struck down at the federal level as interfering with the freedom of religion, in large part because the First Amendment limited only federal action, and most questionable laws were at the state level. In the twentieth century, though, the freedom of religion was held to include and protect those groups that the majority in society might find disruptive, such as the Jehovah's Witnesses who went door to door. It was also held to include the right to refuse medical treatment, as long as the actions did not result in permanent harm to a child. Thus, blood transfusions could be refused as long as those refusing were not directly (and solely) responsible for a young child. In the mid- to late twentieth century, the freedom of religion was held to protect from laws that targeted the impact of religiously motivated behavior, such as missing work on Saturdays if that was the religious Sabbath, but not the taking of peyote. At first the Supreme Court held that the state needed a compelling state interest to restrict religion but then determined that neutral laws could restrict religion, as long as the laws were general in scope. Congress tried to overturn the neutrality decision on two occasions, and the first law was ruled unconstitutional, but parts of it were supported by Congress as recently as 2006, and the second is still under scrutiny in the courts.

Government Involvement in the Teaching of Creationism and Evolution

The controversy over teaching evolution in public schools, nearly one hundred years after it began, is still going strong. It is relatively easy to see, if the issue is considered objectively, why it has such longevity and such public appeal. In ways few other religious controversies do, the contest pits some people's core values against others' core values. For those who believe strongly in evolution, the idea that evolution should not be taught, or that, in their minds "pseudoscience" should be taught along with it, is repulsive. It is to them as if the schools were saying, "science is dead." For those who believe that evolution is a direct contradiction of creationism, as it is taught in the Bible, teaching evolution destroys the very centerpiece of their religion and, in their minds, threatens their souls. It is as if the schools were saying "God is dead." Thus, the debate between creationism and evolution creates much heat and often little light (and no closure). Government involvement between these two groups comes in several forms. School boards, both local and state, are government-backed institutions, court decisions are backed by government authority, and it is the relationship among courts, school boards, and the public that forms the crux of the controversy.

The whole idea of evolution was publicly debuted, in most people's minds, with Charles Darwin and his *The Origin of Species* (1859). However, scientists before Darwin had considered evolution and tried to determine the origins of the vast number of species they studied.

For a variety of reasons, including the fact that his explanations worked better than those of his predecessors and the increasing importance of science generally and biology specifically in the nineteenth century, Darwin received the most attention. He argued for "survival of the fittest" in terms of species. He stated that species tend to be different, that not every representative of a species is the same, and that the organisms with the differentiation most suited to the environment the group is in will tend to survive and then will pass down that difference to their children, for the most part. Over time, argued Darwin, species change enough to create new ones. This idea so far might not seem to be religiously objectionable, but it was (and is) to some. The problem for some is the idea that entire new species can appear today.

Some religious groups believe that the whole Bible is meant to be taken literally, and that the Bible is the only pronouncement from

Author, natural historian, geologist, and botanist Charles Darwin formulated and popularized the controversial theory of evolution in the mid-nineteenth century and published The Origin of Species *in 1859. (Library of Congress)*

God. The first book of the Bible, Genesis, is the one that creates the most controversy with evolution. The creation accounts state that God created the earth and all of the creatures. After that initial creation, there is nothing else in the Bible that discusses God making any more animals. No more animals, according to some literal interpreters of the Bible, means no species originating after the initial creation. A second problem is that evolution (and also other sciences such as geology) suggests that the world is millions of years old. A literal reading of the Bible produces a different age for the planet. The Bible tells us that creation took six days, then Adam was born, and the lives of Adam and all of his descendants are listed and enumerated, up to Jesus Christ, whose birth was later used as a starting point for the Christian era. If the days of creation are six days of twenty-four hours each, a specific age for the earth can be determined, and a Protestant Anglican bishop in the seventeenth century, James Ussher, did the calculation and came up with the date of 4004 B.C. for the earth's creation.

Thus, the very foundations of evolutionary thought come into conflict with some readings of the Bible. Not all Christians believe evolution conflicts with their religion. Some feel evolution could be part of God's plan. Others, however, primarily fundamentalists in the southern United States, feel very strongly that teaching evolution represents a threat to their religion. It should also be noted that the conflict did not start as soon as Darwin wrote his book. The original response to Darwin from religious figures was somewhat muted. The Catholic Church at the time held that evolution and Christianity were not irreconcilably opposed, and many of the Protestant denominations did not oppose it as of the end of the nineteenth century. The period of the late nineteenth and early twentieth centuries, however, saw a rise in fundamentalist Christianity, many of whose followers combined anti-modernism with a belief in the literal truth of the Bible. It was, in many

ways, a return to simplicity—no complicated urban modernization, no complicated religion, and no need for change; the Bible was correct as it was written, word for word, and the family and national system was correct as created in American life in the past. A series of traveling revivalists brought these ideas to a wide audience and millions believed in them, partly because of the perceived challenges of modernism and radicalism—the latter of which included communism, anarchism, feminism, and socialism in many people's minds. Evolution was linked directly to those threatening ideas.

Many fundamentalists in the 1920s campaigned for laws prohibiting the teaching of evolution. Some fifteen to twenty states considered bills, and the first state to pass one was Tennessee. The opposing side in this controversy did not sit by idly but argued against the fundamentalists from the very beginning. Some believers in evolution traveled far and wide to debate the fundamentalists, and the American Civil Liberties Union (ACLU), in its infancy in the 1920s, volunteered to defend anyone fired for teaching evolution. John Scopes in Dayton, Tennessee, was recruited to take the ACLU up on its offer and the Scopes "Monkey" Trial was on. This trial, in many ways, had it all: international media coverage, radio coverage (probably the first trial covered live by radio), famous attorneys (Clarence Darrow for the defense and William Jennings Bryan for the prosecution), and big issues. Scopes was fined $100 for teaching evolution, but Darrow got Bryan to be willing to come to the stand to defend the anti-evolutionary platform and the Bible's literal truth. Bryan did not explain his case well, and his performance caused many to look badly upon fundamentalists. It did not, however, cause many fundamentalists to change their views. The Tennessee Supreme Court overturned the Scopes verdict on a technicality and then dismissed the case, seeking to be done with it, as it had embarrassed Tennessee in the eyes of many. Only two states out of the fifteen considering anti-evolution legislation at the start of the Scopes Trial eventually passed any.

After 1925, many nonfundamentalists believed that the battle was over, that evolution had won, and it would appear in science classrooms thereafter. Many fundamentalists complained about modernism and focused on keeping evolution informally out of the schools. Control over textbooks and teachers became their goal, as opposed to laws banning the teaching of evolution. The events in the world also turned attention away from the controversy as the Great Depression, World War II, and then the Cold War were much more prominent than evolution in people's minds. In 1968, however, attention returned to the issue as the Supreme Court, in *Epperson* v. *Arkansas,* considered the issue for the first time.

The law in *Epperson* was quite similar to that in *Scopes.* It essentially banned the teaching of evolution in state-supported schools and universities because of the perceived conflict with Christianity. However, federal law had evolved in the time between *Scopes* and *Epperson*. Only one month before *Scopes,* the Supreme Court had announced its decision in *Gitlow* v. *New York* that the First Amendment also applied to the states (the text of that amendment applies directly only to Congress) but the decision did not specify how the amendment limited the states in any practical manner. By the time of *Epperson,* the Supreme Court had decided several cases dealing with state laws and the freedom of religion, most notably *Lemon* v. *Kurtzman,* which held that state laws need to have a secular (nonreligious) purpose, among other things. The Supreme Court concluded that there was no secular purpose to the law being contested in *Epperson,* and it was struck. Tennessee, after this decision, removed its statute.

Those opposed to the teaching of evolution denounced the Court, and during the interim between *Scopes* and *Epperson* they had also been working to use science against evolution. Some anti-evolutionists decided that the best way to defeat evolution was to disprove it scientifically.

So scientists formed institutes and groups to promote research aimed at disproving evolution. Some groups hoped to scientifically prove the occurrence of Noah's flood, feeling that this would explain fossils and vanished species. Others believed they could prove the earth could be only 6,000 years old. The name given to this overall movement was creation science, which aimed, as the name suggests, to give scientific support to the idea of a biblical creation. In the classroom, having been largely defeated in their attempts to use laws to forbid evolution's teaching, those opposing evolution sought to combat it in other ways. Some supported the idea of "equal time," which held that evolution was only a theory (misunderstanding and misusing the scientific definition of "theory"), and it should not be taught as fact. From this, people argued that evolution should be given only as much time as the idea of creationism, which they argued was also a plausible theory.

Their mission reached fruition in Louisiana in the early 1980s when that state passed a bill mandating equal time for both positions, if either were taught. The supporters of the bill, for the most part, at least publicly claimed that they were only helping science, as they were testing the idea of evolution just exactly as the scientific method suggests. Thus, they argued that equal time teaching was more scientific and more fair than the mere straightforward teaching of evolution. They also stated, and cited scientists to prove their point, that there was scientific support behind creation science, which is what they labeled the discussion of the scientific aspects of a relatively young earth. Not surprisingly, the law was challenged and went all the way to the Supreme Court, which decided in *Edwards* v. *Aguillard* that the law was unconstitutional, as it did not have a secular purpose. Two justices, Rehnquist and Scalia, dissented, holding that the purpose of the law was to create a balance, and that even if there was a religious purpose, that would have been acceptable as long as the law did not advance a religion. The whole idea, these two suggested, was that laws were supposed to be neutral to religion. Their two votes, of course, were not enough, but they did give some comfort to those supporting this bill.

Opponents of evolution were not dissuaded by this defeat. They continued their research and institutes and worked at the local school board level. Another important development in education during this time was the rise of standardized testing. Use of statewide assessment tests grew as people called for accountability in education. Tests were given to students at various levels, and if students performed poorly on the tests, districts were not funded and teachers were reprimanded, which led some teachers to teach solely what was on the tests. This related to evolution, as states set forth standards for the students to be tested on, and if evolution was ignored in those standards (or given little attention), then students weren't taught it. Educators in some states removed the term "evolution" from their state standards, with Kentucky preferring the term "change over time," for instance. Other states merely gave little attention to the issue.

Other concepts entered the discussion as well, as it grew broader. One of the most prominent at the present time is the idea of intelligent design. That holds that the world is so complex that it could not have arisen merely by chance, which is how some proponents of intelligent design describe the whole idea of evolution. Among the current examples commonly used by proponents of intelligent design are how blood clots and proteins work. Similar arguments in the past have used examples like the human eye and wings. Intelligent design, in its most scientific form, does not specify who the intelligent designer is, or if there is more than one intelligent designer working (or who worked, if the designer has left) on the project. Thus, in this way, the proponents of intelligent design state that this is a scientific theory without any required religious component. The proponents

of intelligent design point out that their idea accommodates all religious perspectives, and intelligent design websites argue that there are agnostics among their supporters.

The opponents of intelligent design (which is often shortened to ID by both opponents and proponents) point out that the idea is not testable, as it is impossible to prove that proteins, for instance, were designed by an intelligent designer. The proponents of the theory admit to using inferences but argue that these are the most probable answers. Opponents of intelligent design also point out that even though there might be a low chance of some things, such as DNA, occurring purely by chance, this does not mean that they did not arise by chance, which is the center of the ID perspective.

Some supporters of ID took over directly from creationists. Some of the creationists shifted their allegiance to the ID movement, and at least one textbook widely used in ID circles was alleged to have been written from a creationist viewpoint but with the term "intelligent design" entered for "creationism" during the editing process after the *Edwards* decision. Other supporters of intelligent design state that their intelligent designer could only be the Christian god, using the same logic, that this is the most probable correct conclusion, as is used to support the entire intelligent design theory. Other supporters of ID, as noted, hold no public religious connection.

The positions and religious views of both the supporters and detractors of intelligent design are often, but by no means always, linked. Supporters of both ideas adopt their views because they do not conflict with their religious opinions. The belief in intelligent design and religion are connected for many Christians who believe in science, because intelligent design is a good way to reconcile the two potentially conflicting ideas. Similarly, many who support evolution but have no religion, finding no evidence of God in the world, believe in evolution because it does not require intervention from a god. There are plenty of non-Christian supporters of intelligent design, and plenty of Christian supporters of evolution, further muddying the waters. And last are those supporters of intelligent design who also believe some form of evolution is a possibility. Some discussants in the evolution debate want to paint the battle as religion versus science, but the discussion today, especially when dealing with intelligent design, is much more complex than that. When this discussion is carried into the science classroom, evolution's proponents argue that with teaching time already extremely limited, the true effect is to completely forestall any understanding of evolution by launching straight into an argument about its merits and detriments. (And some, though hardly all, ID supporters would be very happy with this result.)

Evolution opponents, whatever alternative they propose, were active in twenty-eight states as recently as 2001, and this did not count, of course, those states where quiet efforts to remove evolution are still ongoing through book selection and curriculum control. The most publicly known recent efforts have been in Kansas and Pennsylvania. In Kansas, in 1999, the state board of education removed evolution from those areas tested on statewide high school science tests. With the increased emphasis on testing, this was the equivalent of telling all the high schools in the state that they could ignore evolution. Indeed, it was the equivalent of telling high schools that they probably *should* ignore evolution, as teaching information that will allow a student to pass a test carries more weight in funding circles than does teaching information for which no tests exist. In the 2000 elections, voters effectively overturned this decision by electing new members to the board, but in 2004 the board, again with even more new members, returned to the controversy by supporting intelligent design. One school board in Pennsylvania went one step further by voting to require that teachers use and read a statement suggesting that students

keep their minds open on the question, noting what intelligent design was and noting a specific pro-intelligent design reference book to consider. The action of this board was challenged in federal district court and in late 2005, Federal District Court Judge John Jones ruled that these instructions were unconstitutional as they created a state endorsement of religion, barred by the First Amendment. Jones cited several reasons for the ruling, including that ID was not science, as it was not testable, and that while many of ID's arguments did tend to point out problems with evolution, this was not the same as supporting an opposing viewpoint. Finally, he noted that ID was not generally supported in the scientific community.

Judge Jones's decision hardly ends the debate overall, even though it might end it in this school district. Beliefs about evolution teaching in public school classrooms are and will continue to be deeply held. As the two events that might end the debate will not happen any time soon—those being irrefutable proof of evolution or irrefutable and public proof of the existence of a supernatural being—the debate will extend and change. Similarly, as education increases in importance in the twenty-first century, control over school policies will increase in importance as well. Governments are also responsive to the will of the people, and when one side or the other protests loudly enough, as happened in Kansas twice in four years, the governmental pendulum will swing. The issue even reaches all the way to the presidency, as President George W. Bush in August 2005 stated that intelligent design should be taught as an alternative to evolution, even though he seemingly contradicted that point by saying that school boards, not the national government, should set policy. Whether these remarks were intended to announce his views on the issue or to push people into supporting ID or to satisfy social conservatives (all of which are possible motives), such comments do little to settle the debate. For all of these reasons, it is unlikely that the controversy over the teaching of evolution will go away, even though the Scopes Trial, in many people's views, "settled" the controversy over four score years ago.

Important Organizations in the Development of Religion and the Law

While movies and novels often focus on the one person fighting against the state all alone, the individual litigant stands little chance of success in today's (and most of yesterday's) legal environment. To be successful, an individual often needs backing from an organization, and some of those organizations have played a shaping role in the development of religion and the law. While some unsupported individuals have had legal success, the focus here is on nongovernmental organizations. Indeed, many cases known by the names of individuals also had important organizations involved. For instance, *Brown* v. *Board of Education* is named for litigant Oliver Brown, who sued on behalf of his daughter Linda Brown, but the NAACP, whose backing of Brown provided the means for that lawsuit's success, is an example of a similar situation in another context.

Rather than use judgmental terms that will likely bog down the discussion with arguments of which group's perspective is correct, this essay will admittedly use a wide tent approach to gather those who have litigated into two main groups: the accommodationists and the separationists. The accommodationists are those who argue that, either for policy or historical reasons or both, the First Amendment allows the government, both at the state and federal levels, to accommodate religion. The separationsts argue that, once again for either policy or historical reasons or both, the First Amendment tells the government that church and state should be kept far apart. None of the lists discussed below are either exclusive or definitive, as they try to highlight the most sig-

nificant groups. It should also be noted that, of course, each group believes that it is correct in its view of the First Amendment's religion clause, or how the First Amendment's religion clauses affect its particular interest.

Those groups who have fought for a more accommodationist view of the First Amendment will be discussed first, and they include two main subgroups. The first is those who have appeared in court in general, and the second is those whose interests are in only one area.

Among the important groups who favor accommodation and who have regularly appeared in court is the Rutherford Institute. This group was founded to help conservative causes and early on worked against what it saw as improper actions on the part of school boards. The group was founded in large part with donations from Christian conservatives, among them, Howard Fieldstead Ahmanson, Jr., who was also a large donor to the Discovery Institute, noted later. Among those things protested by the Rutherford Institute were AIDS prevention efforts and condom distribution. The Institute soon moved into areas of the First Amendment, particularly the religion clauses. Among the well-known cases in which the Institute has filed amicus briefs are the *Newdow* case, on the use of the phrase "under God" in the pledge—the Supreme Court decided that the person suing did not have a legal right to bring the case (the Institute believed the phrase to be legal); the *Lee* v. *Weisman* case, in which the Supreme Court struck down prayer at graduation (the Institute again believed it to be legal); and the *Bowers* v. *Hardwick* case, in which the Supreme Court upheld a Georgia law penalizing homosexual sodomy (the Institute filed on the side supporting the law, and the *Bowers* decision has since been reversed). The Institute has also filed amicus briefs or appeared, in the area of religion, in suits defending a Muslim woman's right to wear religious garb to class, defending a church's right to display a religious message in a public light show alongside those of secular organizations, and defending a church against an adverse decision by a zoning board. In other areas of the First Amendment, the Rutherford Institute often takes a libertarian view and sometimes agrees with the ACLU, as court cases make strange pairings. For instance, both groups have opposed the Patriot Act and opposed the detentions without counsel allegedly resulting from the war on terror.

A second important group that has filed amicus briefs in many Supreme Court cases dealing with religion is the Christian Legal Society. This group was founded in Chicago and now is headquartered in Springfield, Virginia. The group requires its members to be Christian but is nondenominational. The society requires its members to accept the Bible as the word of God and to accept a bodily resurrection and the virgin birth. The society also includes law school students, having over one hundred chapters, a sizable number compared to the number of law schools existing. Members do not have to be a lawyers. The Christian Legal Society has founded the Center for Law and Religious Freedom, which, since 1993, has been fighting laws legalizing abortion, as it considers one of its purposes to defend all lives and it believes life begins at conception. Among the recent well-known cases in which the Christian Legal Society, acting through the Center, has filed briefs are *Boy Scouts* v. *Dale,* in which the Boy Scouts were successful in maintaining their policy excluding homosexuals from being Scout leaders; *Santa Fe* v. *Doe,* in which the Santa Fe School District tried unsuccessfully to allow student-led prayer at football games; and *Zelman* v. *Simmons-Harris,* in which the Cleveland School Board was allowed to implement a voucher program that included private religious schools. The society favored the Boy Scouts and both school districts in the above litigation. In other recent amicus briefs, the Center appeared in support of the United States in their passage of the Religious Land Use and Institutionalized Persons Act. This

Dr. Jonathan Wells of the Discovery Institute and a supporter of intelligent design, puts on a presentation on the first day of hearings held by the Kansas State Board of Education on the teaching of evolution in Kansas schools on May 5, 2005. (Larry W. Smith/Getty Images)

statute aimed to increase the rights of those in state prisons partially funded by the federal government. The Center has also appeared in actions recently challenging California's denial of tax-free financing to religious schools and supporting a church that attempted to use the Religious Freedom Restoration Act to defend its members against prosecution for use of an illegal drug during a religious ceremony. The society, in addition to its efforts in defending religious freedom, also aims to provide contacts, create prayer groups, link attorneys to like-minded attorneys and individuals, and try to help the poor.

A third accommodationist organization important nationally is the Catholic League for Religious and Civil Rights, more generally known as the Catholic League, headquartered in New York City. This organization has the most members of any Catholic organization concerned with religious freedom. The Catholic League's positions generally mirror those of the Catholic Church, and it has been in existence since 1973. The Catholic League is active in a number of areas, including countering what it sees as anti-Catholic attacks, working against bills that it considers to be attacking Catholics, and working through the courts for redress of damages done to Catholics. Among the well-known cases that the Catholic League has been active in are *Edwards* v. *Aguillard,* in which the Catholic League defended the right of Louisiana to require equal time in science classrooms for creation science and evolution (the Supreme Court disagreed, striking down the legislation); and *Bowers* v. *Hardwick,* in which the Catholic League wrote in defense of Georgia's law penalizing homosexuality (the Supreme Court agreed; as previously mentioned, however, the Court has since overturned *Bowers*). The less well-known cases that the Catholic League is interested in include the current policy of the New York public schools to prohibit manger scenes while allegedly allowing the menorah to be displayed in schools, and an attempt by New Hampshire to repeal the priest-penitent privilege in the area of child abuse by requiring priests to report any suspected cases of child abuse. The Catholic League opposes the latter, of course, as it infringes upon the confessional. In addition to its legal actions, the Catholic League also encourages boycotts of groups it feels are hostile to Catholicism, defends the Catholic Church in the media, and publishes a journal (and a website) to publicize its efforts.

Among the important specialized areas that have promoted a lot of litigation is that of teaching evolution in the public schools. A wide variety of groups on both sides of the issue have started (or continued) their scientific research into the topic and have also become involved in the legal battles. Of course, those on the accommodationist side say, or at least some groups on that side say, that evolu-

tion can be banned, that only creationism can be taught or that a balanced treatment is needed between the two, and that intelligent design can be taught or that a balanced treatment is needed between those two issues.

Among the important groups on the accommodationist side of evolution is the Discovery Institute, headquartered in Seattle, Washington. This group is a strong proponent of the idea of intelligent design, which argues that the universe must have had an intelligent force involved at some point. The reasons advanced are that the universe has elements too complex to have merely arrived by chance, that certain elements have both a very specified function and a very complex nature and that could not have arrived by chance either, and that the universe works too well together to have just arisen by chance. The Institute's goal, in the area of intelligent design, is to present evolution as a theory with far too many flaws and evolution's defenders as simply unwilling to consider other arguments and hiding from reality rather than pursuing it. Following this second argument to its natural end, the Institute argues that intelligent design should be taught along with evolution to further the pursuit of reality. The proponents of intelligent design, especially the Discovery Institute, state that intelligent design goes beyond creationism, which will be discussed next, and that religion does not have to play a role in classroom discussions of intelligent design. The Intelligent Designer may just be an intelligent designer, and discussions of who that designer might be are not necessary, stresses the Institute.

Another important group, although it has been outshadowed by the Discovery Institute recently, is the Institute for Creation Research, headquartered in San Diego, California. This institute argues that the world is only 6,000 years old. It takes a literal view of the first chapter of Genesis, meaning that the creation account there, having the world created in six days, is correct. Furthermore, the six days are taken to be six twenty-four-hour days, and the rest of the Bible is to be taken literally as well. The biggest problem that is publicly known with this idea is the fossil record, which the Institute for Creation Research explains as having been created by the great flood noted later in the Genesis account. The group requires belief in the inerrancy of the Bible and also produces research that works to square science with religion. Unlike the Discovery Institute's public stance that religion is not a required part of their worldview, the Institute for Creation Research publicly proclaims such a requirement. The Institute for Creation Research was directly linked to the 1980s attempt by the Louisiana legislature to mandate the teaching of both creation science and evolution when either was taught, as the Institute was one of the main places cited to which creation scientists belonged.

The other side of the table from these groups is very often filled by, or at least joined by, those groups who favor a more separationist approach. Similar to the accommodationist camp, there are those who are interested in multiple issues, or in the overall separation of church and state, and those involved in only one issue.

One of the more important groups on the separationist side that is interested in the First Amendment as a whole is Americans United for Separation of Church and State, which often refers to itself as Americans United. That group is headquartered in Washington, D.C., and has existed for roughly sixty years. In contrast to some portrayals of anti-accommodationist views, like Americans United, as atheist, the early founders of the group, along with current members, are very much connected with organized religion. Among the early founders were the president of Princeton Theological Seminary, one of the nation's leading religious training grounds, and the president of the Southern Baptist Convention. The group has been active in the courts over the past six decades, and among the recent lawsuits in which Americans United has filed amicus briefs were *ACLU* v. *McCreary County,* dealing with the posting of the Ten Commandments on public property in Kentucky; *Edwards* v. *Aguillard,* dealing with the required teaching of creation science if one taught evolution in Louisiana; and *Hibbs* v. *Winn,* dealing with tax credits for scholarships to private schools. Americans United believes in the wholesale separation of church and state, and, besides litigation, also works in the areas of public education and with school boards and government in trying to resolve areas of difficulty without litigation. This group is currently involved in a wide variety of areas dealing with religion and the state, believing that the state bans on gay marriage are unconstitutional, as some religions favor allowing gay marriage, the bans favor one religious view over another, and they impose a religious element on marriage, a state-sanctioned status. The group also opposes vouchers for education as it forces the public to subsidize religion and also creates problems with the schools. Also, because many religious schools discriminate on the basis of religion, the group believes vouchers force the state to subsidize religious discrimination. Americans United also opposes faith-based initiatives, which allow money to be given to religious groups to perform social work.

A second important group in the separationist camp is the American Civil Liberties Union (ACLU). This group has been around since the early 1900s, having been founded during World War I to attempt to protect those who protested against that war. The ACLU was originally active mostly in the areas of free speech but gained notoriety in the area of freedom of religion as it served to defend John Scopes in the 1925 Scopes Monkey Trial over the teaching of evolution in Tennessee. The ACLU now fights to keep the government out of religion, in the areas of both establishment and free exercise. An example in the first area would be the ACLU's recent fight to remove an anti-evolutionary sticker from schoolbooks in Georgia. The sticker suggested that evolution needed to be approached with an open mind, but a court struck down use of that sticker as evolution was the only scientific idea mentioned and its selection would cause a reasonable observer to see an endorsement of religion. The ACLU also recently protested against the removal of two jurors for religious reasons unrelated to the case, as a prosecutor had believed that religious people were more friendly to the defense. The court agreed with the ACLU that this was an unacceptable practice. Among the more well-known recent cases that the ACLU has been involved in are the *Kitzmiller* case in Pennsylvania dealing with the attempt of the school board to force biology teachers to read a disclaimer before teaching evolution in biology classes (the federal district court ultimately struck down the disclaimer), and in the *Newdow* case, decided by the Supreme Court in 2004, dealing with the term "under God" in the Pledge of Allegiance (the Court ruled that Newdow did not have standing to pursue the case). The ACLU is also involved in other less well-known cases, such as attempts by districts to force students to stand for or recite the pledge and attempts by transit districts to prevent religious groups from advertising.

A third important overall group on the separationist side is the American Jewish Congress (AJC). It was originally formed in 1918, and its original purpose was to protest against anti-Semitism. While that remains one of its important goals, the AJC has moved beyond that to other issues in America and the world, including defense of the state of Israel and support of its peaceful existence with the rest of the Middle East, and, importantly for this essay, belief in the separation of church and state. The AJC has recently filed amicus briefs in a wide variety of cases, including *Edwards* v. *Aguillard,* in which the AJC protested against the Louisiana legislature's decision to grant equal time to creation science and evolution if either was taught (the Supreme Court eventually agreed with its view), and *Lee* v. *Weisman,* with the AJC

protesting against a school board's decision to invite a rabbi to graduation to deliver an invocation (the Supreme Court decision agreed with the AJC perspective). It has also helped in the litigation of other cases, including appealing against the decision of the government-funded Americorps to support teachers in religious schools, in a case that was denied review by the Supreme Court, which allowed the government grant of teachers to continue. The AJC also protested against a voucher program by the Florida government, which was eventually overturned by the Florida Supreme Court. Besides the courts, the AJC has also been involved in a wide variety of other efforts, including helping the state of Israel by commissioning studies and establishing liaisons, promoting women's causes such as breast cancer research and pay equity, and supporting the Oslo peace process. The AJC has been particularly interested in efforts that bridge its interests, such as studying the incidence of breast cancer in the worldwide Ashkenazi Jewish population; the group also produces a variety of publications.

One of the significant separationist groups favoring separation of church and state in the area of the teaching of evolution is the National Academy of Sciences (NAS). This group was founded in the 1860s as a society for the leading scientists of America, and one becomes a member only by invitation. The NAS is interested in a number of different scientific areas, including futuring, but the main area that combines science, religion, and the law is the teaching of evolution. The NAS lends its scientific weight in the discussion and provides information about the issues. It also has created many different standards in the area of education, and these standards are often the base of statewide standards. The academy has withdrawn copyright permission from some states that discount evolution and lean toward the side of either teaching both evolution and creationism, or that are teaching nothing on evolution in their standards. This group has also filed statements and briefs in evolution cases.

One organization that focuses exclusively on the issue of evolution and desires a strong wall of separation is the National Council for Science Education (NCSE). It claims to be the only group founded for the specific purpose of defending evolution in the schools. Among the organization's activities are the publishing of a journal to keep its members informed on the evolution issue, continuous collection of state-by-state reports of activity in the evolution–anti-evolution tussle, and educating the public about evolution. The NCSE does not itself hire lawyers to fight against anti-evolution efforts, but it does help groups encouraging the teaching of evolution by referring them to like-minded lawyers, and it provides a wealth of materials. This group aims to counter the anti-evolution forces by providing experts who will debate them on national talk shows and other public forums. Thus, the NCSE is an important force in the evolution area of religion and the law, even though they do not directly enter the courtroom as lawyers.

The stereotypical view of the battleground in the area of religion and the law has a single lone plaintiff challenging a government decision about either religious practice or the potential government establishment of religion. However, that view is much too simplistic. Very often the forces on both sides are supplemented by the briefs, arguments, and funding of various interested organizations. Sometimes the federal government also makes arguments in favor of state legislation or vice versa, and the federal government and state government may appear in litigation that seems to be between two private forces. Organizations, as noted, represent a wide variety of viewpoints, and sometimes form strange alliances on some issues. Some organizations are interested in only one issue, while others express opinions on most facets of the church-state relationship. Without such organizations few checks would

exist against the powerful in society and the government, even though the powerful in turn often help to fund these same organizations.

Issues of Taxation and Funding and Religious Groups

The ways in which taxation and funding influence religious groups cannot be considered in isolation from other issues, such as the establishment of religion and the free exercise of the First Amendment. The reason for this is that if the government funds a religious group, then it may be establishing a religion, but if it prevents a religion from being funded the same way any other charitable organization is funded, it may be discriminating against the free exercise of religion. Of course, the issue becomes even more complicated when one religion is treated differently from another. Thus, the issues of how a religious group is funded and how the tax system treats religious groups are complex ones and interact with many other facets of the whole relationship between religion and the law.

Only issues that have a direct effect on how religious groups are funded will be considered here and those with indirect effects will be excluded. For instance, government regulation of the health and safety conditions of a day care program in a church may indirectly affect a church's finances, but that will not be considered here. Whether the government could tax the employees in that day care operation will, however, be considered. Some of these issues are discussed in other essays, as the relationship between religion and the law is many faceted.

First, the issue of taxation is examined—whether the government can (and must) tax a religious organization if it taxes other similar organizations. Generally, it has been held that a government can tax a religion if its taxes are neutral. For instance, the government has been able to put sales taxes upon religious sales. A revival in California was sued for sales taxes on the religious publications that were sold during the revival. The church noted a prior Supreme Court decision not allowing a city to force door-to-door proselytizers to be licensed, but that license was held to be a tax preventing the spread of ideas, or a prior restraint. Prior restraints, as a form of censorship, are especially odious to the Constitution, but taxes after the fact are less so. Property taxes on church property have also been allowed. In both cases, the taxes do result in less money being available to the church and so they have some impact on religion, but this was not held to be sufficient to be a restriction on the free exercise of religion. As religions are generally protected more than (or equal to) religious institutions, if a religion can be taxed, a religious institution such as a religious college can be taxed also.

The issue of income taxes and other employee taxes has also been addressed by the federal court system on numerous occasions with regard to religious institutions. Some churches have claimed that their beliefs require them to follow the law of God and that they do not have to follow the law of man. These churches have generally not come into the court system until they have been forced to do so, but the federal courts have not been generally receptive to their arguments. Freedom of belief is absolute, but freedom of action based on those beliefs is somewhat limited and does not excuse the believer, or the church, from participation in government programs of taxation that are applied on a neutral basis, including income taxes. The courts have also considered direct challenges to the Social Security taxes on the grounds of religious belief. Some churches have argued that their religious convictions require them to take care of their own and have made provisions to do so, desiring no interference of government. The Amish, who have long attempted to live separately from society, are among those issuing such protests, lest it be perceived that these were just contrived

tax protests or new beliefs. It should also be noted that the Supreme Court agreed that religious freedom would be somewhat infringed by taxation. The Court, however, held that the government interest in creating and administering a standardized tax system justified this infringement as the need for a consistent and workable tax system was held to be substantial enough to justify the infringement. Some have also argued for being able to withhold taxes because they or their churches disagree with how the money is being spent. Specifically, a group of Quakers wanted to withhold some of their taxes as they disagreed with taxes being spent to support the Department of Defense. The court, however, disagreed, and held that the taxes were still due, with penalties and interest. Some churches have disagreed with other taxes imposed, such as workmen's compensation taxes (generally gathered at the state level) in a recent case in Ohio. Similar to the arguments made about Social Security, some churches feel that they should take care of their own and that workmen's compensation programs have someone else intervene. Ohio law did allow self-insurance, but the church did not take advantage of this. As with the income tax, with a sufficiently important government interest, burdens on religion are allowed, and in this case, as with the other taxes, the court held that the government interest justified the burden.

A final issue considered by the courts is whether licenses can be required of door-to-door religious proselytizers and whether they can be subject to prior registration. Both of these questions were answered in the negative, as prior registration and prior licensing have been held to be prior restraints and thus censorship. Controls on the time, place, and manner of soliciting have been held to be acceptable, but overall registration and especially the payment of fees for the privilege of discussing one's religion have been struck down.

Besides the issue of whether a tax can be applied to a religion, in taxation there is also the matter of whether (and when) a tax exemption can be removed from a religion or religious institution. That issue was before the Court in 1983, when the Court considered the case of Bob Jones University. The IRS had long given tax exemptions to universities, and these exemptions helped with the university's tax burden and also allowed donors to give money to these causes and then have a tax benefit. The rationale behind this exemption was that the universities conferred a benefit upon the public and thus could merit a tax exemption in return. It should be noted that most universities received (and receive) tax-exempt status. However, if a university violates IRS rules, the exemption can be withdrawn. In the case of Bob Jones University, the exemption was removed because Bob Jones practiced racial discrimination, forbidden by the IRS. The school had claimed that its religion required this discrimination, but the Supreme Court sided with the IRS, holding first that controls on religious action could be justified only by a compelling government interest, but that preventing discrimination was such an interest. While Congress is supposed to be in charge of tax policy, the IRS was set up to determine the specifics, and as past removals of tax-exempt status had not been changed by Congress, Congress was presumed to have affirmed by its silence. Thus, tax exemptions can be removed for actions taken under the color of religion, but that removal has to be justified by a compelling government interest, not just a trivial one. Note that this removal of a tax exemption was from a specific group for a specific act, not from all religious colleges or even all religious colleges of a particular religion. Churches have also had their tax-exempt status revoked because of participation in forbidden political activities. One church lost its exemption because it placed ads in newspapers against a presidential candidate, and this violated the IRS rule against any activity in campaigns against any individual candidate by the church. The courts upheld this revocation upon review, as the ads clearly constituted involvement in a campaign against a candidate.

A more complex question is the relationship between the government and religious groups in terms of the amount of funding the government is allowed to give to churches. The government is generally not allowed to charge more for religious speech than for other noncommercial speech. A school board allowed religious groups to meet, but charged religious groups more than other noncommercial ones that were not religious if the religious group had met for more than five years at the facility. The reasoning of the school board was that it wanted to discourage religious groups from using the facility in a permanent manner to avoid the appearance that the school board was promoting religion. The courts struck down this justification, holding that one could not discriminate against religion, and that the amount of use of the facility by religious groups was not enough to justify that discrimination.

On the other hand, the government can choose not to fund religious speech as long as it does not discriminate against religious institutions in general. The government has been allowed to provide funds and support for religious institutions, such as colleges, and insert the restriction that the funds be used only for secular purposes. Religious colleges have been provided with building grants, with the caveat that these buildings be forever used only for secular activities. These colleges have also received lower-cost government-supported bonds for building purposes, with the caveat that the buildings be used for secular purposes until the bonds are repaid. Thus, while the government can provide religious institutions with money, that funding can also carry government restrictions.

A related question is whether government-regulated universities can distribute money to religious organizations. Some protested against the decisions of state schools to support religious organizations, as they did not want their money going to groups that they found to be objectionable. The courts, though, have found that universities can charge students a general fee, and then redistribute that money to groups that some might find to be objectionable as long as the criteria and process used are neutral with regard to the organization's content. Thus, while groups that some might find objectionable can be funded, the fact that they are religious in nature cannot be used as a criterion to deny their funding. In a related manner, the courts also found that a university can simply choose not to fund all organizations that are generally religious. A university adopted the same test the government uses against laws, the *Lemon* test, which states that an organization, to be funded, must have a nonreligious purpose, must have a general effect of neither advancing nor retarding religion, and must not entangle the school in religion through the oversight of the funding. The court system upheld this test, holding that the university did not have any obligation to fund anyone and that the university had created a limited area for funding; therefore it could discriminate as long as nonreligious criteria were used. Schools, however, have been prohibited from refusing support for religious magazines on the basis of their content. A school wished to deny a religious magazine funding on the basis that it was religious; this was not allowed as the magazine met the school's printed nonreligious criteria for the funding. Thus, secular standards need to be used.

Tied in with this question is the whole issue of whether government grants that are given to individuals and organizations may wind up in the hands of religious schools, and whether religious schools and majors must be treated the same as nonreligious ones. The answer to the first question is yes, if the government is not the one making the decision as to where the money goes. The courts have held that the government may provide support for nonreligious matters, such as interpreters for the deaf or scholarship support for the unemployed, and it is acceptable for this money to be used at religious schools through the choice of the recipient. The courts have gone so far as to say that support should not be revoked when students choose to attend a religious school. Thus, if a deaf child attends a religious mainstream school, the state should still provide that child with an interpreter, if that interpreter would have been provided at a nonreligious school.

States and schools have, however, been allowed to decide not to fund religious studies. A state provided scholarships for students to attend colleges but required that recipients not study religion as a major. A student at a private school sued, claiming religious discrimination, but the Court upheld the state's decision. While the state could have decided to allow study of religion, as one of many majors, it was not required under the First Amendment to make that allowance; thus, funding the study of religion was neither banned nor required.

A related and very intricate matter is the funding of religious education, particularly at the high school and lower levels. The state, at the most basic level, is generally required to allow private religious schools to exist. It may regulate them the same way that it regulates all other private schools and may extend some of the same regulations to those private schools as it does to public ones, such as state-mandated testing. However, the state may not directly fund religious education. In the late 1960s, some states tried to help private education by providing teacher supplements to private schools, including religious schools. The court system struck this program down, and in doing so provided the *Lemon* test, described earlier.

The controversy then shifted from the funding of religious schools to the funding of auxiliary, nonreligious, services for religious schools. Transportation was a large issue, and the courts held that states can provide transportation of students to religious schools, as long as that transportation is provided on an equivalent basis as the transportation to public schools. Other services provided to private schools include the loan of nonreligious textbooks, provision of audiovisual materials, and provision of instructional personnel for remedial instruction. The loan of materials was challenged in a wide variety of cases and produced a quixotic set of rulings. For instance, lending books was held to be acceptable, but not maps, and so, as one justice noted, what about a book of maps? The Court recently has upheld providing materials in general, but by a narrow decision. Different factions of the Court disagree, even among those allowing financial support, how much oversight of the funds is necessary. When the federal government (or states) provides materials to a religious school, the school saves money. The critical question here is whether the private schools should have strict oversight to prevent them from shifting to religious instruction the funds saved by the government grant of materials, as this would have the effect of the government promoting religion. The most accommodationist wing of the Court, led by Scalia and then Chief Justice Rehnquist, would allow almost any program providing sec-

ular materials open to all, regardless of any diversion. A middle faction, led by Justice Breyer and then Justice O'Connor, would desire oversight, and the separationist wing, led by Justice Stevens, would ban all such programs.

A related issue is providing teachers for remedial and assistance services and the use of funds provided for low-income students in private schools. Many private school students, similar to public school students, need some assistance, such as speech therapy, and the federal government programs for low-income students are given to all, regardless of where they go to school. At first, cases required that the assistance not be given on the site of private schools, as the chance for religious indoctrination was too high and would require too much oversight, resulting in entanglement. Such assistance then was often given in temporary buildings, often trailers, set up on the school parking lots of private schools so that the aid was not provided on

With the U.S. Capitol in the background, proponents and opponents of school vouchers take part in a rally outside the Supreme Court in Washington on February 20, 2002. (AP Photo/Rick Bowmer)

school grounds. However, in the late 1990s, the Supreme Court reversed itself and allowed the funding of such education on school grounds.

A more recent battleground, and one more directly related to school funding, is that of school vouchers. Under voucher programs, districts and schools are ranked (similar to what occurs elsewhere) based on student scores on standardized tests. Those graded as failing must allow students to go elsewhere, and the voucher pays a certain amount to the school or district to which the student moves (the school or district receiving students must want more students). Those favoring the programs see them as creating student choice, allowing students and parents to "vote" to leave failing schools. Those opposing them would rather fix the current system and note that the vast majority of students using vouchers who enter private schools enter private religious schools, which in turn creates a massive government subsidy of religious schools. The Supreme Court, however, has upheld this program, stating that the aid is neutrally available, as students can choose to attend a private nonreligious school, a private religious school, or a public school, and that the student choice is what directs the money to religious schools, not the government; thus, there is no government establishment of religion. A voucher program in Cleveland, Ohio, has been approved by the Supreme Court, but one in Florida was struck down by the Florida Supreme Court, relying on language in Florida's constitution. Thus, whether a voucher program is constitutional not only depends on who is on the Supreme Court and what their views are, as is always true, but also what court (state or federal) hears the case, what state the case originates in, and what language is in the state's constitution.

Recently, faith-based programs have come under scrutiny. In these, churches are given funds to provide social services, such as feeding the homeless. This idea is controversial, not because people want hunger to continue but because people do not want the government funding religion. Some religious people op-

pose these grants also because the one who pays the bills often controls the action, and they do not want government interfering with their actions (even though they sometimes would like the money). Other religious people fear that the "wrong" religion will be funded. These programs have been allowed by the courts but continue to be controversial.

The ban on establishment and the allowing of the free exercise of religion, both in the First Amendment, seem like relatively simple ideas. However, there are few hard-and-fast rules in the question of how taxation and funding treat religious groups. The government is not allowed broadly to fund religion or to ban religion from tax exemptions. However, tax benefits for religious groups are allowed when other charitable groups receive those benefits. Government funds are also allowed to flow to religious groups when the stated purpose of the grant is not the promotion of religion and when those funds are available on neutral terms. Thus, while the large ideas seem simple, the building blocks of a program's constitutionality or lack thereof are often in the fine print or in the details of administration.

Major Court Cases Involving Religion in U.S. Legal History

Many significant court cases have shaped American legal and constitutional history in the area of religion. It would be impossible to describe all of them in a short essay or to provide a comprehensive list of such cases. With those disclaimers, however, it is helpful to survey some of the major cases to understand their impact on American society and the fields of the law that they help to establish.

The First Amendment only limits the actions of Congress, but the majority of First Amendment cases that come to the Supreme Court involve the states, and so an introduction to religion and the law should begin with an explanation of this apparent paradox. The whole of the Bill of Rights, not just the First Amendment, was held in 1833 to limit only Congress. Thus, the liberties outlined in the Bill of Rights did not protect the citizens of each state from the state governments, which were reliant upon the state constitution and the state courts for their liberties. After the Civil War, the Fourteenth Amendment both declared that all freed slaves were American citizens with the same rights as every other American and limited the powers of the states in terms of what liberties they could infringe. The exact reach of the Fourteenth Amendment in the eyes of those who wrote it has been (and will forever be) unclear, but in the early days after the Civil War, the Fourteenth Amendment was read narrowly and did not greatly increase the rights of the freed slaves or of anyone else.

However, in 1925, a Supreme Court decision began to change that situation. In 1925, in *Gitlow* v. *New York,* the Supreme Court held that Fourteenth Amendment language mandating that states could not infringe upon a person's liberty did not mean liberty as an abstract concept only but also included some specific liberties, including parts of the First Amendment. Thus, the *Gitlow* case, and other cases building on it, are the root cause of much of our liberty today and consequently the underpinnings of the fetters on power at the state level. While the federal government has more power than any state, state laws have the most impact on liberty in our daily lives. They affect how our schools are operated, how we marry, what monuments are created, and so on. Thus, the *Gitlow* decision was very important in increasing our religious freedom, even though it did not specifically address the freedom of religion portion of the First Amendment. It was the foundation that the Supreme Court used in 1940 to specifically extend the freedom of religion protections to apply against the states in *Cantwell* v. *Connecticut.*

Since *Gitlow,* there have been important court cases in several specific areas of religion and the law, but there have also been important

general cases. The most important general case is that of *Lemon* v. *Kurtzman* (1971), which dealt with the general question of how to determine whether a state program is legal when it involves both the state and religion. The *Lemon* case involved state aid to private education, but it is more important for the test that it established. The *Lemon* test has three parts: first, it requires that the program, to be constitutional, must have a secular purpose; second, the program must neither advance nor hinder religion as its primary effect; and third, the program must not excessively entangle the state and religion. The secular purpose is required because the government is not allowed to enact programs for religious reasons, and a program without a secular purpose is assumed to have a religious one when programs enter the area of religion. The government must be neutral in the area of religion, and that is why the program must neither help nor hinder religion as its main effect. No program that touches religion can have absolutely zero effect, of course, but whatever effect it has on religion cannot be its main goal. This is sometimes viewed as the neutrality test, and according to some justices this is enough: if the program neither advances nor retards any specific religion as its main effect, it should be allowed. Other justices just see this as one part. The entanglement issue is relevant as the government is supposed to stay out of areas of religion, and while some entanglement is inevitable, justices can review precedents and relevant information to determine what level of entanglement is acceptable.

In addition to such general cases, which apply to nearly all religion and the law situations, the courts have also made a number of rulings with more narrow application. One of the most controversial of these areas is school prayer. Many people who feel that American civilization is declining tie that decline, rightly or not, to the ban on vocal prayer and mandated Bible readings in public schools. Originally, many states, but by no means all, allowed local school districts to decide whether prayer was allowed or mandated or banned and to decide whether to have Bible readings to open the school day. Some states, most notably Illinois, banned those readings, but most did not. In the 1950s, the Cold War terrified America, and many looked for ways that the United States was better than and different from the USSR, our main opponent in that contest. The principal difference most often voiced was the status of the United States as, in most people's eyes, blessed by God (and/or Christian, depending on who was asked), compared to the USSR, which was officially an atheistic nation. To differentiate the two countries further, many chose to emphasize the religious difference, and to do that they aimed to increase the amount of religion in public life, focusing particularly on the schools. Several states, including New York, mandated a statewide prayer in the public schools; others instituted (or already had) mandatory Bible reading in the public schools. To challenge these practices was seen by some as equivalent to agreeing with the USSR. Of course, those opposed to these practices saw them as a state endorsement of religion, banned in the First Amendment. In 1962, *Engel* v. *Vitale* came before the Supreme Court, dealing with New York's school prayer. The justices there struck down the practice, holding it to be an endorsement of religion in violation of the First Amendment. The next year, in 1963, the Supreme Court struck down mandatory Bible readings and saying of the Lord's Prayer in *School District of Abington Township* v. *Schempp.*

These two decisions together created a whirlwind of opposition. While the decisions drew support from religious minorities and others who had felt marginalized and pressured to become Christian, the more common reaction was outrage. Many returned to the reason that the policy was adopted in the first place, often charging the Supreme Court with being communist or supporting communism, or being atheistic, or all three. As the United States survived the Cold War, fears proved unfounded that communism would triumph due

to the banning of school prayer. Since the early 1960s, there have been numerous efforts to introduce constitutional amendments to allow school prayer (the banning of Bible reading provoked less controversy), and just as many efforts to get around the prayer ban. Some of the more recent include efforts to allow a moment of silence at the beginning of the day. Supporters state that it allows students and teachers time to reflect, and that students can do whatever they want in that time, including pray, and the school boards officially take no stand on the activity. The Supreme Court has allowed this but has struck down efforts to pass mandates for a moment of silence that added the suggestion that these could be used for prayer. The difference might seem negligible, but in the Supreme Court's eyes, the second rule puts the school boards behind prayer as they are stating that prayer is a good thing. Prayer at public school graduations and other events has also been struck down.

Besides the issue of prayer in the public schools, another area of controversy decided in a major court case is the posting of the Ten Commandments on public property. Similar to those who favor school prayer, those who want to see the Ten Commandments displayed in public places, particularly government buildings and schools, often believe that society has declined and that exhibiting the Ten Commandments in schools and in courthouses will bring about an improved society. Others believe that the government should not support the display of religious documents in public places as this indicates the government's approval, either in truth or in public perception, of the religions that use those documents. A frequent answer to that charge is that Judaism, Islam, and Christianity, listed in reverse alphabetical order, all use the portion of the Bible that has the Ten Commandments in it (although in multiple versions in multiple places). Thus, the argument continues, the government is not promoting any one religion, but is either (a) advancing morality or (b) promoting religion in general—and promoting the religions to which the vast majority of the population belong; some believe that promoting religion in general is constitutional as long as no single religion is favored. The Supreme Court has divided on the issue, hearing two cases on the topic in 2005. In *Van Orden* v. *Perry* and *Mc-Creary County* v. *ACLU,* the Court allowed a display in Texas to continue, but struck down one in Kentucky. The Texas exhibit was allowed to continue for two reasons: first, it contained other items in addition to the Ten Commandments; second, it had been displayed for forty years without any lawsuits against it. The Kentucky display was struck down as it contained only the Ten Commandments at first (others were later added), and it had just recently been erected. The future of other such displays is still an open question and one that provokes controversy while enjoying some support and serving as a good grandstanding issue for politicians; all of these reasons guarantee that attempts to erect such displays and legal challenges to them will not end soon. (Indeed, some areas of Kentucky have already acted against the Supreme Court ruling to post the Ten Commandments again.)

Besides prayer and the Ten Commandments in public schools, the control of schools in general has also been very important and decided in large part by Supreme Court cases. One issue is the right of parents to send their children to the school of their choice. There were some efforts in the early twentieth century to ban private schools, particularly Catholic schools, in large part due to the xenophobia of the era. However, the Supreme Court held that parents could not be forced to send their children to public schools as long as the children were schooled in some way. The major Supreme Court case was *Pierce* v. *Society of Sisters* (1925), which determined that states could not ban private schools. Parents still have a responsibility to send their children to some school or to home school their children in a regulated environment, but states may not say that public schools

are the only schooling avenue available. Nearly fifty years after *Pierce,* the Supreme Court took what seemed to be a significant step back from the rule of universal schooling, at least on the face of it. In *Wisconsin* v. *Yoder* (1972), another major case, the Court ruled that Wisconsin could not order Amish parents to send their children to school beyond the eighth grade. The Court's logic was that the Amish system of values was threatened by the worldly values infused in high school, and to preserve their religion, the Amish could withdraw their children after eight grades. However, the Amish system, the Court held, was successful in presenting their children with enough community support to prevent the children who would drop out after eighth grade from becoming a burden on society, and the Amish society had a long history. Thus, this ruling was unlikely to be (and has not yet been) enlarged beyond the Amish to other religions who feel threatened by school. A court's likely answer to those groups would be for them to establish their own regulated private high school.

A further area of school controversy is that of evolution. Ever since 1925 and the infamous Scopes Trial (and indeed even before that), evolution has burned white hot in schools and courtrooms around the country. Evolution argues that the current species evolved from different ones over millions of years and that human beings represent one of those species. Both these ideas conflict with some religions, especially those that read the Bible literally; for them, the earth is about 6,000 years old; was formed in six, twenty-four-hour days; and after the creation there were no new species. Also, humans were formed in the image of God, in the Christian, Muslim, and Jewish religions, and one implication of that belief is that humanity probably was created as a separate, different species. Thus, humans could not have evolved from some other species. Human evolution is the sticking point for most who disagree with evolution, as humans are seen as different from all the rest of the creatures, while evolution holds that humans share common ancestors with some of those creatures. Several states banned the teaching of evolution in the early twentieth century. The Supreme Court did not deal with one of these bans until 1968 in *Epperson* v. *Arkansas*. There, the Court held that the ban on teaching evolution imposed by Arkansas was unconstitutional as its main reason was the conflict between evolution and the Bible, which in turn meant that the government was creating a curriculum with an eye toward religion. This decision touched off a great amount of criticism, but the Supreme Court has never seriously reconsidered the decision.

Opponents turned to science in order to fight science. Many opposed to evolution started or continued funding research aimed at proving the literal truth of the Bible. Once these groups believed they had gathered enough evidence to prove that the earth was only 6,000 years old, they began a push to have creation science—their name for the scientific evidence behind a 6,000-year-old earth—taught side by side with or in place of evolution. The announced goal was either to widen debate, by bringing in both views, or to correct the errors of evolution. The shadowed goal for many was to either remove evolution entirely or to muddy the waters enough that the students would not learn any evolution. A law mandating equal time for creation science and evolution (school districts could also choose to skip both evolution and creation science entirely) was passed in Louisiana in the early 1980s and came to the Supreme Court in 1987. *Edwards* v. *Aguillard* held that this program's purpose was to advance religion and so was unacceptable.

Undaunted, some creation scientists continued their work and others shifted their focus to promoting an idea called intelligent design. This idea held that some things in the universe were so complex that they could not have arisen by chance, and so there must have been some intelligence directing it. The age of the earth is not posited by this theory, and it holds that evolution can be true in most instances

but not all, and again it suggests that this theory should be taught alongside evolution. Its proponents publicly claim, similar to creation science, to be widening the debate or correcting the errors of evolution. Sometimes publicly, but often more quietly, some proponents also cite the religious benefits of this theory. Several school districts have considered adopting a policy teaching both or a disclaimer to be read before teaching evolution noting the other theory (intelligent design). A school district in Pennsylvania adopted the latter approach, and it was immediately challenged. In *Kitzmiller* v. *Dover Area School District,* a district court ruled that such a policy of forcing the disclaimer was motivated by religion and thus was illegal. While the claimed policy aim was to widen debate, the judge took notice of a wide variety of other comments made by certain school board members to refute this assertion. Although that decision is only at the district court level, it is the highest decision to test a specific school board policy. Neither intelligent design nor creation science have been ruled constitutional, so the debate over evolution in the schools is sure to continue.

Outside of the schools, religion and the law do intersect in a number of ways. The federal government has acted to control state action in several specific ways involving marriage, for example. One major court case in this area is *Reynolds* v. *United States* (1879). Generally, the states have control of marriage, but here, a territory was involved, and the federal government controls those areas of the United States that are territories and not states. The case dealt with the Utah territory, and the church in question was the Church of Jesus Christ of Latter-day Saints, commonly referred to as the Mormons. The Mormon Church at that time advocated polygamy, and many of the church leaders were polygamous. The United States passed laws to outlaw the practice and eventually removed the charter of the Mormon Church for its advocacy of polygamy. Justification for the law was that it was illegal to advocate an illegal act, and so religions could be restricted for doing so. On several occasions in the late nineteenth century, but especially in *Reynolds,* the Supreme Court upheld the government's attempts to outlaw polygamy and eventually to seize the property of the Mormon Church. In the 1890s the main branch of the Mormon Church changed its views and so was allowed to be rechartered and to regain its property. Today, some offshoots of the Mormon Church that are not recognized by the main church advocate polygamy, and the federal government still encourages prosecution for polygamy.

A related important court case in the area of religion and personal relations dealt with homosexual rights. Much of the justification for criminalizing homosexual relations and for treating homosexuals differently from heterosexuals comes from religion. The Supreme Court until recently allowed such different treatment by states in the area of homosexual sexual relations, based on its 1986 *Bowers* v. *Hardwick* decision. Many states penalized homosexual sex more stringently than heterosexual sex, while others phased out these laws. Some remained, though, and the Supreme Court, in *Lawrence and Garner* v. *Texas* (2003), held that having increased penalties for homosexual sodomy (over what exists for heterosexual sodomy) was illegal, overturning the *Bowers* decision. Where *Lawrence and Garner* intersects with *Reynolds* is in the area of homosexual marriage, and these two cases obviously suggest different results. The Court was clear in *Lawrence and Garner* that homosexual marriage was different from penalizing homosexual sex and that they were not ready yet (if ever) to rule that states must allow gay marriage under any federal constitutional provision. Thus, the cases of *Lawrence* and *Reynolds* are major ones as they state some of the areas of personal relations in which the Supreme Court will allow religious influence and what areas of personal relations shaped by religion the Supreme Court will allow to be regulated by the state or federal government.

Some areas of personal relations have been greatly shaped by Supreme Court decisions, and religion has been seen by the public to be a shaping influence, even though the Supreme Court tried to steer clear of religion at the time. The major issue in this area is abortion, and the major case is *Roe* v. *Wade* (1973); it created a framework for telling when abortion was allowable, and created a general right, in the first trimester, for women to have abortions. The original decision, for the most part, tried to keep religion and the state separate, but it did not ignore religion. It noted that religions have greatly varying ideas of when life begins, and thus there is no clear answer from the area of religion; to pick one specific date would be to put those religions into law. This moved religion off to the side of the discussion, focusing more on the individual's privacy rights against the state's right in protecting what was eventually a life. The Supreme Court noted that the woman's right to control her own body and her privacy conflicted with the state's interest, which caused the Court to create this system of allowing the woman the majority of control in the first trimester and the state an increasing amount of control after that. While unwieldy, it was the only possible solution in the Court's eyes. The Court mostly, as noted, steered clear of religion, but negative reactions since have largely been based in religion. Many who favor outlawing abortion do so because of their belief that life begins at conception, a view based in their religious outlook. Some who favor allowing the woman to choose have the belief that life begins at birth, which often again is based in their religious outlook. However others believe in a woman's right to choose regardless of their own position on when life begins, as they do not feel that their own religion gives them the right to tell others what to do in this area. The controversy continues today, and later Supreme Court decisions have limited *Roe* without overturning it. *Roe* is thus clearly a good example of a case whose public profile is shaped by religion even though the

Court tried to avoid religion when originally reaching the decision.

Besides the areas of control over marriage and control over one's body, another important area decided by a major court case is that of door-to-door proselytizing. Several religions, including the Jehovah's Witnesses and the Mormons, require their members to go door to door spreading their faith, at least at certain times. However, this effort has also provoked opposition from those who wish to be left alone in their homes. Cities have often regulated door-to-door salesmen (or simply tried to ban them), and cities have also tried to ban these religious travelers. These religions have fought their convictions in court and carried their cases all the way to the Supreme Court. The major Supreme Court case on this issue is *Cantwell* v. *Connecticut* (1940), and it was one of the first that extended the First Amendment's protection, as applied to the states through the Fourteenth Amendment; and *Gitlow*, to the area of religious liberty. *Cantwell* held that freedom of religion included the freedom to act, and that otherwise legal conduct would not be illegal just because it involved religion. The Cantwells had been opposed and arrested due to their religious views, and the Supreme Court held that religion could not be a basis for the arrest. Regulations could still be put on door-to-door travelers but not on the basis of whether they were religious. This decision was important for the protections that it gave to those who wished to travel and promote their religion, but it was even more important as it was the first time the Supreme Court specifically said that the states had to follow the First Amendment's religion clauses in the same way as the federal government.

One final area actually returns this discussion to its beginning, as both cases involve the interaction of religion, the law, and public schools. However, these cases differ from the others in that they examined the significance of the Pledge of Allegiance and its role in American life. In the 1940s, *Minersville School District*

v. *Gobitis* (1940) and *West Virginia* v. *Barnette* (1943) addressed mandatory flag salutes and sayings of the Pledge of Allegiance in public schools. In the 2000s, *Elk Grove* v. *Newdow* (2004) addressed the inclusion of the phrase "under God" in the pledge. The first cases dealt with a mandatory salute to the American flag and a mandatory saying of the Pledge of Allegiance. The Jehovah's Witnesses objected to these items as they saw them as a form of idol worship specifically banned in the Bible. Thus, the Witnesses concluded that to salute the flag would be a violation of their religion. In the late 1930s and early 1940s, the storm clouds of World War II were hanging over the world, and many in America wanted to increase America's patriotism; they felt that mandatory flag salutes and pledge recitations were a good way to do this. Initially, in *Gobitis,* the Supreme Court held that the nation's need to encourage patriotism trumped any religious objection, and that the mandatory salutes and pledge recitations were constitutional. The Jehovah's Witnesses, however, still resisted saluting and found themselves the victims of frequent assaults. The freedoms that the United States was fighting for abroad seemed, to many, to be denied to Witnesses at home. As the fortunes of the U.S. forces in World War II improved, the Court reconsidered the issue. How these three factors—the assaults, denial of freedoms, and improved wartime outlook—weighed in the mind of the Court is difficult to determine. Regardless, in 1943, the Supreme Court held that a forced salute and saying of the pledge violated the religious liberty of the Witnesses.

In the 1950s, in the midst of the Cold War, Congress added the phrase "under God" to the Pledge of Allegiance. People objected from time to time, and some school districts made the pledge voluntary to all, not just to those whose religions opposed a flag salute, but no case reached the Supreme Court until 2004, in *Newdow.* The Supreme Court did not address the issue, as they used a procedural matter to dismiss the case, but some on the Court noted that they thought the pledge was allowable with that phrase. Thus, *Barnette* established that our religious liberty trumps government efforts to force or encourage (depending on one's point of view) a flag salute, but *Newdow* shows that the issue is far from over.

How we are educated, who we marry (and if we can marry), what we can and cannot be forced to see (or encourage others to see) in our public buildings, whether we can follow the dictates of our religion, whether the government can force us to violate our religion (and when it can do so), and when the government can promote a religion or a religious agenda are all areas that affect us deeply. As they are so personal, they also are subject to a wide array of interpretations, as one person's establishment of religion may very often be another person's promotion of morality, and a third person's freedom of religion very often might constitute trespassing to a fourth. It is thus clear that while the First Amendment is only forty-five words long, it will not be decisively limited or protected by forty-five million words of the Supreme Court, nor will it be settled by that many, and the controversy will continue over exactly what the First Amendment means. It is also clear that the major cases of the Supreme Court in the area of religion, some of which were detailed here, do still play an important role in the life of America.

Personal Issues of Religion and State

There are issues of personal freedom in which religion creates a clash between an individual and the state or federal government. Among the areas discussed here are marriage, polygamy, gay marriage, divorce, abortion, and the right to refuse medical care. A more general discussion of the issues surrounding freedom of religion receives treatment in a different entry.

The state generally has considerable control over defining marriage, particularly any marriage that moves away from the perceived norm. In the area of marriage the term "state" used here does not mean government in general, but specifically state government, as the federal government has little control over marriage. Each state generally controls its own marriage and divorce laws. Thus each state can set minimum age, residency requirements, and so on for marriage and divorce. States also impose restrictions on how long applicants must wait after getting a marriage license to actually marry. Different states have long had different standards. Most states now use the age of eighteen as the age of consent, but a couple require people to be older than that to marry without parental permission. For instance, the Nebraska age requirement is nineteen. Some states impose additional requirements for those under twenty-one as opposed to those over twenty-one, such as the presentation of a birth certificate for anyone between eighteen and twenty-one. States also sometimes allow those between sixteen and eighteen to marry, but only with certain stipulations, such as parental consent or marriage counseling. Most states also have restrictions on who one can marry—the most common of which is that most states allow marriage only between people of different sexes. There are also restrictions on marriage within the immediate or extended family, as many states have bans on marrying first cousins. Some states used to have restrictions on interracial marriage, but those restrictions were declared unconstitutional by the Supreme Court in the 1960s. These requirements have been upheld as legal and generally have no direct connection to religion, other than the belief that religion helped to form morality.

States often also impose restrictions on who can perform marriages. Preachers and judicial officials are the most common individuals allowed to perform marriages, but in some states captains are allowed to perform marriages at sea. Some states have very liberal requirements on who can be qualified to serve as a preacher, and some states have even allowed marriages via the telephone or Internet. In the past, proxy marriages, in which the bride, groom, or both sent stand-ins to the wedding due to their own inability to attend, were not uncommon. Thus, states have a large amount of control over the marriage process, even though the controls are much less restrictive than they used to be.

The federal government and all states have barred polygamous marriages. The Mormons were the main religious group to argue for polygamous marriage, and they officially ceased the practice in 1890. The Latter-day Saints was not originally a polygamous group, but polygamy had developed as a church practice by the 1840s; this was around the time the Mormons were driven to the deserted Utah territory by the society of the rest of the United States, who disliked their secrecy. Mormon church leaders decided polygamy was supported by the Old Testament and so adopted it. For a time in the mid-nineteenth century, the church argued that all good Mormons should be polygamous.

This threat to the traditional family was strongly opposed by the American government. In 1862, during the American Civil War, the federal government passed an anti-bigamy act, covering the federal territories. (Marriage was, and is, generally under control of the states, but in those areas which were not states, or not states yet, the federal government generally set policy. Today the federal government sets policy for only Washington, D.C. and a few small island territories.) A major concern of the Grant administration was wiping out polygamy. After the federal government banned polygamy, the practice declined, although not fast enough or with enough certainty to please Congress. The 1887 Edmunds-Tucker Act eliminated the Mormon Church and removed the vote from women (women in Utah were seen as more favorable to the Mormon Church than men were as most women there were in Mormon families). Before 1887, however, the Supreme Court had already had a chance to consider whether the ban on polygamy was a violation of the First Amendment. In 1879, the Court decided *Reynolds* v. *United States,* in which George Reynolds, secretary to Brigham Young, the leader of the Mormon Church, was prosecuted for bigamy. The Supreme Court upheld the conviction, ruling "laws are made for the government of actions, and while they cannot interfere with mere religious belief and opinions, they may with practices" (98 U.S. 145: 564). This differentiation between belief and practice has been continued in Supreme Court doctrine until today.

The Supreme Court continued, over the next two decades, to enforce strongly the prohibition against polygamy and to rule against the Mormons. In 1890, prior to the Church of Jesus Christ of Latter-day Saints' renunciation of polygamy, the Supreme Court upheld a decision removing the right to vote from a man who had lied when he took an oath stating that he did not believe in polygamy and did not belong to any group who believed in polygamy (i.e., was not a member of the Mormon Church). Even though this was clearly focused on belief and not on action, the Court held that it was illegal to advocate illegal acts (making it illegal to advocate polygamy then), and so the state could remove the vote from people who supported groups that did illegal things. The same year, the Supreme Court upheld the 1887 law eliminating the Mormon Church and seizing their assets, holding that it was illegal to belong to a group doing illegal things for whatever reason, religious or otherwise, and thereby revoking the church's charter, the general belief in the sanctity of contracts notwithstanding. The same year the leader of the church issued a statement urging all Mormons to follow federal law and not engage in polygamy. After that time, the federal government allowed the church to recharter. However, breakaway sects maintained the practice, and in 1896, when Utah wanted to become a state, the federal government forced Utah to forever ban polygamy in its constitution. The issue slowly died down and is now heard of infrequently. However, some sects throughout the United States still advocate and maintain the practice, leading to renewed concerns about the health and safety of the women and children involved in such practices.

The Supreme Court has continued to uphold its polygamy decisions, including upholding a conviction for violating the White Slave Act (the Mann Act) for polygamous men who took their underage wives across state lines and upholding a Utah state decision removing custody from those who had told their children that polygamy was acceptable even though they themselves did not practice it. Thus, polygamy is one area where personal control, religious belief, and legal practice have interacted much more heavily in the past than in the present.

Polygamy has also been trotted out recently in the whole gay marriage debate, as some gay marriage opponents argue that gay marriages represent the same threat to the traditional family as polygamy and, indeed, that gay marriage can be equated with polygamy. However, such opponents forget that very few people ever strongly advocated polygamy, and no church has supported it since the Mormons officially banned the practice in 1890; gay marriage, on the other hand, has many well-known supporters whose morals are generally acknowledged to be among the highest, and the idea is accepted by a growing number of religions.

Indeed, gay marriage is probably the best-known current area where the personal issues of religion and state interact. Those opposing gay marriage believe that if the state allows it, the state would be mandating that gays be accepted as equals in the area of marriage, and these opponents consider this a violation of their religion. Many of the opponents believe their religion bans gay marriage, either because God (as most of those opposing gay marriage are Christians and see the Christian God as opposing the practice) set up marriage for only a man and a woman or because God ordained sex as between a man and a woman and so banned homosexuality in general (or, of course, both). Those in favor of gay marriage see its opponents as imposing individual religious qualifications on marriage, which they believe the state should treat solely as a legal issue. Gay marriage supporters also point out that there are religions, indeed, Christian religions, that accept gay marriage and believe it *should* be equal with heterosexual marriage. Remember that if one couple is married in a church and another is married before a justice of the peace, in the eyes of the law, the weddings are equally valid. Thus, the religion of those opposed to gay marriage, in the eyes of the supporters of gay marriage, should not enter into the question of the practice's legality. Some supporters of gay marriage believe there should be no interaction between the state-controlled union of two individuals and religion. It is not as simple as that for others, however, both supporters and opponents. Marriage was originally a church matter, and though it is now controlled by the state, religion is still intertwined with marriage in the eyes of many, even if the exact reasons for the connection cannot be articulated.

Some churches fear being ordered to marry gay couples if gay marriage is legalized, but that is simply not true. Currently, churches cannot be ordered to marry any particular heterosexual couple, and the same would be true of any gay couple; if the church decided not to perform gay marriages, the church could not be ordered to do so. Indeed, in Canada, where gay marriage was recently legalized, Parliament officially declared that no church in that country would be required to marry a gay couple.

Gay marriages were originally legalized by the courts in the state of Hawaii in 1993, but by 1996 Hawaiian voters had amended the state constitution to prohibit gay marriage. In the interim, a firestorm raged as the whole issue of marriage and respect of one state for another was reconsidered. As of 1993, all states respected every other state's decisions on marriage and divorce: if married in one, married in all, and if divorced in one, divorced in all. It had not always been that way, but as of 1993 this had been the practice so long that it was accepted. However, many states did not want their morality disturbed by another state's decision to legalize gay marriage. Supporters of gay marriage were thrilled, in 1993, thinking that they did not have to fight to legalize gay marriage anywhere anymore, as the courts had done it in Hawaii. In 1996, Congress passed and President Clinton signed the Defense of Marriage Act (DOMA), which held that one state did not have to respect another state's marriage if the marriage was between two people of the same sex and the first state did not allow gay marriage. This issue is far from settled as Canada has legalized gay marriage, Massachusetts has acted to legalize gay marriage, and California will likely soon be considering a law relating to the practice.

Connecticut, New Jersey, and Vermont all permit civil unions to both gay and straight couples. Civil unions are an interim step between having no legal relationship and being married, and those states that have adopted them grant the people in civil unions the same tax benefits and status that married couples have, without declaring the couples to be legally married. Importantly for the rest of the country, no other states have to recognize that status, as most states do not have civil unions. Thus, Vermont, Connecticut, and New Jersey's decisions to create civil unions and the civil unions created there remain there. Some gay marriage advocates feel these unions are not stepping stones toward an eventual acceptance of gay marriage but permanent roadblocks relegating gay couples to second-class status; some gay marriage opponents, on the other hand, oppose giving any rights (or formal recognition) to any gay couples. As the imposition of belief stemming from religion causes many to deny the recognition of gay marriages, this issue shows the interaction of religion, personal freedom, and the state.

Divorce is another area in which state law influences one's personal life. Similar to mar-

riage, most regulations on divorce are created at the state level. Unlike the Defense of Marriage Act, there are no divorce regulations created by the federal government and applied to the whole nation—no Defense of Divorce Act, if you will; therefore, all states must still honor one another's divorces. Divorce standards vary from state to state. Some states are quite strict about divorce, while others are quite liberal. The requirements differ in a number of ways, including how long applicants for divorce must be residents of the state in which the divorce is applied for and the causes that have to be given for the divorce. Many states have no time limit if both spouses are residents of the same state at the time of the divorce. The time limit if only one spouse is a resident varies greatly. For instance, New York requires that the resident spouse be a resident for two years, while Nevada only requires six weeks; some, like Alaska, require no residency period, even though applicants must reside in the state.

The acceptable causes for a contested divorce also vary. For example, in a contested divorce in New York, if the divorce does not come after a separation decree, the state still requires that the filing spouse either prove adultery, long-term abandonment, imprisonment, or cruel and inhumane treatment. Nevada, on the other hand, requires only that the filing spouse in a contested divorce prove that he or she is mismatched with his or her spouse or that the couple has not lived together for at least a year. Of course, if the divorce is uncontested, most states allow relatively easy disjoining of the couple.

In many ways, state regulations are directly related to religion, and religious ideas have always shaped divorce law. Historically, divorce was believed to violate the will of God, so very strict standards were imposed on who could divorce. For instance, Massachusetts, the earliest colony in New England, allowed divorce only in cases of adultery, bigamy, desertion, and physical cruelty. Such cases were difficult to prove, and divorce was rarely granted. In the first century of Massachusetts' existence, it allowed about one divorce every other year. This was still more than the rate in England, however, where Parliament, the ruling body for the entire country, had to grant a divorce, and the official church rarely granted annulments. At times, states did not recognize divorce decrees from other states, but now nearly all states do, at least in general. Fewer courts now allow attacks on divorces from neighboring states than in the past. Such a policy has actually led to a loosening of divorce regulations in some states, as stricter regulations merely mean that rich people can go and live for a short time in another state and be divorced, while poor people must stay married. Thus, divorce is another area where personal freedom and the state connect, with the regulations based at least in part on religion.

Another area where personal freedom interacts with state regulations, which originate, at least in part, from religion, is the area of abortion. The main rationale advanced behind most laws banning abortion wholly is that life begins at conception. The belief that life begins at conception, in turn, comes in large part from the religion of those supporting the position, though anti-abortion organizations also point to such factors as a fetus's heartbeat beginning eighteen days after conception to support their perspective. Biblical and religious quotes can be seen on many of the bumper stickers and billboards advocating an anti-abortion stance. Courts have also recognized that there is a religious element to the abortion controversy. The case legalizing abortion on a national level, *Roe v. Wade,* stated, "We need not resolve the difficult question of when life begins. When those trained in the respective disciplines of medicine,

Abortion rights advocates and anti-abortion activists square off during a demonstration outside the U.S. Supreme Court on December 8, 1993. Ever since the court upheld the legality of abortion in the landmark case Roe v. Wade *(1973), abortion has been one of the most divisive personal and political issues in American society. (AP/Wide World Photos)*

philosophy, and theology are unable to arrive at any consensus, the judiciary, at this point in the development of man's knowledge, is not in a position to speculate as to the answer. It should be sufficient to note briefly the wide divergence of thinking on this most sensitive and difficult question" (410 U.S. 113: 159–160). While *Roe* v. *Wade* claims that religious positions are too fragmented to state a consensus, many people move from their own religious beliefs to positions on abortion, particularly those in the pro-life camp, as it is called by its adherents.

The Supreme Court doctrine on abortion started with *Roe* in 1973. That case held that states cannot ban abortions in the first trimester, can regulate them in areas related to maternal health from the end of the first trimester up to the point of viability (where the fetus is able to live, should it be necessary, outside the womb), and can regulate and even ban the practice after viability, except when the life of the mother is at risk. That case sparked a huge controversy, in part because it was the first time the Supreme Court had ruled on abortion, a very sensitive subject, and in part because it relied on the right to privacy, a right that was not directly stated anywhere in the Constitution. Those opposed to abortion called it legalized murder, while those in favor of allowing women to choose viewed it as leveling the field across the nation and giving women control over their bodies. Not all states banned abortion before *Roe*, as roughly one-third of the states allowed some access to abortion, and most states granted an abortion when the mother's life was at risk. Also, there was a thriving practice in foreign abortions (for those who could afford to fly out of the country) and back-alley abortions (for those who could not), and there were medical risks associated, particularly with the latter. Other women disappeared for six months at a time, ostensibly to visit an unknown aunt, in order to avoid the shame of an unwed pregnancy. The baby would be given up to an orphanage or for adoption, and no one, public thought went, was the

wiser. Thus, the absence of legal abortion did not mean that abortions were not performed or that no one had premarital (or extramarital) sex, as some commentators suggest.

Since *Roe,* abortion has become a hot-button political item. Most Republican presidential candidates have promised to appoint pro-life Supreme Court justices, and most Democratic presidential candidates have promised to appoint pro-choice Supreme Court justices. Many Supreme Court decisions have limited the holding in *Roe,* but no decision has overturned it. Among the most important decisions since are *Harris* v. *McRae* (1980), which held that the federal government could refuse to fund abortions under Medicaid, and *Planned Parenthood* v. *Casey* (1992), which held that the key point now was viability and that burdens were allowed on abortions as long as they were not undue burdens, even while *Roe* in general was affirmed. Thus, even after thirty years of attempts to place justices on the Supreme Court to overturn *Roe*—and all of the justices but two appointed since 1973 were appointed by Republicans—*Roe* still stands. *Roe* and the cases that follow have little direct connection with religion, as religion has not been used often as a rationale for deciding the cases, but abortion as an issue has a lot to do with religion, as religion greatly helps to form most people's opinions on the issue.

A final area to be considered is the right to refuse medical care. Dying adults are generally allowed to refuse medical care, so long as they make the decision while conscious and lucid. Therefore, many people make living wills, dictating that their lives not be maintained artificially in the event that such a decision must be made while they are not conscious or lucid. These living wills can specify whether a hospital should resuscitate an individual who has stopped breathing as well as what measures should be done to keep alive an individual who has passed into a vegetative state. Without proper medical documentation, this becomes a quite complex issue, as was shown in the Terry

Schiavo case in Florida in 2005. Religion did not enter directly into the *Schiavo* case, but it could have, as different religions take different stands on the amount of medical assistance that should be allowed, and many of the groups supporting Terry Schiavo's parents, who wanted to keep her alive after she had passed into a medically vegetative state, were religious. Some religions go so far as to prevent consultation with regular medical personnel, rather referring one to medical healers within the faith. Adults who makes the express wish to avoid care or avoid extraordinary care can generally expect to have their desires granted. However, the issue becomes more complicated when children's rights become involved. The child's rights to care are then weighed against the religious rights of the adult. When someone is a sole caregiver, the right to refuse treatment may be denied, as the child would be left with no one to care for him or her; but if there are other caregivers for the child, even if the person refusing treatment is the primary caregiver, then the interests of the adult are often held to outweigh the interests of the child.

When the person is a child and the parents are the ones making the decisions, the state may step in to protect the interests of that child. Many parents who belong to churches that do not believe in Western medicine and/or blood transfusions want to have their children follow these practices, and so refuse that care for their children. Of course, the children are not old enough to decide on their own, and so the state will try to force the care when it is needed to save the child's life to allow the children to grow up to make their own decisions. The state has often won these legal battles and treatment has been forced. Thus, if only the individual is concerned and is an adult, the state is generally not allowed to interfere in this personal area. However, when the person concerned is a child, the state can interfere and force the child to be treated. Here, the question is not religion motivating the state law, as in other areas, but the state law, which is religiously neutral, coming into contact with religiously motivated personal actions.

Religion moves large parts of many people's daily lives, and also motivates, directly and indirectly, many state laws. When religiously inspired state laws intersect with individual action, or when individual action that originates in religious belief clashes with state laws, the First Amendment's bans on state establishment of religion or state interference with religious freedom no longer seem as clear as they might have at first blush. Religion is seldom used as the main defense for a state law, as doing so would run afoul of the First Amendment's establishment clause, but religion does still push some state laws, many of which have been upheld on nonreligious grounds. Likewise, religious conduct that violates state law is neither always upheld nor denied, as the actions taken, how much they violate the social mores, and the people affected always need to be considered. Personal issues of religion and the state are thus as varied and as intense as the people from whom they emanate.

Prayer and Bible Reading in Public Schools

The issue of prayer and Bible reading in the public schools is one of the more heatedly discussed topics today, even though there is little prospect for any real change on either of those issues. To understand this issue further, several areas should be examined, including the practices of the states in the period leading up to the 1960s, the Supreme Court cases dealing with prayer and Bible reading in the schools, the reaction to these cases, and the current state of the law.

Most states did not have uniform policies dealing with Bible reading and prayer prior to the 1960s. As late as the early twentieth century, only one state had a law mandating Bible reading, that being Massachusetts, and the reading was supposed to be done without comment.

This does not mean that other states did not have Bible reading or prayers to start the day, but control of this was left to the local school boards. To determine the actual percentage of students who had Bible reading or prayers in their public schools would require an analysis of every school board's policy in a certain year and then to assume that schoolteachers were following the board's directions. Thus, until the twentieth century, no real uniformity existed. The twentieth century saw some attempts at uniformity in the area of Bible reading and prayers for a number of reasons. First, states became convinced that a good way to fight communism, during the Cold War, was to inject God into the classroom both with Bible reading and prayer. The adoption of Bible reading had not been without controversy at the local level, and part of the widespread reform movements of the early 1900s was aimed at settling that controversy. People were convinced of the need for prayer but knew also that a prayer that satisfied Catholics would not satisfy Protestants, and vice versa, never mind the religious minorities or those who did not belong to (or believe in) organized religion. Some states developed official state-mandated prayers that aimed to satisfy Catholics, Jews, and Protestants (but not other groups).

Another issue of concern was whose Bible to use and what part of the Bible to read. Catholics and Protestants used quite different Bibles at the time, with the Catholics using the Douay version and the Protestants generally using the King James Version, and thus, even the decision of which Bible to read from provoked controversy. Some school boards tried to defuse the issue by turning it over to even more local control than the school board—in the neighborhoods where Catholics were in the majority, the Douay would be used, and in the neighborhoods where Protestants were the majority, the King James would be used. Another consideration was what part of the Bible to read from. In order not to anger Jews, the Old Testament was often used from Christian Bibles, either Douay or King James. Neither of

these reforms, of course, pleased those who wanted government to stay wholly out of the issue of religion.

While the 1960s are seen as the time when God was removed from the classroom (and, correspondingly, by those supporting Bible reading and prayer, as the time when America began to decline), the 1960s were not the first time that the courts had heard the issue of Bible reading and prayer, merely the first time that the U.S. Supreme Court had ruled on it. In the 1800s, Cincinnati had seen great controversy over the question of which Bible to use for Bible reading, so much so that the whole episode came to be called the Cincinnati Bible Wars. The final decision of the school board was to end the practice of Bible reading altogether, and an appeals court held that a school board was not able to do this as it exceeded the school board's powers. The Ohio Supreme Court, however, declared that the policy was allowable, as parents were supposed to be teaching religion to their children, not the local school system. The Illinois Supreme Court decided a similar issue in 1908, dealing with the forced use of the King James Bible in public schools for Bible reading, and it struck down this practice, as the Illinois constitution prohibited religious discrimination or instruction in religious subjects in the public schools, and the court found that both occurred.

Other states had similar conflicts. Wisconsin agreed with Illinois, but Maine held that a parent could not remove his child from the public schools and teach the child at home if he disagreed with the use of the King James Bible. Thus, in a few areas, the state supreme courts had removed the reading of the Bible from the public schools, but in most places, the decisions were left to the school boards, and appeals to the courts, if any, were unsuccessful. These decisions of the courts provoked controversy at the time but later were overlooked, so when the Supreme Court decided to visit the issue in the 1960s, many people believed, erroneously, that the practices of Bible reading and prayer were nationwide, beneficial, and previously unchallenged.

The Supreme Court considered dealing with the issue of Bible reading in the 1950s. In *Doremus* v. *Board of Education,* in 1952, the Vinson Court accepted for review a case dealing with the mandatory reading of five Old Testament verses. (Five seems to have been a common number of verses to read for an unknown reason.) However, the student who challenged the law had graduated by the time the case came to the Court, so it was dismissed as moot; and the Court denied standing to the other plaintiff, a taxpayer. In 1962, the Supreme Court returned to the issue in *Engel* v. *Vitale.* There, the New York State Board of Regents (a powerful board that sets standards for education and exams across New York) had constructed a prayer that they felt should be acceptable to Catholics, Jews, and Protestants (groups listed alphabetically). The Regents stated that prayer in the public schools would protect students from atheism and juvenile delinquency, and encourage them to lead moral lives. (Lee, Francis Graham. *Church-State Relations: Major Issues in American History.* Westport, CT: Greenwood Press, 2002.) The prayer was not mandated in schools, but each school board could choose to adopt it. The Hyde Park School Board did, and their decision was challenged in *Engel* v. *Vitale.*

The Supreme Court, in a 6–1 ruling, struck down use of the prayer as unconstitutional. The prayer in question read "Almighty God, we acknowledge our dependence upon Thee, and we beg Thy blessings upon us, our parents, our teachers and our Country" (370 U.S. 421: 422). Justice Black wrote the opinion of the Court, and he believed in a strong wall of separation between church and state. For Black, this prayer was clearly religious and so clearly a violation. However, he believed that history proved his case and reviewed the development of religious freedom in this country and why he thought the First Amendment established an absolute wall. The fact that no coercion was used and no denomination was promoted was no reason to

allow the prayer, nor was the reason that many people in America's history were religious. Black answered that last argument by stating, "There were men of this same faith in the power of prayer who led the fight for adoption of our Constitution and also for our Bill of Rights with the very guarantees of religious freedom that forbid the sort of governmental activity which New York has attempted here. These men knew that the First Amendment, which tried to put an end to governmental control of religion and of prayer, was not written to destroy either. They knew rather that it was written to quiet well-justified fears which nearly all of them felt arising out of an awareness that governments of the past had shackled men's tongues to make them speak only the religious thoughts that government wanted them to speak and to pray only to the God that government wanted them to pray to" (370 U.S. 421: 434–435). As New York had stepped in and promoted a religion by writing an official prayer, it had pierced the wall between church and state. One dissent by Justice Stewart pointed out the instances of government invocation of religion, including the cry of "God save this honorable court," before each Supreme Court session, and that none of these established a religion. However, Stewart did not carry the day.

This decision was widely criticized. In the politicized Cold War atmosphere, many thought it was removing God when America needed religion most. Many church leaders, but by no means all, criticized the decision, and many Americans, but once again by no means all, disagreed with it. Notably, though, President Kennedy and Governor Rockefeller (of New York) supported the decision. Much of America was challenged in the 1950s and 1960s, and many did not like at least parts of the changes. However, the Supreme Court is not supposed to rule by public opinion polls.

If they had ruled by such polls, to take it a step further, they would not have put forth the *Abington Township* v. *Schempp* decision the next year. That decision dealt with Bible reading in the schools, and the companion case *Murray* v. *Curlett* dealt with Bible reading and the saying of the Lord's Prayer. In Pennsylvania, origin of the *Schempp* case, ten or more verses of the Bible had to be read each day, and in Maryland, origin of the *Murray* case, either five verses of the Bible had to be read, or the Lord's Prayer had to be said, or both. The Supreme Court struck down both practices. The Supreme Court first noted that religion was important in American history, holding, "It is true that religion has been closely identified with our history and government" (374 U.S. 203: 212). But the Court noted that religion was not the only factor to consider: "This is not to say, however, that religion has been so identified with our history and government that religious freedom is not likewise as strongly embedded in our public and private life" (374 U.S. 203: 214). Thus, neither factor ruled, and the Court turned to past cases.

After reviewing past cases, the Court reminded the public that the overriding principle was one of neutrality, and that the First Amendment limited the states just as much as it limited the federal government—and the government cannot favor religion over nonreligion just as it cannot favor one religion over another. The Court then stated a direct test for constitutionality of a legislative enactment under the First Amendment: "The test may be stated as follows: what are the purpose and the primary effect of the enactment? If either is the advancement or inhibition of religion then the enactment exceeds the scope of legislative power as circumscribed by the Constitution. That is to say that to withstand the strictures of the Establishment Clause there must be a secular legislative purpose and a primary effect that neither advances nor inhibits religion" (374 U.S. 203: 222). The Court held that Bible reading was clearly a religious activity and that this program violated the First Amendment, as its purpose was not secular but religious. The majority opinion answered the charge that has been made often since, that by removing the Bible the Court was

being hostile to religion and thus establishing a religion of hostility to religion, or a religion of secularism. However, the Court here held that merely removing the Bible did not create hostility to religion.

Justice Douglas wrote a concurrence. He outlined the various ways that an establishment could be created, noting that in all of the ways "the vice of all such arrangements under the Establishment Clause is that the state is lending its assistance to a church's efforts to gain and keep adherents" (374 U.S. 203: 228). He added that the establishment clause "also forbids the State to employ its facilities or funds in a way that gives any church, or all churches, greater strength in our society than it would have by relying on its members alone" (374 U.S. 203: 228). The funding of a religion was illegal, but it was also illegal to promote religion indirectly through the schools for which the public spent its funds. Justice Brennan also concurred, looking not at the history but at the effect, holding that "a more fruitful inquiry, it seems to me, is whether the practices here challenged threaten those consequences which the Framers deeply feared; whether, in short, they tend to promote that type of interdependence between religion and state which the First Amendment was designed to prevent" (374 U.S. 203: 236). He held that the programs did. Brennan also argued that the First Amendment needed to evolve with the times, as education had, and religious practices in America had. He also pointed out that the churches should be concerned with attempts of the state to mandate religion, as "it is not only the nonbeliever who fears the injection of sectarian doctrines and controversies into the civil polity, but in as high degree it is the devout believer who fears the secularization of a creed which becomes too deeply involved with and dependent upon the government" (374 U.S. 203: 259). Brennan noted that even though prayer had long opened school days, a mandated prayer and Bible reading was much newer, and that these practices were innately religious, even if they had other benefits as well. That religious element could not be overlooked, and so the Court struck down the practice. Brennan concluded, as a principle, that "what the Framers meant to foreclose, and what our decisions under the Establishment Clause have forbidden, are those involvements of religious with secular institutions which (a) serve the essentially religious activities of religious institutions; (b) employ the organs of government for essentially religious purposes; or (c) use essentially religious means to serve governmental ends, where secular means would suffice. When the secular and religious institutions become involved in such a manner, there inhere in the relationship precisely those dangers—as much to church as to state— which the Framers feared would subvert religious liberty and the strength of a system of secular government" (374 U.S. 203: 295).

Justice Stewart dissented. He argued that more of a record was needed and held that "religion and government must necessarily interact in countless ways . . . there are areas in which a doctrinaire reading of the Establishment Clause leads to irreconcilable conflict with the Free Exercise Clause" (374 U.S. 203: 309). He argued that the Court used too mechanical a definition in the establishment clause, and that the free exercise clause was superior here, "for there is involved in these cases a substantial free exercise claim on the part of those who affirmatively desire to have their children's school day open with the reading of passages from the Bible" (374 U.S. 203: 312). He also suggested that the cases should be remanded to see if any coercion existed. Concerning the argument that children needed to be saved from the religious influence of the Bible, Stewart held that "even as to children, however, the duty laid upon government in connection with religious exercises in the public schools is that of refraining from so structuring the school environment as to put any kind of pressure on a child to participate in those exercises; it is not that of providing an atmosphere in which children are kept scrupu-

lously insulated from any awareness that some of their fellows may want to open the school day with prayer, or of the fact that there exist in our pluralistic society differences of religious belief" (374 U.S. 203: 316–317). This presaged Justice Scalia's argument, much later, that tolerance in a society needs to run both ways, with those children who do not like prayer being tolerant of those who do.

After *Schempp* and *Engel,* the Supreme Court experienced a large amount of criticism. Also criticized was the plaintiff in the *Murray* case, Madelyn Murray, later Madelyn Murray O'Hair, who had sued on behalf of her son. She was viewed by many as a gadfly, and she was proud of her militant atheism and of her vigorous efforts to oppose what she saw as the state's establishment of religion—which brought down firestorms of criticism from time to time. At the national level, though, the Supreme Court received most of the negative press. Many called for a constitutional amendment allowing prayer in the public schools (less effort has been made to allow Bible reading in the public schools). Part of the reason for this firestorm has been political gamesmanship: it is very easy and very good for a politician's political standing to introduce an amendment allowing voluntary prayer when constituents favor it, even when that amendment will never be voted on and will never cost the politician anything in political capital. Roughly 300 amendments that would make voluntary prayer or Bible reading constitutional were introduced in 1962 and 1963 alone. Only three such amendments promoting voluntary prayer as constitutional, total, have made it to the floor of the Senate for a vote since *Schempp,* and all three have failed to pass, generally by at least ten votes (out of the sixty-seven generally needed).

The Supreme Court did not again hear any case directly calling for prayer in the public schools or Bible reading. This is in keeping with its general practice of not hearing cases dealing with the same situation as established law unless two lower courts conflict or the law generally

First-graders share a moment of silent prayer at the start of their day in a South Carolina school on September 8, 1966. Though the Supreme Court banned school prayer as unconstitutional in 1962, many state legislatures have supported the practice of providing a brief moment of silence during the school day that could be used for prayer. (UPI/Bettmann/Corbis)

changes. The opposition from below did not abate, though. Many states passed laws calling for voluntary prayer, and many school districts may have just ignored the Supreme Court's ruling and had prayers until someone sued. It is interesting that prayer, as in the proposed amendments, was the main focus, not Bible reading. The Supreme Court, however, did hear other cases on prayer, including moments of silence.

In 1978, Alabama passed a law calling for a moment of silence. That law was twice amended until it allowed a moment of silence "for meditation or voluntary prayer" (472 U.S. 38: 40). As amended, a suit was brought against it, and the Supreme Court ruled on that case in *Wallace v. Jaffree* in 1985. The Supreme Court held, "Just as the right to speak and the right to refrain from speaking are complementary components of a broader concept of individual freedom of mind, so also the individual's freedom to choose his own creed is the counterpart of his right to refrain from accepting the creed established by the majority" (472 U.S. 38: 52). The Supreme Court looked at the purpose of the two amendments and held that they, especially the latter one adding voluntary prayer, were aimed at encouraging religion. However, the decision did not strike down the moment of silence. Thus, moments of silence are constitutional as long as the legislature and school board do not indicate, either in the wording or in the hearings accompanying it, that they would like prayers undertaken in that moment of silence. In the dissent, however, Justice Rehnquist argued that the only thing banned was preference for one religion over another, that the purpose test should be abandoned in favor of a neutrality test, and that the First Amendment's history was silent here, and so a moment of silence, even explicitly perhaps to be used for prayer, should be allowed. Lower courts have considered moments of silence, and as long as a secular purpose has been noted and no call for prayer has been made, they have been allowed.

The Supreme Court also has considered occasional prayers in the public schools, such as those at graduation and at football games, and has ruled against both of those. The Supreme Court first dealt with prayer at graduations in 1992. This practice was held unconstitutional. The procedure was that the principal would invite a local clergyman and tell him to deliver a nonsectarian prayer. Even though the prayer was offered by a private individual, he was invited by the school board (through the principal), and the Supreme Court held that people were being coerced by the prayer. The dissent argued that people who did not like the prayer simply had to remain silent, but the majority held that this was too much, as peer pressure would encourage individuals to pay attention, and the government was compelling participation in a religious exercise, a violation of the First Amendment. In the area of prayers at football games, decided in 2000, the procedure was that students would vote on whether to have a prayer before the game, and then, if the vote was yes, there would be another vote on who would give the prayer, and it had to be a student. Even though attendance at the football games was theoretically voluntary (at some high schools, expectation of attendance at the football games on Friday night is greater than expectation of presence in school on the weekdays), the Supreme Court held that the process forwarded the will of the majority, whereas the purpose of the First Amendment was to protect minorities and prevent the government from taking a stand on religion. The dissent held that preventing a prayer was hostile to religion and that having the occasion "solem-

nized" (which was the official purpose of the occasion) was acceptable. Thus, occasional prayer at public schools, whether at graduation or at football games, is supposed to be illegal—of course, as noted before, whether everyone follows the wishes of the Supreme Court is another matter entirely. Thus, prayer, whether occasional or often, and Bible reading, when not done for clear curriculum-related purposes, are currently unconstitutional.

Several areas of current Supreme Court doctrine are the subject of widespread dispute, including prayer in public schools, abortion, and the death penalty. Of those, the area of prayer, particularly daily prayer, seems to be the most settled. Politicians from time to time push for an amendment allowing prayer, but the Supreme Court has settled that issue, seemingly (one must say seemingly as the Supreme Court doctrine is never truly permanently settled) or at least until such an amendment would pass. Even with the new 2005 and 2006 appointments, a full five justices have held that prayer cannot be offered at graduation, which means clearly that daily prayer cannot be offered in public schools, even while a moment of silence, with no religious mention in its statement of purpose, is allowable. The exact difference may not be clear to a layman, but the issue is seemingly settled to those on the Supreme Court. Also, even the dissent arguing against a ban on prayers at football games did not suggest that it was time to reconsider *Engel* v. *Vitale,* which had banned prayer in the schools in the first place. Thus, while creating much heat and little light, like many discussions over religion, the battle over prayer in the public schools continues, even while not being likely to see any significant Supreme Court changes in the near future.

Religion and Issues of Employment

Religious tests for public office, at the federal level, have been prohibited since the ratification of the Constitution in 1789. On the state level the practice, however, continued until much more recently. Of more importance to most workers today is how religion is allowed to affect the workplace, and what protections exist against religious discrimination.

The federal Constitution specifically prohibited religious tests for public office. This was a direct break from practices in England and most of Europe where there were state religions and religious qualifications for public office. The federal government, though, did not pass regulations prohibiting specific types of religious discrimination for nearly another 170 years. The Supreme Court also did not strike down religious tests for state office for about the same period of time, finally acting in 1961. Thus, for much of America's history, only the federal government specifically prohibited discrimination, and then only for public office. Furthermore, policies have not always dictated federal practices. Until the 1880s, the main qualification for public office was to be well connected, and if the party and candidate for whom a political functionary had encouraged public appeal won public office, the reward might be a job, most often in the post office. This was called the "spoils system." Thus, publicly, *who* you knew was more important than *what* you knew, and most political connections also involved religious connections.

After the late 1880s, applicants had to take tests for federal jobs, and while there were no religious qualifications for those, being connected still helped, and not all jobs were covered by the civil service. Eligibility for federal service jobs was also affected by the overall religious discrimination dominating the era. For example, many universities did not accept certain religious minorities, most often Jews. Because they could not graduate from some of the top universities and did not have the same educational credentials as Christian candidates, they were not seriously considered for some federal jobs. One specific note about the prevalence of this in the American legal system: the

first Jewish Supreme Court Justice was Louis D. Brandeis, appointed in 1916, a full 125 years after the creation of the Supreme Court.

The same system affected those in the private sector, and often more harshly. Connections, including graduating from the same university and being in the same fraternity, were enormous helps to people seeking white-collar jobs in the nineteenth and early twentieth centuries, and those jobs often had religious tests. It was also important to belong to the right country clubs and move in the right social circles, which sometimes meant attending the right churches. While the focus of this encyclopedia is the relationship between religion and the law, it is important to realize that these same criteria were also used to exclude women and African Americans. This system did not change largely until the 1960s, with the passage of Title VII of the 1964 Civil Rights Act. This act barred discrimination, generally, on the basis of religion. It stated, as amended, that it was illegal "to fail or refuse to hire or to discharge any individual, or otherwise to discriminate against any individual with respect to his compensation, terms, conditions, or privileges of employment, because of such individual's race, color, religion, sex, or national origin; or . . . to limit, segregate, or classify his employees or applicants for employment in any way which would deprive or tend to deprive any individual of employment opportunities or otherwise adversely affect his status as an employee, because of such individual's race, color, religion, sex, or national origin" (U.S. Code, *Pub. L. 88–352,* Vol. 42, Title VII of the Civil Rights Act of 1964).

For religious organizations, the act held that religious discrimination was acceptable "where religion, sex, or national origin is a bona fide occupational qualification reasonably necessary to the normal operation of that particular business or enterprise" (U.S. Code, *Pub. L. 88–352,* Vol. 42, Title VII of the Civil Rights Act of 1964). For universities, the act held that religious discrimination was acceptable when "such school, college, university, or other educational institution or institution of learning is, in whole or in substantial part, owned, supported, controlled, or managed by a particular religion or by a particular religious corporation, association, or society, or if the curriculum of such school, college, university, or other educational institution or institution of learning is directed toward the propagation of a particular religion" (U.S. Code, *Pub. L. 88–352,* Vol. 42, Title VII of the Civil Rights Act of 1964).

Religion included both practice and belief, as the act stated that "the term 'religion' includes all aspects of religious observance and practice, as well as belief, unless an employer demonstrates that he is unable to reasonably accommodate to an employee's or prospective employee's religious observance or practice without undue hardship on the conduct of the employer's business" (U.S. Code, *Pub. L. 88–352,* Vol. 42, Title VII of the Civil Rights Act of 1964).

Thus, employers are generally not allowed to discriminate on the basis of religion, particularly those companies that have little to do directly with religion. For corporations that employ individuals whose job is directly shaped by religion and thus for whom religion is a "bona fide occupational qualification" (BFOQ), religious discrimination is allowed, but the BFOQ must be part of the business's necessary operation. For nonreligious corporations, that would generally be difficult to prove. For religious corporations, when a religious group runs the corporation or is directly involved, preference for a specific religion is allowed. Religious accommodation is also required of employers, but only at a reasonable cost.

An examination of the various areas affected by Title VII will demonstrate how religion interacts with types of employment. First, the federal and state sectors are considered. The federal government has been subjected to relatively fewer claims of discrimination than the private sector. One area that has had claims of religious discrimination is the military. Religious claims to be exempt from the draft are dealt with elsewhere in this volume and will not be discussed here. Once indoctrinated into the military, all soldiers become subject to the same regulations, regardless of religion, within reason. In 1986, a suit made it all the way to the Supreme Court dealing with whether a Jewish person could be forced to remove his yarmulke while on duty. It did not interfere with his work at all, and other factors may have been behind this person's suffering the forced removal, but the Supreme Court still upheld the action. The policy did not last long, as the next year Congress reversed the policy. However, general conformity in dress is required in the military. This is less of a problem now than it was in the past, as the draft no longer exists, and so participation in the military is voluntary; people who enter the military now generally know about and accept these regulations. By contrast, in the past, people would be unwillingly drafted and forced to wear military garb, even those strict pacifists who did not support the military in any way, and their claims of religion were not enough then to change the regulations or secure for them a religious exemption from the military.

The whole educational sector is also affected by Title VII of the Civil Rights Act of 1964. For instance, a school district was allowed to order that a teacher put away the Bible he was reading during quiet reading time. This was considered an improper endorsement of religion by the teacher, allowing the school district to ban the activity. School districts have also been allowed to tell employees what to teach and what not to teach. They have been upheld in ordering teachers not to teach creationism and intelligent design and in ordering teachers to teach evolution. Public education institutions have also not been allowed to promote religion by the calendar, meaning public schools are generally not to close on Good Friday. Schools are also allowed, somewhat, to control the dress of employees, but this varies based on circumstance and setting. One school district banned religious clothing while teaching, and its firing of teachers for violating this policy was upheld. Another district, however, fired a third-grade teacher for wearing a head covering, claiming that it was religious dress recognizable to students, which represented an unacceptable promotion of religion. However, that decision was overturned, as the Court held that third-grade students would not recognize the head covering as religious and so would not view it as an endorsement of religion. Some general statewide laws banning religious clothing have also been upheld.

Most private sector employers are generally prohibited from exhibiting religious discrimination. Of course, complainants still have to prove that discrimination occurred and that it was due to religion, both of which may be difficult. Once one becomes an employee, policies can legally discriminate against a religion in their effect, but they cannot be written or aimed at doing so. Promoting only those in a single church would be illegal, if that were the stated policy, but it would be hard to prove that such a practice occurred without a written policy to support the claim. Employers also have to try to accommodate religious practices, but they only have to make reasonable accommodations. One school board (this is an example based in education, but it works in other areas as well) fired an employee who wished to take paid leave for religious holidays, over and above the three paid days for personal reasons, including religion, that were negotiated. Personal business days were allowed, but the policy specifically banned their use for religious services. Another employer was upheld in refusing to give an employee Saturdays off for worship (his worship day was Saturday) as it would have cost the employer overtime to have other employees to work the person's shift, a cost held to be more than a "reasonable" one.

Some state laws forcing accommodation of religious days have been upheld, but others have been struck down. Blue laws, which require a business to close on a Sunday, have

been upheld, even against complaints suggesting that they discriminated against those businesses whose religious day was not Sunday, as it forced them to close two days a week. Some people have also been fired for refusing to work on their Sabbath. Unemployment laws require people to search for work in order to qualify for unemployment compensation, and some who refused to work Saturday and were fired for doing so could not obtain work that did not require them to work on that day. They were initially denied unemployment compensation on the grounds that they were not making a reasonable attempt to work, but the Supreme Court struck down that denial. In a seemingly similar case, the Supreme Court ruled that a law guaranteeing Sundays off was unconstitutional. Thus, the entire area concerning work on religious days is fraught with complications. Unlike the laws for accommodating religious practices, Title VII does not even carry the somewhat clear notation that an employer must make reasonable accommodations for religious holidays.

Companies that claim religious justification for their actions but are not directly religious in their own natures have generally had little success. One private school that had been established with a bequest that required all of its teachers be Protestant was held to be in violation of the law. The school was not aimed at increasing Protestantism, and so requiring one to be Protestant was not a BFOQ. Another corporation claimed to be a "religiously" oriented corporation; it had a mandated church service and penalized employees for failure to attend, but the beliefs of the owners were not held to be sufficient to make the company religious. A press was held to be a religious corporation, as it was directly tied to a specific church, but it could not point to a specific religious doctrine that would allow it to discriminate on the basis of sex, and so the discrimination was not allowed. Discriminating on the basis of religious qualifications for ministerial positions was held to be acceptable.

Religious groups are generally allowed more leeway by Title VII but are not allowed total control. Congress originally set the exemption for religious groups to cover only religious activities but then broadened it to encompass all activities, and religiously oriented colleges are also covered here as long as the church has a significant amount of control over the college. For instance, a gynasium run by a church but open to the public was allowed to discriminate against an engineer on the basis of religion, and a religiously oriented college, part of whose mission required it to have "an adequate Jesuit presence," was allowed to have a religion test for hiring in some departments. Schools must announce such requirements in job ads and other areas. Schools are also allowed to restrict the behavior of their employees by forcing them to follow the rules of the sponsoring church. A Catholic school was allowed to fire a Protestant teacher when the teacher divorced and then remarried without getting an annulment of the first marriage. At religious colleges, statements slurring the sponsoring religion or arguing against the beliefs of the majority religion very well might be justification for firing, even if such statements would be allowed at a public college.

Schools also cannot mask anything they wish to do under the cover of religion. Schools that wish to discriminate on the basis of sex, not religion, need very specific doctrinal support for that discrimination and need to be hiring for religious positions. One church refused to hire a minister because she was a woman (the seminary allowed women students as the church allowed women to serve in positions that required seminary training, but the church as a whole did not employ women ministers), and the courts upheld this. However, some colleges that wanted to discriminate on the basis of sex were not allowed to, even though the courts stated that the schools would have been allowed to discriminate based on the viewpoints of those hired. The Salvation Army was allowed to discriminate against a woman minister as the Salvation Army was sufficiently religious and the position considered was that of a minister, and the courts have been reluctant to interfere with the relationship between a church and its ministers. On the other hand, those church-affiliated colleges, even when their churches banned women ministers, were not hiring for minister positions, and so were not allowed to discriminate on the basis of sex. Thus, some gender discrimination by religious groups was allowed, but the groups were sufficiently religious and the discrimination was carefully based on religious doctrines.

The federal government also has crafted for itself a continuing role in overseeing these groups for the most part. State and federal commissions have generally been allowed to investigate the practices of religious institutions. A local religiously oriented school required, as a condition of employment, that people waive their right to sue, and the Supreme Court held that this was illegal and that a civil rights commission could investigate. Another school claimed that the Age Discrimination Employment Act did not cover it as the school was religious, and the courts ruled against that school as well; the Fair Labor Standards Act was also held to cover church schools. The Equal Employment Opportunity Commission was prohibited from gathering data from religious schools for some types of employment, but only about those employees chosen on the basis of religion. Thus it could gather information about staff and administrators who were not chosen on the basis of religion. One seminary claimed that the faculty, staff, and administrators were all ministers whom the EEOC was therefore prohibited from surveying, but its claim was denied.

Of course, with any of these, discrimination must be proven, and this is often difficult to achieve. Prohibitions of discrimination on the basis of religion are not nearly as cut and dried as discrimination on other bases, such as that based on race, sex, national origion, and religion, and the system is much more even-handed than it has been in the past. The system is not perfect, but discrimination is generally harder to prove, and the law is now on the side of the employee. Also, discrimination on the basis of religion is generally not allowed unless the employer is religious and/or the religious element is part of a bona fide occupational qualification. Employers also need to make reasonable concessions to the employee's religious desires, but defining what is religious can be difficult. Spelled-out policies, if they are reasonable, are usually enforceable as well, particularly in the area of religion and religious practices.

For those interested, the entire text of Title VII of the Civil Rights Act of 1964 can be viewed online at *http://www.eeoc.gov/policy/vii.html*.

Religion and Politics in American Public Opinion and Public Attitudes toward the Free Exercise of Religion

Many people believe a democracy is consistently ruled by the majority. However, the Constitution and the Bill of Rights also limit government infringement upon specific rights. What the government is supposed to do when politics and public opinions run into the Constitution and Bill of Rights is a vexing question, particularly in the area of religion.

The battle between religion and politics began early in American history. The second colony, Massachusetts, was attempting to set an example for the rest of the world, and particularly to England, in the right way to live and govern. The colony's leaders believed they had a divine mandate to pursue perfection; as a result, they believed God should have an influence on the state, and so they had a state-established church. Disagreements from individuals were looked upon very unfavorably by the church/state leadership, and the church pushed the state to expel the early religious radicals, including Anne Hutchinson and

Roger Williams. There were no early public opinion polls, but the Puritans and John Winthrop, the leader of the time, did maintain power for years afterward.

Massachusetts was also the scene of another case where religion and politics intermixed, this time with more tragic results. In 1692, the Salem Witch Trials brought accusations of witchcraft against hundreds. Here, the state allowed religious matters to be brought into the courts in two ways. First, the witchcraft charges were brought in state courts. Second, the use of "spectral" evidence was allowed. Spectral evidence was the report of ghosts, spirits, or shadows in the shape of the alleged witch that the accusers said they had seen, particularly at night. Religion and politics also interacted in more subtle ways. Not surprisingly, it was often the social pariahs, who failed to achieve acceptability in the eyes of "upright" religious citizens, who bore the brunt of the accusations, though some stalwarts were accused as well. Moreover, political strife, including Native American attacks, is now thought to be one of the aggravating factors in Salem. The question is not really why people were accused at Salem, but why the village turned to mass hysteria, accusing some 300 people of witchcraft before the state acted to curb the excesses. Across America, there were frequent allegations of witchcraft, but the mass hysteria of Salem is somewhat unique. In the end, 20 were hanged for being witches, 1 was pressed to death by stones, another 100 were convicted, and another 200 were accused—and politics probably helped end the crisis as the governor became more involved with the case after his wife was accused of being a witch.

Religion and politics continued to interact freely throughout the eighteenth and nineteenth centuries. One sign of this is the political backing received by the religiously motivated reform movements of the early and late nineteenth century. In the early nineteenth century, reform movements included temperance and abolition, both of which came largely from religious motivations, with early nineteenth-century religious revivals arguing all people could be perfected and made to live without sin. If all could be saved, the logic followed, then alcohol abuse could be ended, and no one would be enslaved as no man deserved to own another. These movements in turn had effects on politics; one state banned alcohol, and others took faltering steps toward that end. And the abolition movement helped to break up the Whig Party and start the Republican Party, even though the latter initially only argued for "free soil," meaning no slaves moving into the federal territories, rather than the abolition of slavery in the South. In the late nineteenth century, social gospel movements arose, arguing that it was God's will to raise up (and potentially convert) all those living in poverty and slums, and the social gospel idea was one of many behind the Progressive movement, which radically transformed politics.

Politics also interacted with religion in the 1924 and 1928 presidential elections. In 1924, Al Smith and William McAdoo were the leading candidates for the Democratic Party nomination. Al Smith was from New York and a Catholic, and William McAdoo was from the South. Smith had more support but could not garner the two-thirds vote of the convention then necessary for the nomination. The main opposition to Smith stemmed from his Catholic religion, as many felt that the Catholic pope would be in control of America if Smith was elected. Neither candidate was willing to withdraw, and the Democratic convention produced vote after vote, with neither candidate amassing the two-thirds majority. Eventually, after over one hundred ballots, both withdrew and a relatively unknown candidate, John Davis, was selected. Davis suffered a stunning defeat by Calvin Coolidge. While Coolidge was popular, and no candidate might have been able to defeat him, if not for the Catholicism issue at the Democratic convention Smith would have probably received the nomination and fared much better than Davis in the na-

tional polls. Smith ran for the nomination again in 1928, receiving it this time, and losing to Herbert Hoover by a sizable margin. Many Catholics voted for Smith, perhaps more than the number that voted for the average Democratic candidate, but many others voted against Smith due to his Catholicism. It is unclear what the exact effect of Smith's Catholicism was on his vote total, but it is clear that religion directly shaped many people's votes in the 1928 election, as it had also done in the 1924 battle for the Democratic nomination.

While none of these events deal directly with American public opinion, these elections are a good indicator of American public opinion, as few accurate public opinion polls existed before the 1950s. Of course, voting records have a lot of flaws as reflectors of public opinion: disenfranchised groups often do not vote, and there is no way to measure how informed the average voter is. It is unclear whether Smith's Catholicism hurt or helped him in the 1928 election, but it definitely hurt the Democratic Party in 1924 by causing them to promote a weak compromise candidate. The polls that Americans are so familiar with today are a late twentieth-century phenomenon. Polls were taken only haphazardly in the early twentieth century and often brought inaccurate results. In 1936, the magazine *Literary Digest* forecast a stunning victory for Alf Landon over Franklin Delano Roosevelt in the presidential election. Of course, the stunning victory was the other way around. The reason was that the *Literary Digest* essentially surveyed only its own readers, all of whom could afford to subscribe to the magazine, and so failed to sample any other groups of voters. In 1948, polls predicted that Thomas Dewey would handily defeat Harry Truman in the presidential race—to the extent that Dewey stopped campaigning and some polls ceased surveying. The *Chicago Tribune* even printed newspapers announcing Dewey's defeat of Truman before voting results showed the opposite result. At that time, most polls were conducted via telephone, and this naturally limited the respondent base to those who could afford to be hooked up to the local exchanges. Dewey appealed largely to the affluent, who represented the largest percentage of the polling base at that time. With few working-class votes actually taken into account, pollsters had only a partial grip on the nation's opinion when they thought they understood the country's perspectives quite well indeed. Thus, surveying the public response to the interaction of politics and religion is somewhat hit and miss in the pre-1950 era.

After 1950, religion continued to interact with politics, but public opinion became easier to survey with the introduction of random opinion polls, particularly the Gallup poll, which attempted to garner responses from a much wider base than the straw polls and readership surveys conducted by magazines and newspapers up until that time. One of the most noted public responses to the interaction between religion and politics was in the 1960 election. Many people did not want to vote for John F. Kennedy, because of his Catholicism. Some 51 percent of the respondents to one poll said that they would vote for Kennedy if he were not Catholic, whereas only 40 percent said they would vote for Nixon (Gallup Poll #627: 04/26/1960). This was a much more lopsided result than the actual election, which was nearly a 50–50 split, suggesting that a significant percentage of the respondents really did feel that a Catholic should not occupy the White House. Similar to the 1928 election, many people believed that if Kennedy were elected, the pope would direct U.S. policy, particularly U.S. foreign policy. Catholics, on the other hand, voted heavily for Kennedy.

Public opinion also has been used in two of the more heated topics in the political arena over the last half century: school prayer and abortion. After the 1963 *Schempp* decision, which banned Bible reading in the public schools, and the 1962 *Engel* decision, which banned school prayer, people were outraged, at least according to the polls. Both of these cases were decided under the establishment of religion part of the First Amendment, with the Court holding in both that forcing Bible reading and forcing school prayer created a government establishment of religion. However, the supporters of school prayer and Bible reading (more prayer than Bible reading) argued that such a ban interfered with their freedom of religion and that removing the Bible from classrooms would lead to the decline of American civilization. Regardless of exactly the reasons used, a number of polls showed great public opposition to both decisions. Nearly five out of six people polled favored a constitutional amendment allowing school prayer (Gallup Poll #682: 12/12/1963–12/17/1963). In another interesting poll, however, when asked if school prayer took place in their communities, about 30 percent said it did, about 25 percent said it did not, and some 45 percent said they did not know (Gallup Poll #661: 07/26/1962–07/31/1962). Politicians used the polls supporting school prayer to argue for just such an amendment allowing school prayer or to say that the Supreme Court was wrong.

With the second argument, and similar arguments against Supreme Court decisions, a valid question is the exact relationship between public opinion and the Supreme Court. The Supreme Court is not immune to public opinion, but the role of the Court, in our justice system, is to protect against constitutional infringements. If a policy truly does infringe upon the Constitution, is the Supreme Court supposed to be overruled merely because of public opinion, as recorded in polls? And if so, what percentage of the public has to agree before a constitutional violation is considered permissible? And does the percentage have to be even higher if more than one constitutional amendment is violated? Some believe the Court should follow the intent of the founders, who insulated the Court from the public partly for that reason—they wished to avoid the influence of mass opinion as part of the government's system of checks and balances. Politicians have generally answered this question by saying that the will of the people should rule. This is a compelling reelection argument, if not a particularly constitutional one. Although efforts to amend the Constitution to allow prayer failed in the 1960s and 1970s, two efforts at the end of the 1960s did at least come to a vote, as did one in 1984. All have fallen at least eleven Senate votes or twenty-five House votes short of the needed majority.

In the area of abortion, politicians have also appealed to public opinion to try to overturn a court case, in this situation *Roe v. Wade.* Unlike school prayer, however, where the question is relatively simple ("Do you favor having prayer in public school?") and the poll data relatively uncontested, responses to abortion polls often revolve around how the questions are worded or how the results are interpreted. In one poll in 2005, 26 percent of people favored keeping abortion legal regardless of the circumstances, another 16 percent thought abortion should always be illegal, and the majority, some 56 percent, favored keeping abortion legal under certain conditions (Gallup Poll November Wave 1 2005: 11/11/2005–11/13/2005). Thus, one could argue from these results that 71 percent of people favor abortion restrictions (combining the second and third groups) or that 82 percent of people favor keeping abortion legal (combining the first and third groups). It is important to remember that often the wording of a question will affect a person's answer, and that conflicting replies often cast doubt on the accuracy of the polls and the consistency of our opinions.

The creation of questions aimed at reaching the results the pollsters want has come to be called push polling. Thus, in the area of abortion, there is both the question of whether public attitudes should control the Supreme Court and exactly what those attitudes are. Politicians opposed to *Roe,* however, have not worried themselves about these constitutional issues but instead have clamored to appoint Supreme Court justices who agree with their views and to propose a constitutional amend-

ment overturning *Roe.* The second effort has been much less successful than the first, as a vote has never been held on such an amendment, and the first has been much less successful than those opposed to the decision hoped. Since 1973, some eleven justices have been appointed to the Supreme Court, with all but two appointed by Republicans and all but three believed to be opposed to *Roe,* but *Roe* still stands, even though it has been limited by later rulings. Of course, it is unknown how Justice Alito and Chief Justice Roberts will vote on a case asking them to overturn *Roe* v. *Wade.*

Besides *Roe* and school prayer, religion has also been used in American foreign policy throughout the second half of the twentieth century, and in American domestic policy in general. In foreign policy, religion was used as a way to differentiate the United States from the USSR. The USSR was officially an atheist nation, and some in the United States in the 1950s thought that there was not enough, in the average person's mind, to distinguish the United States and USSR. A few writers even suggested that one could read the Pledge of Allegiance and substitute the words "the Union of Soviet Socialist Republics" for the words "the United States of America," without having to change anything else. For this reason, they advocated adding the words "under God" to the pledge, and, to further remind people of the Christian nature of the country, changing the national motto to "In God We Trust." Opposition to these measures was equated with communism, and a general Cold War paranoia existed, and so the measures passed. Similarly, most of the country continued their view that "God" blessed America, apparently to the exclusion of other nations around the world. Politicians and presidents invoked God's blessing on America, and they still take their oaths of office on the Bible, adding "so help me God" to their oaths of office in the present day. Thus, politicians used religion to reinforce their legitimacy and to try to reinforce the legitimacy of America throughout the 1950s, 1960s, and 1970s, and religious references from the president are still considered acceptable today.

Religion was again invoked in the 1980s to justify a militaristic policy toward the USSR. The 1980s was not the first time that the United States took an aggressive stance toward the world. Woodrow Wilson viewed America's mission as including the spread of democracy around the world and believed that the United States should be an example. Ronald Reagan continued this theme in the 1980s, repeatedly invoking the image of America as a model to the rest of the world, a "shining city on a hill"—words that had been used by John Winthrop and the Puritans to describe the Massachusetts colony. More subtly, but arguably present because of his heavy fundamentalist religious backing, was the idea that challenging Reagan's ideas on America and foreign policy was tantamount to challenging God, as God was the one who had set up this city and made it shine. Reagan early in his political career linked the idea of a city on a hill to God and later used it as an example in foreign policy. Reagan enjoyed high popularity ratings and was able to involve the United States in a high-spending, high-stakes race that ultimately concluded peacefully (fortunately) with the Cold War's end in 1989.

Both wars in Iraq had (and have) indirect religious elements. Democracy was a more frequently cited motive for the first Gulf War as George H. W. Bush frequently insisted the logic for the war lay in Iraqi aggression. However, as did his predecessor, the elder Bush had heavy fundamentalist backing, and his perspectives often carried religious overtones. After the attacks on 9–11, the younger Bush said that the United States was being attacked for its role in spreading freedom around the world. Bush then argued for attacking Afghanistan and Iraq in order to spread freedom. During the two Gulf Wars, anti-Islamic sentiment in the United States has run high. Many, including news analysts and media fig-

ures, incorrectly assume that anyone Arab in the Middle East is Muslim, and they often then equate being Muslim with having an anti-American sentiment. Some have also suggested that the second Gulf War carries the assumption that the idea of democracy will instantly appeal to all in Iraq. While this simplistic assumption is largely cultural, it does retain some religious elements. The religion and the overall culture of the Middle East are assumed to be less advanced than those of the United States. Those who believe this further assume that as soon as America's superior culture and political system are shown, a conversion of sorts will occur. Ideas of this sort have been part of U.S. foreign policy, unfortunately, for over a century.

One piece of evidence cited to demonstrate that the nation's leaders believed this argument is that the federal government in Washington repeatedly proclaimed that once the war had been declared successful, the troops would come home soon afterward. This slogan was in fact used by George W. Bush once the official invasion was over, but the fighting did not end, nor were many troops recalled. While not solely religious, there are definitely religious elements to this paradigm of foreign policy.

Public attitudes toward the limits of the free exercise of religion are more difficult to determine. Very few polls have asked questions directly about each clause of the First Amendment's religion guarantees, and few consider the rights of others to their free exercise of religion when considering their own freedom of religion. For instance, in one poll about a Ten Commandments display in Alabama, some three-quarters of all respondents believed that the display should remain due to the freedom of religion, but no question was asked about how this squared with others' freedom of religion as other people also had a right not to have the government suggest which religion was correct (Gallup Poll Social Series: Governance: 09/08/2003–09/10/2003). In that same poll, only about 20 percent of the respondents believed that complete freedom from government establishment of religion should cause the display to be removed. Thus, the answer seems to be that personal individual freedom of religion matters, but extending that right to those with divergent views is much less important.

This is not to suggest that people do not find freedom of religion at an abstract level to be important, only that freedoms are personal and one is often more concerned with one's own freedom than anyone else's. Freedom of religion was one of FDR's Four Freedoms in World War II, and after the war ended, some 80 percent of people answered that a government ensuring freedoms, such as those of religion and the press, was more important than a government ensuring a good paycheck to people (Gallup Poll #416: 04/07/1948–04/07/1948). In 2003, nearly sixty years later, a poll asking how important freedom of religion was found 84 percent of those responding, or five out of six people, saying that it was at least very important (Gallup Poll November Wave 1 2003: 11/10/2003–11/12/2003). Thus, freedom of religion matters, but where that freedom of religion stops for one person and begins for another, and where the prohibition against governmental establishment of religion enters into the picture in general are not well understood. On particular issues, like school prayer and abortion, people have strong responses, but the general issues are often not as well thought out as they could be.

The First Amendment states four freedoms in fewer than fifty words, but brevity does not guarantee clarity. Similarly, something as important as freedom is often thought to be enduring, and not to be related to public opinion. Thus, many people's answer to the question of how public opinion impacts religious freedom might be that it should not at all, but such is truly not the case in a democracy. Others might argue that the majority should always rule, but if the majority rules, then how enduring is freedom? This tension between majority rule

and the freedoms that are supposed to endure, combined with the difficulty that freedoms are neither self-defining nor self-executing, has produced many landmark Supreme Court cases in the area of religion, among others. America, to its credit, has accepted those rulings, even when many of the people (and more of the politicians) have railed against them and sometimes worked to overturn them, and that fact, never reflected in a public opinion poll, perhaps should be remembered first when considering religion and politics in the area of American public opinion.

For further reading

Gallup Poll footnotes with complete interviewing dates and sample sizes and the inclusion of a URL.

Gallup Poll #627. Question 30. Sample size: 2759. 4/26/1960. Available *http://brain.gallup .com/documents/question.aspx?question= 95124&Advanced=0&SearchConType=1&Search TypeAll=kennedy%20nixon*

Gallup Poll #682. Question 48. Sample size: 4126. 12/12/1963–12/17/1963. Available *http://brain.gallup.com/documents/question.aspx? question=89464&Advanced=0&Search ConType=1&SearchTypeAll=school%20prayer*

Gallup Poll #661. Question 6a. Sample size: 4040. 7/26/1962–7/31/1962. Available *http://brain .gallup.com/documents/question.aspx?question= 87903&Advanced=0&SearchConType= 1&SearchTypeAll=school%20prayer*

Gallup Poll November Wave 1 2005. Question 15. Sample size: 1006. 11/11/2005–11/13/2005. Available *http://brain.gallup.com/documents/ question.aspx?question=155110&Advanced= 0&SearchConType=1&SearchTypeAll=abortion*

Gallup Poll Social Series: Governance. Question 43. Sample size: 1025. 09/08/2003–09/10/2003. Available *http://brain.gallup.com/documents/ question.aspx?question=145536&Advanced= 0&SearchConType=1&SearchTypeAll=ten%20 commandments*

Gallup Poll #416. Question 10. Form T. Sample size: 3367. 04/07/1948–04/07/1948. Available *http://brain.gallup.com/documents/question.aspx? question=115392&Advanced=0&Search ConType=1&SearchTypeAll=religion%20press*

Gallup Poll November Wave 1 2003. Question 36c. Sample size: 1004. 11/10/2003–11/12/2003. Available *http://brain.gallup.com/documents/*

Religion and Politics in the Framing of the Constitution

Religion was an important issue for many Americans in their personal lives at the time of the American Revolution and the ratification of the Constitution, but it does not appear to have played a significantly formative role in the Constitution's creation. Politics and negotiation did play an important role, but politics do not seem to have had much of a publicized interaction with religion. For this reason, it is difficult to determine what role our Founding Fathers expected religion to play in the nation.

Religion played a formative role in many of the colonies at the time of their founding. Several, including Massachusetts and Virginia, established official state-supported churches, and others limited the role of religious minorities. Freedom of religion did increase in the period between the founding of Virginia in 1607 and ratification of the Constitution, specifically with Maryland's Toleration Act and the formation of Rhode Island and Pennsylvania as colonies with mandated religious freedom. It also increased in England, with the English Toleration Act following the Glorious Revolution. The latter act protected only Protestants, but that was an increase in religious liberty from before, when the Anglican Church had been the only one protected.

In America, during the first three-quarters of the eighteenth century, religion had varied in significance, though it remained quite important. In the early 1700s, Enlightenment ideas dominated American thought, particularly among the elite. However, life was not easy in America, with epidemics, crop failures, and occasional Native American (and French) attacks. Thus, most attended church regularly. Estimates of church attendance vary, but 80 percent of the population may have belonged at some level and at some time. This attendance, along with the need for religion, helped to spark the First Great Awakening in the 1730s and 1740s, which revived religion for a time and caused many to think for themselves. As a result, many people, or their children, were willing to rebel against England when the time came, even though they may not have thought of rebellion in religious terms. New denominations also came out of the First Great Awakening, including the Presbyterians and the Baptists.

At this same time, a less Christian religion came about in Deism. This held that Jesus was not divine but merely a great teacher, and that all religion should be tested, similar to the way scientific ideas were tested. Deists also believed in a Watchmaker God who had created a working universe and then stepped aside, similar to a watchmaker making and winding a watch. Among the adherents of Deism in America were Thomas Jefferson, Benjamin Franklin, and John Adams. Many more people were believers in the Enlightenment, it should be noted, than were Deists, and most Enlightenment believers were still members of traditional congregations. There is still dispute about whether George Washington was a Deist.

Religious liberty was slowly emerging as an idea at the time of the Declaration of Independence, but that document still notes that "God" entitles nations to exist and that a "Creator" gives people rights. The document as a whole is relatively unreligious in terms of the colonists' complaints, but it does contain two other references to a God. Religion also was important in the American Revolution as ministers who favored the colonists' side preached sermons that said colonists were doing the right thing in the eyes of God, and other ministers predicted that the founding of a new nation would be the first step to the Second Coming.

Benjamin Franklin, a Deist, achieved worldwide renown as a writer, scientist, statesman, and diplomat. (National Archives)

During the period between the American Revolution and the Constitutional Convention, the government under the Articles of Confederation did little for anyone, never mind for religion. The Articles of Confederation said little about religion. That government did, however, see some role for religion, appointing chaplains in the armed forces and attempting to promote Christianity among the Native Americans. It also promoted the publication of Bibles and issued proclamations aiming to increase religious devotion. The Continental Congress (which was the ruling body under the Articles of Confederation) also passed the Northwest Ordinance, which set up schools in the Northwest Territory, and part of the schools' goals included the promotion of "religion, morality and order."

State governments in the period between 1776 (America's independence) and 1787 (the Constitutional Convention) were very busy. Every one of them had to establish a new constitution, as all of the old constitutions had been charters issued by England; America was then independent of England, so these were invalid. Some passed wholly new constitutions, while others edited their former charters slightly to remove the language referencing the Crown. The colonies also greatly varied on their view of official churches. As noted, certain of them had already created some level of religious liberty, and others took this period to do so, although not without controversy, and still others kept their state-supported churches. Some states, in their new constitutions, passed a tax to support the official church but also allowed taxpayers to divert that support to whichever church they chose. Massachusetts was among these, and in the new constitution were the words that "it is the right as well as the duty of all in society, publicly, and at stated seasons, to worship the Supreme Being, the great Creator and Preserver of the universe. And no subject shall be hurt, molested, or restrained, in his person, liberty, or estate, for worshipping God in the manner and season most agreeable to the dictates of his own conscience, or for his religious profession of sentiments; provided he doth not disturb the public peace or obstruct others in their religious worship" (Article II). Thus, in Massachusetts, freedom of religion existed, but only for those who still worshiped regularly without disturbing the public.

Other states attempted to keep the publicly supported church, but failed. Virginia is the most well known of these. Virginia attempted to pass a tax, under the new state constitution, to support ministers, but James Madison and Thomas Jefferson, among others, defeated the attempt and instead passed the Bill for Establishing Religious Freedom, which had been written by Jefferson. Jefferson was in Paris at this point and so did little directly to pass the bill, even though he had written it. Madison is also one of the main proponents of the eventual Bill of Rights, so his support of the bill is often surveyed to attempt to see his views on religion. Virginia and Massachusetts provided the first six presidents of the United States, and so they are worthy reflections of American leaders' opinions on that score, but they also show the range of opinion about religion in America at the time the federal Constitution was written.

The religion of those at the Constitutional Convention has been a much studied topic. It is often referenced by those who want to introduce religion into America today, backed by the federal government. The argument goes along these lines: most of the Founding Fathers at the Constitutional Convention in 1787 were religious, and thus they would not have objected to ____ (insert topic here: prayer in the public schools, the phrase "under God" in the Pledge of Allegiance, etc.). That argument merits a bit of discussion. First, it assumes that whatever our Founding Fathers wanted, we should uphold, perhaps always, or perhaps only until we have a constitutional amendment ratifying the change. However, many things have changed since 1787, and only some of those have been changed by amendments. Slavery was banned by an amendment, but women have many more rights than they did in 1787, and only their right to vote was given in an amendment. Other changes of this nature can also be enumerated. Second, the argument assumes that religious men necessarily thought it was the role of the federal government to advance religion. Many religious people at the time and since, from Roger Williams on, wanted religion and the state to be separate, not to protect the state but to protect the church from the state's corrupting influence. Others thought that religion should be left to the states rather than the federal government. A third view notes the vast religious divisions of the times, holding that many of the founders thought that religion was a very

divisive topic, which is why they left it out of the Constitution. If that view did prevail, of course, then the Founding Fathers would have wanted the federal government not to take a stand on religion at all. That does not mean, however, that they would not have wanted the states to take a role. The states were seen as more united and able to do things that the federal government could not, particularly after the federal government was limited by the First Amendment. Thus, the religiosity of the Founding Fathers is informative but not determinative of what they would have wanted the government to do in the area of religion, nor does that end the debate on what religion should do today, without an agreement of the current populace that it should do so. This does not mean that religion should or should not be a part of our federal government today, but only that America needs to move beyond the belief that the federal government should promote religion because the Founding Fathers were mostly Christians.

The religion of the Founding Fathers who attended the Constitutional Convention needs to be considered, along with their occupations. Of those attending the Constitutional Convention, only one, Abraham Baldwin, had been a minister, a Congregationalist, even though his primary occupation by the time of the convention was as a lawyer. Several others had studied the ministry for a time but were not practicing ministers. Of those fifty-five who were Convention delegates, over half, thirty-one, were identified as Episcopalian by one source or another; the others were, among other denominations, Presbyterian, Congregationalist, Quaker, and Catholic. The most common thread among the delegates, it might be noted, was the law, as some thirty-five, or about two-thirds, had a connection to the law, either at the time or before. Several of the delegates were adherents at one time or another of more than one religion, and some attended multiple services at different times. All founders were adherents of at least one religion at some time in their lives. For instance, Benjamin Franklin, widely regarded as one of the more scientific of the founders and generally thought to be a Deist, attended a revival by George Whitfield, a leading preacher, and even publicly admitted making a significant contribution to him. Thus, the whole web of religion and the founders is a very tangled one, even as we try to figure out what religion each one belonged to (never mind believed in), much less determine the effect of that religion in the founding of the nation.

Politics played a large role, much more so than religion, in the ratification of the Constitution. The document did not command unanimous support, even among those delegates who attended the convention—of the fifty-five who attended, only thirty-six, or a little over two-thirds, signed the Constitution. Many who liked the Articles of Confederation wanted those to continue, and many others thought the Constitution gave the federal government too much or too little power or had other flaws. Thus, a battle erupted over the Constitution. The name given those who favored the Constitution was Federalists; those who opposed the Constitution were the anti-Federalists. Among the complaints about the Constitution was that it lacked a Bill of Rights that would protect the liberties of the people. The whole process by which the United States has a Bill of Rights will be considered in a bit, but the Federalists eventually did carry the day, and the Constitution was ratified.

Important in convincing the nation to ratify the Constitution were the Federalist Papers, a series of essays written by Alexander Hamilton, James Madison, and John Jay. Their views of religion and national government are quite important for three main reasons: first, they demonstrate what three of the founders thought about the Constitution; second, they were influential in helping the Constitution to be adopted; and third, they are often still cited today by scholars and the Supreme Court when making arguments about the Constitution's meaning. The Federalist Papers, on the topic of religion,

had very little formal to say. In one, Jay advanced the argument, in passing, that all Americans professed the same religion and so should unite (he was arguing against a looser confederacy, such as that existing under the Articles of Confederation). Religion was often used as an example of things groups could form factions about, and statements about religion and government were quoted, but the focus was more on government. In the main place that religion was mentioned directly, the famous Federalist No. 10, Madison wrote, "A religious sect may degenerate into a political faction in a part of the Confederacy; but the variety of sects dispersed over the entire face of it must secure the national councils against any danger from that source" (Madison, 1787) *(http://www.yale.edu/ lawweb/avalon/federal/fed10.htm)*.   Madison's overall argument in that document was that the larger nation is safer from tyranny than the individual state, but if the nation was to have no power to check the tyranny in an individual state, little would be gained for the protection of that state. Madison mentioned no solution for the state, within the nation, that succumbed to tyranny, but his focus here was more the virtues (and benefits) of forming the United States under the Constitution, not helping the individual states. Thus, the Federalist Papers have little to say on the whole issue of religion.

As mentioned before, one demand placed upon the Federalists by the anti-Federalists was that the nation adopt a Bill of Rights, something lacking in the national constitution that was present in many of the state constitutions. James Madison had been opposed to the whole idea of a Bill of Rights, thinking that such documents did little in practice to protect rights and that any rights excluded from the Bill of Rights might be considered as not guaranteed to the people; in this way, a bill of rights would actually limit the rights of the people rather than assure them. He believed in a limited government, meaning that if the government had no specified power to legislate in an area—for example, religion—then it could not do so constitutionally. Thus, as religion is not mentioned as an area for congressional power in Article II of the Constitution, there was no need for a religion clause in the Bill of Rights. Madison was not able to convince others of his argument, and the Federalists were pushed into supporting a bill of rights. There was little interest in the topic, though, in the First Congress, and Madison became the one pushing Congress to consider the bill. Madison, it is thought, introduced the Bill of Rights at least in part to safeguard the Constitution and to avoid calls for another Constitutional Convention, and so his interest was not wholly in the rights of the people. It is unclear from the House debates exactly what was meant by the "freedom of religion" eventually adopted by the group, and the Senate's debate (as well as that in the states) was even shorter. It is clear, however, that the freedom of religion, as proposed in the Bill of Rights in 1789, applied only to Congress, as Madison's suggestion that the amendment should also prohibit the states from infringing upon freedom of religion was not adopted by those writing the Bill of Rights. It should be noted that the current First Amendment was originally third when the Bill of Rights was sent to the states; the first two, dealing with apportionment and congressional pay, were rejected at the time, so what was third became first. (The original Second Amendment was eventually passed in the late twentieth century, becoming the Twenty-Seventh Amendment). Of course, the Fourteenth Amendment, added in 1868, did prevent the states from infringing on a person's liberty without due process of law. Whether the term "liberty" included religious liberty, of course, remains open to debate.

Politics played a much larger role than religion in the Constitution's creation. Religion was a matter, it seemed, for the individual states, and those states with an established church did not even manage to block the First Amendment. Probably they felt that the federal government would never interfere with their state

churches, but this is not clear, and there were no public opinion polls to tell the view of the public toward the Bill of Rights or the Constitution in any area, much less in the area of religion. It appears that religion was largely left up to the states, some of which, in turn, left it up to the individual (and some of whom still pushed for a church or churches with state support). Thus, religion, while important to the generation that created the Constitution, did not have much impact on that document, and we have little guidance about the limitations that should be placed upon either part of the First Amendment's religion clauses today.

Religion in Times of War

It has often been said that law is silent in times of war. Religion, by contrast, can often be clearly heard when a nation goes to battle. It has been used to justify and oppose wars throughout U.S. history. Surveying the role of religion in America's wars will help readers understand the interaction between religion and warfare in this country. It will also help to clarify the role religion plays for many conscientious objectors (COs) to war.

In the American Revolution, religion, particularly the Christian religion, was used by both the British and American sides to defend their causes. Preachers in congregations supporting the revolution would praise revolutionary efforts in their sermons, when previously their sermons would have praised the king. This was particularly true in those Anglican churches that had been, of course, controlled by England and that now favored the revolutionary cause. Preachers thus reassured the revolutionaries and their families that what they were doing was right in God's eyes. Religion was also used by Loyalist preachers to rally their followers. The Continental Congress appointed military chaplains to serve with the troops, and some ministers even fought. The Quakers, on the other hand, were a pacifist group. They, therefore, opposed the war, regardless of whether they thought the colonists were in the right. During the end of the American Revolution, the Articles of Confederation were passed, and the Continental Congress became the Confederation Congress. That body also had some dealings with religion, telling the American troops to live justly (even though it did not regularly pay them). Moreover, during the American Revolution, Congress appointed a chaplain for itself, and toward the end of the war it approved the printing of a Bible in the United States as the British blockade cut off delivery of all the Bibles from Europe. Thus, the Continental Congress and the people of America had a very active religion during the American Revolution.

Most of America was not directly affected by the War of 1812. Other than naval clashes, there was very little activity on land. The British invaded in only four places: Baltimore-Washington, New Orleans, the Great Lakes Region, and a portion of Vermont, and none of these incursions constituted a serious threat to the nation. The United States, for its part, invaded Canada on three occasions, even burning present-day Toronto in 1813, but there was never really any chance to conquer the country. This was a significant war for American morale, but it had few battles, and its battles did not represent particularly decisive victories for either country. Not surprisingly, therefore, the War of 1812 had only a small impact on religion. Religious revivals, on the other hand, created divisions among the people over the War of 1812. Both those who favored and those who opposed the war spoke their views at the pulpit. The war was most opposed in the Northeast, and it was those preachers, especially the Congregationalists, who inserted the most anti-war views in their sermons. Southern preachers, particularly the Baptists, felt that God was giving the United States approval to become involved in the war. England was painted as a corrupt and diseased nation, and God was shown as therefore favoring the United States. Political divisions from before the war were largely maintained during it, even while the war was integrated into sermons as an issue. Remember that the War of 1812 was fairly unpopular, and the minority party, the Federalists, opposed it all along, wanting to end it by negotiation right up to the point that a peace treaty arrived. After the war, both northern and southern religionists turned their attention to reforms of various kinds, particularly of the individual.

The next formal war involving the United States was the Mexican-American War. This was over quickly in most areas, except for a somewhat extended campaign in Mexico. Religion played a small role with the troops but a larger one at home as it was a major factor in promoting both general and specific opposition to the war, especially in terms of the war's potential effects. Oppositionists believed it had been undertaken at the behest of pro-slavery forces as the conquered areas would be new territories for the spread of slavery. Thus, those opposed to slavery, some of whom based their opposition in religion, generally also opposed the Mexican-American War. Among those in opposition were Ralph Waldo Emerson, Henry David Thoreau, and former president (and at the time congressman) John Quincy Adams. It was in this period that Thoreau wrote his "Civil Disobedience" essay to explain his views on the war and spent a day in jail for refusing to pay his taxes for the past six years. (The Mexican-American War was one of his reasons not to pay.) Abraham Lincoln opposed the war as well, but not on religious grounds; he felt that the incident that started the war had occurred on Mexican, not U.S., soil, and that this should have been enough to keep the United States out of the conflict. Some also opposed the war on generally pacifist grounds, such as the Quakers, who opposed all war. On the other side of the coin, religion, in a nationalistic sense, was also a cause of the war. Many people felt that the United States, as part of its Manifest Destiny, had the patriotic and religious right and duty to expand to the Pacific and to civilize all of the lands that would be conquered. The war's end result was a large territory gained by the United States but no peace achieved between the pro- and anti-slavery forces who disagreed about the war's necessity.

In many ways the Mexican-American War led directly to the U.S. Civil War. The territory gained provoked even more fierce debate over slavery, and the admission of California as a state touched off another fierce debate as it broke the balance between the number of free and slave states. Before California there had generally been as many slave as free states, but California tipped the balance toward free, and the resulting Compromise of 1850 only served to further inflame passions. Thus, in many ways, there is a straight line from the Mexican-American War to the U.S. Civil War.

The Civil War had many ties to religion. First, both the North and the South thought that God was favoring their side. The "Battle Hymn of the Republic," written by Julia Ward Howe in 1861 and praising the northern forces, includes in its lyrics, "Mine eyes have seen the glory of the coming of the Lord . . . Glory! Glory! Hallelujah! His truth is marching on." Its tune was taken from another northern anthem, "John Brown's Body," which had among its lyrics, "He's gone to be a soldier in the Army of the Lord" and "The stars above in Heaven now are looking kindly down." The South felt equally sure of God's blessings, as at least one version of "Dixie," probably the best-known song today from the Civil War, contained the lyrics, "Swear upon your country's altar . . . Never to submit or falter— . . . To arms! To arms! To arms, in Dixie! . . . Till the Lord's work is completed!" "Dixie" was not the only southern song to reference God, as one southern tune was titled "God Save the South."

Second, religion was one cause for the war, especially for some Northerners. As noted before, religion was a motivating factor in some people's opposition to slavery; this caused the North to oppose the spread of slavery, which in turn angered the South. However, few politi-

cians called for the removal of slavery from the South, as this would have required a constitutional amendment. Even with the admission of California and Oregon, there were only seventeen free states and fifteen slave states. Thus, thirteen more free states would have had to enter the union before the free states would have had the two-thirds majority necessary to pass an amendment banning slavery (and that assumes, of course, that all of the free states' representatives would have voted to abolish slavery).

Religion also affected the way women worked during the war. The United States Christian Commission played a significant role in providing nurses to the war, using women in its work (although they were unpaid). Clara Barton and Dorothea Dix both were instrumental in organizing nurses and medical supplies. Barton was motivated largely by her father, who had told her always to serve others as Christians should. Many of those serving on this commission, also called the United States Sanitary Commission, were motivated by religious reasons. In the South, women also served significant roles as nurses, often motivated by religion.

Opposition to the war, especially to the Union draft, also had a religious component. Many Irish Catholics were Democrats and opposed the war both from the Democratic perspective and because they feared African American competition for their jobs. The draft act told these men that it was their duty to fight and also allowed rich men to purchase their way out of the draft. These factors produced the 1863 draft riots in New York City, where four days of riots produced lynchings and much property damage. Thus, religion did lead some to oppose the war, and religion played a significant role in the overall Civil War.

While not officially a war, the movement to eliminate the Native Americans from the western part of the United States (and earlier from the eastern part) was influenced substantially by religion. Most white Americans considered themselves superior to Native Americans, and religion was one reason for this opinion. They believed God had given America to the white people for their use, and since Native Americans were not using it—as the white population thought it should be used —they could be removed. White Americans also gave little consideration to the religion of the native people, considering all aspects of Native American society, including religion, to be primitive. The enlightened plan for Native Americans was to herd them onto reservations, teach them how to be yeoman farmers on small plots of land (similar to the lifestyle of white settlers), and give them a Protestant culture, which included Protestant religion, of course. The unenlightened plan was simply to exterminate all of the Native Americans. Somewhere between the two lay the idea that Native Americans would simply die out of their own accord. Thus, religion played a part in the idea of rounding up Native Americans, herding them onto reservations, and "civilizing" them.

Civilization was an important theme of America's next war as well, the Spanish American War. That war erupted, at least in part, due to American jingoism and boisterism in the late nineteenth century, as America aimed to make a mark for itself on the world stage. Manifest Destiny was also important. Similar to the Manifest Destiny of the mid-nineteenth century, the late nineteenth-century version said that it was America's God-given right to take its place in the world alongside other nations, but instead of instructing Americans to expand across America to the Pacific, it instructed them to expand across the Pacific and create an American dominion there. America originally claimed that its goal in the Spanish American War was only to help Cuba against the Spanish, but the United States soon launched an attack in the Philippines, a Spanish possession halfway around the world from Cuba. When the smoke cleared, the United States had gained not only the Philippines but also Guam and Puerto Rico, and it was not sure that Cuba was ready for independence. The reason that Cuba and the Philippines were not ready for independence, in most minds, was that they were not "civilized" enough, and part of civilization, to white Americans, was Christianity. America's goals in the Philippines included converting and civilizing its population. Fighting raged in the Philippines for four years, and over 4,000 U.S. soldiers and 20,000 Filipinos died. Cuba was not given its freedom until 1901, and the Philippines were not given theirs until 1946. During the initial war, religion did not play a large part, but the campaign to subdue the Philippines was quite brutal; one reason for this was the idea that the United States was superior due to its cultural, religious, and racial strengths vis-à-vis those of the Filipinos. Thus, religion played a role in the initial reasons to go to war, in the fighting to subdue the Philippines, and in the justifications for keeping the Philippines (and Cuba for a time) as American territories.

America next became involved in World War I, and religion played a substantial factor in the decisions of many about whether to support the U.S. war effort and about their initial approach to the European conflict. When World War I broke out, many pacifists, who opposed all wars, opposed this one as well, and many others saw the United States as superior to the Old World of Europe, which was mired in a conflict reminiscent of the imperial mindset Europe represented. Over time, many of the U.S views, particularly that of Woodrow Wilson, changed, and Wilson began to believe that the United States had a religious and civilizing mission to go into Europe, create a just peace, and "make the world safe for democracy." Wilson, at least in his own mind, saw America as being able to create a peace so that this war would be "the war to end all wars." Other reasons existed for the change in public opinion as well, including British propaganda that portrayed the Germans as un-Christian and uncivilized Huns. (The war pitted the British and French on the one side against the Germans and Austro-Hungarians on the other for the most part, at least on the Western

Woodrow Wilson was a distinguished professor of political science and president of Princeton University before he began his remarkable political career as governor of New Jersey (1911–1913) and president of the United States (1913–1921). (Library of Congress)

Front.) While not always expressed in religious terms, Wilson's stern moral ideas and upbringing (he was the son and grandson of preachers) showed through in his rhetoric.

Pacifists who had backed Wilson's call for neutrality throughout his first term often acted from ideas based in religion as well, and most did not change their views when Wilson did. Those who had favored Germany all along also had a religious basis for their views. Irish Catholic Americans supported Germany largely because it was opposed to Great Britain, which had owned Ireland and treated it questionably for centuries; not surprisingly, they were opposed to the United States entering the war on the side of the British. Other reasons for opposing U.S. involvement included the socialist perspective that this was a rich man's war and a poor man's fight, even though their ideas were not expressed in purely religious terms.

Once the war started, religion did not go away. Many stories about the war emphasized the morality and goodness of the side the United States was fighting on and stressed the evil of the other side, using religious or pseudo-religious terms to do so. This view of the war continued until its end, and the victory was proclaimed as a righteous one. Wilson in part believed his own rhetoric and expected the rest of the victors (including Great Britain and France) to follow his lead—being magnanimous to the losers and proclaiming a just peace. This mistaken belief created great problems at the Paris Peace Conference and may have been largely due to Wilson's own religious bearing, which held that those who agreed with him were on the side of God and that all others belonged in hell.

Many pacifists before the U.S. involvement in World War I remained so, even at the risk of, or in the face of, government persecution and prosecution. Often those who opposed the draft did so because of their religious views. Among these were the forerunners of the group that would become the Jehovah's Witnesses, and they tried to be exempted from the draft as they were against all war. Some offshoots of the Amish religion found their members jailed as they proclaimed pacifism and refused to wear the army uniform. Pacifists also found themselves physically assaulted on many different occasions. Quakers were active in opposing the war and the draft, and they found themselves accused of being un-American as well, even though they had been in America for more than two centuries. Some ministers were fired for opposing the war. The whole selective service system did not have a good way to evaluate who should be exempted as a conscientious objector or one whose religion forbade him to be involved in any war. Consequently, many religious pacifists were either jailed for opposing the draft or inducted into the armed forces, and then dealt with by the military justice system; this system of justice resulted in even harsher penalties than meted out by civilian courts and at least some deaths from mistreatment in the prisons of the armed forces. Thus, pacifists found themselves abused by both the public and the military system for their religious views.

World War II saw fewer problems related to religion. Part of this was because World War II in general was a much more popular war than World War I—many people did not understand why we were fighting World War I, but few had this difficulty about World War II, resulting in less opposition to the war for religious reasons. Also, the draft system had been revised, which led to an easier time for those who were pacifists and wished to request a conscientious objector exclusion. Most conscientious objectors were allowed to perform alternative service, and only a very few (especially when compared to the overall number drafted) totally refused any service at all, claiming that taking any part was still supporting the war. However, most pacifists were willing to serve in hospitals or in noncombatant positions. Some groups, however, were more likely to be given conscientious objector status than others. It has been estimated that only 500 African Americans were granted conscientious objector status out of the three-quarters of a million drafted. (To give a frame of reference, roughly 34 million were subjected to the draft in World War II.) In total, only some 72,000 individuals applied for conscientious objector status in World War II. Of those, some 25,000 performed noncombatant service (they agreed to serve in the military but in a noncombat status), 12,000 did alternative service (they served on the home front in a hospital or as a test subject for vaccines, etc.), around 20,000 were denied conscientious objector status overall, and about 15,000 had claims that were never acted on (their request was not considered by the draft board or they were rejected for other reasons). Of the 20,000 denied conscientious objector status, some 6,000 were imprisoned for refusing to serve.

Religion also played a role in how World War II was defined. It was not one of the stated reasons for why the war began, as there really was only one: Pearl Harbor. As for why we were fighting the Germans, technically it was because they had declared war on us after we declared it on Japan, and so we returned the favor by declaring war on Germany. However, in the popular estimation, German fascism was considered evil and immoral. Most Americans also viewed Japan as evil and had a similar feeling toward the Nazis in Germany, and religion colored Americans' understanding of evil. One of the Four Freedoms, which Roosevelt sought to preserve through fighting the war, was freedom of religion. Thus, at both the diplomatic and popular levels, religion was a factor in the popular understanding of why we were fighting World War II, even though it was not one of the most direct reasons.

Of course, Hitler had decidedly religious motivations for his own involvement in the war. He wanted nothing less than Aryan world domination and the extinction of all Jewish people. He equated race and religion as one and the same and applied stereotypes to justify his position. The concentration camps housed members of a number of unpopular religions, including Catholics and Jehovah's Witnesses. However, the Holocaust became well known only after the fact, and most Americans supported the war for more patriotic reasons. Indeed, America was among the countries that denied entry to many Jews fleeing Europe, refusing to grant them protection from annihilation.

The next war, the Korean War, was somewhat ignored at the time in the public perception. The troops in the Korean War came generally from the regular armed forces and the National Guard and also from the draft. The Korean War was more popular than the Vietnam War, so fewer problems occurred with that draft than the one for Vietnam. Also, as fewer people were needed than in World War II, fewer chances arose for problems, even though there were certainly conscientious objectors. During the Korean War, about 25,000 people received conscientious objector status, a rate relatively comparable to that of World War II (when many more people were considered by the selective service system). From the start of World War II to Vietnam, most who received CO status were Mennonites, and of all COs during this same period, 98 percent had a specific religious affiliation. Thus, most conscientious objectors were religious, as the system required an applicant to request the status because of religious belief and training; in 1948, Congress added language requiring belief in a "Supreme Being." It was not until the Vietnam War that the category was widened.

Religion was a significant factor in the reasons the United States fought against communism in Korea and later in Vietnam. The Soviet Union, who backed the U.S. opponents in Korea and Vietnam, was officially an atheist country, and the United States had always viewed itself as religious, a perception that Congress underlined in the 1950s. At that time the United States adopted as its motto "In God We Trust" and added "under God" to the Pledge of Allegiance. Both of these actions were taken to differentiate the United States from the atheist USSR. Cold War attitudes often carried a zeal reminiscent of the medieval crusades, which encouraged the United States to fight communism everywhere, including in Korea and Vietnam.

During the Vietnam War many problems arose with the issue of religion in wartime, as the number of conscientious objectors skyrocketed—some claiming religious reasons but many objecting on nonreligious grounds. Compared with 72,000 who applied for conscientious objector status in World War II, more than 162,000 were granted this status between 1964 and 1973 during the Vietnam War. These figures become significant in the context of the overall draft: about one-fifth as many men were drafted by the selective service during the Vietnam War as in World War II (10 million were drafted during World War II, and slightly fewer than 1.8 million in the Vietnam War). Conscientious objectors were not

the only people opposed to the Vietnam War, even among those of draft age; some 200,000 were charged with violating the draft laws, and probably another 350,000 violated the laws but were never indicted.

Around 1966, the need for military manpower became acute, and the selective service was asked to provide about 300,000 men a year to the armed forces; between 1966 and 1969, the military grew from 2.5 million to 3.5 million troops, most of whom were drafted. The majority of these did not serve in Vietnam, but the risk of being sent into the war zone greatly shaped people's reaction to the draft.

During this war, the allowable reasons for claiming to be conscientious objectors were expanded. At first, one had to believe in a Supreme Being and oppose the war on religious grounds. However, in 1965, the Supreme Court considered the case brought by Dan Seeger, who was truly opposed to war but did not claim belief in a Supreme Being, and the Supreme Court allowed Seeger to be excluded from the draft. They held that although Seeger did not profess a religious belief, elements of his philosophy were parallel to belief in a Supreme Being, among others. In 1970, in *United States* v. *Walsh,* the Supreme Court considered the case of a person who was opposed to war due to his beliefs. The Court again widened the definition of religion, holding that if a person's beliefs occupied a place in his or her life similar to the place held by religion in others and these beliefs were in opposition to all war, an exemption should be granted. This wide definition held until 1973, when the draft was canceled and an all-volunteer army was put in place.

Since the Vietnam War, the draft has not existed in practice, even though all young men since 1980 have been required to sign up with the selective service system at the age of eighteen. A system for a draft is in place, with the necessary requirements and procedures, should the country ever need to mobilize a large military service, but doing so would be very unpopular. Recent calls during the second Gulf War for a renewed draft garnered two votes in the U.S. House of Representatives out of over 400 voting. Some of those in the military did apply for conscientious objector status during the first Gulf War (technically named Operation Desert Storm) as they protested America's actions in the area, and some were given discharges, but many more were jailed: although estimates vary, about 100 were discharged and another 2,000 were jailed. During the second (and much longer) Gulf War (technically named Operation Iraqi Freedom), soldiers who were conscientious objectors were still allowed out of the military, and it is estimated that hundreds have applied for CO status, with probably many more looking for other ways out or not re-enlisting. These numbers are undoubtedly much lower than they would have been under a draft, as everyone who joined the service was a volunteer. Although some of these volunteers chose the armed forces as the only way to afford a college education rather than out of devotion to combat of any kind, they did so with awareness of the possibility of war. Particularly those who enlisted after September 11, 2001, have done so knowing that they would probably be sent into battle. Some of these opposed to war probably have religious objections, but those who were religiously opposed to all war are not very likely to have signed up in the first place. This is not to imply that those conscientiously objecting to the war in Iraq do not have real objections to it, but that they are not likely to be religious pacifists, like most of those who were COs in World War I, World War II, and the Korean War.

Religion has also figured in America's military involvement since Vietnam. Although many motives were stated for going to war in Iraq both times, a definite factor was the religious beliefs of the opponents. The initial reasons for the first Gulf War were not religious (Saddam Hussein headed a Baathist or secular

regime), nor were they religious for the first part of the second Gulf War; however, most Americans (and probably most policy makers) see our opponents as Islamic, and some express this opinion using racial, religious, or ethnic slurs. This attitude definitely was a factor in the decision to go to war. The popular media regularly analyze Islamic beliefs and discuss the religious positions of the Iraqis. Country radio stations play Lee Greenwood's "God Bless the USA," which expresses the sentiment that God favors U.S. military actions, with the implication that all U.S. military actions are undertaken to secure American freedom and democracy. Irving Berlin's "God Bless America" is also frequently played as a less politically charged but still religious anthem for the country.

Thus, conscientious objectors who are (or were) motivated by religion have long existed in American history. Similarly, religion has long figured in our motives for fighting wars and in our national commitments. America tends to view itself as a country spreading goodness and light and freedom and fostering religious plurality; also, the decline of religion or increasing secularization is frequently cited as a threat to Western civilization. But deep down, religion still plays a large role in influencing America's actions and colors many people's views of war—one war or all wars in general.

Religious Proselytizers and the Law: One Person's Religion versus Another's Right to Be Left Alone

A well-known area of religion where the establishment and free exercise clauses of the First Amendment clash, and the law often gets involved, concerns door-to-door religious proselytizers. Very often, believers of a certain faith are instructed to promote their religion to those who are not members of the faith and to spread the word. Some religions, though, go further than most, ordering the active conversion of others rather than just welcoming interested parties at their temple doors. Thus, the followers of certain religions, including the Jehovah's Witnesses and the Mormons, feel that the only way to spread the religion effectively and find new converts is to go door to door promoting the faith. However, many of those contacted often feel offended, irritated, or trespassed on by the spreading of that word and wish to be left alone. They sometimes feel that their freedom to believe something else, or at the very least their freedom to be left alone, is being infringed on by these conversion efforts. Thus, the law often has been asked to step in and determine where the proselytizer's freedom of religion ends and the other person's freedoms, religious and otherwise, begin.

This note considers those proselytizers who are sincere in their efforts to promote their religion to others. In religion, as in other areas, there are those who use religion as a cloak for their desires to get rich. This group includes some televangelists, revivalists, and door-to-door preachers who are sometimes more interested in their own wallets than in anyone's salvation. However, the issue in those situations is fraud, not the freedom of (and from) religion, which is what this note considers. All authorities are allowed to prevent fraud and have less concern about religious infringement in those situations than in the area of sincere door-to-door religious proselytizers.

Two of the best-known groups that go door to door are the Latter-day Saints, referred to often (and in this essay) as the Mormons, and the Jehovah's Witnesses. The Mormons' founder, Joseph Smith, believed he had been visited by an angel of God, who led him to golden tablets in upstate New York. These tablets, when translated with a special key on stones also revealed to Smith, told of Jesus' visit to the area that is now the United States after his death and resurrection. According to the tablets, the people who lived in that area were descendants of the tribes of Israel, and Jesus had revealed himself to them, but they did not fol-

low him. The tablets said that God had become angry at this and, as a punishment, turned the Native Americans' skin dark. (This curse is similar to the curse of Ham in the Old Testament, used by some to try to justify white supremacy.) The message of Mormonism soon spread, and Smith moved west with his followers. He was met with a violent response, and a mob killed him in Carthage, Illinois, in 1844. Most of the Mormons then traveled to the Utah territory, initially isolating themselves from the world.

Relatively quickly, the Mormons began looking outward to spread their message and came to believe that all male Mormons should serve a two-year mission in their late teens or early twenties (generally late teens), with the purpose of telling non-Mormons (whom the Mormons call Gentiles) about the Mormon

Mormon missionaries talk with a pedestrian in Cambridge, Massachusetts. The Idaho natives, both twenty-one years old, were on a two-year mission. (AP Photo/William B. Plowman)

faith. Even in the mid–1800s, while most Mormons lived in Utah, Mormon missionaries were spreading the word about their faith. Young Mormon women are not under the same obligation, although some do serve, and they are expected to spend only a year and a half in missionary work, not two years. It is estimated that about one-half of Mormon boys will be involved in such a mission. The Mormons serve these missions both in the United States and around the world. The total number of Mormons worldwide is now estimated to be 11 million to 12 million, with 6 million in the United States.

The second group of door-to-door preachers, as noted, are the Jehovah's Witnesses. The Witnesses were founded, although not under that name, in 1879 under the leadership of Charles Taze Russell. Russell was a pastor who organized study groups and did research on the Bible, becoming convinced, as did many others over time, that the end of the world was near. Russell set the ending date as 1914; he believed that only a certain number of people would be saved, and that it was important to be among the fellowship of those relative few. Russell originally limited the focus pretty much to the group itself, as only 144,000 were supposed to be saved. The group was originally called Russellites after their founder. The second leader (Russell died in 1916), Joseph Rutherford, transformed the group, explaining that after the original 144,000 were saved, the rest of the people on earth who behaved properly would live on earth after the Second Coming, and so the Witnesses needed to spread the word. They began their practice of going door to door, giving away magazines, playing records, and spreading the doctrine of the faith.

The group attracted attention early for other reasons than the proselytizing, as they opposed World War I, believing that all war was immoral, and also refused to salute the flag, because Exodus 20 held that graven images should not be worshiped, and they believed the flag to be a graven image. The title Jehovah's Witness was based on Isaiah 43, and the name, Jehovah's Witnesses, was adopted in 1931. The group grew internationally, and total membership is now estimated to be over 5 million, but might be as high as 15 million, with about 1 to 2 million of those in the United States.

The Jehovah's Witnesses seem to provoke more opposition than other movements, and they definitely have been involved in more Supreme Court cases, particularly in terms of proselytizing, than the Mormons or other groups. Historically, this may be explained by the Mormons' significant head start in time over the Jehovah's Witnesses, and currently it may have to do with the Mormon Church's tendency to work with the local authorities in the areas where they do missions. Another source of opposition may stem from the claims of the Jehovah's Witnesses concerning the Second Coming of Jesus Christ. They have predicted five different dates for this event, the first said to have occurred in 1914. Currently, most Witnesses claim that Jesus came in 1914 but only in an invisible state, and some of the official Jehovah's Witnesses' literature and websites note how much the world did change in 1914 (which was, of course, the start of World War I). Another reason for opposition is the strongly held beliefs of the Witnesses. These strong beliefs make the Witnesses perhaps more noted than the Mormons and thus perhaps more opposed. A third reason for opposition to the Jehovah's Witnesses is their ideas that deviate from the mainstream, such as a refusal to salute the flag, to have blood transfusions, or to participate in the military.

The first well-known case of a Jehovah's Witness gaining Supreme Court attention for his treatment by the legal system was *Lovell* v. *City of Griffin* (1938). Alma Lovell was a Jehovah's Witness in the city of Griffin in Georgia. Griffin, like many other municipalities, required people to have permits before distributing literature. Other cities who had such ordinances claimed that their purpose was to prevent fraud and litter and to protect the public against strangers coming to their doors. Lovell, for her part, refused to listen to any city regulation, as she claimed that she had to listen only to God. The Supreme Court, deviating from Lovell's freedom of religion concern, found Griffin's permit requirement to be a restriction on the freedom of the press, as it was a prior restraint on the distribution of information. Prior restraints, in the area of the press, are viewed as particularly odious both because they were used by Great Britain in the colonial period and because they operate as a total ban on dissemination of information.

The second noted case was *Cantwell* v. *Connecticut* in 1940. The Witnesses, under Rutherford, were increasing their efforts to draw in new members and, with this, increasing their attacks on those who did not agree with them, particularly Roman Catholics. Jesse Cantwell and his sons were Jehovah's Witnesses who played records for those who would agree to listen to them. The record leading to their arrest was called "enemies," and it basically described the Roman Catholic Church as an enemy of everyone, and provoked resistance in a Catholic community. Cantwell was arrested for breaking the peace and for not registering. His convictions were overturned, as he had not posed a threat in any way (in fact, the state admitted that he had moved along when asked and had requested permission before playing the record), and his religious freedom gave him the right to play the record and to witness.

Throughout the 1940s, the Witnesses were involved in a number of legal battles. Some of these involved refusals to salute the flag or cooperate with the draft, but a fair number involved door-to-door operations. Twice the case of *Jones* v. *Opelika,* when Roscoe Jones challenged the right of Opelika, Alabama, to require a license to go door to door, came in front of the Supreme Court. This case was different from that of *Lovell,* in that the licenses were not predicated on what was being distributed. Rather, the law was intended as a control on who went door to door. At first, the

Supreme Court held that a city could require a license, especially if it guaranteed all applicants universal approval, so long as the license tax was paid. Taxes were allowed, as were controls on the time, place, and manner of distribution of literature. The next year, 1943, however, the Supreme Court reversed itself and held that ideas cannot be taxed, as that ran counter to the First Amendment, which aimed for an open marketplace of ideas.

The Jehovah's Witnesses very often involved their children to pass out magazines and help in witnessing, and this attracted attention from the police. Whether it attracted more attention than would have been directed at someone of a majority faith doing something similar is, obviously, unknown, but several cases of charges against parents for allowing their children to be involved in witnessing also came before the courts. One of the earlier such cases was *Pierce* v. *Massachusetts* in 1944. There the Supreme Court upheld the conviction of a parent for violating child labor laws for unlawful selling of magazines by a child and for having her work in an illegal way. The child in question was nine years old and was selling magazines at nearly nine o'clock on a school night. The Supreme Court narrowly upheld the rule, saying that the interests of the state needed to be balanced against the interests of the child and parent in religion.

Some have suggested over time that the door-to-door solicitation practiced by the Jehovah's Witnesses does not have as much claim to religious protection as more formal types of worship carried on in places of worship such as sanctuaries and synagogues, but the Supreme Court rejected that rationale, holding that door-to-door contact for religious purposes did have ancient roots and so needed to be protected.

Martin v. *City of Struthers* (319 U.S. 141, 1943) focused on the delivering of handbills door to door, in which the Witnesses rang the doorbell to hand the flyers to a home's inhabitants. This case dealt with a blanket ordinance that prohibited ringing doorbells (or knocking on doors) to pass out such material, and the person involved had been fined $10. The Supreme Court pointed out that the ability to distribute literature and ring doorbells was important to many groups, including those selling war bonds (the case occurred during World War II) and held that a blanket prohibition was illegal. Thus, even though the Jehovah's Witnesses were the groups bringing these issues, the courts did not feel that the Witnesses were the only ones affected by such statutes. The Supreme Court has also always been reluctant to allow bans on certain practices, particularly in the area of religion, on the grounds that only one small group is affected and thus not that many people's rights are violated. The Court in the door-to-door handbill case also pointed out that a home owner could still post a "no soliciting" sign and the city could still arrest those violating that sign. The Court has felt that the reasoning of the prohibiting law, in and of itself, represents religious discrimination banned by the First Amendment, which prohibits the government from favoring one religion over another, at the very least. Judicial authorities over time have also pointed out that freedom of speech and of the press in many of the cases litigated by the Witnesses also applied in other areas such as labor union organizing.

The Jehovah's Witnesses have not ceased coming before the Supreme Court. One of the most recent cases was *Watchtower* v. *Stratton* (2002) (Watchtower is the name of the Jehovah's Witnesses formal organization, the Watchtower Bible and Tract Society of New York). There the village of Stratton, Ohio, required all people going door to door to promote "causes" to first register and get a permit. The Supreme Court struck down this regulation in an 8–1 vote, holding that it violated the First Amendment in the areas of religion, speech, and press. The main offenses appear to be that the regulation was overly broad and it made the registrants too easily identifiable to later hostile

groups as registrations were made public. The ban covered not only commercial activity but all activity. Two concurrences accompanied the decision. The first noted that crime, which was cited in the lone dissent by Chief Justice Rehnquist as a reason for the ordinance, was not even advanced by the village in the lower courts and so could not have been very much of the justification. The other argued against some of the justifications advanced for striking down the ordinance in the majority opinion, including that getting a permit would violate some people's religions. Justice Scalia, who wrote the second concurrence, stated that a religious objection to a statute should not be a reason for its being invalid if it was otherwise acceptable. As noted, the only dissent was by Rehnquist, who suggested that rampant crime might result if such ordinances were not allowed, and he cited some examples of crime and assaults by door-to-door salesmen and people posing as such.

Most of these stated cases have involved the Jehovah's Witnesses, not the Mormons. The reasons are not exactly clear, particularly in the early cases, but possibly the more recent founding of the Jehovah's Witnesses, established in the twentieth century, has some impact. In its early years, the Mormon Church had no federal recourse against state and local laws. It was not until 1925 that *Gitlow* applied the First Amendment against the states, making the Witnesses' complaints against state and local ordinances possible at the federal level. In later years, the Mormon national headquarters has worked strongly with local communities and law enforcement agencies to attempt to inform those groups about the constitutional rights of the traveling Mormon missionaries in their towns. These efforts probably decreased the arrests and prosecutions of Mormons, particularly relative to the Jehovah's Witnesses, as the Mormons are a larger church than the Jehovah's Witnesses in the United States, having approximately 5 to 6 million members in the United States to the 1 to 2 million members of the Jehovah's Witnesses. Also, all Jehovah's Witnesses are expected to witness, whereas only those who are on missions are expected to be active frequent witnesses for the Mormons. Thus, there are more Jehovah's Witnesses who witness and a smaller organization to back them.

It should be noted that individuals do not have an absolute right to be left alone, nor is that right stated in the Constitution. There is definitely the right to not be disturbed by the authorities in one's home without a search warrant, and there is, throughout, a sense of the right to privacy, but such a right is not expressly stated. Thus, the right to privacy is less clear, especially in terms of its boundaries, than the right to freedom of religious expression, against which privacy is being balanced. In addition, in their own homes, people do not have to answer the door if they choose, and thus home owners do not have to deal with religious proselytizers. Similarly, if a resident displays a "no trespassing" or "no soliciting" sign, he or she has a legal right to expect those signs to be honored; and if they are not, cities can pass regulations criminalizing a refusal to obey those signs (as does the state). Thus, when considering this topic, the nature of the rights needs to be kept in mind.

Most court cases dealing with the conflict between those who travel door to door to spread religion and the people's right to be left alone have dealt with the Jehovah's Witnesses. Many different laws existed to prevent door-to-door solicitation, and the Witnesses have been subjected to most of them. It has been estimated that the Witnesses have been involved in over fifty Supreme Court cases in the area of door-to-door witnessing and other areas. However, the Mormons are also involved in door-to-door proselytizing, even if they have been less often visibly prosecuted for performing this activity. The Supreme Court has clearly stated that Witnesses and others have a right to travel and proselytize—and the Latter-day Saints now regularly post amicus curiae

briefs in the Witnesses cases—and that areas cannot uniformly ban door-to-door religious activities. Individual home owners, on the other hand, can act to prevent unwanted visitors with "no trespassing" signs. It also must be remembered throughout the discussion, when considering the interaction of home owners' (and other individuals') rights and the right to religious proselytizing, that this is a balancing act for our society and the courts, and neither side can expect complete victory. Thus, the desire to ring doorbells and the desire to not have them rung, which exist often throughout society, will continue to be balanced by the court system for the foreseeable future.

The Development of Religion and State in America and the World

The United States of America does not exist in a vacuum. Thus, the interaction of religion and the state in America needs to be considered in light of current and historic world events. This topic is broken up into two areas: first, the development of religion and the state in Europe and the Mediterranean area, and then the development of religion and the state in the rest of the world. For each, the history of the development will be considered first, and then the current state of the interaction of religion and the state.

This essay is limited to developments since the founding of the Greek city-states around 500 B.C.E. While this is an arbitrary date, the Greeks are often the society the United States looks back to as initiating democracy, and Greek society therefore makes a good starting point for what is, ultimately, an analysis of U.S. political culture. Each Greek city-state had its own patron god, such as Athena at Athens. Greek leaders allowed the worship of other gods, but each state focused on its patron god or goddess, who was consulted through divination before major decisions. To obtain a divine command, the political leader would go to an oracle and ask the god/goddess for advice on such things as wars. Greeks, as Greek philosophy developed, began to focus more on the individual, and in varying amounts, the state allowed this philosophy to develop. With the rise of Greek democracy, more power in the area of one's own beliefs was given to the individual, in turn allowing individuals to choose which gods to follow. In the classical Greek period of Socrates, shrines to many gods existed, and many different Greek gods had followers; the state supported these groups by building temples, but did not force idolization.

After Greece, the next major power in the area was Rome, and Rome had its own set of gods and goddesses, closely modeled after those of the Greeks. Rome was more interested in power than philosophy, and the interest in the gods was similarly practical. Leaders of the republic of Rome and the ensuing Roman empire both wanted the gods to bless their endeavors, and so Roman religion was very polytheistic, with gods for home, wars, city gates, and so on. The early Roman Republic did fairly well and so seemed to be in favor with the gods. With the political upheaval at the end of the Roman Republic and the founding of the empire, religion became less important, and the Roman emperors made themselves into gods. Augustus publicly proclaimed himself as divine. Most people were happy with the general developments of the period, even if they did not believe Augustus to be divine, as the empire, particularly Italy, prospered. Augustus did promote religion, rebuilding temples and providing for priests who had been neglected financially during the turmoil of the fall of the republic.

Rome, under the emperors, was generally tolerant of most faiths, even though it was notably intolerant of Christianity. This was primarily because Christians refused to make the same sacrifices to the emperor made by the followers of other religions. Christians also worked in small groups and covertly, as a new faith

Roman emperor Constantine I, known as Constantine the Great, restored order to the Roman world and laid the foundation for the empire's success for centuries to come. He is particularly significant for his conversion to Christianity. (iStockPhoto)

might, and so were suspect, as many societies fear those who act in secret and by themselves. From time to time, Christians were persecuted and some were even used in public spectacles, such as the infamous feeding of Christians to the lions. However, for the most part, Roman emperors wished to have peace, and they left religion largely separate from the state, so long as the appropriate sacrifices were made. Around the start of the fourth century C.E., the Roman Empire was undergoing many difficulties, and the emperor Diocletian undertook one of the most brutal persecutions ever. His successor, Constantine, went in exactly the opposite direction, converting to Christianity, proclaiming it the religion of the Roman Empire, and putting the force of the Roman Empire behind the new state faith. This was the first formal state religion in a long time in Western civilization.

The Roman Empire, in the era of Constantine, split in two—the Eastern (or Byzantine) Roman Empire, headquartered in Constantinople (present-day Istanbul) and the Western Roman Empire, headquartered in Rome. The Western Roman Empire continued the use of Christianity, but its main concern for the next century (after Constantine) was survival. It failed in this effort, finally collapsing in 476 C.E. The Eastern Roman Empire continued, surviving until 1453. In the East, the emperor was also the head of the church and used the state to promote religion (and religion to promote the state). For the next ten centuries, with varying amounts of success, the Byzantine Empire promoted Christianity and spread the Orthodox religion with a view of the state and the religion as one. This concept strongly influenced much of eastern Europe, particularly Russia. There, once a state formed, the rulers installed a state-controlled bishop to maintain local order, but they used the Cyrillic alphabet to stay away from full Byzantine control. The same idea permeated the Balkans. Thus, the concept that the church and state should be united was prevalent throughout eastern Europe, and the Byzantines were directly responsible for this in large part, even while the Byzantines were unable to fully control the area politically. Local rulers, in order to maintain their power (and hoping to increase it), promoted their own culture, language, and writing while allowing the Byzantine Church, with an eye toward limiting the Byzantine influence.

In western Europe, for three centuries after the formal end of the Western Roman Empire, small-scale states existed where any existed at all. The bishop of Rome created for himself a position as leader of the Western Christian Empire, titling himself pope of the Catholic Church, where Catholic means universal. The pope determined that Peter was the key figure in Christianity following Jesus, that Peter had

become bishop of Rome, and that successors to that seat should also be the religion's key figure, meaning that the bishop of Rome, now pope, could appoint bishops and work to determine church doctrine. The popes did just that, establishing an official translation of the Bible, with an official list of the correct books to be included, and trying to establish direct control of all of the church. Of course, the church in the Byzantine Empire did not listen to the pope, and many local princes opposed him when it was in their interests, but princes also sought the pope's blessings when it served their purposes, and the princes and popes worked together to keep out other religions. Thus, although religion and the state fought each other, there was no separation of church and state in any practical way. This situation of anarchy in politics and growing power for the pope continued until 800 when the Holy Roman Empire under Charlemagne was established.

Charlemagne was a Frankish leader who managed to unite much of central Europe, including most of present-day France and Germany, and he believed that humans should not wait for God to establish a kingdom in the future, or to wait for an afterlife, but that humans should try to establish a City of God in the here and now, borrowing from St. Augustine. Membership in this city depended on following God in the right way rather than on race. God ruled in the heavens, and God wanted Charlemagne to rule on earth. Church and state worked hand in hand for Charlemagne, and he rescued Pope Leo III in 799. Pope Leo then crowned Charlemagne Holy Roman Emperor the next year. Charlemagne's empire did not last long, being divided within the next fifty years, but the idea of church and state unity continued throughout the next several centuries in western Europe.

The other main religion affecting Europe in this period was Islam. That religion was founded in 622 by Muhammad. Muhammad claimed to have had visions over the past dozen years or so and used what was seen in those visions to create a new religion. Unlike other prophets, most notably Jesus, who clearly differentiated between Caesar and God, Muhammad combined religious and political aims and created a new kingdom. With that combination, it is not surprising that Islamic kingdoms did not have separation of church and state. What is surprising is that the Islamic kingdoms did not demand fidelity to Islam as a precondition to remaining in their realms. Christians and Jews were allowed to stay in the areas conquered but did have to pay higher taxes, and others very often were forced to convert. Thus, while there was no separation of church and state in Islamic territories, there was not only one religion in those territories, unlike other places where church and state were unified. The Islamic empires conquered most of North Africa, much of what we generally call the Middle East, and parts of Spain. Most of what is generally considered the Western world was controlled by either the Islamic world, the Byzantine Empire, or the fragmented Holy Roman Empire.

This situation pretty much prevailed in Europe and the Mediterranean world from 600 C.E. to about 1500 C.E. Western Europe eventually developed larger states and more of a state apparatus, but the Catholic Church was still the choice of nearly all kings, as was true of the Orthodox Christian Church in eastern Europe. Separation of church and state was nonexistent. Those in the majority fared well in terms of how the ruling forces treated their religion, which is always the case, but a better estimation of the interaction of church and state can be gained by considering the fate of religious minorities in these areas. The Jews were the main religious minority in both areas. Jews were usually treated better in Muslim lands than in Europe. The stated goal of European rulers was forced Jewish conversion, whereas Muslim nations merely wished to encourage conversion. Jews were also more able to supervise their own affairs in Muslim lands—they did not have full power over their communities

but generally had more than they did in Europe. The same was true for Christian communities in Muslim lands. In Europe, however, whole communities of Jews were sometimes wiped out, and Jews were forced to live in only certain areas of the city, which is where the term ghetto comes from: it refers to the Jewish quarter of the city. Jews were prominent in the banking area for two reasons: first, Jews were not accepted in other businesses, and second, Christianity for a time had a rule against lending money with interest, meaning Jews were able to make a profit from banking while Christians were not. This made Jews more likely to be bankers than Christians but also fostered Christian hatred of the Jews. This hatred showed clearly in the Elizabethan era in the stereotypical picture of the usurer displayed by Shylock in Shakespeare's *Merchant of Venice*. Jews were also blamed for the Black Death in the thirteenth century. All the Jews in Spain were expelled in 1492, and the Spanish government followed this up by expelling all Muslims in 1504. Thus, minorities often fared better in Muslim lands, even if the idea of toleration, as understood today, was not a possibility.

In South America, with the arrival of the Christian conquerors, the native religions, which were greatly tied in with the states, were almost completely destroyed. The conquerors' goals were often summed up as God, Gold, and Glory, with God being the extending of Christianity to the Native Americans. If the local people did not want Christianity, they had little choice, as they were soon conquered. Christianity was then forced on those natives who lived through the conquest and the diseases brought by the conquistadors.

Today, in most of Europe, the church is generally far separated from the state, even if the state does support the church at times. For instance, in France, the state pays for all religious schools, but the church is expected to stay out of state matters. In Eastern Europe, religion was generally banned under the communist regime, and some communist states, such as Albania, went so far as to close down all of the churches. In the Americas, church-state separation varies greatly. Separation of church and state is the norm in Canada, but a good deal of power is allowed at the provincial level for each province to adapt to its religious groups. In the United States, the level of religious involvement in the state often varies depending on what political party is in power. The country seems contradictory, proud of both its separation of church and state and its religious heritage, with many invoking "God bless America" every chance they have. In the Muslim countries of the Middle East and North Africa, in those states where a religious group has influence, very often religion forms the basis for the state law. In Saudi Arabia, for instance, even visiting women are required to dress in relative conformity with local law. In states where the state is the controlling influence—for example, in dictatorships—much less power is given to religion as the state reigns supreme. Thus, the relative ratio of toleration, which favored the Middle East over Europe in the Middle Ages, has now shifted to favoring Europe.

Besides Europe and the Americas, of course, there are also Africa and Asia to consider when discussing the interaction of religion and the state. In Africa, before European colonialism, most societies had established sets of gods, or a single god, and an afterlife was generally believed in. In addition to its own set of gods, some societies adopted Islamic or Christian beliefs. If one belonged to a particular society, one at least publicly worshiped its god or gods. Islam moved into the area in the 600s, reaching Africa soon after its establishment. In the Islamic societies in Africa, similar to those in the Middle East and elsewhere, other religions were tolerated, even if they were taxed more heavily. This is not to suggest that all Islamic societies were the same, as each mixed items of the local culture into it. Ethiopia, by contrast, was a Christian kingdom, Axum. In West Africa, the kings originally ruled by assuming the mantle of divine right, but many of these

kings adopted Islam as a state religion, as that religion also allowed the kings to increase their authority. While less is known about southern Africa, it is relatively safe to assume that at the very least, culture often reinforced religion. With the arrival of European colonial conquerors in Africa, which occurred on the edges of Africa until the nineteenth century and then all across Africa, Christianity was introduced in large scale.

In Asia, the Hindu and Buddhist faiths coexisted in India before the seventh century C.E. The upper classes tended to prefer the Hindu faith, in part because it gave them special rights and privileges, while the lower classes tended more toward Buddhism, often because it claimed equality for all. In time, starting in the 700s, Muslim forces, such as that of the Mahmud of Ghanzi, moved into India, crossing the Indus River. Over the next six centuries, up to about 1300, Islamic forces increased their empires and promoted the religion of Islam by imposing increased taxes on the non-Muslims.

In Southeast Asia, spirit worship was originally prevalent, but Hindu and Buddhist beliefs made a strong entrance as well, between 1 and 1000 C.E. Many of the local rulers liked this as it increased their power and allowed the kings to perform rituals, giving the king an air of legitimacy.

In China, by the early centuries C.E., three main religions competed for influence: Buddhism, Daoism, and Confucianism. Confucianism provided little emotional satisfaction in the eyes of many, who turned to Buddhism or Daoism. Buddhism was supported by some rulers in the early seventh century C.E., when the Tang dynasty was beginning, but eventually many rulers turned against it, promoting Daoism and Confucianism instead. Eventually, most Chinese emperors promoted Confucianism, as it melded well with the Chinese tradition of focusing on the family and hard work. Thus, for Chinese dynasties, it largely was not a question of whether to support religion but which religion to support. China was largely ruled by government officials who had studied Confucianism, and this both continued the support of Confucianism and decreased change.

In Japan, the main religion was Shinto, and this religion was strongly promoted by the state. The spirit worship common to Southeast Asia was also apparent in Japan, and this worship evolved into Shinto, which focuses on nature and purification. The Japanese state linked the divine emperor with Shinto.

In Asia, in the sixteenth century C.E. and after, the arrival of Europeans played a large role in shaping the relationship between church and state. Most Asian countries became colonies of European powers, which, in turn, allowed Christian missionaries to attempt to convert the local populace. The Europeans did not universally remain, however. For instance, in the Philippines, the Spanish established a colony that would remain from the 1500s until the defeat of the Spanish in 1898 in the Spanish American War. However, the British and French were forced out of Burma and found Vietnam to be unprofitable and so left by the end of the seventeenth century. England and France and many other European nations would soon return, however. The British focus turned to India, conquering it between the mid-1700s and the beginning of the nineteenth century. Christian missionaries followed, and the British rule, often through colonial allies, promoted these missionaries, although it did not force conversion. France returned to conquer Vietnam and much of the rest of Southeast Asia from the 1850s to the 1890s. England and France, unlike 300 years earlier, were not as motivated by religion, but their conquest of the areas did allow missionaries, supported by the colonial powers, to move in.

Africa and Asia threw off the colonial yokes in the 1950s and 1960s and assumed a relative level of independence. A listing of all the countries' current policies on religion would take a volume of its own, but a survey will help in understanding how the United States interrelates with these areas. In Algeria, for instance, Sunni Muslim is the state religion. To go to the other end of the pole, in China, similar to most communist countries, religion is severely marginalized; religion is opposed by the state rather than just separated from it, as the country is officially atheist. North Korea, also socialist in government, takes things in a different direction; there are government-sponsored religious activities, as the state wishes to appear tolerant of religion. In the Middle East, Islamic law forms the basis for several states' legal systems, including those of Saudi Arabia and Jordan. In Africa, the basis for law varies, as does the treatment of religion. For instance, in Chad, the legal system is based on French law and Chadian custom, leaving religion largely up to individuals; in Kenya, the bases include English common law, Kenyan common law, Islamic law, and tribal law, to cite a few. Thus, law comes from a huge variety of places in some African countries, resulting in a more hands-off approach to religion. Much of Africa is also attempting to move toward democracy, which promotes a greater separation of church and state, at least in theory.

Religion and state have typically been united throughout most of world history, with the notion of separating church and state developing only recently. Even since the 1700s, when this idea developed, most states and ruling entities, particularly in the colonies, did not allow separation of church and state, with some promoting a certain religion and others trying to ban all religion. However, in the last few years, more areas have moved toward allowing a separation of church and state, and the United States continues to promote this policy that is written into its Constitution.

The Supreme Court and the Establishment Clause

Freedom of religion as described in the First Amendment is made up of two parts, known as the establishment and free exercise clauses.

The first is often referred to as the freedom from religion and the second as the freedom of religion. They state, "Congress shall make no law respecting an establishment of religion, or prohibiting the free exercise thereof." The first part is generally called the establishment clause, as it means, in a near universal reading, that the federal government, and since 1925 the states, cannot create an establishment of religion. (The second part is the free exercise clause, discussed generally in a separate essay.) However, the question remains, what is an establishment of religion?

The establishment clause is sometimes less debated than the free exercise clause, as more cases arise from questions about how an individual worships than from claims that the government is establishing a religion. However, this does not mean that the establishment clause is irrelevant. Far from it, as those cases stemming from the establishment clause have been among the most controversial in the nation's history. School prayer, school vouchers, and the Pledge of Allegiance are all issues that deal with the establishment clause. Many of the hottest debates come out of areas where one side feels tradition is being wiped away and civilization threatened, and the other feels that the government is trying to tell them which god to worship (and whether to worship a god).

Many people have the idea that the Founding Fathers came to America for religious freedom, and this is partially correct. Many of the original immigrants to America, of those who came willingly, came for the opportunity to practice their own religion. This is not, however, the same idea as religious freedom. Often one religious group generally controlled a colony or settlement, and their religion was considered the state religion. So the colony or settlement founders had freedom to practice *their* religion, but there was truly no religious freedom as the rest of the colony had to practice that religion as well. Many different colonies established their own religions as the colony-approved religion (and the only op-

tion): Massachusetts was Puritan, Connecticut was Congregationalist, and Virginia was Episcopalian. Famous religious dissenters also dot our early history, including Anne Hutchinson and Roger Williams. In the late eighteenth century, in the period leading up to the American Revolution, several colonies had established the idea of religious toleration and freedom, including Pennsylvania and Rhode Island, but others still had a state-supported church.

Religion was not a large element in the American Revolution, as issues of taxation, general economics, and power were greater motivating forces. The original Constitution is also relatively silent on the whole issue of religion, save for one clause, which holds that no religious test can be used for holders of federal offices. This meant the central government could not require officeholders to profess a certain religion. However, the original Constitution did play an important role, in hindsight, in the development of religious freedom in America. It did this through its opponents, known as the anti-Federalists. One complaint of the anti-Federalists was that the Constitution gave too much power to the federal government, and early in the first session of Congress in 1789, James Madison proposed a series of amendments to the Constitution to satisfy these critics. With revision, most of these amendments became our Bill of Rights. The freedom of religion has become part of what we now know as the First Amendment, but it was actually third in the original list sent out to the states—the first two were not ratified. Madison was relatively silent on the meaning of the religion part of the First Amendment, as he was fairly silent on what he thought the whole Bill of Rights meant. Regardless, the Bill of Rights became law in 1791 and has remained so since. One first needs to realize that the First Amendment is explicit in that its restrictions bind only Congress, and the whole of the Bill of Rights may have been intended to limit only Congress. This, at any rate, was what the Supreme Court said in 1833. The

First Amendment would be applied to the states only later, after the addition of amendments specifically referring to the states.

There are several possible interpretations of what the First Amendment aimed to do. One of these is that the main goal was to move away from any governmentally mandated or supported church on the federal level. The federal government could still support religion as an idea but could not favor any one church over another. Another is the idea that the First Amendment is intended to protect the churches by prohibiting the government from interfering in ideas of the church. This goes back in many ways to the arguments of Roger Williams, who thought that the secular state, sinful by nature, should have no role in religion, as such interaction would commute the sins of the state into religion and pollute that area as well. A third is that the government should have nothing at all to do with religion. Thomas Jefferson, in 1802, wrote that the First Amendment created a "wall of separation" between government and religion, and some people take those words to be their metaphor for how the government and religion should interact. Jefferson was a good friend of Madison, but it is hard to know what Madison thought the First Amendment should mean in 1789.

Others describe Madison as not overly interested in any individual liberty but more interested in protecting federal power as a whole and the federal Constitution. These scholars argue that he managed the Bill of Rights debate and process with an eye toward that end, which would suggest that Madison had thought little about what the establishment clause really meant. Each of these positions have merit, and as Madison left relatively few clues about what he thought the clause meant, it has been up to the Supreme Court to determine its meaning.

In 1833, the Supreme Court declared that the Bill of Rights limited only the federal government, and the federal government did little to directly control religion. Thus, few cases arose under the First Amendment's religion clauses before 1900. Some that did dealt with the issue of polygamy in the Utah territory. In the 1850 to 1890 period, Congress passed many laws outlawing polygamy in federal territories (the main Mormon settlement was in the Utah territory, centered around modern-day Utah), and these laws were eventually challenged. All of them, including disenfranchisement of people for believing in but not practicing polygamy and the disestablishment of the Mormon church, were upheld. Utah was even required to insert into its state constitution an irrevocable provision stating that polygamy would not be practiced. These were, however, the main cases testing the freedom of religion on a national level before the 1920s.

In the 1920s, challenges arose, and slow change began. After the Civil War, the federal government passed laws guaranteeing civil rights to African Americans, with the aim of offering some protection to former slaves. To make these rights more permanent, the federal government passed (and the states approved) the Fourteenth Amendment, which guaranteed the rights of due process and equal protection for all against any state infringement. It was not clear what these rights meant though, and early court interpretations of them limited the scope of the Fourteenth Amendment, along with the reach of the Thirteenth and Fifteenth Amendments, which had also aimed to protect the former slaves. In 1925, this all took a radical change. The case of *Gitlow* v. *New York* dealt with the conviction of Benjamin Gitlow under an anti-sedition law. The conviction was upheld, but Gitlow had argued that the Fourteenth Amendment, by its guarantee of due process, also guaranteed the rights stated in the Bill of Rights against state infringement. To put it more concisely, Gitlow argued that the Bill of Rights should also protect the people against the states. The Supreme Court in an almost casual manner, said "for present purposes we may and do assume that freedom of speech and of the press—which are protected by the First Amendment from abridgment by Congress—are among the fundamental personal rights and 'liberties' protected by the due process clause of the Fourteenth Amendment from impairment by the States" (268 U.S. 652: 666). The Supreme Court never explained its logic for applying the freedom of speech and the press against the states, and did not at the time enumerate in any more detail what other rights were part of the fundamental rights and liberties applied against the states. However, since that ruling in 1925, the whole idea of incorporating at least part of the Bill of Rights against the states has not been seriously challenged at a national level (even while the debate over what to incorporate raged), and the idea that the First Amendment's guarantee of religious liberty and nonestablishment, once accepted, has also been generally applied.

The Supreme Court continued to develop the idea of applying the Fourteenth Amendment against the states over the next decade and a half. In 1937 the Court stated that fundamental liberties were within the idea of liberty guaranteed by the Fourteenth Amendment and in 1938 stated that the specific guarantees of the Bill of Rights also applied against the states. Religion was added to the list later, coming in 1940 in *Cantwell* v. *Connecticut.* In that case, three Jehovah's Witnesses were going door to door and playing a record vilifying the Catholic Church. They were arrested for a breach of the peace. The Supreme Court read the First Amendment rather widely, incorporating the actions these men were taking to be included in the freedom of religion. The Court also included that freedom of religion in the overall idea of liberty created in the Fourteenth Amendment and thus applied the First and Fourteenth Amendments against the states, overturning the Witnesses' convictions. The Supreme Court also stated that the establishment clause of the First Amendment applied against the states but did not use that clause to strike down any laws for

a few years after the *Cantwell* case. In 1947, the first time an establishment clause case came before the Supreme Court after *Cantwell,* the Court upheld a law repaying the costs of parents who paid bus fare for their children to attend private school.

Many of the establishment clause cases are somewhat similar to the first one in one significant aspect—they deal with education, largely because schools are where the government has a captive and easily molded audience. (The government also has a captive audience in the military, but soldiers are generally adults and not considered to be as easily molded as children in schools.) The cases in education dealing with the establishment clause can be divided into three areas: aid to private schools, prayer in public schools, and religious education for public school students, or what is often called released time.

One of the most litigated issues has been that of aid to private schools, most of which are religious. This issue hinges on both the establishment and the free exercise clauses of the First Amendment: if states provide too much aid to religious schools, they are seen to be establishing religion, but if they provide none at all or provide too many obstacles to these schools, they may be interfering with the free exercise of religion or parental liberty. Early in the twentieth century, some states tried to ban private religious schools, but this was held to be unconstitutional, both for contract reasons (as schools that already had charters could not have them summarily voided) and for reasons of liberty (as parents have the right to raise their children as they see fit, within certain parameters).

The issue of aid was first litigated in the 1940s, dealing with reimbursements to parents of schoolchildren who took the city bus to private schools. This aid was held to be constitutional, as it paid the fares of children to attend any private (or public if necessary) school, and it was not aimed specifically at helping religious schools. The Court said that all public safety programs, such as road maintenance and traffic safety, aid religious schools indirectly, and the Court was not about to ban all such programs. The issue returned to the Court in the late 1960s. New York had a program of lending secular textbooks to private schools, with the goal of maintaining neutrality between teaching in the public and private schools. The state argument was that the public school students did not have to pay for their textbooks (which were all secular), and private school students should not have to pay for their secular textbooks. The Supreme Court agreed, allowing these loans, as the program was neutral, having neither the purpose nor the primary effect of advancing religion. Those two tests, the purpose test and the primary effect test, have continued to play an important part in First Amendment jurisprudence ever since.

In 1971, the Supreme Court created what has proven to be the most lasting test of whether a legislative act related to religion is constitutional. The case was *Lemon* v. *Kurtzman,* and the programs at issue gave supplements to private schools for the salaries of teachers who taught secular subjects. The Supreme Court struck down the programs, holding that they overly entangled the state in religious matters, as the state would have to monitor the teachers to be sure they were teaching only secular subjects. A three-part test emerged: first, the legislation must have a secular purpose; second, the primary effect of the legislation must be to neither advance nor retard religion; and third, the legislation must not create excessive entanglement with religion. The legislation here violated the third part of the test. The Supreme Court, for most of the 1970s, continued to move in the direction of limiting governmental programs that were involved with religion. It struck down a program providing tuition reimbursement or tax credits to parents who sent their children to private schools because the program advanced religion.

By the 1980s, however, the Supreme Court began to swing in the other direction; with the appointment of more generally conservative

justices, programs began to be allowed if they were "neutral" and if they allowed the individual to have a choice in where the aid was directed. Tax deductions for expenses of sending students to schools, including religious schools, were allowed, even though tax credits had earlier been struck down. In one case, a student was receiving government assistance because he was blind, and the Supreme Court allowed him to attend a religious school and to keep his aid as the program was neutral and the student chose where to attend. However, in 1985 the Supreme Court struck down programs in which public employees drawing state salaries taught secular subjects in private schools on private school grounds. The solution was to allow them to teach such subjects just off private school grounds. By the 1990s, the Supreme Court had reversed this trend, allowing aid to both private and public schools when that aid was distributed on a neutral basis.

The Court in 1997 reversed its 1985 decision and allowed the public employees to teach directly on private school grounds. Their reasoning was that the teachers could be trusted not to teach religious subjects and that the aid was neutral. The Court next, in 2002, ruled that a voucher program that allowed students to select from a wide variety of schools was constitutional, even though most students picked religious schools; in determining the constitutionality, the Court ruled that the aid was neutral and the parents' choice directed the aid. Thus, by the early years of the twenty-first century, neutrality of a program with regard to religion became the guiding idea in many of the decisions, even though calls to abandon the *Lemon* standard did not meet with success. Many different justices announced a disagreement with the *Lemon* standard and crafted their own alternatives, but no other standard has, as of 2006, received a majority of the Court's approval.

The next major topic is probably the most contentious of the three and one of the most divisive issues the Supreme Court has had to deal with, except for civil rights and abortion:

the issue of school prayer and Bible reading. School prayers were quite common in many public schools, although by no means all, as was the practice of Bible reading. Many programs of school prayer and Bible reading acknowledged the religious diversity of this country, requiring readings from the Old Testament, which were generally acceptable to Catholics, Jews, and Protestants, and prayers that were supposed to be acceptable to all three religions. Muslims, adherents of less popular religions, agnostics, and atheists were all ignored. The first challenge to Bible reading, on a state level, occurred in 1908, with the Illinois Supreme Court declaring that the practice violated the state constitution. The main issue at that time was not so much whether to read the Bible, but which Bible to read, as Catholics and Protestants favored different versions of the Bible. The U.S. Supreme Court first took up the issue in the 1950s, but once the case reached the Court, dismissed it on a technicality. In 1962, the Court returned to the issue in *Engel* v. *Vitale,* striking down New York's program of prayer, as it created an establishment of religion, even though the prayer was written to be broad. This created a firestorm of criticism, as one reason school prayer was being pushed in the period was to differentiate America from the atheistic USSR, the nation's opponent in the Cold War.

The next year, the Supreme Court struck down the practice of Bible reading, and some saw the Court as attacking all that was traditional in America—prayer, Bible reading, and, for white Southerners, segregated schools. Many railed against the Court's decisions, and signs appeared in some places in America suggesting that America should impeach Earl Warren, who was chief justice at the time. However, attempts to pass a constitutional amendment allowing school prayer or Bible reading failed every time it was introduced, both in the 1960s and later. President Kennedy and Governor Rockefeller (of New York) supported the school prayer decision, and this may have caused some in the middle to accept it. The rationale for striking down both programs was the same—that the programs created a government religion and put the government's force behind a certain religion. The Bible reading cases added an idea that would have increasing importance as the century progressed, that the government should be neutral in the area of religion.

These decisions did not lead to acceptance from much of the country. Many school districts continued to have prayers, sometimes publicly, sometimes quietly, and lawsuits over the issue continue. State legislatures also passed statutes calling for school prayer or for the posting of the Ten Commandments. Hundreds of amendments have been proposed on both the school prayer and Bible reading issues, with more being offered on the school prayer issue. One main element in many of the statutes and proposed amendments was that participation was theoretically voluntary. Some also called on Congress to remove school prayer from the jurisdiction of the Supreme Court. As with the amendments, though, the efforts failed. Those supporting school-sponsored prayer (and fighting publicly for it, as opposed to those who were quietly praying in school and, having the support of the community, not worrying about being caught) argued instead for a "moment of silence" rather than a prayer. The supporting idea was that those who wanted to pray could do so, but those who did not want to were not being forced to—they simply had to remain silent. The U.S. Supreme Court has never ruled directly on the issue, even though they did strike down a moment of silence statute that had added that the moment could be used for silence or voluntary or spoken prayer. Other moment of silence statutes, not mandating a purpose for the moment, have been generally accepted, even though the Court has never directly ruled on the issue.

The other main area of school prayer is occasional school prayer, either at football games or graduations. The U.S. Supreme Court has

Billboard in Decatur, Illinois, in 1963 demands the impeachment of U.S. Chief Justice Earl Warren who supported racial desegregation in public schools. (AP Photo)

generally held both of these practices to be unconstitutional, with a variety of rationales. It seems relatively clear that the 1962 *Engel* decision is here to stay, no matter how despised or circumvented it is in many parts of the country. The edges might be chipped away by moments of silence or prayer at certain events, which some suggest might be allowed in certain forms, depending on how the new justices rule on the issue.

Finally, the issues surrounding released time programs were contentious in the middle of the twentieth century but have decreased in significance. Most released time programs (called such as students were released from public schools to attend religious classes) also included an element of physical release, as students left the school campus to attend religion classes elsewhere. In 1948, the Supreme Court considered a system of religious classes that were conducted on public school grounds and struck down the program. The reasoning of the Court, through Justice Black, was that government and religion were supposed to be wholly separate, with a tall wall of separation, and the wall was clearly breached with the schools and churches working together. The minority of the Court agreed with the idea that the schools and churches were working too closely together but did not condemn all released time programs, just those with too much collusion. One dissenter, Justice Reed, suggested that all things short of a national church should be allowed. In 1952, the Court somewhat reversed itself, allowing a released time program that occurred off the premises of the school. Changing political climates, with the heating up of the Cold War and increasing attention to public religion in the nation, also may have helped to shape the Court's decisions, as did the fact that four new justices were appointed between 1948 and 1952. Released time is not as much of an issue now as it was then, as students are generally able to commute from their schools to religious classes outside of school hours, negating the need for released time programs, and fewer students take religious classes after school.

The Pledge of Allegiance has also been controversial under the establishment clause, as have Christmas displays. In the 1950s, Congress added the phrase "under God" to the pledge, in order to differentiate the United States from the USSR, which was officially an atheistic nation. This addition brought little legal challenge at the time, but with the easing and then end of the Cold War, challenges came in the 1980s and 1990s. In 2004, the Supreme Court heard the case *Elk Grove* v. *Newdow,* in which a father challenged his daughter's recitation of the pledge every day. The claim was that by forcing students to say "under God" in the pledge, the government was taking a stand on religion. Similar challenges to the national motto had been turned away in the past—in the 1950s, the phrase "one nation under God" was adopted as the motto. The Supreme Court decided the case on a legal issue, but three justices did argue that had the case been heard, the pledge with the words "under God" would have been declared constitutional. One reason given is that some justices, including just retired Justice O'Connor, felt that the phrase "under God," whether in the pledge or in our motto, have so entered our national fabric that

they have ceased to be purely religious and have become more nationalistic.

Displays of nativity scenes have not fared as well. The Supreme Court in the 1980s heard several cases on displays of nativity scenes and other religious symbols, such as menorahs, during the holidays. The basic rule that seems to have emerged is that if the symbol has a mixed meaning combining the religious and the secular, such as Christmas trees and Santa Claus, it will probably be allowed, or if the nativity is combined with many other items, it might be allowed. However, if a nativity scene is placed by itself, it may very well be disallowed.

The final issue to emerge recently is the posting of the Ten Commandments on public grounds. Some groups have called for placing the Ten Commandments in public places on moral grounds, arguing that these are the basis for many of our modern laws and should be displayed. Others, of course, call for their place-

Stephen Breyer, an associate justice of the U.S. Supreme Court, is considered a moderate liberal. (Collection of the Supreme Court of the United States)

ment on religious grounds, but such a religious purpose would never be allowed, either under the neutrality principle or the *Lemon* standard. In Alabama, Kentucky, and Texas, among other places, monuments and placards were erected and then challenged. Cases concerning two displays in Kentucky and one in Texas reached the Supreme Court. In all three cases, the commandments were displayed with other texts, such as the Bill of Rights. The Supreme Court, in a narrow decision, struck down the exhibits in Kentucky, but allowed the one in Texas, as the Texas display had been in place for an extended time. Because it had existed for a long time without protest and the Ten Commandments were combined with other documents in the display, Justice Breyer (the swing vote in the decision) was convinced that the commandments had enough of a historical meaning that most people considered them historical and part of a moral message rather than religious. Breyer was the key justice as he voted to strike down the Kentucky displays while allowing the one in Texas.

The establishment clause has produced many of the hottest issues concerning the First Amendment's treatment of religious liberty. The Supreme Court did not hear many establishment cases until after 1950, but the magni-

tude of the cases in many ways has made up for the lost time. The Court first held that some aid to private schools was allowed, even while overt religious activities were not. Thus, busing and textbooks for private schools (when allowed for public students also) were acceptable, but a prayer and Bible reading were not. In the 1970s, the Supreme Court moved to its strongest position, denying programs that aided religious schools, striking down the loan of maps and tax credits for public schools, holding that allowable programs had to have a secular purpose, had to have a primary effect of neither helping nor hurting religion, and had to avoid excessive entanglement with religion. The Court then reversed itself for the next two decades, allowing programs that resulted in aid to private schools as long as these programs were neutral and the aid was directed to the private schools through an individual's choice, not the state's choice. While the whole question of the establishment clause is certainly not totally resolved, it appears that the states will continue to be limited by that clause, that public debate over exactly how that provision limits the states and federal government will continue to rage, and that no clear and easy test will soon emerge for the Supreme Court to use.

A

"Absolutist" interpretation of the First Amendment

When approaching the U.S. Constitution, Supreme Court justices can take the position that the words of our forefathers were intended to be unraveled by the Supreme Court and that they were written with room for a variety of interpretations. Or the justices can take the position that the words of the country's founders should be interpreted literally, and that this is the only way to ensure the appropriate dispensation of justice. This second position is known as the "absolutist" interpretation. Hugo Black was among the most famous justices favoring an absolutist interpretation of the Constitution with regard to the First Amendment.

In order to interpret the First Amendment and relate it to American laws, the justices must decide several important things. They must consider, especially when dealing with the question of the freedom of and from religion, what the amendment means as a whole. The amendment reads "Congress shall make no law respecting an establishment of religion, or prohibiting the free exercise thereof; or abridging the freedom of speech, or of the press; or the right of the people peaceably to assemble, and to petition the government for a redress of grievances" (U.S. Constitution, Amendment I, 1787). The Supreme Court has been repeatedly called on to define the phrases "establishment of religion" and "the free exercise thereof." However, another question, one often overlooked and one the absolutist interpretation focuses on, is "what does the phrase 'Congress shall make no law' mean?" Several interpretations are possible.

The first interpretation says the amendment means Congress cannot legislate in the areas of freedom of speech, press, or religion. Under this, the absolutist interpretation, what these freedoms are still needs to be determined, but once something is accepted to be in one of them, then it is off limits to the legislation of Congress and the states. One note should be made here: this does not necessarily mean that the freedom of religion is going to be overly broad. It means that the absolutist takes a literal view of the phrase "no law" in the First Amendment. Absolutism asks only whether a legislative act creates an establishment of religion or interferes with the free exercise of religion. Having once answered yes, for the absolutist, the law must be stricken, because "no law means no law" (*New York Times* v. *US,* 403 U.S. 713: 717).

A second possible interpretation is that the Constitution needs to be read as a whole and that the powers granted to Congress and the executive branch throughout the document sometimes allow them to restrict the freedom of speech or religion when it is necessary. Historically, Supreme Court justices who have taken this position did not favor an absolutist interpretation of the First Amendment. This non-absolutist attitude would suggest that while some activities, such as protesting the draft, would generally be allowed, laws calling for the arrest of draft protestors might be acceptable in the case of a national emergency. Such an emergency might only include a war, or might also include a "police action" like what occurred in Vietnam and what is occurring currently in Iraq.

A third possible interpretation, suggested by Eugene Volokh, among others, is that interpretation is necessary in all areas of the Constitution and that the "no law" clause is as subject to interpretation as any other. Volokh argues that it is impossible to work with the concept that "no law" means exactly that. He suggests areas in which regulation is clearly allowed. His suggestions fall outside the scope of religion, but the parallels can be clearly seen. He writes, "The text of the First Amendment sounds categorical— 'Congress shall make no law . . . abridging the freedom of speech, or of the press'—but it can't be taken as a literal protection of all speech, all the time. Is Congress forbidden from restricting the use of loudspeakers in residential D.C. neighborhoods? Do people have a constitutional right to send death threats to the president, or publicly threaten other forms of terrorism?" ("First Myths: Some on the Right Are Getting the First Amendment Wrong"). Many of these regulations can be justified. For instance, the loudspeaker regulation is a typical "time, place, and manner" restriction that limits when and where loudspeakers can be used without banning their overall use (general bans have typically been overturned). These laws still clearly restrict "freedom of speech," which is Volokh's point. A clear ban on such laws is not workable.

Hugo Black was the main defender of a literal interpretation of the "no law" clause. (It should be noted, however, that he never carried the Court to agree with him on this issue, and that he applied this position more often to the "freedom of speech" part of the First Amendment than to "freedom of religion.") He would frequently carry a copy of the Constitution and pull it out, noting exactly where the Constitution says "no law" and thunder "no law means no law" (*New York Times* v. *US,* 403 U.S. 713: 717). Black used this position in *New York Times Co.* v. *US* (also known as the Pentagon Papers case). In that case, the *New York Times* wanted to publish government documents, known as the Pentagon Papers, relating to the Vietnam War. These documents tended to show that the United States had known, as early as 1965, that it was losing the Vietnam War, even while publicly claiming it was winning. The government, therefore, had clear reasons (the twin desires to avoid negative publicity and retain public trust) for wanting to prevent publication of the papers. They also wanted to avoid having sensitive

material revealed while the Vietnam War was still in progress. In general, governments also try to avoid allowing the publication of classified material (which this material was). A preliminary injunction against publication was issued, and the case made it quickly to the Supreme Court. The majority held for the paper, and publication was allowed. Black went even further than the majority, holding that the injunction should never have been issued, writing "I believe that every moment's continuance of the injunctions against these newspapers amounts to a flagrant, indefensible, and continuing violation of the First Amendment" (*New York Times* v. *US,* 403 U.S. 713: 714–715).

If Black's position were extended to the First Amendment in the area of religion, no restrictions would be allowed on the freedom of religion, and the government could not in any way create "an establishment of religion." Of course, some concerns are immediately apparent, as one individual's freedom of religion may interfere with another's. For instance, some religions require their participants to go door to door to profess their beliefs. This often comes into conflict with the religions of those who answer the doors. Under absolutist interpretations of the First Amendment, Congress should make no laws supporting either party. However, the Supreme Court has ruled in favor of the right of groups like Mormons and Jehovah's Witnesses to carry their religion door to door. The "no law means no law" position, on the other hand, comes to mind whenever the Supreme Court strikes down a case as a government establishment of religion, or as going too far in allowing freedom of religion.

Thus, even though vexed by complexity and problematic, to say the least, in its implementation, the absolutist interpretation is still considered one valid approach to the First Amendment. Indeed, one of the best-known Supreme Court Justices of the twentieth century, Hugo Black, supported this method.

See also Hugo Black; First Amendment; Felix Frankfurter

For further reading

Ball, Howard. 1996. *Hugo Black: Cold Steel Warrior.* New York: Oxford University Press.

Dennis, Everette E., and Donald M. Gillmor. 1978. *Justice Hugo Black and the First Amendment: "'No Law' Means No Law."* Ames: Iowa State University Press.

Simon, James F. 1989. *The Antagonists: Hugo Black, Felix Frankfurter and Civil Liberties in Modern America.* New York: Simon and Schuster.

Volokh, Eugene. 2004. "First Myths: Some on the Right Are Getting the First Amendment Wrong." *The National Review.* http://national review.com/comment/volokh200401050906 .asp (accessed June 7, 2005).

Abstinence, government grants to force teaching of

Sex education in schools is a controversial subject aimed at preventing unwanted pregnancies and limiting the spread of sexually transmitted diseases (STDs). However, some feel that these classes do more harm than good or that the classes are too sexually explicit. Others feel that discussion of some topics is taken by students as permission to do certain things. For instance, some feel that a discussion of birth control tells students that it is acceptable to have sex so long as pregnancy does not result. Those defending the teaching of various methods of birth control argue, on the other hand, that students are having sex anyway, and it would be better to try to prevent pregnancy than to naïvely assume students will act with restraint or wholly abstain from sex.

Public schools generally teach what they have been funded to teach. Funds are very often provided through federal grants, the lifeblood of many school districts, which often spell out conditions for spending the money. If funding is not provided for music, for instance, music is not taught. It is no different for sex education. If funds are provided to teach about preventing pregnancy through birth control methods, then that is what will probably be taught by many school districts. If funds are provided to teach only abstinence, that is what will be taught. Re-

Protester yells at a rally outside the Centers for Disease Control–sponsored National STD Prevention Conference on March 10, 2004, in Philadelphia, Pennsylvania. About 250 demonstrators attended the rally to criticize President Bush's plan to expand abstinence-only education in the fight against sexually transmitted diseases. (Jeff Fusco/ Getty Images)

cently the Bush administration created the SPRANS (Special Programs of Regional and National Significance Community-Based Abstinence Education) program (among others), which grants money only for those agencies that teach abstinence solely as the way to avoid pregnancy. A report from the U.S. House of Representatives Committee on Government Reform Minority Staff noted that the programs funded by this initiative often present erroneous information, including errors about the effectiveness of contraceptives, inject religion into the area of science, reinforce stereotypes, and contain errors in their scientific facts. Among the ways that religion is inserted into the curriculum are the use of the term "Creator" (capitalization in original) and statements that life begins at conception.

The impetus behind the abstinence programs is largely religious based. The religious belief of the current administration has an impact on its funding of sex education programs, and thus in this way religion affects the law.

The question of what method of birth control empirically best prevents pregnancy and STDs is one that is fraught with controversy, and many different studies have been done in this area. Some reports have concluded that abstinence programs are of little value. Planned Parenthood offers a pamphlet stating that just under 90 percent of those who pledge virginity break their vows. Reports discussing the federal initiatives that are currently being promoted also may demonstrate that the abstinence-only programs have little effect. The group Advocates for Youth surveyed the results available for ten states (the only results released so far), and that concluded abstinence programs had no long-term success.

These funding issues are not limited only to educational programs in school districts. The federal government, over the last two decades, has often refused to fund any United Nations (UN) programs that help to pay for abortions, and UN programs that provide family planning services but also may fund abortions have been de-funded. The reason for this funding withdrawal is religious, with advocates arguing that abortion goes against God's will. Some religions, including the Catholic Church, are opposed to any method of birth control.

Some of the abstinence programs are offered through churches, and indeed the funding carries a clause requiring schools to involve religious and other charitable organizations. A policy of the federal government requiring one to "involve religious and charitable organizations" in return for funds came in front of the Supreme Court in 1988 (487 U.S. 589: 596). The Court upheld that program, stating that it had a secular purpose—to reduce teen preg-

nancy, did not advance religion even though religious groups could receive funds, and did not excessively entangle church and state via the reporting requirements that had to be followed to monitor how the money was spent. This means the federal government can require that schools involve religious organizations as long as those organizations do not spend the funds to advance religion.

Thus, religious organizations can be mandated to be involved in programs, and the federal government can mandate that abstinence be taught, even though religion and state are directly mixed by the first consideration, and the second is based in religious considerations and beliefs rather than science.

See also Celebration of Halloween and singing Christmas carols; *Harris v. McRae;* 1995 statement on "Religious Expression in Public Schools"; *Roe v. Wade*

For further reading

Advocates for Youth. 2004. "New State Evaluations Show Federally Funded Abstinence-Only Programs Have Little Effect." http://www.advocatesforyouth.org/news/press/092704.htm.

Eberwein, Robert T. 1999. *Sex Ed: Film, Video, and the Framework of Desire.* New Brunswick, NJ: Rutgers University Press.

Levine, Judith. 2002. *Harmful to Minors: The Perils of Protecting Children from Sex.* Minneapolis: University of Minnesota Press.

Melody, Michael Edward, and Linda M. Peterson. 1999. *Teaching America about Sex: Marriage Guides and Sex Manuals from the Late Victorians to Dr. Ruth.* New York: New York University Press.

Planned Parenthood of America, Inc. 2006. "Abstinence Only Sex Education." http://www.plannedparenthood.org/news-articles-press/politics-policy-issues/teen-pregnancy-sex-education/abstinence-6236.htm.

Roleff, Tamara L., ed. 2001. *Teenage Sexuality: Opposing Viewpoints.* San Diego, CA: Greenhaven Press.

United States House of Representatives Committee on Government Reform—Minority Staff. Special Investigations Division. 2004. *Content of Abstinence-Only Education Programs.* http://www.democrats.reform.house.gov/Documents/20041201102153-50247.pdf.

Abuse of nonreligious conscientious objectors in World War I

Conscientious objectors to World War I routinely experienced abuse. Those whose resistance to the war was based in something other than religion often fared the worst. In order to understand the relative conditions faced by religious conscientious objectors, it is necessary also to be aware of the nonreligious conscientious objectors. Economic, cultural, and personal factors could also act as bases for nonreligious objections to the war. Those who objected on economic grounds were opposed to the war because they saw it as a tool of capitalists and/or of the wealthy. Cultural objectors felt an affinity to either the nation or the ethnic group that they had emigrated from or still belonged to, which was at war with the United States. An Austrian immigrant, for example, might not want to support a war against the Austro-Hungarian Empire, which was fighting alongside Germany in World War I. Finally, those who objected to the war on personal grounds were opposed to any war but did not base their pacifism, and therefore their claim for conscientious objector status, in religion. These objections were greatly opposed by both the government and the public. The government generally refused to assign conscientious objector status for other than religious reasons and then only for those in recognized pacifist faiths.

Those who refused to register for political reasons were often made to kiss the flag or were tarred and feathered. These punishments

Conscientious objector is publicly humiliated for refusing to join the U.S. Army in 1915. (Hulton Archive/Getty Images)

were used against other people who objected to the war as well. Often war protestors were tarred and feathered, and then, assuming they survived, fired from their jobs or horse-whipped, and then handed over the authorities, who might induct them into the army anyway and then subject them to army discipline.

Pacifists were viewed as pro-Germans in general, and police shut down meetings of pacifist groups and arrested people who attended such meetings for disturbing the peace and obstructing traffic. Those who argued against the war in public and refused to enlist on grounds of conscience were, if they were lucky, arrested by the government and tried for obstructing the draft, and many of these were sentenced under the Espionage and Sedition Acts to years in jail. Unlucky objectors were forcibly registered by the government and then tried by the military courts. Some 540 were court-martialed, with nearly all being convicted. Nearly 200 of these were sentenced to either death or life imprisonment. "All of the death sentences were reversed," and many of the rest were reduced later, but some individuals spent up to three years in jail, the last person being released in 1920 (Peterson and Fite, 1957: 138). The objectors were also treated very poorly, with many beaten and some dying from the abuse. Others were so tormented that they committed suicide. The aim of these beatings very often was to convince the pacifist to serve in the armed forces. At times this worked, as some people's resistance was weakened, others chose survival over principles, and still others became so debilitated that they could not prevent others from taking their hands and forcing signatures.

See also Abuse of religious conscientious objectors in World War I; African American draft resisters during the Vietnam War; African American religious conscientious objectors in World War II

For further reading

Kohn, Stephen M. 1994. *American Political Prisoners: Prosecutions under the Espionage and Sedition Acts.* Westport, CT: Praeger.

Peterson, H. C., and Gilbert Fite. 1957. *Opponents of War.* Madison: University of Wisconsin Press.

Abuse of religious conscientious objectors in World War I

During World War I, conscientious objectors who cited religious grounds routinely experienced abuse. While the United States fought for freedom abroad, we did not allow much of it at home, especially for those who claimed religious reasons not to fight. Unlike in wars closer to the present, most religious conscientious objectors were lumped, by the public, into one category. (In World War II and Vietnam, certain conscientious objectors, like members of the Quaker faith, which was viewed as an established religion, were given more of a "pass" by the public and so were subjected to less abuse.) The government also, in World War I, was less forgiving of religious conscientious objectors than in recent conflicts.

The government in World War I allowed people to avoid serving as a combatant if they could prove membership in "a well organized religious sect or organization" (Peterson and Fite, 1957: 122, quoting the Secretary of War's Statement Concerning the Treatment of Conscientious Objectors in the Army) whose beliefs "forbade members to engage in war" (Peterson and Fite, 1957: 122). These men were, however, still inducted into the army. The army then tried to break the men and either force them into the fighting army or, at the very least, force them to do work. A sizable percentage of religious conscientious objectors refused to have any connection with the army, even attempting to refuse to wear the uniform. The military often forced them to wear the uniform over their objections and court-martialed them for refusing to work. At least a dozen members of the Mennonite faith were sentenced to jail terms of over twenty years for refusing to cut down flowers (the banal task they had been assigned as an alternative to combat duty), and another group was given similar terms for refusing to wear uniforms. Other difficulties resulted with those whose faiths taught them to dress or live in a manner not in accordance with the army's regulations. Several Hutterites, who believed that for religious reasons they could not cut their beards, experienced forced shaves. Scores were treated badly enough to die as a result of the abuse, and some were even dressed in military uniforms before their bodies were shipped home. The majority, though, who were willing to work at non-combatant jobs, were treated relatively decently by all reports, even though they were looked down on by the rest of the military.

The public often was not as kind. Very often conscientious objectors were beaten up or given forced haircuts, and their homes were destroyed or their wells polluted. They were also brought before the legal apparatus. Those who spoke out against the war and suggested that God did not want the members of their religion, or people in general, to fight were charged with opposing the draft or "creating insubordination"; they were often convicted and then sentenced to up to twenty years in prison. In rural areas, many Holiness preachers opposed the war and found themselves in front of district courts when the public reported them. Vigilante incidents against people who objected to the war on religious grounds occurred frequently. Thus, those who were religiously opposed to the war were treated well by the army only so long as they helped out in a non-combatant fashion. They were treated poorly by the public in general, and very badly by the military if they refused to cooperate at all.

After World War I, the public came to view those opposed to war with a bit more kindness. Part of this was because more people supported World War II, and with less opposition came less hatred (relatively) of those opposed. In World War II, and in Vietnam also, there was less vigilante violence against those opposed, as

the nation moved away from vigilante methods. Thus, after the "Great War," religious conscientious objectors were treated somewhat better, but those opposed to war in general, rather than on religious grounds, still faced an uphill battle for exemption from the draft.

> **See also** Abuse of nonreligious conscientious objectors in World War I; African American draft resisters during the Vietnam War; African American religious conscientious objectors in World War II; *United States* v. *Seeger*

For further reading

Kohn, Stephen M. 1994. *American Political Prisoners: Prosecutions under the Espionage and Sedition Acts.* Westport, CT: Praeger.

Peterson, H.C., and Gilbert Fite. 1957. *Opponents of War.* Madison: University of Wisconsin Press.

ACLU—goals and efforts of the ACLU in the area of religion

The American Civil Liberties Union (ACLU) has long been involved in religious issues, although issues of free speech and freedom of the press were its main concerns early in its existence. Indeed, the ACLU often has greater recognition for its efforts in fighting for freedom of speech. Religious freedom, however, is one of the group's central goals. The ACLU fights for freedom of religion, to have a free choice among religions or not to have a religion, and freedom from religion—to have no imposed religion at all.

The ACLU was directly involved in the *Scopes* case in 1925 when the state of Tennessee wanted to ban the teaching of evolution, claiming that it went against religion. Clarence Darrow defended John Scopes in this trial, and his services were provided by the ACLU. The ACLU also made headlines over fifty years later in 1977, when it defended the right of the Nazi Party to march through Skokie, Illinois. This case mixed the issues of religion and freedom of speech. The ACLU was on the side of freedom of speech, as it felt that the civil liberties of the Nazis were being restricted by the refusal of Skokie to allow the march. Certainly, the

ACLU did not endorse the Nazi message, but it felt that even groups making a repugnant statement have a legal right to do so in this country. The city of Skokie had a high Jewish population, many of whom had survived or had relatives who had survived the Holocaust. Not surprisingly, many residents felt their right to believe and live without being harassed due to religion was being violated. The ACLU finally won but lost many members over its stance.

The ACLU is today much more involved in fighting against what they view as religious indoctrination by the states or federal government or, and this is less reported, fighting against what they view as interferences with the free exercise clause. For instance, the ACLU in 2004 filed amicus curiae briefs in a case against a prosecutor who removed two potential jurors from a pool for religious reasons. The prosecutor claimed that their outward shows of religion would cause them to be the sorts of people who favored defendants. (One of them wore Muslim attire, and the other was a missionary.) The court, however, held that such a removal was illegal as it would lead to having fewer jurors from those groups who tend to show religion with their clothing or activities. The ACLU also continues to be active in its support of those who oppose teaching intelligent design theory side by side with evolution in the classroom. Intelligent design theory argues a scientific basis for belief in an intelligent creator of the universe and is often promoted by Christian groups as an alternative to evolution theory. Recently, in Georgia, a school district proposed a sticker to be placed in schoolchildren's biology textbooks. The sticker would have read, in its entirety, "This textbook contains material on evolution. Evolution is a theory, not a fact, regarding the origin of living things. This material should be approached with an open mind, studied carefully, and critically considered" (*Selman et al.* v. *Cobb County,* CIVIL ACTION NO. 1:02-CV-2325-CC).

The ACLU filed suit. The District Court for the Northern District of Georgia used the *Lemon* test, and first turned to the purpose of the legislation, holding "the Court continues to believe that the School Board sincerely sought to promote critical thinking in adopting the Sticker to go in the textbooks" (*Selman et al.* v. *Cobb County,* CIVIL ACTION NO. 1:02-CV-2325-CC, 25). Thus, the stickers' secular purpose was accepted by the court. However, the stickers failed the other two prongs of the *Lemon* test. The second prong holds that a government cannot endorse a religion, and the court believed "an informed, reasonable observer would interpret the Sticker to convey a message of endorsement of religion. That is, the Sticker sends a message to those who oppose evolution for religious reasons that they are favored members of the political community, while the Sticker sends a message to those who believe in evolution that they are political outsiders" (*Selman et al.* v. *Cobb County,* CIVIL ACTION NO. 1:02-CV-2325-CC, 31). The court went on to say that the sticker was unconstitutional, as it had the effect of promoting religion. Therefore, the sticker was not allowed.

In March 2006, Georgia's lawmakers enacted a law allowing Bible literacy classes in public school classrooms. The law did not require any school district to adopt the policy.

Similarly, a Little Rock, Arkansas, school board agreed to remove stickers from their textbooks when the ACLU protested. The ACLU's concerns hinged on the description of evolution as a controversial theory and their suggestion that the origins of life could not be explained only by evolution but must include an intelligent designer.

The ACLU is also part of an ongoing case in Dover, Pennsylvania. Teachers in Dover have been required to read their classes a statement to the effect that Darwin's theory of evolution is not a fact, and that, indeed, gaps in the theory cannot be explained by any existing evidence. They are required to inform students that the book *Of Pandas and People* is available for independent reading in the subject of intelligent design.

The book in question, *Of Pandas and People,* was written by Percival Davis and Dean H. Kenyon and was published by the Foundation for Thought and Ethics, a group the ACLU describes as a Christian organization designed to promote Christian understanding of the Bible. The ACLU has opposed both the statement and the teaching as they see them as an imposition of religion on the schools. In 2004, the ACLU filed a lawsuit in Pennsylvania against the suggested Dover school board policy, along with Americans United for Separation of Church and State, and other groups. The ACLU's involvement is consistent with its aims of protecting the rights of individuals to the freedom of and from religion. The trial was decided in favor of the ACLU and the parents in late 2005, and thus the ACLU is quite active presently.

Looking at the past, it was not until the 1940s that the Supreme Court first ruled on the interaction of government and religion, and later still before the ACLU became involved in this issue. In the 1940s, two flag salute cases involved Jehovah's Witnesses; the question was whether the government could force students to salute the flag. The Witnesses did not want to salute the flag as they considered it worshiping a graven image, and thus blasphemous. However, the ACLU did not participate in either case and did not defend Jehovah's Witnesses in 1940, when a case came in front of the Supreme Court on the charge of creating a breach of the peace. A Jehovah's Witness had played a recording on a street, and the recording was deemed insulting. The Jehovah's Witness moved on, as asked, after playing the record, but he was arrested. The Supreme Court held that the Witness did not create a "clear and present menace to public peace and order" and so should not have been arrested (310 U.S. 296: 311). The Court also ultimately found the Jehovah's Witnesses could not be forced to salute the flag, but only after the second time it ruled on the issue.

However, the ACLU reversed its early trend and has been active in recent Pledge of Allegiance challenges. It was involved in the recent Supreme Court case *Elk Grove Unified School District* v. *Newdow.* It there supported Michael Newdow, who opposed his daughter's being forced in school to recite the Pledge of Allegiance because of its phrase "under God," which Newdow viewed as a violation of his daughter's First Amendment rights. Newdow was unsuccessful, but not on First Amendment grounds. The Court dodged the First Amendment question, holding that Newdow lacked legal standing as he did not have custody of his daughter.

The ACLU is active in the area of the forced recitation of the Pledge of Allegiance in other areas beyond their support to recent Supreme Court challenges. The ACLU in Virginia protested a decision of a school board to force students to stand during the saying of the pledge. The ACLU had protested a planned law forcing students to both stand and to say the pledge, and the law was amended to allow students to sit and/or to remain silent. However, one school board was still going to try to force students to stand until the ACLU protested against it, when the school board returned to their original policy of allowing students to sit.

The ACLU is also active in some areas of religion that would surprise many conservatives, who often paint the group as an extremist liberal organization that exists to harm conservative and religious causes. The ACLU in 2002 challenged the right of the Massachusetts Bay Transportation Authority (MBTA) to reject ads based on their content and filed suits against decisions by the MBTA to reject ads arguing for a wider discussion of the anti-drug laws, and ads, supported by a different group, arguing against the current secularization of Christmas. The ACLU won in the first case but lost in the second; it criticized the Court's ruling, arguing that this was a violation of the church's right of free speech and a restriction of the freedom of religion of the church.

Thus, the ACLU is a strong fighter for freedom *of* religion and freedom *from* religion. It fights for the rights of religious groups not to be treated any differently than any other group and also fights for the rights of those who choose not to believe in a dominant religion not to be treated disparagingly. The ACLU also fights what it sees as government endorsement of religion. Not all religious groups are always happy with the ACLU, of course, as many religious groups might favor a government endorsement of their religion; and sometimes, as with Skokie, the ACLU's activities in favor of freedom of speech may ultimately seem to some to be harmful to the freedom of religion.

> ***See also*** American Civil Liberties Union (ACLU) establishment; *Cantwell* v. *Connecticut; County of Allegheny* v. *Greater Pittsburgh ACLU; Elk Grove Unified School District* v. *Newdow; McCreary County* v. *ACLU;* 1995 statement on "Religious Expression in Public Schools"; Saluting the flag; *Scopes* v. *Tennessee*

For further reading

Benedict, Michael Les. 1987. *Civil Rights and Civil Liberties.* Washington, DC: American Historical Association.

Cottrell, Robert C. 2000. *Roger Nash Baldwin and the American Civil Liberties Union.* New York: Columbia University Press.

Gibson, James L., and Richard D. Bingham. 1985. *Civil Liberties and Nazis: The Skokie Free-Speech Controversy.* Urbana, IL: Praeger.

Johnson, Donald Oscar. 1963. *The Challenge to American Freedoms: World War I and the Rise of the American Civil Liberties Union.* Lexington: University of Kentucky Press.

Kersch, Kenneth Ira. 2004. *Constructing Civil Liberties: Discontinuities in the Development of American Constitutional Law.* New York: Cambridge University Press.

Walker, Samuel. 1990. *In Defense of American Liberties: A History of the ACLU.* New York: Oxford University Press.

ACLU of Kentucky v. *McCreary County*

354 F.3d 438 (6th Cir. 2003)

Whether a public building can display a religious symbol has long been a contested topic.

Concerning seasonal religious symbols, the Court has allowed a cross, as long as that cross was not displayed in isolation. The Court, though, has struck down a large picture of Jesus in a high school. The case here turns on the question of the display's context.

A note about the history of the case is first in order. In McCreary County, Kentucky, in 1999, the county had established a display of the Ten Commandments; similar displays had been made in Pulaski County, and the school board had done something similar in Harlan County. After the ACLU filed suit, all three agencies added documents to the displays such as the Bill of Rights, the Declaration of Independence, the Star-Spangled Banner, and the Magna Carta. Other than the Declaration of Independence, of which the Ten Commandments were said to "provide the moral background," none of the documents were linked in any way to the Ten Commandments. The district court granted a preliminary injunction against the displays and the case was appealed.

The Sixth Circuit Court of Appeals, sitting as a three-judge panel, first noted that an injunction should not be issued unless the case had "a strong likelihood of success on the merits." The decision then turned and examined that issue. The court first held that the *Lemon* test, regardless of what the circuit court felt about it, still applied, and the court considered the first part of that test, the "purpose" issue. While governments are "given some deference" in what they state to be the purpose of an action, courts still must decide whether the stated purpose is the real one. Here the court stated that the governments had five stated purposes: to display the commandments constitutionally, to show how those commandments led to the American government, to show how they led to the Declaration of Independence, to "educate" the citizenry about important past documents, and to "create a limited public forum" to display these important documents. The court held that the first goal was irrelevant, as simply wanting something to be constitutional did not make it so. The court then said that the commandments could be displayed constitutionally if they presented a secular message, as the Supreme Court had stated in *Stone* v. *Graham* (1980).

Even though the district court had not considered these factors, the circuit court did so. First, in the school board displays, the court noted that the Ten Commandments were in no way integrated with the other documents, and thus the Ten Commandments, even with the other documents as a whole, still presented a message that was "patently religious and in no way resembles an objective study of the role that the Ten Commandments, or even the Bible generally, played in the foundation of American government" (354 F.3d 438: 451). The courthouse displays made the further claim that the Ten Commandments had influenced the Declaration of Independence. The circuit court agreed with those defending the commandments that the commandments had influenced laws in the colonial period, but held that no influence on Jefferson's Declaration of Independence could be found.

The court next examined the "context of the displays," holding that even though no extra emphasis was given to the commandments, the commandments were still seen as religious. Also, as the commandments began by themselves and had other documents added, the purpose of this display was religious and that the activities of the government in first showing the commandments by themselves could be considered by the court in order to determine the purpose of the display. The court then turned to the "endorsement" part of *Lemon*. The court held that as the historical documents (the Bill of Rights and the other historical documents) were not related in any clear way to the Ten Commandments, and as the documents were in the courthouses and the schools, the display clearly endorsed religion. The majority opinion closed by noting that the high probability of success by the ACLU in its suit against the Ten Command-

ments was enough to cause the court to grant the preliminary injunction.

One judge filed a concurrence, agreeing with the court's opinion, but also noting that he offered "no opinion as to whether the displays violated the 'effect/endorsement' prong of the *Lemon* test" (354 F.3d 438: 462). The concurrence also argued against the dissent, claiming that the dissent is wrong to argue that the majority held that religion did not influence the government, and that the dissent is wrong to hold that the majority established broad law as it spoke only to the facts of this case.

Circuit Judge Ryan dissented, holding that *Lemon* did apply, but that *Lemon* has difficulties. Even so, Ryan held that this display passed the *Lemon* test. The dissent then examined all five of the cited purposes for the display, holding all to be legitimate, and that religion did play a role in the founding of the country. He then cited several historians to back up his view, noting that the Fifth Circuit and Third Circuit upheld displays, even while the Eleventh Circuit had struck them down. The dissent also said that the majority wrongly relied on *Stone* and should instead rely on *Allegheny*, which had allowed other religious symbols and would, in his opinion, allow the display. For all these reasons, he held the display to be constitutional as the various agencies had secular purposes for establishing the displays. Ryan also held that the display does not create an endorsement and thus does not violate the second prong of *Lemon*, as it is made up of nine secular documents and one that is religious.

The court, sitting as a whole, held a hearing on the state's motion for a retrial of the case in 2004, but denied the request. Two justices of the court answered a dissent of two other justices by noting that the display needed to be considered as a whole and with relation to its purpose, and that the court had not applied a higher standard for courthouses but had held that people were forced into courthouses, which made them a "captive audience."

This decision did several things. It reaffirmed the *Lemon* test; noted that since those suing were likely to win at trial, a summary judgment was in order; and held that the use of the Ten Commandments was religious. It ruled that merely adding other documents was not enough to keep the Ten Commandments display from violating the First Amendment; the decision also set up a test to determine whether a display of the Ten Commandments violated the First Amendment. The Supreme Court, in 2005, ruled on this case again, and a companion display in Pulaski County, in *McCreary County v. ACLU.*

> **See also** Celebration of Halloween and singing Christmas carols; *County of Allegheny v. Greater Pittsburgh ACLU;* "In God We Trust" on U.S. currency; *McCreary County v. ACLU; Stone v. Graham*

For further reading

Ahdar, Rex J., ed. 2000. *Law and Religion.* Burlington, VT: Ashgate/Dartmouth.

Alley, Robert S., ed. 1985. *James Madison on Religious Liberty.* Buffalo, NY: Prometheus Books.

Gilbert, James Burkhart. 1997. *Redeeming Culture: American Religion in an Age of Science.* Chicago: University of Chicago Press.

Owen, J. Judd. 2001. *Religion and the Demise of Liberal Rationalism: The Foundational Crisis of the Separation of Church and State.* Chicago: University of Chicago Press.

Wood, James Edward. 1999. *Church-State Relations in the Modern World: With Historical, National, International, and Ecclesiastical Documents and an Annotated Bibliography.* Waco, TX: J. M. Dawson Institute of Church-State Studies, Baylor University.

Addition of "under God" to Pledge of Allegiance

I pledge allegiance to the Flag of the United States of America, and to the Republic for which it stands, one Nation under God, indivisible, with liberty and justice for all.

Like many other national symbols, the Pledge of Allegiance did not start out being widely used. First written in 1892 by Francis Bellamy (1855–1931), a Christian socialist, the original pledge read, "I pledge allegiance to my Flag and the Republic for which it stands, one nation, indivisible, with liberty and justice for all." (Baer, "The Pledge of Allegiance," 1992). The word "to" was added before "the" a short time later. Bellamy originally considered adding the word "equality" to liberty and justice, but he left that word out, knowing many of his contemporaries did not believe in equality for certain groups, including women and African Americans. Bellamy was related to Edward Bellamy, author of *Looking Backward,* a utopian novel that anticipated the United States in the year 2000 to be a nation in which wealth was evenly distributed, national industry kept everyone employed, and class divisions were erased. It is ironic that a document written by a socialist was later changed to distinguish the United States from the USSR (Union of Soviet Socialist Republics), a country that used the word "socialist" in its name, in the Cold War.

Bellamy drew his ideas and ideals from several contemporary models. He had previously written a Columbus Day proclamation, in which he discussed "divine providence," but he did not include a reference to "God" or "divine providence" in his pledge. Bellamy was also not the first to create a flag salute. In New York City, with one of the largest student populations, George Balch had developed a flag salute. "The students in his New York Public Schools gave his 'American Patriotic Salute' as follows: students touched first their foreheads, then their hearts, reciting, 'We give our Heads—and our Hearts—to God and our Country.' Then with a right arm outstretched and palms down in the direction of the flag, they competed the salute 'One Country! One Language! One Flag!'" (Baer, *"Under God,"* 1992).

Bellamy was charged with creating his pledge for a Columbus Day celebration of the 400th anniversary of Columbus's landing in the Americas. He developed the above pledge and also a way to honor the flag. Near the start of the pledge, here is what was supposed to happen: "At the words, 'to my flag,' the right hand is extended gracefully, palm upward, toward the Flag, and remains in this gesture until the end of the affirmation; whereupon all hands immediately drop to the side" (Baer, *"Under God,"* 1992). This pledge was first used in 1892, but there is no record of how quickly it spread. In 1923, the First National Flag Conference adopted the pledge but varied it slightly, revising it to read "I pledge allegiance to the Flag of the United States and to the Republic for which it stands, one nation indivisible, with liberty and justice for all" (Baer, *"Under God,"* 1992). The Second National Flag Conference the next year added the words "of America" after United States. The pledge remained unaltered (and still not a formal national symbol) until World War II, when Congress in 1942 adopted the 1924 version, added it to the National Flag Code, and later in 1942 refined the flag salute, adopting the current one of hand over heart in place of the upraised hand, palm downward, apparently noticing (a full decade after Hitler took power and a full year after the United States entered the war against Germany) the similarities between the U.S. and Nazi salutes.

The next modifications did not come until 1954. In that year, Congress added the term "under God" after "one Nation." There is no comma after "one nation" although most people pause there. God in the pledge was not the only Cold War change made by Congress in the 1950s. Congress also changed the country's official motto from "E Pluribus Unum" (one out of many), which it had been since the founding of our nation, to "In God We Trust." Both of these changes can be traced to anti-communist hysteria during the period. The United States, wanting to distinguish itself from the USSR and its atheist positions, went to great extremes to demonstrate that God was still supreme in this country.

Who was important in the drive in the 1950s to add those words to the pledge? One group was the Knights of Columbus, a fraternal organization originally founded for Catholics,

Francis Bellamy was a Christian socialist and author of the original Pledge of Allegiance in 1892. (Library of Congress)

in part to give them a place to socialize as they were excluded from many other fraternal groups. By the 1900s, the group's aims included aiding the Roman Catholic Church and "do[ing] good works." With the start of the Cold War in the 1940s, fighting communism became part of one of those "good works." The Sons of the American Revolution (SAR) were also involved in the push to add "under God" to the flag pledge. This organization allows into membership only those men who can trace their ancestry back to a person who fought in the American Revolution (women can join the Daughters of the American Revolution, the DAR). In Illinois, in 1948, Louis Bowman had added "under God" after "one Nation" and claimed that his idea originated from President Lincoln's alleged inclusion of the phrase in the Gettysburg Address. It should be noted that the phrase "under God" does not appear in the written versions of his address, meaning Lincoln must have added it while speaking, if at all. Over the next few years, Bowman convinced the SAR and DAR to back the addition. The SAR also enlisted the help of the Hearst newspaper chain. The early 1950s was the height of the Red Scare. Joseph McCarthy, who influenced the nation from 1950 to 1954, created an atmosphere in which the USSR, with its perceived hordes of Godless communists, was feared across the nation. It must be remembered that McCarthy attacked first, berated second, created evidence third, and proved never.

However, the early 1950s also saw the Soviet Union explode its first hydrogen bomb, catching up to the United States in that technology in only nine months. Thus, public pressure, real fear, and the created hype of McCarthyism all pushed the country to want to be more anti-communist. The addition of "under God" to the pledge was seen as an important part of this process. One of the most direct supporters to link the two (the "under God" and anti-communism) was the Reverend Dr. George M. Docherty from Washington, D.C. "His point was that a Soviet atheist could easily recite the Pledge without compunction by substituting the 'Union of the Soviet Socialist Republics' for the 'United States'" (Baer, "*Under God,*" 1992).

After the end of McCarthyism and the second Red Scare, several years passed before the phrase was publicly challenged. Those who support the phrase often cite its historic nature without being aware that it was added only in the 1950s. Those who oppose the phrase do so on the basis of U.S. efforts to promote freedom of religion. Those who originally inserted the phrase may not have considered that the USSR, by asserting universal atheism, removed from its people the right to choose whether or not to have a religion. Some of those who argue against the phrase "under God" in the American Pledge of Allegiance hold that it hinders our ability to have freedom of or from religion. Indeed, Bellamy's daughter believed

her father would have opposed the addition. Considering the phrase's history of revision, it may well be changed in the future. The Supreme Court declined to judge the constitutionality of the phrase "under God" in 2004. However, any final decision about retaining the phrase as a part of the Pledge of Allegiance is likely to be decided by that body.

See also Elk Grove Unified School District v. Newdow; Saluting the flag

For further reading

Baer, John W. 1992. "The Pledge of Allegiance: A Short History." In The Tisbury History and Genealogy Website. http://history.vineyard.net/pledge.htm (accessed June 13, 2005).
Baer, John W. 1992. *"Under God" and Other Pledge of Allegiance Questions and Answers (Q&A).* http://pledgeqanda.com/ (accessed June 13, 2005).
Canipe, Lee. 2003. "Under God and Anti-Communist: How the Pledge of Allegiance Got Religion in Cold War America." *A Journal of Church and State* 45 (No. 2): 305+.
Ellis, Richard. 2005. *To the Flag: The Unlikely History of the Pledge of Allegiance.* Lawrence: University Press of Kansas.

African American draft resisters during the Vietnam War

The military has long had a mixed relationship with its African American soldiers, especially after the Civil War when independence and technical equality were theoretically given to all. On the one hand, the army, particularly in the late nineteenth century, provided a job with some level of independence for African Americans, as all soldiers lived on army bases with set rules and regulations. On the other hand, the army did not give them equality even though they were fighting for the rights of all.

The situation was not any better in the declared wars, including the Civil War, the Spanish American War, World War I, and World War II. In the Civil War, African Americans were kept in segregated units, and until late in the war they were paid less than whites and charged for their uniforms, which the whites were given free. The African Americans in the last three wars were very often trained in the South in segregated cities and were always in segregated units. African Americans generally unloaded ships and served as mess boys in the navy. During World War II, African Americans took a step forward and argued for a "Double V" campaign—Victory over the enemy abroad and Victory over discrimination at home. Many African Americans were quite proud to serve their country, as they felt it to be worth defending, but they felt strongly that the military needed to give them equal treatment. The armed services desegregated in 1948, some twenty years before the rest of America, but some racism lingered.

Given this history of mistreatment, even in wars that were generally popular with the public, it is not surprising that the Vietnam War, which was controversial and largely unpopular at home, also brought its share of racial inequality. Young African American men subject to the draft generally did not want to serve any more than did young white men who were draft age, but the African Americans actually were called on in greater numbers. There were three reasons for this. The first was the overall draft system. One way to avoid the draft legally was to gain a student exemption. Undergraduate students—and, for a time, graduate students—were automatically exempted. As more colleges were available for white students, who were generally better off financially, more of them proportionately could go to college (and did so) than could African Americans. A second reason was the composition of draft boards, which were usually predominantly white. Twenty-three states did not have a single African American on their draft boards. These boards often ignored conscientious objector claims from African American draftees and sent them to Vietnam much more often than white individuals. A third reason was the National Guard. Many white draftees who still had to serve chose the National Guard, which generally kept them out of Vietnam. The same power structure controlling the draft boards dominated the National Guard assignments, and fewer African Americans were assigned to the National Guard for this reason. Class also played an issue—the poor were twice as likely to wind up in combat than the middle class, and when race and class combined, poor African Americans were up the proverbial creek without a paddle.

For all these reasons, many African Americans asked for conscientious objector status and other legal exemptions from the armed forces. Those who objected to the draft on a racial basis were not likely to receive much sympathy. One man who objected to being drafted on the grounds that his draft board was all white was given a five-year sentence, which was one of the longer sentences given. Many African Americans argued that the war was unfairly targeting them and they had nothing against the Vietnamese, so they had no business fighting in Vietnam. Many said it was a rich man's war and a poor man's fight. Others, at least in the lore of the period, asked that the following, or something similar, be put on their tombstones: "Here lies a black man killed fighting a yellow man for the protection of a white man." Many Black Muslims opposed the war, but the Nation of Islam was not given much consideration as a faith back then, and the draft boards were even less kind to Black Muslim requests for deferments than to African American ones in general.

The civil rights movement had an odd relationship with those who opposed the draft. Most civil rights groups, at least for a time, tried to separate themselves from black draft resisters as the civil rights groups did not want to be seen as unpatriotic. SNCC (the Student Nonviolent Coordinating Committee) was one of the main groups willing to protest the draft. Some SNCC protestors got three-year sentences merely for picketing draft centers. Martin Luther King, Jr., in time, moved against the war but lost some of his influence because of this stance. Thus, the civil rights movement was not as supportive of African Americans protesting against the draft as it could have been, and those who protested against the draft by using racial issues were not very successful.

African Americans had a long history of involvement with the armed forces in America's defense. However, like much of America, most African Americans questioned the war in Vietnam, and also questioned, quite rightfully, why such a large percentage of African Americans were being sent into that conflict. Such protests were not well received, and many African Americans were sentenced to jail terms for either protesting the war and draft or for draft resistance. This issue has not returned with such force, as America began to use an all-volunteer army toward the end of the Vietnam War and since, but many still question whether this all-volunteer army is really a cross section of America or if it is disproportionately made up of the poor and minorities who see the armed forces as the only way to an education or the only job available.

> **See also** Abuse of religious conscientious objectors in World War I; African American religious conscientious objectors in World War II; Religious elements of the civil rights movement; *United States* v. *Kauten*; *United States* v. *Seeger*

For further reading

Buckley, Gail Lumet. 2001. *American Patriots: The Story of Blacks in the Military from the Revolution to Desert Storm.* New York: Random House.

Terry, Wallace. 1984. *Bloods: An Oral History of the Vietnam War.* New York: Random House.

Tischler, Barbara L., ed. 1992. *Sights on the Sixties.* New Brunswick, NJ: Rutgers.

Westheider, James E. 1997. *Fighting on Two Fronts.* New York: New York University Press.

African American religious conscientious objectors in World War II

African American religious conscientious objectors were generally treated poorly during World War II. A history of African Americans fighting in America's wars sets the stage for this discussion. African Americans had been a part of U.S. fighting efforts since before there was a United States. During the period before the American Revolution, African Americans had answered the call. Crispus Attucks was one of the five men killed in the Boston Massacre and was the first African American to die fighting for America's freedom. African Americans continued to serve valiantly in the War of 1812 and the Mexican American War. During the Civil War, African Americans wanted to enlist even before the Emancipation Proclamation, but enlisted in droves after that. Perhaps the best-known troop of USCTs (United States Colored Troops), as African American soldiers were known back then, was the 54th Massachusetts Infantry, whose gallantry was recounted in the film *Glory.* African Americans also served during the Spanish American War. Most African Americans during World War I had answered the call to fight when asked, falling behind W. E. B. Du Bois who urged African Americans to put away their dislike for America's racism and "close ranks" behind the president. Many of those serving in World War I, though, expected America to repay its African American veterans and all African Americans with equal treatment after the war. This did not occur, and so by the time World War II rolled around, African Americans were not willing to have a repeat of World War I. Some followed the protest methods of A. Philip Randolph, which resulted in the executive order banning discrimination and setting up the Equal Employment Opportunity Commission (EEOC). Others decided to refuse to serve for political reasons or decided not to muffle their religious protests.

One must realize that most African Americans who were called to serve did so. Few deferments were granted in general, and few African Americans became conscientious objectors. The number of conscientious objectors varies from source to source, but all accounts agree that fewer than 500 African Americans, which is minuscule compared to the nearly three-quarters of a million who eventually served, were given conscientious objector status. In general, few deferments were given African Americans, as the percentage of deferments in each area was smaller than the percentage of African Americans in the population, except for agriculture, which was only slightly larger (and probably less than the percentage of the agricultural population who were African Americans). One must also realize that fewer African Americans served than could have been because of the general U.S. draft policy. Draftees were taken based on racial quotas, as the U.S. Army did not want any more than 10 percent of its forces to be African American. Thus, once a draft board achieved its given quota of African Americans, it stopped calling them, even if this meant going through many more white men's files. African Americans also were not allowed to serve in combat, and because of this many poor whites, much more than their percentage of the population, became combat troops. Some college students were given exemptions (few African Americans went to college in this period and so few received exemption), and more-educated whites were supposed to be given skilled jobs; this policy was administered poorly, however, so unskilled people might be given desk jobs, and greatly skilled people might be sent to the infantry.

In the area of religious exemptions, during World War II a person did not officially have to belong to a pacifist sect to be exempted, and in practice this made the exemption much easier. How established one's church was also played a role. Those in the Quaker religion were generally given a much easier road to exemption than those in newer faiths, including newer African American faiths. The makeup of the draft board also played a role, and here African Americans suffered markedly. Across the nation, less than 1 percent of draft boards, or about one-tenth of the percentage of African Americans in the population, were

African American. Across the South, where most African Americans still lived, only seventeen draft board members (in only three states) were African American, and these members, not surprisingly, were given power to rule on only African American draftees. That was the situation African Americans were dealing with in the war.

As noted before, most African Americans served when called rather than receiving exemption. Those who desired exemption on religious or moral grounds did not fare well. Many who desired exemption on religious grounds were members of newer churches, and this may have played a role as well. Many members of the Nation of Islam, or the Black Muslims, were turned down for exemption, and over sixty were arrested in 1942 in a mass raid in Detroit. Elijah Muhammad, leader of the Nation of Islam, was sent to prison for five years for opposition to the draft. Muhammad opposed the draft as he was a Muslim and as he did not want to participate in war with "infidels," or non-Muslims, which most of the U.S. troops were, in his opinion. The Espionage and Sedition Acts were not used as widely as in World War I, but some of those who came under it were African Americans who opposed the war. These African Americans generally based their resistance in their religion, even though the religion also had political overtones. Other members of African American religions had a similar lack of success. A member of the Black Hebrews was sentenced to fifteen years in prison for promoting resistance to the draft. Others combined their political and religious issues. Some twenty-one members of the Church of Freedom League were imprisoned as they tried to combine a general opposition to this war and how the United States was handling their troops with a general religious opposition to war.

More African Americans opposed being involved in the war because of the segregation in the military, but few of these had any success in preventing their being drafted, if they were called. Ernest Galloway opposed the war and refused to serve when called but did not ask for conscientious objector status; he was sentenced to three years in prison. Winnifred Lynn refused to serve, citing the segregation existing in the army, and he was told that he would have to join the army to be able to sue it. He did this and was eventually shipped overseas. When his case came up for trial, the courts refused to rule on it because he was not present, and because no one could produce him (because he was overseas, of course), the case was declared moot.

The level of segregation was pervasive in the army, as there was only one African American general, and the army actually segregated some northern bases. However, protests against this segregation in the army in the legal arena to avoid service had little success. Note that African Americans who refused to serve generally did so with an eye on only the Pacific Theater, noting that they should not be sent to fight "the yellow man" (as some described the Japanese), and some even noted an affinity for all other non-white races. Gunnar Myrdal was allegedly told by an African American that he wanted the following put on his tombstone: "Here lies a black man killed fighting a yellow man for the protection of a white man" (Mintz, 2003). Most African Americans were more supportive of the fight against Hitler, noting that he hated African Americans (and all black people) worse than white Americans did.

Thus, most African Americans who were called served, and they were called less than they could have been, but they also received few exemptions. Specifically, African Americans were generally unable to be granted exemptions to induction on religious grounds, and protests on political grounds seem to have been universally unsuccessful.

See also Abuse of nonreligious conscientious objectors in World War I; Abuse of religious conscientious objectors in World War I; African American draft resisters during the Vietnam War; Religious conscientious objectors in World War II; *United States* v. *Kauten; United States* v. *Seeger; Welsh* v. *United States.*

For further reading

Foner, Jack. 1974. *Blacks and the Military in American History: A New Perspective.* New York: Praeger.

McGuire, Phillip. 1983. *Taps for a Jim Crow Army: Letters from Black Soldiers in World War II.* Santa Barbara, CA: ABC-CLIO.

Mintz, S. 2003. "America at War: World War II." *Digital History.* http://www.digitalhistory.uh .edu/database/article_display.cfm?HHID=545 (accessed July 25, 2005).

Mullen, Robert W. 1973. *Blacks in America's Wars: The Shift in Attitudes from the Revolutionary War to Vietnam.* New York: Monad Press.

Scott, Lawrence P., and William M. Womack, Sr. 1994. *Double V: The Civil Rights Struggle of the Tuskegee Airmen.* East Lansing: Michigan State University Press.

Westheider, James E. 1997. *Fighting on Two Fronts: African Americans and the Vietnam War.* New York: New York University Press.

Wynn, Neil A. 1975. *The Afro-American and the Second World War.* New York: Holmes and Meier.

Agostini v. *Felton*

521 U.S. 203 (1997)

Aid to parochial schools has provoked many lawsuits, with one of the first being *Everson* v. *Board of Education* (1947), which held that transportation to school at state expense was allowable. Direct aid to schools was even more controversial, and for a dozen years before *Agostini,* the ruling case was *Aguilar* v. *Felton,* which declared that aid to private schools was allowable as long as that aid did not occur on parochial school grounds.

Agostini was a 5–4 decision overturning *Aguilar* v. *Felton.* The same parties who had sued in *Aguilar* sued again, this time to have the injunction of *Aguilar* lifted. The Court, in an opinion written by Justice O'Connor and joined by Justices Scalia, Kennedy, and Thomas and Chief Justice Rehnquist, granted that request, holding that remedial education for private school children could now be provided on private school sites rather than having to be provided in mobile classrooms or vans off site, or in an off-site location to which the children were transported. The Court held that changes in the law since *Aguilar* required lifting of the injunction, and some five justices had noted the same in a past case, *Kiryas Joel* (512 U.S. 687 [1994]), which had encouraged the filing of the lawsuit. The Court first noted that for the order issued in *Aguilar* to be lifted, either the facts or the law had to be changed, and that the facts had not. The Court then looked at the law, and used the three-pronged *Lemon* test. The test, as announced in *Lemon,* was "first, the statute must have a secular legislative purpose; second, its principal or primary effect must be one that neither advances nor inhibits religion; finally, the statute must not foster an excessive government entanglement with religion" (403 U.S. 602 [1971]: 612–613). The Court noted the violations of the *Lemon* test that the 1985 Court had found in *Aguilar* and then noted that the *Lemon* test still stood as the standard to use, but that the Court's attitude toward two particular practices had changed.

The Court then stated changes in this area of law since *Aguilar.* First, they noted that decisions no longer presumed, as they had before 1985, that the very presence of public school officials on private school grounds meant that states were promoting religion or that states were creating a union of church and state. The Court stated that in past cases, decisions had moved away from *Ball's* strict rule that "all government aid that directly assists the educational function of religious schools is invalid" (521 U.S. 203: 225). *Ball* was a companion case to *Aguilar,* decided at the same time.

O'Connor wrote that contrary to *Ball* and *Aguilar,* the current Court did not believe that public school employees would indoctrinate the students (a concern voiced in those earlier cases) and that no symbolic union was created between church and state by these programs. As these aid programs were allowable for private school students on public school grounds, they should also, the Court held, be allowable in pri-

vate school classrooms. The Court rejected Justice Souter's argument made in his dissent that these services provided by the state would save the private school money and held that since the services were allowable provided off site, there was no reason not to allow them to be provided on site. The Court also noted that the test used to determine whether a student received aid was neutrality on the issue of religion, which meant that the program did not violate the *Lemon* test on that basis. The last test was whether an excessive entanglement of religion was created by this program—that is, did the program force the secular authorities to become overly involved, thus entangling them more than necessary in religious issues. *Aguilar* had held that it did, as the employees would need to be watched to prevent them from making religious comments. Cases in the interim, though, had held that teachers were to be trusted, and that no difficulties had occurred in past programs of a similar nature. For those reasons, no excessive entanglement was seen. The Court ended with an examination of stare decisis, trying to see if the fact that *Aguilar* had been good law for ten years prevented its being overruled. They concluded that if the facts changed, stare decisis did not prevent a change in decision, particularly when the change desired was a lifting of the injunction created by the previous case.

Four justices, however, dissented. The first dissent was filed by Justice Souter and joined by Justice Stevens and Justice Ginsberg, and Justice Breyer joined it in part. Souter argued that *Ball* and *Aguilar* were both correctly decided, and he focused more on the fact that programs, such as the one desired here, to put teachers directly on school grounds, and the ones in *Ball* and *Aguilar,* subsidized religious education. This direct aid, the dissent argued, violated the First Amendment. The courses provided, Souter argued, would have been provided by the religious schools if the state had not done so, and this helped out the religious schools. Souter held "there is simply no line that can be drawn between the instruction paid for at taxpayers' expense and the instruction in any subject that is not identified as formally religious" (521 U.S. 203: 246). Souter's solution was to allow teaching only off site, as that would make the school probably offer remedial classes, and thus the school would not be expected to save money. The dissent also argues that the majority opinion has stretched far beyond its boundaries; *Zobrest*'s holding that sign interpreters are acceptable. Souter also argued that the program here is far wider than that approved in *Zobrest* and must be considered as such. He ended by suggesting that stare decisis should rule and that while the goals of this program are noble, they are still unconstitutional, and drawing "constitutional lines [is] the price of constitutional government" (521 U.S. 203: 254).

The second dissent was by Justice Ginsburg and she argued that the Court should not have heard the case. This case was brought by the defendants seeking an overturning of the previous decision, and Ginsburg held that the Court should have waited until a new case came along to reconsider its decision rather than hearing this one. She disagreed with the analysis of the majority that the law had changed sufficiently for a rehearing, instead suggesting that the Court should have waited.

Since *Agostini*, the issue has been relatively quiet at the Supreme Court level, even while being heard at the circuit court and district court levels. School aid is thus allowed on private school grounds. Recently the controversy has shifted more to voucher plans in which the state provides funds for schoolchildren in public schools to choose what school to attend. These have been challenged as unconstitutional, as most of the schools chosen are private and also often religious schools, but the Supreme Court in 2002, in *Zelman*, upheld the vouchers as legitimate and not a violation of the separation of church and state.

See also Aguilar v. Felton; Everson v. Board of Education; Lemon v. Kurtzman; McCollum v. Board of

Education; Sandra Day O'Connor; *Zelman* v. *Simmons-Harris*

For further reading

Agostini v. *Felton (1997).* 1998. Bethesda, MD: University Publications of America.

Bayer, Linda N. 2000. *Ruth Bader Ginsburg.* Philadelphia: Chelsea House.

Devins, Neal E., ed. 1989. *Public Values, Private Schools.* London: Falmer Press.

Maltz, Earl M., ed. 2003. *Rehnquist Justice: Understanding the Court Dynamic.* Lawrence: University Press of Kansas.

Monsma, Stephen V. 2002. *Church-State Relations in Crisis: Debating Neutrality.* Lanham, MD: Rowman & Littlefield.

Randall, E. Vance. 1994. *Private Schools and Public Power: A Case for Pluralism.* New York: Teachers College Press, Teachers College, Columbia University.

Rubenstein, Michael C. 1998. *Title I Services for Private School Students under the Reauthorization of ESEA: A Snapshot of Federal Assistance in Transition.* Washington, DC: U.S. Dept. of Education, Office of the Under Secretary, Office of Educational Research and Improvement, Educational Resources Information Center.

Aguilar v. Felton

473 U.S. 402 (1985)

Aid to parochial education has long been one of the more divisive issues in church-state education. Those who run parochial schools desire the aid generally, as do parents who send their children to these schools, but their desires are opposed by those who prefer a total separation of church and state, as well as by others. The program in question here dealt with remedial education in parochial schools.

This decision was a 5–4 decision with Justices Marshall, Brennan, Blackmun, Powell, and Stevens voting in the majority and Justices O'Connor, Rehnquist, White, and Chief Justice Burger dissenting. The majority decision was written by Brennan. He first examined the program, noting that the program originated in the 1965 Elementary and Secondary Education Act, which provided funds to help low-income children. For the private schools, it was administered to provide remedial education. The teachers who worked in this program were regular public school teachers who had volunteered to be in it, and there was oversight of the program. The Court then noted the similarities between this case and *Grand Rapids* v. *Ball*. The Court focused first on the issue of entanglement, as the *Lemon* test had banned programs that created "excessive entanglement of church and state" (473 U.S. 402: 410). The precedents were reviewed, with the Court noting that the unique nature of the high school environment must be considered, and so precedents from the college level did not apply. The Court then held that there was entanglement here similar to that banned before. "First, as noted above, the aid is provided in a pervasively sectarian environment. Second, because assistance is provided in the form of teachers, ongoing inspection is required to ensure the absence of a religious message" (473 US 402: 412). As continual monitoring was needed to prevent state support of religion, which is illegal under *Lemon,* this continual behavior would in turn create an entanglement. Thus the program was ruled unconstitutional.

Justice Powell filed a concurrence. Powell emphasized the issue of entanglement and wrote to explain "why precedents of this Court require us to invalidate these two educational programs that concededly have 'done so much good and little, if any, detectable harm'" (473 U.S. 402: 415). Powell noted that precedents of the Court required that the Court invalidate the program on the issue of entanglement and added that "there remains a considerable risk of continuing political strife over the propriety of direct aid to religious schools and the proper allocation of limited governmental resources" (473 U.S. 402: 416). Powell suggested that aid in a state with many different religions like New York was bound to cause controversy and strife, which gave another reason to strike down the program on the issue of entanglement. The concurrence noted that this program also aided education in that it "amounts

to a state subsidy of the parochial schools by relieving those schools of the duty to provide the remedial and supplemental education their children require" (473 U.S. 402: 417). Powell, though, did hold that some aid might be allowable, but the current program "provides a direct financial subsidy to be administered in significant part by public school teachers within parochial schools—resulting in both the advancement of religion and forbidden entanglement" (473 U.S. 402: 418).

Chief Justice Burger filed a short dissent. He argued that the program had many beneficial features and that the majority opinion did not "identify any threat to religious liberty posed by the operation of Title I." He also argued against the sole use of the *Lemon* criteria and viewed the majority as finding religion everywhere, while the only thing really there was helping children to read.

Justice Rehnquist also dissented, and accused the majority of taking "advantage of the 'Catch–22' paradox of its own creation . . . whereby aid must be supervised to ensure no entanglement but the supervision itself is held to cause an entanglement" (473 U.S. 402: 420– 421). Rehnquist also saw the Court as violating the intent of the First Amendment, suggesting "we have indeed traveled far afield from the concerns which prompted the adoption of the First Amendment when we rely on gossamer abstractions to invalidate a law which obviously meets an entirely secular need" (473 U.S. 402: 421).

A final dissent was filed by Justice O'Connor, who looked at the actual practice that had occurred under this program in New York. Rather than religion being advanced regularly or even occasionally, O'Connor reminded the Court that "in 19 years there has never been a single incident in which a Title I instructor 'subtly or overtly' attempted to 'indoctrinate the students in particular religious tenets at public expense'" (473 U.S. 402: 424). O'Connor also argued that on-site remedial instruction should be allowed as the Court would have allowed off-site remedial instruction. O'Connor argued against the Court's holding in *Meek,* that public school teachers might indoctrinate students when those teachers were teaching in religious settings. She also noted that the level of supervision was not enough to create an entanglement and that no real controversy had been created by this program, other than the current case. O'Connor suggested that just because public and private schools worked somewhat together, this did not create an entanglement, remarking "if a statute lacks a purpose or effect of advancing or endorsing religion, I would not invalidate it merely because it requires some ongoing cooperation between church and state or some state supervision to ensure that state funds do not advance religion" (473 U.S. 402: 430).

O'Connor closed by noting that the majority decision did not end the program, even for parochial schoolchildren, but just moved it off the school grounds, ending it only for those whose school could not create such an arrangement. She criticized the Court for this, holding "for these children, the Court's decision is tragic. The Court deprives them of a program that offers a meaningful chance at success in life, and it does so on the untenable theory that public school teachers (most of whom are of different faiths than their students) are likely to start teaching religion merely because they have walked across the threshold of a parochial school" (473 U.S. 402: 431).

Thus, in a very split decision, the Court held that aid to schoolchildren who went to parochial schools was not allowed on school grounds but was allowed off school grounds. One result is that many parochial schools had auxiliary services, such as working with disabled children, provided in trailers on the school's property where the trailers were provided by the state and thus the aid was not on parochial school grounds. Only certain aid was allowed and only in certain places, which produced a minefield for parochial school administrators and public officials trying to navigate it. The situation remained this way until *Agostini* v. *Felton* in 1997.

See also Agostini v. Felton; Everson v. Board of Education; Lemon v. Kurtzman; McCollum v. Board of Education; Sandra Day O'Connor

For further reading

Irons, Peter H. 1994. *Brennan vs. Rehnquist: The Battle for the Constitution.* New York: Knopf.

Marion, David E. 1997. *The Jurisprudence of Justice William J. Brennan, Jr.: The Law and Politics of "Libertarian Dignity."* Lanham, MD: Rowman & Littlefield.

Monsma, Stephen V. 2002. *Church-State Relations in Crisis: Debating Neutrality.* Lanham, MD: Rowman & Littlefield.

Muller, Carol Blue. 1982. *The Social and Political Consequences of Increased Public Support for Private Schools.* Stanford, CA: Institute for Research on Educational Finance and Governance, School of Education, Stanford University.

Rubenstein, Michael C. 1998. *Title I Services for Private School Students under the Reauthorization of ESEA: a Snapshot of Federal Assistance in Transition.* Washington, DC: U.S. Dept. of Education, Office of the Under Secretary: Office of Educational Research and Improvement, Educational Resources Information Center.

Van Sickel, Robert W. 1998. *Not a Particularly Different Voice: The Jurisprudence of Sandra Day O'Connor.* New York: P. Lang.

Airport Commissioners v. *Jews for Jesus*
482 U.S. 569 (1987)

City councils, airport commissioners, the police, and other public officials have always had a hard time balancing one group's right to worship in public versus the right of others using the facility to use it and be somewhat left alone. Of course, this assumes that those in power want to allow protest or worship in public, which is not always the case. The First Amendment, though, allows freedom of religion, and this constitutional right of one's freedom of religion came into play in this case, as a group believed that their religion required them to solicit in public.

The airport commissioners had tried to deal with a large number of people, religious and nonreligious groups, who tried to have activities in the airport. To control this in a simple way, and perhaps to prohibit the presence of Jews for Jesus, the commissioners banned "all 'First Amendment activities'" in the airport (482 U.S. 569: 570). The case reached the Supreme Court, and the regulation was struck down.

Justice O'Connor wrote the decision for the Court, and held that the Court did not need to decide what type of a "forum" the airport was, as the regulation was unconstitutional regardless. The type of a "forum" is relevant, as, if something is a "traditional public forum," individuals have more rights to speak, and the regulations generally can only apply to the "time, place, and manner" of the activities. The Court held that this regulation was extremely overbroad, banning everything, up to and including talking, and that "no conceivable governmental interest would justify such an absolute prohibition of speech" (482 U.S. 569: 575). O'Connor went on to say that the regulation had no way to be constitutionally narrowed and so must be struck down. The Court of Appeals had ruled it unconstitutional as violating the First Amendment, but the Supreme Court struck it down as being overbroad.

Justice White and Chief Justice Rehnquist concurred, but also noted that they did not see the Court as holding that the airport was a "traditional public forum." Reading between the lines, this suggests that these two justices did not think that the airport was such a place, and so people there deserved less protection of their First Amendment rights than would have happened in a "traditional public forum." What White and Rehnquist appear to have been hinting was that regulations adopted by boards governing airports might be legal if they treated the airport as a public forum created by government designation or as a nonpublic forum. In the former, the protections are similar to those in a traditional public forum, but in the latter, as noted in O'Connor's opinion "access to a nonpublic forum may be restricted by government regulation as long as the regulation 'is reasonable and not an effort to suppress expression merely because officials oppose the speaker's view'" (482 U.S. 569: 573). However, the problem for all the justices here, without question, was the sweeping nature of the ban and the fact that the religious pamphleteers were clearly being singled out due to the nature of their activities and their views. Thus, restrictions on pamphleteers, or others worshipping in public, might be legal, but total bans were not.

Balancing the rights of one group against a larger society is a tricky call, and this case did little to make that process easier. It did, however, send a clear sign that the rights of the minority (in this case Jews for Jesus) needed to be respected and that a ruling body could not simply solve the issue by banning all activities of a religious nature.

See also *Bronx Household of Faith v. Community School District No. 10; Cantwell v. Connecticut; Chapman v. Thomas; Employment Division v. Smith; Good News Club v. Milford Central School; Heffron v. International Society for Krishna Consciousness, Inc.; International Society for Krishna Consciousness v. Lee; Watchtower Bible and Tract Society of New York v. Village of Stratton*

For further reading

Davis, Derek. 1991. *Original Intent: Chief Justice Rehnquist and the Course of American Church-State Relations.* Buffalo, NY: Prometheus Books.

Hutchinson, Dennis J. 1998. *The Man Who Once Was Whizzer White: A Portrait of Justice Byron R. White.* New York: Free Press.

Lipson, Juliene G. 1990. *Jews for Jesus: An Anthropological Study.* New York: AMS Press.

Rochford, E. Burke. 1985. *Hare Krishna in America.* New Brunswick, NJ : Rutgers University Press.

Tushnet, Mark V. 2005. *A Court Divided: The Rehnquist Court and the Future of Constitutional Law.* New York: Norton.

United States Supreme Court. 1988. *Board of Airport Commissioners of Los Angeles v. Jews for Jesus (1987); Meese v. Keene (1987).* Frederick, MD: University Publications of America.

Van Sickel, Robert W. 1998. *Not a Particularly Different Voice: The Jurisprudence of Sandra Day O'Connor.* New York: P. Lang.

American Civil Liberties Union (ACLU) establishment (NCLB at founding)

The American Civil Liberties Union (ACLU) was originally called the National Civil Liberties Bureau (NCLB); it changed its name in 1920. Largely the work of Roger Baldwin, the NCLB grew out of efforts to defend those who refused to fight in World War I and those who were more generally opposed to the war. The NCLB also had origins in the American Union Against Militarism (AUAM), founded in 1914. One of the founding members of the AUAM and the NCLB, Roger Baldwin received a firsthand taste of government repression during World War I. Opposed to war, he refused to register for the draft and was sentenced to a year in jail. Fortunately for Baldwin, he was not forcibly inducted into the army over his objections and then tried, as this course of action generally resulted in longer sentences. Other founders included Albert De-silver and Crystal Eastman. The NCLB's success defending those who were opposed to the war was limited during World War I.

Baldwin had graduated from Harvard and taught at Washington University in Missouri. He had formed the Fellowship of Reconciliation, a Christian pacifist group whose main

Roger Nash Baldwin was the principal founder of the American Civil Liberties Union (ACLU) in 1920 and its director for thirty years. (UPI-Bettmann/Corbis)

claim to historical note was that it helped to form CORE (the Congress on Racial Equality), which became a leading civil rights group. After the fellowship, Baldwin helped to form the AUAM and served as its executive director in 1916; the NCLB followed in 1917. Crystal Eastman was one of the earlier woman lawyers, graduating from New York University School of Law in 1907. She was the sister of Max Eastman, one of the defendants in the infamous *Masses* case during World War I. (In that case, *Masses Publishing Co.* v. *Patten,* the Second Circuit Court of Appeals decided in 1917 that a revolutionary journal, the *Masses,* was eligible for prosecution under the Espionage Act.) Other famous people in the AUAM included Lillian Wald, Oswald Garrison Villard (grandson of William Lloyd Garrison, the abolitionist), and Jane Addams. Also noted on the NCLB's active roster was Norman Thomas, later six-time Socialist Party candidate for president.

The NCLB tried to defend people during World War I, especially those who resisted the draft. The bureau, though, had a significant number of difficulties. First, its position on the war conflicted with the standard American perspective, so it had difficulty raising funds. Second, of course, each battle it undertook was an uphill fight. It did, however, have a great advocate in Roger Baldwin. Baldwin had been active in the AUAM, and he became head of the Civil Liberties Bureau (CLB) of the AUAM, which then became the NCLB. The CLB told young men who were opposed to war to register and "when you register, state your protest against participation in war" (Cottrell, 1997). The CLB also tried to get decent treatment for those who opposed the war and communicated often with government officials like Secretary of War Newton Baker. Baldwin and the CLB were placed under government surveillence, even while the CLB tried to stay within the law. Baldwin protested the Espionage Act, the later Sedition Act, and the treatment received by those opposed to the war. In August and September 1918, Baldwin

started his own long trip down the road to jail for failure to register. The NCLB was also raided on August 31 of that year, and many documents were taken. Thus, the NCLB was, not surprisingly, not extremely effective during World War I.

Roger Baldwin emerged from jail a changed man. He was originally a Progressive, believing in the force of government to bring about a better society. His time in jail, however, convinced him that another force was needed to restrain government. In 1920, Baldwin moved to help create this force with the establishment of the ACLU. He would serve as its leader until 1949—nearly thirty years.

The ACLU was established to fight for the rights of the people. At its founding, it identified the Bill of Rights as a document designed to protect Americans' rights and the rights of minorities of all persuasions—racial, cultural, and ideological. This was a revolutionary idea, as in 1920, the Bill of Rights was not yet applied against the states in any way. The ACLU was originally somewhat conservative, attempting to limit its membership to the top of society who would work to protect the rest. The ACLU also, through the first decades of its existence, tried to avoid having radical members, believing this would bring criticism. Baldwin banned communists from being officers of the ACLU. The ACLU was originally interested largely in civil rights and free speech cases, defending John Scopes in the Scopes Monkey Trial, defending James Joyce's *Ulysses,* and originally defending the Scottsboro Boys. (It dropped out of that defense once it became clear that the communist-dominated International Labor Defense, ILD, would play a major role.)

In the early years, and when Baldwin remained active, religion was not one of the major topics of the ACLU's efforts. However, the organization did become active in this area later, fighting against what it saw as erosions of the separation between church and state, including government attempts to put up the Ten Commandments in public places.

See also ACLU—goals and efforts of the ACLU in the area of religion; *County of Allegheny* v. *Greater Pittsburgh ACLU; McCreary County* v. *ACLU*

For further reading

Cottrell, Robert C. 2000. *Roger Nash Baldwin and the American Civil Liberties Union.* New York: Columbia University Press.

Cottrell, Robert C. 1997. "Roger Nash Baldwin, the National Civil Liberties Bureau, and Military Intelligence during World War I." *Historian* (Fall). http://www.findarticles.com/p/articles/mi_m2082/is_n1_v60/ai_20150897 (accessed June 13, 2005).

Walker, Samuel. 1990. *In Defense of American Liberties: A History of the ACLU.* New York: Oxford University Press.

American Indian Religious Freedom Act

The goal of this 1978 act was to help Native Americans protect their religion. The act, however, was not effective, doing little to help Native Americans practice or preserve their religion. In the past quarter of a century, this act has been ineffective, and little has been done since its passage to help protect Native American religion. The act itself refers to the group as American Indians; this note will use the term American Indian only where it directly refers to government descriptions of Native Americans.

Native Americans, in the centuries before 1978, were largely ignored or abused by the larger white society. The goal of past government policies was largely one of extermination and land seizure, moving the Native Americans onto reservations. In the 1880s, government decided to encourage Native Americans to become white with the 1887 Dawes Act, which gave land to individuals rather than tribes, encouraging the breakdown of the tribe into family units of sedentary farmers. (Naturally, the land offered to these families was substandard, at best.) Landholdings had previously been largely at the tribal level, where any idea of ownership existed at all, and so this was a radical change.

Because of the poor quality of the land, many Native American farms failed, and white people then bought the land from them, often unethically. Another portion of the Dawes Act encouraged the Native Americans to adopt white religions, in the hope that they would eventually become good white citizens, melting away their Native American identity.

This process largely failed, but it did immeasurable damage to Native Americans. Little was done before the 1960s to try to restore the Native American culture that was lost. In the 1960s, many facets of American policy came under attack, including Indian policy. Native Americans lobbied and marched for change. Like many other groups, some Native Americans became more militant in the late 1960s, seizing Alcatraz Island and the site of the Wounded Knee Massacre. They particularly protested against religious restrictions and against museums that held Native American bodies and sacred relics.

In 1978, President Carter signed the American Indian Religious Freedom Act. The act was intended to respond to Native American concerns about federal policies that affected opportunities for Native Americans to worship and protect their religious practices in general. The first part of the act stated this intention and noted that the government would begin a policy of respecting Indian rights. The second part ordered the president to evaluate all of the current laws and within a year have all of the divisions under him report on what actions were taken to improve the treatment of Indians. However, no actions were mandated. It was, in many ways, more of a moral comment that the U.S. government should be nice to Native American culture rather than a specific command. The act also did not contain any specific enforcement provisions.

Indeed, the act has really done little to improve the treatment of Native Americans. It did cause some places to return artifacts that they had acquired from Native American grounds, but that was its main positive effect.

The Supreme Court, both times it has prominently dealt with Native American religion, ignored the spirit of the act. In 1988, in *Lyng,* the Supreme Court upheld a decision by the U.S. government to build a road through a sacred religious area, stating that as long as the government's action did not prohibit the Native Americans from practicing their religion, it was permissible. It determined that a mere burden on religion should not be considered and thus ignored the purpose of the American Indian Religious Freedom Act. The Court did consider the act, but noted it was merely a resolution of Congress, not a specific prohibition. In 1990, the Supreme Court returned to the issue in *Employment Division* v. *Smith,* in which two Native Americans had taken peyote and been fired, and then were refused unemployment benefits as they had been fired for illegal behavior. The Supreme Court held that the law in question was religiously neutral and should be upheld, and the Court once again ignored the spirit of the act.

The act also ran into difficulties in its wording, even when it was considered. It provides that Native Americans should have visitation rights to sacred lands but if religious worship depends on those lands, then more permanent rights are needed. Native Americans tried twice to block construction of dams that would put their religious grounds underwater, but the courts used a balancing test—balancing the effect on religion versus the need to build a dam, and both times held that the dam was more important.

In 1990, Native Americans did gain some measure of comfort from the Native American Graves Protection and Repatriation Act. This act ordered museums to make an inventory of all human bones, to publish that inventory, and to allow Native Americans to make claims for return of their relics. This differed greatly from earlier policy in which governments did not consider the stealing of Native American artifacts grave robbery, as it would have of any white grave. This act does prohibit future looting of graves. Though it does not cover private land or private collections, it is a significant improvement that has led to the return of many Indian artifacts.

Thus, the American Indian Religious Freedom Act led to little improvement for Native Americans, even though it was an important symbolic step. The courts have ignored the spirit of the act, and the act itself had no enforcement provision. Thus, if Native American religious freedoms and grounds are to be truly protected, more will need to be done.

See also Dawes Severalty Act; *Employment Division* v. *Smith; Lyng v. Northwest Indian CPA;* Native American combination of religion and law

For further reading

Cousineau, Phil, ed. 2006. *A Seat at the Table: Huston Smith in Conversation with Native Americans on Religious Freedom.* Berkeley: University of California Press.

Long, Carolyn Nestor. 2000. *Religious Freedom and Indian Rights: The Case of Oregon v. Smith.* Lawrence: University Press of Kansas.

Steinmetz, Paul B. 1998. *Pipe, Bible, and Peyote among the Oglala Lakota: A Study in Religious Identity.* Syracuse, NY: Syracuse University Press.

Wunder, John R., ed. 1996. *Native American Cultural and Religious Freedoms.* New York: Garland.

American Revolution's effect on religion

The American Revolution shaped religion in America in a number of ways. It did not create an American religion, which many European political upheavals did, but instead it helped to create an American system of religion. Particularly, the Revolution brought an end to state-sponsored churches as the states drew up new constitutions promoting an increased diversity in religion. And the push for democratization in politics coming out of the Revolution spread to a push for democratization in church structure, supporting the growth of new Christian churches.

The American colonists were very religious in the eighteenth century. Nearly 80 percent of the colonists regularly attended church and some colonies had state-supported churches. Religious variety was also increasing at this time with the development of new denominations such as the Presbyterians and the Baptists.

The American Revolution directly affected what preachers said in many pulpits. Before the American Revolution—and especially before the Stamp Act in 1765, which effectively touched off the resistance—English monarchs were directly praised, but after the Revolution, anti-British preachers stopped praising the king and instead praised the nation. In time, the Revolution also caused people to revere the early documents of the United States, like the Constitution and the Declaration of Independence, with the kind of ardor normally reserved for religious symbols. Thus, in the Revolution, America made it possible to create for itself political-religious icons.

The American Revolution also, in time, brought fewer public references to God. Many early references to God were, in part, attempts to gain legitimacy for America. God was combined with public celebrations, but the Founding Fathers, in some ways, did attempt to move God out of the center, the place He held in the European mind. One sign of this is the ban in the Constitution of a religious test oath for federal officeholders. One probable reason that the founders did this was to remove the issue of religion from the national discussion, as states varied in terms of their religious fervor and which religion(s) they favored.

The American Revolution had two direct effects on the Anglican Church in Virginia. There (and elsewhere), the Anglican Church in the colonies looked to its headquarters in England for leadership. After the American Revolution, the Anglican Church in America had to establish its own church headquarters, doing so in the Episcopal Church. The Anglican Church had also been state established in Virginia, but after the American Revolution, Patrick Henry's efforts to reestablish a tax for supporting the church failed. Therefore, the Episcopal Church was not state sponsored as the Anglican had been.

This trend continued after the American Revolution. Some colonies that had established churches did not reestablish them when the colonies became states, instead increasing religious diversity and freedom and decreasing church-state interaction. Other states reimposed the tax that had existed to support churches when they were colonies but allowed their citizens to choose which church received the money. Thus, there was more church freedom and diversity than before the Revolution. The reason all the colonies had to pass new constitutions, which in turn caused them to consider the role of the established churches, was because they had received their charters (which created them and allowed them legally to exist) from the Crown, and the American Revolution had declared the colonies free from the Crown. After the Revolution, the newly formed states had to justify their very existence. The states looked to their citizens and, through representative bodies (theoretically), created new constitutions justifying their own existence.

In time, states moved even further away from established religion until all of them removed all support for an established church. Connecticut, for example, ended its support of churches in 1818. Massachusetts was the last to act, in 1833. The democratization movement, sparked in some ways by the Revolution, helped to decrease the appeal of some of the older religions and increase that of new ones. For example, the Methodists argued against the rational appeal of the Congregationalists, instead preferring a ministry of passion, and thereby gained many followers in the first half of the nineteenth century. All can participate in a ministry of passion, whereas a ministry of ideas, like that of the Congregationalists, can be directly understood only by those who have more sophisticated ways of thinking. The new ideas of democracy that were shaping the nation politically also shaped it religiously, as more people wanted to be able to participate directly in their relationships with God.

Democratization helped to promote the argument that people can play a role in their own salvation, and this idea was the spark of the Second Great Awakening in the early 1800s. In addition to spawning the growth of the Methodist religion, this movement ignited revivals across the country. One central idea was that all could choose either good or sin, and so could save their own souls. This idea also helped people become interested in saving each other, leading, in part, to the ideas of abolitionism and temperance, among others. In these ways, the American Revolution had long-lasting and far-flung effects tied to religion directly for another ninety years and indirectly for many more than that.

See also Bible controversy and riots; Establishment of Pennsylvania as religious colony for Quakers; Anne Hutchinson; Punishment and religion

For further reading

Albanese, Catherine L. 1976. *Sons of the Fathers: The Civil Religion of the American Revolution.* Philadelphia: Temple University Press.

Bonomi, Patricia U. 1986. *Under the Cope of Heaven: Religion, Society, and Politics in Colonial America.* New York: Oxford University Press.

Phillips, Kevin P. 1999. *The Cousins' Wars: Religion, Politics, and the Triumph of Anglo-America.* New York: Basic Books.

Americans United for Separation of Church and State

This group is one of the leading forces, along with the ACLU, fighting against the support of religion in the public sphere. It tries to educate the public about the need for the separation of church and state, and files lawsuits to remedy situations when it believes that the wall of separation between church and state has been breached. It also advises public officials about potential violations and tries to work with those who it feels have breached that wall in order to end violations without resorting to lawsuits.

This group was founded in 1947, in response to several incidents, including the *Everson* v. *Board of Education* decision in that year and President Truman's proposal for an official U.S. ambassador to Vatican City. A group of people met in Chicago and generated a statement noting their apprehension over the eroding of the church-state barrier, which they titled "A manifesto." Among the group's founders were Louie Newton, president of the Southern Baptist Convention; John McKay, president of Princeton Theological Seminary; and William Scarlett, an Episcopal bishop. The group's early goals included informing the public about the historical basis for the wall of separation, opposing President Truman's proposed ambassador, and opposing public support for religious schools. Many attacked Americans United for its opposition to school prayer, and with the 1950s Red Scare, it is not surprising that the organization was painted by their opponents as soft on communism. Among the recent cases in which Americans United has filed briefs are *ACLU of Kentucky* v. *McCreary County,* which dealt with the posting of the Ten Commandments; and *Hibbs* v. *Winn,* which dealt with tax credits for scholarships to private schools. Among current issues of interest to Americans United are the proposed federal amendment defining marriage as being between a man and a woman, vouchers for public schools, faith-based initiatives, the posting of the Ten Commandments on public property, and prayer in public schools.

Americans United is opposed to the current move for an amendment to define marriage for three main reasons. The first is the one that people would expect, as the current drive for the amendment is backed by several large churches, including the Southern Baptists and the Roman Catholic Church; for those reasons, Americans United sees this amendment as imposing a religious dimension on marriage, and, as the organization is opposed to the interaction of church and state, it opposes this. Americans United also cites the decision of several denominations, including the Unitarians and the United Church of Christ, to allow gays and lesbians to be married. As these denominations allow marriages to occur, while others do not, to state that these marriages were invalid would show a preference for one religion over another, a position that is prohibited, in the view of Americans United, by the First Amendment. Finally, the group points out that the amendment, as currently worded, goes well beyond just denying marriage rights, removing a whole host of other rights that have been granted to gays and lesbians.

Americans United also opposes vouchers for private, religious-based education. It sees vouchers as underwriting churches and argues that taxpayers should be able to contribute only to the religious groups to which they wish to contribute. Most schools that participate in voucher programs, particularly most private schools, are religiously affiliated, and Americans United argues that the use of vouchers creates taxation without representation, as the vouchers subsidize education that the public has no control over. Americans United also points out that many religiously affiliated schools discriminate on the basis of religion, thus vouchers support either (a) having tax dollars subsidize discrimination or (b) forcing religiously affiliated schools to change to get tax dollars. Even though the Supreme Court upheld vouchers in 2002, Americans United argues that these two factors make the vouchers an unacceptable breach of the wall between the church and the state envisioned by the Constitution. The group also points out that in religion-based schools, the views of the religion generally influence the education, which is not supposed to be the goal of secular education.

Finally, Americans United opposes faith-based initiatives in which tax dollars are used to fund charity programs run by churches. One reason for its opposition is that the churches providing the aid often discriminate in employment and in other things on the basis of religion; this, in turn, means that government dollars are being used to support discrimination. Those groups who receive funds are even allowed to continue discriminating in

hiring, even when using government funds. The group also points out that people who receive services might very well be coerced to attend church or become members of the church where the services are provided. Americans United also notes that even though the government is giving these groups a fair amount of leeway, there will be increased regulation with the funds given, and this creates the risk of entanglement between the church and the state. This whole concern is relatively new, as only under George W. Bush have these initiatives really been pushed at the federal government level.

Americans United has been active in a wide variety of areas dealing with the separation of church and state. It has filed a large number of lawsuits and briefs in cases, with some success, and, as it was founded nearly sixty years ago, its historical basis demonstrates a long-term commitment from its members.

> ***See also*** Abstinence, government grants to force teaching of; *ACLU of Kentucky* v. *McCreary County; Everson* v. *Board of Education;* Gay marriage; *Hibbs* v. *Winn; McCreary County* v. *ACLU; Zelman* v. *Simmons-Harris*

For further reading

Americans United: Vouchers/Religious School Funding. http://www.au.org/site/PageServer?pagename=issues_vouchers.

Boston, Rob. 1997. "Watchdog on the Wall: The Americans United Story." *Church and State* 50 (November): 7–12.

Gaustad, Edwin S. 2003. *Proclaim Liberty throughout All the Land: A History of Church and State in America.* Oxford: Oxford University Press.

Segers, Mary C., and Ted G. Jelen. 1998. *A Wall of Separation?: Debating the Public Role of Religion.* Lanham, MD: Rowman & Littlefield.

Ansonia Board of Education v. *Philbrook*

479 U.S. 60 (1986)

The state and federal governments are not supposed to discriminate against religion, and hiring or firing on the basis of religion is a clear indicator of discrimination. However, when a policy that seems neutral nevertheless hurts one because of his or her religious choice, it is harder to state whether religious discrimination occurs. That was the issue addressed in this case, which dealt with a school employee whose religion required him to miss school days for religious observances. His contract allowed him only three days, but he missed six. He would have been permitted to use sick days for personal business but not for a religious observance. The school board refused to allow him to use his sick days for religious observances, even after he repeatedly requested to do so. They instead offered him the three additional days as unpaid leave. He therefore sued under Title VII of the 1964 Civil Rights Act, which requires employers to reasonably accommodate an employee's religion (479 U.S. 60).

The case came before the Supreme Court, which initially remanded the case to a lower court for further research. When the case once more reached the Supreme Court, it found in favor of the school board and against Philbrook. Chief Justice Rehnquist wrote both the initial opinion for the court, remanding the case to a lower court, and the second opinion, finding for the school board. In his first decision, he was fully joined by six other justices. Justices Marshall and Stevens concurred partly and dissented partly. After reviewing the history of the case and the collective bargaining agreement that covered Philbrook, Rehnquist turned to what the Court saw as the crux of the issue: whether an employer had to make reasonable accommodations when those accommodations were not shown to cause an undue hardship on the employer (479 U.S. 60: 66). The court of appeals had held that an employer was required to adopt the employee's desired solution unless that accommodation caused such a hardship. The Supreme Court disagreed, holding that "by its very terms the statute directs that any reasonable accommodation by the employer is sufficient to meet its accommodation obligation" (479 U.S. 60: 68).

Rehnquist argued that the legislative history supported this view, and that both the needs of the employer and the employee were supposed to be taken into account. The Court then considered whether the bargaining agreement took into account the needs of Philbrook, holding that unpaid leave for religious observances would generally be acceptable.

However, the court believed the personal business clause was extremely open-ended, and so might discriminate against religion, as one was generally allowed to take three more days of sick leave for most sorts of personal business as long as it was not religious. It was on this point that the Court remanded the issue to the district court for more fact finding. The district court found then that the personal leave days were administered consistently with the contract and did not discriminate against religion, allowing only some specified types of personal business and nothing else.

Justice Marshall agreed with the finding of the Court that more factual inquiry was needed at the district court level. However, he disagreed that the undue hardship issue was irrelevant, holding that if other teachers were allowed six days of paid leave for religious and personal business, then the school board could allow Philbrook the same without undue hardship, and he argued that the employer still had a duty to accommodate. Even though the statute was supposed to allow for both sides to have their needs taken into account, according to Marshall, the school board still needed to work with the employee. Marshall also pointed out that unpaid leave was not really a solution, as that forced Philbrook "to choose between following his religious precepts with a partial forfeiture of salary and violating these precepts for work with full pay" (479 U.S. 60: 74). Accordingly, Marshall wanted to return the case to the lower court "for factual findings on both the intended scope of the school board's leave provision and the reasonableness and expected hardship of Philbrook's proposals" (479 U.S. 60: 74).

Stevens dissented in part and concurred in part, holding that the Court should have merely reversed the court of appeals' ruling. He held that neither claim had merit: neither Philbrook's claim of discrimination in the leave policy nor his claim that the board should be required to have proven an undue hardship before rejecting his accommodation. The leave policy, Stevens suggested, was neutral as it denied leave for other things besides religion. Indeed, he went so far as to say the board's policy might even benefit religion, as it allowed three days off a year for religious observances, which occurred annually, while the other occurrences allowed for paid leave, such as weddings, occurred rarely. Stevens also held that the only harm that occurred to Philbrook was having to make up missed work (he ignored the issue of lost pay), and he held that all people who missed work experienced this harm, which meant that Philbrook could not claim religious discrimination.

Upon remand, Philbrook lost the case, appealed again to the Second Circuit, where he lost, and, finally, requested another review by the Supreme Court, where he lost for a final time. This issue has not been litigated frequently in the Supreme Court in the two decades since the *Ansonia* decision, but it remains one that is still important today. Some firmly believe that any employer's policy that would force an employee to choose between religion and paycheck is discrimination; others feel that even granting three days off for religion, and not counting those against the total number of days off, benefits religion, which is also illegal.

See also *Braunfeld* v. *Brown; Cheema* v. *Thompson; Corporation of Presiding Bishop* v. *Amos; Employment Division* v. *Smith; Goldman* v. *Weinberger; Trans World Airlines* v. *Hardison*

For further reading

Bureau of National Affairs. 1987. *Religious Accommodation in the Workplace: A Legal and Practical Handbook*. Washington, DC: Bureau of National Affairs.

Burstein, Paul. 1998. *Discrimination, Jobs, and Politics: The Struggle for Equal Employment Opportunity in the United States since the New Deal.* Chicago: University of Chicago Press.

Feldman, Stephen M., ed. 2000. *Law and Religion: A Critical Anthology.* New York: New York University Press.

Hauck, Vern E. 1997. *Arbitrating Race, Religion, and National Origin Discrimination Grievances.* Westport, CT: Quorum Books.

U.S. Equal Employment Opportunity Commission. 2001. *Employment Discrimination Based on Religion, Ethnicity, or Country of Origin.* Washington, DC: U.S. Equal Employment Opportunity Commission.

Answers in Genesis

Answers in Genesis is a twentieth- and twenty-first-century creationist group that interprets the Bible as literal truth. Answers in Genesis argues that the Bible answers all questions, with a particular focus on Genesis 1–11. The group is planning to build a Creation Museum, set to open in 2007. The group holds that God created the earth in about six twenty-four-hour periods. It also holds that all genetic defects are because of the Curse of Eve eating the apple and believes that the current generation is not as smart as previous ones. Those participating in this group sponsor research and publish materials arguing against the scientific basis for evolution. The group opposes evolution and its teaching because they consider it not to be scientifically supported, and because they believe that some atheists think that evolution, if proven true, would destroy Christianity, and so the atheists want it taught for this reason.

In an interesting twist, this group allows for some natural selection, the very mechanism on which evolution is dependent and the most controversial element of Darwin's theory. Under the theory of natural selection, evolution takes place because those traits most suited to a particular environment are the ones most likely to survive in a species, because those members of the species possessing the traits are the ones who will live to procreate. Answers in Genesis allows that changes within a species can occur, but still disagrees with the theory of evolution. In evolutionary theory, natural selection eventually leads to new species, but Answers in Genesis holds that no new species can grow up. The group accepts the possibilities for new types within a species to occur, so that wolves, dingoes, and dogs all have a common ancestor. However, the group denies the possibility that these changes can produce any new species, which is the key component in evolution. Answers in Genesis believes, for instance, that humans have similarities to apes, not because they evolved from a common ancestor, but because they had a common creator and common habitats.

In another interesting twist, the group holds that only those things in Genesis that are directly stated and commonly thought to have happened actually did happen, and those things that are not stated but go along with the common theme could also have occurred. For instance, the reason they believe the six days of creation must be six twenty-four-hour periods is because that is what the Bible says. However, the Bible does not mention Cain's wife's origins, and this group explains that Cain's wife was descended from another son of Adam, who came after Cain, but before Cain killed Abel, and who had a daughter who then married Cain.

This group is important in the religion and law debate primarily in the area of evolution. If evolution can be scientifically discredited, or if the majority of people come to believe it less than they do now, then evolution can either be removed from the schools or another theory, such as intelligent design, can also be taught. While the aim of Answers in Genesis is to destroy evolution theory, other groups, including those such as the Discovery Institute, which supports intelligent design, may be just as interested in the secondary effects of this group in the evolution versus creationism or evolution versus intelligent design debate, as an Answers in Genesis success in the evolution debate would help intelligent design advocates as well.

See also Avoidance of the issue of evolution in many teaching standards; Creation Research Society; Creation Science Research Center; Disovery Institute; Intelligent design; *Scopes* v. *Tennessee*/Scopes Monkey Trial

For further reading

Answers in Genesis. 2006. http://www.answers ingenesis.org/ (accessed June 15, 2005).

Understanding Evolution. 2006. http://evolution .berkeley.edu/ (accessed June 15, 2005).

Avoidance of the issue of evolution in many teaching standards

Religion and law interact in many unexpected places. Other issues, however, have become such common points of contention that their regular appearance in the news comes as no surprise to most viewers. One such issue in the expected places is teaching evolution in public schools. Those who oppose the teaching of evolution believe that it violates their religion and is untrue. Those who believe evolution should be taught think that it has nothing whatsoever to do with religion and is part of accepted scientific doctrine. This second group often feels that any restriction represents an imposition of fundamentalist Christianity on public education. A related area that has sparked noted interest concerns national and state teaching standards. These are lists of items or goals or points decided by a national commission (or a state commission) to be covered in classroom instruction, and very often these standards are tied to an exam that all students must take. As the exam reflects what is on the list, and generally only that, the list content generally governs what material teachers cover in their classrooms. Thus, from the point of view of the evolution controversy, if evolution is listed, it probably will be taught, and if not listed, it probably will not be taught.

At the national level, the main standards for testing teachers are covered by the PRAXIS exams, and students are tested by the Advanced

Placement (AP) exam. The PRAXIS system, created by the Educational Testing Service, tests potential teachers in areas of content knowledge and knowledge about teaching. It has a number of different exams that cover high school biology. The most in-depth one, a two-hour exam covering biological content, which represents 45 percent of the test's content, covers evolution in two areas: genetics and evolution, and diversity of life, plants, and animals. Over forty states use PRAXIS as part of their licensing standards. High school students in advanced classes generally take the AP exam, created by the College Board. High scores on an AP exam are rewarded by many colleges with college-level credit. The AP biology exam includes one hundred multiple choice questions and four essay questions, with the multiple choice section taking slightly less than one-half of the time and counting for 60 percent of the exam score. Roughly 25 percent of the multiple choice and one of the four essays focus on heredity and evolution, meaning that college-bound high school students need at least some knowledge of evolution if they hope to receive pre-enrollment college credits.

Besides the national teaching standards, each state has its own teaching standards and tests. Most states require students to pass these tests either to graduate or to receive certain types of diplomas. Many require tests to cover specific issues. This is one way in which some states have evaded the evolution debate. While many states do require students to deal with evolution, others avoid it and still others avoid the use of the specific word but cover the concept. Other states have changed their positions over time. For instance, the state of Kentucky used to use the term "change over time" to refer to evolution, but beginning in 2007, students will be tested using the term "evolution."

Other states have had more controversy with their treatment. Kansas became involved in a controversy with its teaching standards on the issue in 1999 because it removed evolution entirely. A new board, elected in 2001, restored evolution to the standards. In 2004, a conservative board was elected again, and it decided to revert back to its 1999 stance, once more removing evolution. In 2006, a school board favorable to evolution was again elected. Such frequent shifts make it difficult to ensure any level of standardization in the testing at all and can do more to turn the science classroom into a political field than to confirm that all students receive a basic education.

Federal standards, developed in large part in the No Child Left Behind legislation, also encourage judging education based on the results of standardized tests, further encouraging teachers to teach with the tests in mind. These tests are no small matter either, as they govern the amount of funding a district receives and the need for state intervention in a district. As mentioned, as long as teachers deal with the teaching standards, they are generally permitted to skip anything that falls outside the perimeter. If evolution is not, therefore, included in the standards, a teacher could probably exclude it from the curriculum with no repercussions. This is especially true since over a quarter of the school year, ten weeks, is consumed by either formally reviewing for the tests or actually taking them. That leaves only thirty weeks for teachers to cover new material, for students to understand that material, for the school to test students on that material outside of the standardized testing and to grade the students, and for all of them to deal with all non-academic matters.

Thus, standardized tests, especially those given at the state level, generally govern an individual school's willingness to teach evolution. The content of the standardized tests varies by state and can even vary from year to year within a state, depending on who sits on the state board. While this change can help to ensure that test material does not get stale, it can also lead to schools becoming political Ping-Pong balls for controversial issues like evolution, which may be included by one state board but excluded by the next. One thing is certain. This area is sure to remain a point of intersection for religion and the law for the foreseeable future, as the evolution debate carries with it overtones of both the freedom of religion and the freedom of speech clauses of the First Amendment to the Constitution.

See also Edwards v. *Aguillard; Epperson* v. *Arkansas;* Equal time laws; *Kitzmiller* v. *Dover Area School District;* National Academy of Sciences; *Scopes* v. *Tennessee/*Scopes Monkey Trial

For further reading

Campbell, John Angus, and Stephen C. Meyer, eds. 2003. *Darwinism, Design, and Public Education.* East Lansing: Michigan State University Press.

Educational Testing Service. 2005. Praxis at a Glance. http://www.ets.org/Media/Tests/PRAXIS/pdf/0235.pdf (accessed April 29, 2006).

Kentucky Department of Education. Core Content for Assessment v. 4.0. 2006. http://www.education.ky.gov/users/jwyatt/Core Content/New%20Science/CCA%2040%20 Science%20HS%20rev%20nov%209.doc (accessed April 29, 2006).

Larson, Edward J. 2003. *Trial and Error: The American Controversy over Creation and Evolution.* New York: Oxford University Press.

National Academy Press. 1998. *Teaching about Evolution and the Nature of Science.* Washington, DC: National Academy Press.

B

Baehr v. *Lewin*

852 P.2d 44 (1993)

This decision, addressing at the state level the issue of gay marriage, came before Hawaii's Supreme Court and had national, and, indeed, international, repercussions, because it determined that to forbid gay and lesbian marriage was unconstitutional in Hawaii. It dealt only with Hawaii law, creating a standard of review for Hawaii's marriage law. However, the law would have consequences elsewhere, as every state in the United States was generally supposed to recognize marriages (as of the time of the ruling in *Baehr*) performed in other states. Thus, while only a procedural ruling, *Baehr* was much more important (and created much more sound and fury) than most procedural rulings.

Plaintiffs in the Hawaii same-sex marriage trial, Ninia Baehr, left, and Genora Dancel appear at a news conference on December 3, 1996, in New York. The judge barred Hawaii from denying marriage licenses to gay couples, a decision that influenced similar cases in other states. (AP Photo/Serge J. F. Levy)

The opinion was written by Judge Levinson and joined by Chief Judge Moon. Levinson first reviewed Hawaii's marriage law, noting that sex was the sole reason that the marriage application of the plaintiffs was denied (the plaintiffs were three same-sex couples). He then turned to the legal matters of the case, noting that the evidentiary record was very light, that judgment should not have been granted for Lewin, head of Hawaii's Department of Health (DOH), which granted marriage licenses. He examined Hawaii's constitution, stating that it considered privacy a fundamental right. However, he also said that the court did not "believe that a right to same-sex marriage is so rooted in the traditions and collective conscience of our people" that "failure to recognize it would violate the fundamental principles of liberty and justice that lie at the base of all our civil and political institutions" (852 P.2d 44: 57). The court then considered the equal protection issue, noting that marriage did create benefits, and holding that "the applicant couples correctly contend that the DOH's refusal to allow them to marry on the basis that they are members of the same sex deprives them of access to a multiplicity of rights and benefits that are contingent upon that status" (852 P.2d 44: 58). The court then ruled that "HRS § 572–1, on its face, discriminates based on sex against the applicant couples in the exercise of the civil right of marriage, thereby implicating the equal protection clause of article I, section 5 of the Hawaii Constitution" and that the state would need to provide a "compelling" reason for the discrimination (852 P.2d 44: 59). The opinion noted that Hawaii's constitution went further than the U.S. Constitution and prohibited any discrimination based on sex. Levinson considered Lewin's answer to the charge, which basically was that same-sex couples could not marry because marriage was defined as being between a man and a woman, and found that argument to be circular. The court reviewed past court decisions in other states advanced as defense of marriage being between one man and one woman

and argued that in the past, interracial marriage had been banned on the same rationale and reminded the parties that the Supreme Court had overturned bans on interracial marriage in 1967. From this, the Hawaii court held that "constitutional law may mandate, like it or not, that customs change with an evolving social order" (852 P.2d 44: 63).

The main question remaining was what standard of review to use when considering questions regarding regulations based on sex. The court reviewed various Hawaii and U.S. Supreme Court decisions and held that "accordingly, we hold that sex is a 'suspect category' for purposes of equal protection analysis under article I, section 5 of the Hawaii Constitution n33 and that HRS § 572–1 is subject to the 'strict scrutiny' test" (852 P.2d 44: 67). From this, the court took the next step and held that the marriage regulation "is presumed to be unconstitutional . . . unless Lewin, as an agent of the State of Hawaii, can show that (a) the statute's sex-based classification is justified by compelling state interests and (b) the statute is narrowly drawn to avoid unnecessary abridgments of the applicant couples' constitutional rights" (852 P.2d 44: 67).

Judge Burns concurred in the decision. He agreed with the remand to the lower court, holding that judgment for the defendant had been too early. He added an issue that he thought should be considered, though— whether homosexuality was biologically determined. Burns believed that the Hawaii constitution protected only those elements of sex that are biologically determined, and so the lower court needed to decide whether homosexuality was controlled by our biological makeup.

Judge Heen dissented, holding that sex and race were not analogous, and so the logic of *Loving* could not be extended to this case. He also held that no sex discrimination occurred as both sexes were treated equally, as both were prohibited from being involved in same-sex marriages. He also stated that since no sexual discrimination occurred, there was no need for an evidentiary hearing and no need to remand the case to a lower court. Heen also stated that the court was entering into an area better reached by the legislature and accused the majority of "creating" a civil right.

The case was remanded to a lower court, which set the issue for trial. It did return to the Hawaii Supreme Court as *Baehr v. Miike* in 1996, as the Latter-day Saints (the Mormons) had asked to intervene in the case. (To intervene, legally, means to be allowed to be heard by the court on a case because the group intervening has legal interests at stake.) The Mormons claimed that this case might force them to perform same-sex marriages, giving them an interest in the case. The court, however, found that no church would be forced to perform marriages ever against their precepts and forbade the Mormons from intervening. At trial in the lower court, witnesses for both sides were heard, and the state was not held to have met its burden of proof. Thus, the regulation was struck down. The case then headed back to the Hawaii Supreme Court, but in 1998 Hawaii acted to amend its constitution, defining marriage as being between one man and one woman, ending the debate. On a national scale, while this case was going on, Congress in 1996 passed the Defense of Marriage Act (DOMA), which held that states did not have to recognize marriages unless they were between a man and a woman, and that in federal law, marriage was defined similarly. Just north of the United States, Canada legalized gay marriage in most of its divisions in 2003, and the whole issue of whether to recognize Canadian marriages is still controversial, as is the whole issue of gay marriage itself. *Baehr v. Lewin* was one of the first state supreme court decisions to deal with gay marriage, but by no means will it be the last.

See also Comity doctrine between states in the area of marriage and divorce; Divorce, marriage, and religion; Gay marriage; *Loving* v. *United States; Pace* v. *Alabama*

For further reading
Eskridge, William N. 2002. *Equality Practice: Civil Unions and the Future of Gay Rights.* New York: Routledge.
Goldberg-Hiller, Jonathan. 2002. *The Limits to Union: Same-Sex Marriage and the Politics of Civil Rights.* Ann Arbor: University of Michigan Press.
McKenna, George, and Stanley Feingold, eds. 1997. *Taking Sides: Clashing Views on Controversial Political Issues.* Guilford, CT: Dushkin.
Mello, Michael. 2004. *Legalizing Gay Marriage.* Philadelphia: Temple University Press.
Mohr, Richard D. 2005. *The Long Arc of Justice: Lesbian and Gay Marriage, Equality, and Rights.* New York: Columbia University Press.
Wardle, Lynn D., ed. 2003. *Marriage and Same-Sex Unions: A Debate.* Westport, CT: Praeger

Jim and Tammy Faye Bakker scandal

Jim (1940–) and Tammy Faye (1942–) Bakker were two of the leading televangelists during the 1980s. Tammy Faye's fondness for huge amounts of makeup was long the subject of public mockery, and after the scandal erupted, she became an object of even greater ridicule, thanks to bouts of copious weeping. The scandal centered around a swindle Jim was orchestrating with their Praise the Lord (PTL) Network, but it included their extravagant lifestyle and Jim's sexual affair with PTL secretary Jessica Hahn as well.

Married in 1961, the Bakkers went touring as revival preachers. The puppet show they developed led to their being invited to appear on Pat Robertson's Christian Broadcasting Network (CBN). Jim then helped to create and launch the *700 Club,* and he co-hosted it for a time before Robertson claimed it for himself.

In 1974, Jim and Tammy Faye created the PTL (the initials also stood for "People That Love"), and worked as the show's primary televangelists. It featured tears, interviews with celebrities, and, particularly, Tammy's singing. Stations in every state and many foreign countries aired the show, and about 10 percent of

Televangelist Jim Bakker addresses an audience with his wife Tammy Faye Bakker in 1986. Jim Bakker was implicated in a sex scandal involving his former secretary Jessica Hahn in 1987 and two years later was sentenced to forty-five years in federal prison for fraud, tax evasion, and racketeering. (AP Photo)

America watched it. The Bakkers then went on to found the Heritage USA theme park, which used Christianity as its basis and trailed only Disneyland and Disney World in attendance. However, anti-Bakker televangelist Jimmy Swaggart, along with the *Charlotte Observer,* revealed that Jim had been involved in an adulterous relationship with PTL secretary Jessica Hahn in 1980 and later used PTL funds as part of an apparent payoff to her. This scandal broke in the late 1980s, and the financing of Bakker's theme parks and other ventures came under scrutiny as well.

The PTL's scam was to sell people lifelong access to nonexistent hotel rooms at Heritage USA for $1,000 deposits or memberships. After this was revealed, the network quickly went bankrupt, and Jim Bakker went to jail, eventually serving over five of the forty-five years to which he was sentenced. The Bakkers had lived quite well, holding that God re-

warded those who served him and that Jesus did not teach poverty. Eventually that high life, along with Jim's sexual scandals and creative financing schemes, caught up to them.

Tammy Faye divorced Jim in 1992, marrying Roe Messner, who later went to jail for bankruptcy fraud. Jim Bakker is generally acknowledged to have been more culpable, but he was also further from the spotlight. He is now attempting to return to ministry, and he continues to earn royalties from his books. Tammy Faye also lost her notoriety. She has since attempted a talk show (failed) and a business creating wigs. After serving his five years in jail, Jim wrote a book, *I Was Wrong,* apologizing for his behavior, and remarried. Tammy Faye endured a bout with cancer and lost a lot of the weight that had haunted her in her PTL days. She, too, has written several books, including *I Will Survive,* which discusses her divorce from Jim. The PTL was taken over by televangelist Jerry Falwell and ultimately filed for bankruptcy.

See also *Bob Jones University* v. *United States; Swaggart Ministries* v. *California Board of Equalization*
For further reading
Barnhart, Joe E., and Stephen Winzenburg. 1988. *Jim and Tammy: Charismatic Intrigue inside the PTL.* Buffalo, NY: Prometheus Books.
Martz, Larry, and Ginny Carroll. 1988. *Ministry of Greed.* New York: Weidenfeld and Nicolson.

Banning of suicide in law and its interaction with religion

Most states consider both suicide and attempted suicide to be crimes. The fact that suicide is viewed as a crime, rather than a decision made by an individual regarding his or her body, is at least partially related to religion. Religious views still shape our legal and personal conceptions about suicide today.

Christian philosophers ranging from St. Augustine to Thomas Aquinas describe suicide as both a sin and a crime. Nonreligious philosophers were less likely to condemn suicide. Rousseau described it as being caused by society, and Hume thought that suicide was simply a change that one made in his nature, similar to other changes that people made in nature.

Much of the early logic for viewing suicide as wrong and therefore illegal is religious in nature. Life was viewed as a gift from God, one that suicide threw away. People were expected to show gratitude to God for the gift of life, and suicide obviously showed none of that. Additionally, it was argued that God established a link with humans by creating them, and suicide broke that link. Moreover, suicide was seen as a cowardly means to evade mortal suffering, and God did not like cowards. Thus, there were many religious reasons (and justifications) to ban suicide.

Some used nonreligious, natural law arguments against suicide, arguing that suicide changes the laws of the universe, changes one's natural end, and violates the will to live that most people have deep down. This logic believed that, as suicide violated natural laws, man's law should also ban it.

Some philosophers have actually offered religious reasons for allowing suicide. Margaret Battin, in her book *Ethical Issues in Suicide,* notes that among these religious-based arguments are that suicide is "self-sacrifice," and that it allows "reunion with the deceased" and "release of the soul" (Battin, 1995: 58–59). Sacrifice is something that many religions, including Christianity support as a concept, at least in the abstract. Of course, there are also many Christian martyrs, or people who allowed themselves to be killed for the cause of Christianity, and these include many of the early saints. Their deaths, however, are generally not considered suicides.

Religious arguments that oppose suicide have been more influential than those that favor allowing it, as suicide remains banned in most places, and nearly all of these also make assisting a suicide a crime. This issue is far more than merely theoretical, of course, as it figures into the battle over assisted suicide and the right to die, which deal with whether those who are terminally ill should be allowed to take their own lives to end their suffering.

See also Battle against pornography—religious elements; Capital punishment and religious-based opposition to it; Right to die and religion
For further reading
Battin, M. Pabst. 1995. *Ethical Issues in Suicide.* Englewood Cliffs, NJ: Prentice-Hall.
Shneidman, Edwin. 1985. *Definition of Suicide.* New York: John Wiley.

Battle against pornography— religious elements

The overall battle over pornography often has religious overtones. These overtones are seen both in who is active in the battle against pornography and in how they view their opponents.

One area that religion influences is how one defines pornography. Two authors, Louis Zurcher and R. George Kirkpatrick, describe one effect of religion on the definition of pornography. They comment that some studies "have demonstrated that persons who are older, less educated and more religiously active are more likely to judge a film, book or magazine to be pornographic" (Zurcher and Kirkpatrick, 1976: 255). They also note that these people have not, in their own estimation, generally seen pornography but still believe they know what it is. This idea is somewhat parallel to the statement of Justice Potter Stewart, who said he knew pornography when he saw it, even though he was unable to define it.

Another area that religion influences is how the two sides in battles over pornography see each other. Those arguing for restrictions on material (which one side sees as censorship and the other sees as protecting morality) describe their opponents in religious terms. Zurcher and Kirkpatrick note that the producers of questionable material are often defined as essentially faithless by their opponents, whose arguments strongly imply that no good religious soul would enjoy pornographic material. The pornography opponents studied also believed they had stronger religion as well as better self-control and better backgrounds (Zurcher and Kirkpatrick, 1976: 257). Those opposing this censorship, Zurcher and Kirkpatrick went on to say, saw their adversaries as "religious fanatics" (Zurcher and Kirkpatrick, 1976: 259).

There are also larger issues at work here with religious overtones. Those wishing to restrict materials believe they are participating in a battle between good and evil, in which they represent the good and pornography supporters represent the evil. This whole concept, of course, originated in religion. Finally, many of the groups promoting restrictions are religiously linked. The Knights of Columbus, which limits its membership to Catholic men, has been active for a long time in arguing against what it sees as pornography. The Moral Majority, a fundamentalist Protestant group, also opposes what they consider pornography.

The battle over pornography is and has been greatly shaped by religion. Issues of sexism and abuse are also raised by the issue of pornography, but this entry is concerned with the religious elements of the debate. Those on each side of the debate sometimes define their opponents and themselves in religious terms. Also, religion can influence who is active in the battle. Indeed, it can be argued that religion creates the overall concept of pornography, as restrictions on pornography assume that there is one correct standard, at least in each community, and that community leaders have been given the power by someone to impose that standard on all.

> *See also* Abstinence, government grants to force teaching of; Banning of suicide in law and its interaction with religion

For further reading

Lederer, Laura, ed. 1980. *Take Back the Night: Women on Pornography.* New York: Morrow.

Zurcher, Louis, and R. George Kirkpatrick. 1976. *Citizens for Decency: Antipornography Crusades as Status Defense.* Austin: University of Texas Press.

Berg v. *Glen Cove City School District*

853 F. Supp. 651 (U.S. Dist. Ct. for Eastern District of New York, 1994)

This case dealt with the effect of religious belief on law, specifically in the area of vaccination. The Bergs wanted to send their children to public school, but they did not want their children to be vaccinated. In a variation from typical vaccination controversies, the Bergs did not belong to a religious group who opposed vaccination (it is unclear [and irrelevant to the law] whether the Bergs belong to any temple), but professed themselves to be Jewish, a faith that did not oppose vaccination. The Bergs wished to have their children put into public kindergarten, and the school district opposed them. The Bergs sought a temporary restraining order, which was granted, allowing the children's admission.

The parents detailed the biblical basis of their belief; however, the school board did not find this defense adequate, resulting in the litigation. Judge Wexler first noted the background of the case and the statute. The statute required immunization, except where the parents held "genuine and sincere religious beliefs which are contrary to the practices herein required" (853 F. Supp. 651: 653). Wexler then noted that past versions of the legislation had required membership in a religion that opposed immunization, that the legislation had been redrafted as it favored membership in certain churches over others, and that the old version had been made a violation of the establishment clauses. The court held that the only tests were those in the statute, that the belief had to be genuine and sincere as well as religious in nature. Wexler noted that the objections were religious, even though the Bergs' interpretation of what it meant to be Jewish differed from the school board's experts. He then held that their beliefs were apparently sincere and genuine, noting that the Bergs had acted consistently with them for the last six years, and so granted the exemption.

Nonreligious opposition to vaccination would surely result in only a minute chance of success, no matter how sincere and genuine the belief, as the medical evidence heavily favors vaccination, and the right to privacy has not been extended to cover vaccinations. One does not, however, have to belong to an established religious group that opposes vaccinations to have a religious objection to them.

See also *Duro* v. *District Attorney, Second Judicial District of North Carolina; Employment Division* v. *Smith;* Failure to treat due to religious beliefs; *Goldman* v. *Weinberger; United States* v. *Board of Education for the School District of Philadelphia*

For further reading

Goldberg, Robert M. 1995. *The Vaccines for Children Program: A Critique.* Washington, DC: AEI Press.

Liang, Bryan A. 2000. *Health Law and Policy: A Survival Guide to Medicolegal Issues for Practitioners.* Boston: Butterworth-Heinemann.

Sealander, Judith. 2003. *The Failed Century of the Child: Governing America's Young in the Twentieth Century.* New York: Cambridge University Press.

Bible controversy and riots

Some of the worst riots over religion were the 1844 Bible riots in Philadelphia. Mob riots over religion were not uncommon in the late eighteenth and early nineteenth centuries, with over twenty-three disturbances in New York City alone. In the nineteenth century, rather than a debate to test whether public schools were even the correct sphere in which to teach from the Christian Bible, there was instead great controversy in the public schools over which Bible to use. This battle is evidence of the larger cultural struggle between Protestants and Catholics taking place at the time.

Many Protestants wanted Catholics to be required to use the Protestant Bible so as to convert them, believing that if Catholics saw the "correct" Bible they would cease to follow the pope. Many Protestants also did not want any Catholic influence, feeling that all political or other decisions made by Catholics would be dictated by the pope. This feeling was directly tied to the larger question of how much influence Catholics should be allowed to have. Schools were also sometimes hostile to Catholics, and some teachers called the Catholic Church "the whore of Babylon" and called the pope the "antichrist" (Feldberg, 1980: 11). Catholics generally wanted to use the Douay Bible in the classroom, and Protestants, by the nineteen century, generally wanted to use the King James Bible.

In addition to general fear about Catholic control, Protestants also had concerns about the Douay Bible's origins. In 1578, English-speaking Catholics worked on an English language translation of the Bible, as they knew that priests and others needed to be able to quote the Bible in their own language. This was not to communicate specific passages to the parishioners but more to allow the priests to argue with others who focused strongly on religion. Latin was still held to be the best language for the Bible and services overall, and it was used in mass. This translation of the Bible was started by the College at Rheims and finished at Douay, when the college moved there—hence its title of Douay or Rheims Bible. The purpose of the translation was not to make the Bible understandable to the common man, and it adhered closely to the Latin. The King James Bible, by contrast, was the translation made at the request of King James I of England. Its purpose was, in fact, to make the Bible readable by the common literate man. Services using the Bible were held in English so the parishioners could better comprehend God's words.

One specific difference between the Douay Bible and the King James is that the Douay contains more books, particularly in the Old Testament. Protestants generally took their cues about the Old Testament from the Jewish Bible, while the Catholics allowed more books in and organized them chronologically. The books generally not included in the Protestant Bible are the texts often called the Apocrypha. Sometimes today these are included in Protestant Bibles in a separate section called by that name. Some seven books appear in the Douay Bible that do not generally appear in the Protestant Bibles, including the King James Version of the Bible.

The books of the Apocrypha were generally given little credence in many Protestant churches. The Westminster Confession of 1648 declared the Apocrypha useless (to Protestants) as these books had no real value beyond their historical interest. In the Protestant view, therefore, treating the Apocrypha as biblical truth was tantamount to heresy, and Protestants did not want it taught in their children's schools.

The Philadelphia school board ordered its schools to use the King James Version, and the Catholic bishop there quickly asked for approval to use the Douay Version. The request, of course, was denied. With a Protestant majority on the board and in the district, the school board did not want to create the perception that it was giving Catholics special privileges. This was tied in with larger issues, as many calling themselves nativists wanted to remove from public schools all influences they considered un-American, including the influence of the Mormons, the Irish, and indeed all immigrants. Schools were sometimes quite hostile to Catholics. This nativist campaign was also related to the whole idea of Christian reform, with some reformers' goals including the removal of Catholicism, the preservation of Sunday as a holy day by banning all amusements (including the sale of alcohol and mail deliveries, practices that persist today in many places), and supporting the colportage movement, which aimed to give the Protestant Bible to all. The Catholic bishop in Philadelphia, Francis Patrick Kenrick, basically asked for equality of the two Bibles, allowing both to be used. However, most people at the time saw any such action as equivalent to removing the Bible from public schools entirely—and this was of course unpopular. The school board denied the request, but the superintendent did allow teachers to suspend Bible reading until a compromise was worked out. The public, again, saw this as removing the Bible from the schools.

There was a nativist rally on May 3 in an immigrant, largely Irish Catholic, area. Shooting from some of the immigrants drove the nativists out. They returned on May 6, and a battle erupted. Some nativists died, and so the group, by now a mob, returned on the following day, May 7. Again, there was shooting, and the nativists set fire to immigrant buildings. Rioting continued over the next two days, and then martial law was declared by the city government. Six people were killed, fifty were injured, and much destruction took place. The destruction was very targeted, including the superintendent of the public school's house, immigrant churches, and the homes of those believed to have housed snipers. Rioting returned after the Fourth of July, resulting in another battle between nativists and Irish Catholics.

The Bible riots in Philadelphia were a good example of how religious disputes in eighteenth- and nineteenth-century America could turn violent. There were also riots against some German Catholics, although less frequently than riots against Irish Catholics. The Mormons were ultimately driven out of Illinois by riots. Ultimately, this violence led to general use of the Protestant Bible in public schools until the twentieth century, when the appropriateness of any Bible in the public school classroom came under heavy fire.

See also *Engel* v. *Vitale; Lee* v. *Weisman; Santa Fe Independent School District* v. *Doe; School District of Abington Township* v. *Schempp*

For further research

Feldberg, Michael. 1980. *The Turbulent Era: Riot and Disorder in Jacksonian America.* New York: Oxford University Press.

Gilje, Paul. 1987. *The Road to Mobocracy: Popular Disorder in New York City, 1763–1834.* Chapel Hill: University of North Carolina Press.

Hugo Black was a strong advocate of judicial activism during his thirty-four-year career as an associate justice of the U.S. Supreme Court. Black was appointed by President Franklin D. Roosevelt in 1937 and served until his death in 1971. (Library of Congress)

Hugo Black

Supreme Court Justice
Born: February 27, 1886
Died: September 25, 1971
Education: Birmingham Medical School (1903–1904) and then attended law school (graduated in 1906)
Sworn in: August 19, 1937
Retired: September 17, 1971

Hugo Black considered becoming a doctor and actually attended medical school for a year, but ultimately chose law school, graduating at the age of twenty. He immediately began practicing in Ashland, Alabama, where he was born, interrupting his practice in 1915 to become county solicitor for Jefferson County (Birmingham's location) for two years. In 1917, he joined the U.S. Army and served until 1918. After the war, he resumed his legal practice and served until 1927, when he was elected to the U.S. Senate. He was re-elected in 1933. Black was a strong supporter of President Franklin Delano Roosevelt (FDR), and he backed FDR's controversial court-packing plan. To reward him, in 1937, the president appointed him to the first court seat that opened up.

Black had some difficulty being approved by the Senate, considering that it was 1937 and presidential appointees generally were accepted without question. Black had been a member of the Ku Klux Klan (KKK) in Alabama, and knowledge of his membership led to protests by some of his fellow senators. In a speech over the radio he tried to explain why he had become a member and then later left the Klan. He said his membership had been trifling and he did not consider himself a Klansman. Though his explanation proved unsatisfactory to many, he was still approved by a vote of 63 to 19. (However, his approval was with the second-largest number of negative votes cast against any successful nominee in the 1930s.)

Black, once on the Court, gave little evidence that any of the KKK's views influenced him. He was a literal interpreter of the Constitution, especially the First Amendment, and a general supporter of civil rights. He claimed that the term "no law" in the First Amendment meant just that, that Congress could not make any law that restricted free speech or freedom of the press.

In general, he believed that the Constitution's provisions should be read more broadly and should limit Congress. He also believed that judges should not hesitate to strike down legislation that was unconstitutional. This second view has sometimes been called judicial activism. In this, he differed from Felix Frankfurter, who believed that the provisions of the Constitution should be read narrowly, and that legislation should be upheld except when there was a clear violation of the Constitution, generally something written directly into the Constitution. This second view has sometimes been called judicial restraint. Black also believed that the whole of the Bill of Rights should be applied against the states, which is called total incorporation, while others believed that only parts of the Bill of Rights should be applied against the states, in what is been called selective incorporation.

Black was not always hesitant to grant the government's wishes, however. In 1940, he agreed with the majority when it allowed the state government to order schoolchildren to salute the flag in *Minersville School District* v. *Gobitis.* He did reverse his position by 1942, suggesting, along with Douglas and Murphy, that *Gobitis* had been wrongly decided. In 1943, Black concurred with the majority and wrote his own position as well in *West Virginia State Board of Education* v. *Barnette.* This case determined that Jehovah's Witnesses could not be forced to salute the flag. This decision reversed

Gobitis. Also during World War II, Black agreed with the majority, writing no separate opinion, in *Hirabayashi* v. *United States* (1943), which held that Japanese Americans could be interned. The next year, he wrote the opinion for the court in *Korematsu* v. *United States* (1944), which upheld the internment, and he argued that military necessity justified this policy exclusion.

However, in the 1950s and 1960s, Black began to lean more toward granting power to the individual, serving as the anchor for the liberal wing of the court in those years. He was much more interested in crafting majorities and working for some level of consensus, even if it was in dissent, than his fellow liberal, Justice William O. Douglas.

When asked, later in life, which of his opinions he considered most important, he cited, among others, one dissent and one majority. The dissent was *Adamson* v. *California* (1948). In *Adamson,* the majority had held that the Fifth Amendment's protection against self-incrimination did not apply against the states, allowing the state to use against a defendant the defendant's refusal to testify. Black dissented, arguing that all of the Bill of Rights should apply fully against the states, but this view never has been adopted. In *Chambers* v. *Florida,* Black wrote the majority opinion. This opinion held that improperly obtained confessions could not be used to bring about a conviction for a capital crime. In this case, four young black men had been sentenced to death after five days of continuous questioning had brought about confessions from three of them. These confessions were then used in Court against all four. Forced confessions were thus held to violate due process, which the Fourteenth Amendment applied against the states, and this opinion is the start of today's constitutional interpretation that requires the states to follow minimum standards of justice in their legal systems.

Besides those cases that Black considered the most important, he also was instrumental in several cases that have reshaped constitutional law up to the present. These include *Everson* v.

Board of Education (1947), which allowed the state to repay parents for their expenses in transporting their children to private schools; *McCollum v. Board of Education* (1948), which struck down a system of voluntary religious classes in the public schools on public school grounds; *Engel v. Vitale* (1962), which struck down a mandatory state-approved prayer used daily in some public schools; and *Gideon v. Wainright* (1963), which created a defendant's right to an attorney at state expense for anyone too poor to afford legal representation. Thus, several cases that are still important in litigation over the issue of church-state relations or still generally cited today were written by Justice Black.

Black suffered a severe stroke in the summer of 1971 and retired on September 17 of that year. He died eight days after his retirement.

> **See also** *Engel v. Vitale; Everson v. Board of Education;* Felix Frankfurter; *Lemon v. Kurtzman; McCollum v. Board of Education;* Saluting the flag; *Zorach v. Clauson*

For further reading

Ball, Howard. 1996. *Hugo L. Black: Cold Steel Warrior.* New York: Oxford University Press.

Ball, Howard, and Phillip J. Cooper. 1992. *Of Power and Right: Hugo Black, William O. Douglas, and America's Constitutional Revolution.* New York: Oxford University Press.

Hockett, Jeffrey D. 1996. *New Deal Justice: The Constitutional Jurisprudence of Hugo L. Black, Felix Frankfurter, and Robert H. Jackson.* Lanham, MD: Rowman & Littlefield.

Simon, James F. 1989. *The Antagonists: Hugo Black, Felix Frankfurter and Civil Liberties in Modern America.* New York: Simon and Schuster.

Yarbrough, Tinsley E. 1988. *Mr. Justice Black and His Critics.* Durham, NC: Duke University Press.

Blaine Amendment

America's treatment of its Catholic citizens has not always been stellar. During the nineteenth century, there were repeated instances of anti-Catholic bias in national politics. One such instance was the 1840s Bible riots when anti-Catholic riots raged through several cities due

James G. Blaine was frequently proposed as a Republican presidential candidate, but his main influence was as Speaker of the House and as secretary of state under President Benjamin Harrison. (Library of Congress)

to disagreements over which Bible, the Catholic (Douay) or Protestant (King James), should be used in the schools. A second example is the formation of the Know-Nothing, or American, Party, formed in the 1850s to attempt to decrease recent immigrants' influence and limit immigration, particularly of Irish Catholics. A third attempt, at both the state and national levels, was the Blaine Amendment, which aimed at preventing any federal money or federal lands from going to help parochial schools in any way.

The Blaine Amendment was first proposed in 1875. It held that no tax money, either raised for schools or otherwise, and no state lands could be given to any church, and thus by extension not to church-controlled schools. It was drafted in response to fears that the Catholic Church was gaining too much influence and that the state would begin to funnel money to the Catholic Church, particularly under the influence of administrations controlled by Catholic voters. Thus, no federal money could go to help a church, but students could still pray in school. The federal government was given power to enforce the amendment, so the issues of state versus federal power and monies to churches were already involved. The Senate altered the amendment specifically so as not to prohibit prayers in school, weighing it down with a third church-state issue. The amendment passed the House easily but stalled in the Senate, where, though the majority of senators voted for it, it failed to receive a full two-thirds majority support. However, it did not go away. It was reintroduced several more times between 1875 and 1930 before it was finally abandoned.

Although it had failed on a federal level, the effort was not totally abandoned. On the contrary, its failure in Congress spurred its supporters on the state level to more action. Indeed, the whole issue had started at the local level. In the nineteenth century, other than setting aside land for schools and colleges, the federal government did little for education. Nearly all of today's federal grants (Title I, which provides funding to school districts with low-income students; the National Endowment for the Humanities, NEH, which supports education and access to the arts, among other things; the National Science Foundation, NSF, which supports science education, etc.) are products of the second half of the twentieth century. It should be noted that the amendments at the state level were not called Blaine amendments at the time but have been given that title later. Most school boards were controlled by Protestants, so a Protestant Bible and prayers acceptable to Protestants were used in most schools, and most voters in many states were Protestants, so money would not have been expected to go to Catholic schools, even without Blaine-type amendments. However, the Republicans in the North were fighting the Democrats for supremacy, and many Democrats were

Catholics; therefore, demonizing the Catholics to influence swing voters was a strategy that appealed to some politicians. Some states adopted such measures in political fights, but more adopted them into newly established constitutions. Unlike the federal government, which has had the same basic constitution (albeit with twenty-seven amendments) for the last 200 years, most states have revised their constitutions from time to time by amending them and by calling conventions and adopting new constitutions. Kentucky, for instance, has had four constitutions, and New York, to use a northern example, has had five, and both states adopted Blaine-type amendments at their constitutional conventions.

Between provisions inserted in the new state constitutions and the amendments adopted separately, some thirty-three states (there were at most forty-eight states in this period) adopted Blaine-type amendments. New York's constitution prohibited aid of any kind, including land, money, or financial backing for any school controlled by a church or in a school where a particular religion was practiced. Of course, it should be noted that this was not held to prohibit prayer in the public schools, as long as the prayer was nondenominational. Prayer in the public schools became much more of an issue in the 1960s, and the Supreme Court has had to address the issue several times. New York's current constitution was approved in 1938, and it contained a prohibition against aid to religious schools at the time it was adopted. The current constitution continues that prohibition, although it allows districts to pay for transportation to parochial schools (a provision that was also in the 1894 constitution). It was New York, in fact, that created the prayer struck down in the *Engel* v. *Vitale* case (1962), which banned any mandatory prayer in the public schools across the nation.

The Blaine amendments on the state level have not been removed from most state constitutions, and they still influence the public sphere to some degree. For instance, in Florida,

Governor Jeb Bush's plan to implement school vouchers—which would allow students in poor-performing schools to choose where they go to school, even to attending private schools partially at state expense—was recently declared unconstitutional at the state level due to the Blaine-type amendment in place in Florida. Thus, the Blaine Amendment's influence is alive and well at the state level, even if never passed at the federal, and the anti-Catholic bias underlying its original creation has greatly diminished in favor of more general concerns about church-state separation.

> **See also** Bible controversy and riots; *Engel v. Vitale;* 1960 election and role of anti-Catholic sentiment; State constitutions and the federal First Amendment; *Zelman v. Simmons-Harris*
>
> **For further reading**
> Crapol, Edward P. 2000. *James G. Blaine: Architect of Empire.* Wilmington, DE: SR Books.
> Howard, Victor B. 1990. *Religion and the Radical Republican Movement, 1860–1870.* Lexington: University Press of Kentucky.
> Kyvig, David E. 1996. *Explicit and Authentic Acts: Amending the U.S. Constitution, 1776–1995.* Lawrence: University Press of Kansas.
> Noll, Mark A., ed. 1990. *Religion and American Politics: From the Colonial Period to the 1980s.* New York: Oxford University Press.
> Summers, Mark W. 2000. *Rum, Romanism, and Rebellion: The Making of a President, 1884.* Chapel Hill: University of North Carolina Press.

Board of Education Kiryas Joel Village School v. *Grumet*
512 U.S. 687 (1994)

This case dealt with New York's decision to establish a special village made up of residents of only one religion. New York had allowed a group of Hasidic Jews to establish its own village. Village children were mostly raised in religious schools, and the public school took care of serving handicapped children only and for providing transportation to the religious schools for the other children. The action creating the school district was then challenged.

Justice Souter wrote the opinion for the Court. He first noted that the statute delegated authority to a religious group. Even though the school board had been elected, this was irrelevant as the village had been limited to Hasidic Jews, guaranteeing that the school board would consist solely of Hasidic Jews. Souter concluded that "we therefore find the legislature's Act to be substantially equivalent to defining a political subdivision and hence the qualification for its franchise by a religious test, resulting in a purposeful and forbidden 'fusion of governmental and religious functions'" (512 U.S. 687: 702). In other words, the legislative action was not neutral to religion and was therefore illegal. Souter held that "here the benefit flows only to a single sect, but aiding this single, small religious group causes no less a constitutional problem than would follow from aiding a sect with more members or religion as a whole, . . . and we are forced to conclude that the State of New York has violated the Establishment Clause" (512 U.S. 687: 705). Souter then considered the dissent's claims that the decision had held that religiously oriented groups could never hold power, and he disagreed, as these groups could hold power, as long as that power was "conferred on it without regard to religion" (512 U.S. 687: 708).

Justice Blackmun concurred, mostly writing to note that he still agreed with the *Lemon* test, first announced in 1971. That three-part test held that policies had to have a secular purpose, had to have a primary effect other than promoting or retarding religion, and had to avoid an excessive entanglement with religion. Justice Stevens also concurred. He noted that the state had a proper interest in helping out the Hasidic schoolchildren who were seen as different by many in the state, but held that the state had many ways of promoting good interaction other than creating a separate school district.

Justice O'Connor concurred in part, though she reached her conclusion by different logic. O'Connor first pointed out that some accommodation is acceptable, noting "religious needs can be accommodated through laws that are neutral with regard to religion" (512 U.S. 687: 714). She found the fatal flaw in this law to be that it was specific legislation that benefited only this one district, commenting, "There is nothing improper about a legislative intention to accommodate a religious group, so long as it is implemented through generally applicable legislation" (512 U.S. 687: 717). She also noted that the *Lemon* test did not work in all cases and should not, in her opinion, be applied in all cases.

Justice Kennedy also concurred in the judgment. He wrote to argue against a possible reading of the Court's holding "that an accommodation for a particular religious group is invalid because of the risk that the legislature will not grant the same accommodation to another religious group suffering some similar burden. This rationale seems to me without grounding in our precedents and a needless restriction upon the legislature's ability to respond to the unique problems of a particular religious group" (512 U.S. 687: 722). Kennedy stated that the problem with this district was that the state had used a religious test to create its boundaries. Kennedy also noted that the problem might not have occurred had not the Court forced schools to stop treating handicapped children from religious schools on public school grounds, which was one of the factors leading to the creation of this district.

Justice Scalia dissented, joined by Justice Thomas and Chief Justice Rehnquist. Scalia mocked the holding of the majority, suggesting that they had held that this particular sect, Satmar Judaism, was being established as a state religion. He commented, "I do not know who would be more surprised at this discovery: the Founders of our Nation or Grand Rebbe Joel Teitelbaum, founder of the Satmar. The Grand Rebbe would be astounded to learn that after escaping brutal persecution and coming to America with the modest hope of religious toleration for their ascetic form of Judaism, the Satmar had become so powerful, so closely allied with Mammon, as to have become an 'es-

tablishment' of the Empire State" (512 U.S. 687: 732). Scalia viewed this decision as being misguided and wholly divorced from either the law or history. "Once this Court has abandoned text and history as guides, nothing prevents it from calling religious toleration the establishment of religion" (512 U.S. 687: 732).

Scalia gave several reasons why he thought that this decision moved away from precedent. He first noted that no aid was going to private religious schools, which had prompted many past cases. He also argued that segregating students by religion had been allowed by past cases. In response to the majority's suggestion that the state had transferred power to the Satmar Jews, Scalia said that power could be given to a religious group, but not a church. Scalia also noted that there was a secular purpose for the law, that of educating the handicapped children, and that it was acceptable for New York to create the specialized school district, as it could have focused on cultural issues, not religious ones when it created the school district. He also argued that even special accommodation on the basis of religion was allowed, as the only reason, in Scalia's mind, that such as system was seen as unconstitutional by the majority was that a similar religious minority might not be given favorable treatment in the future. Scalia closed by disagreeing with the three concurrences. Scalia commented on O'Connor's discussion of the problems of *Lemon* by arguing that he thought *Lemon* should be wholly abandoned. "The foremost principle I would apply [in place of *Lemon*] is fidelity to the longstanding traditions of our people" (512 U.S. 687: 751). On the whole, Scalia held that the decision of the plurality was "unprecedented—except that it continues, and takes to new extremes, a recent tendency in the opinions of this Court to turn the Establishment Clause into a repealer of our Nation's tradition of religious toleration" (512 U.S. 687: 752).

See also *Agostini* v. *Felton; Employment Division* v. *Smith; Mitchell* v. *Helms; Valley Forge College* v. *Americans United*

For further reading

Alexander, Kern, and M. David Alexander. 2001. *American Public School Law.* Belmont, CA: West/Thomson Learning.

Boyarin, Jonathan, and Daniel Boyarin. 2002. *Powers of Diaspora: Two Essays on the Relevance of Jewish Culture.* Minneapolis: University of Minnesota Press.

Endelman, Todd M., ed. 1997. *Comparing Jewish Societies.* Ann Arbor: University of Michigan Press.

Ryden, David K., ed. 2000. *The U.S. Supreme Court and the Electoral Process.* Washington, DC: Georgetown University Press.

Sarna, Jonathan D. 2004. *American Judaism: A History.* New Haven: Yale University Press.

Board of Education of Cincinnati v. Minor

23 Ohio St. 211 (1872)

This case was one of the first in which a state court held that reading the Bible in public schools could be prohibited. The case involved a well-known controversy at the time, the Cincinnati "Bible wars," and Judge Alphonso Taft, who was fairly well known himself, but he is better known to history as the father of future president (and Supreme Court chief justice) William Howard Taft.

Cincinnati had erupted into controversy in the 1860s. The root of the conflict was disagreement about which Bible to use—the Protestant King James Bible or the Catholic Douay Bible. Part of the difference between the two Bibles is in the books they contain, and the larger issue was whether to favor the Catholic or Protestant way of thinking. Cincinnati was particularly torn because the city was about equally divided between Protestants and Catholics. No easy solution seemed possible, so the Cincinnati School Board took the radical step of simply removing the Bible from the schools. Those in favor of keeping the Bible were outraged, and so they first asked the city attorney, called the city solicitor, to sue the school. This did not produce any lawsuit, so those opposed, some of whom were taxpayers, sued the school board. Most of those who sued favored keeping the Bible that had been in use at the time of the division—the King James (Protestant) Bible.

The main argument that took hold with the courts at the superior court level (the name of the lower state court in Ohio at the time) was whether the school board could ban the Bible. Legally the school board had no existence of its own but existed only at the request of the state. Thus, could such an agency ban the Bible from the schools? While that question might seem a bit ridiculous to us today, as present-day school boards set the policy in all areas, the lower court found that the school board had gone beyond its powers. Alphonso Taft was a member of that court and strongly disagreed. Taft did not focus on the school board's own powers but on the Ohio Constitution and Bill of Rights. The Ohio Constitution had within it a guarantee of religious liberty, and Taft found that teaching the Bible in schools interfered with that guarantee. As keeping the Bible in the schools violated the Ohio Constitution, of course the school board could ban it, in the mind of Taft.

The school board then appealed the case to the Ohio Supreme Court, who agreed with Taft and held for the school board in 1872. In addition to arguing that the school board had gone beyond its powers, those opposed to the change argued that the Bible had been in schools since the first Ohio Territory schools had been established, and that many students' only exposure to the Bible was in the public schools. Those opposed also made the interesting argument that biblical passages were in other school materials, such as the readers, and so it made no sense to ban the Bible. The school board, on the other hand, argued that the readers were not religious and that the schools were not responsible for providing religious instruction, even to those who received none elsewhere.

The Ohio Supreme Court first found that the school board was within its powers to pass a ban on Bible reading. The court then asked quite the opposite question, the one asked in most Bible-reading cases today: whether Bible reading is allowed. However, in 1872, the question was whether Bible reading was required by the Ohio Constitution or Ohio's laws. The court shied away from the larger questions of whether Christianity was the best religion or how much religion was allowed. The court focused on whether courts were allowed to step in to the point of banning or forcing religious instruction, and answered the overall question in the negative, leaving it up to the legislature, which had, in turn, already delegated the power to the school board. While the Ohio Constitution did order moral instruction, the legislature had never acted to order Bible reading, and, the court held, until the legislature did act, the courts were unable to intervene. The court also went forward and answered the claim that this was a Christian country and so Christianity should be taught and added into the laws, as, the claim continued, Christianity was implied in the original laws and constitutions when they were written. The Ohio Supreme Court did not agree with that, finding that even if they agreed that it was so, there were no provisions in the Ohio Constitution for forcing the nation to be Christian. The court also added that Christianity saw a separation between God and man, and as Christianity's laws came from God, it did not want the help of man. Religion was to be left up to the individual. For all of these reasons, the Ohio Supreme Court held that the lower court had gone beyond its powers in ordering the Bible back into the classroom.

See also *Donahoe* v. *Richards; Lee* v. *Weisman; McCreary County* v. *ACLU; Santa Fe Independent School District* v. *Doe; School District of Abington Township* v. *Schempp; Wallace* v. *Jaffree*

For further reading

Greenawalt, Kent. 2005. *Does God Belong in Public Schools?* Princeton, NJ: Princeton University Press.

Haas, Carol. 1994. *Engel v. Vitale: Separation of Church and State.* Hillside, NJ: Enslow Publishers.

Marty, Martin E., with Jonathan Moore. 2000. *Education, Religion, and the Common Good: Advancing a Distinctly American Conversation about Religion's Role in Our Shared Life.* San Francisco: Jossey-Bass.

Murray, William J. 1995. *Let Us Pray: A Plea for Prayer in Our Schools.* New York: Morrow.

Sikorski, Robert, ed. 1993. *Prayer in Public Schools and the Constitution, 1961–1992.* New York: Garland.

Board of Education v. Pico
457 U.S. 853 (1982)

This decision dealt with the level of discretion that a school board had in removing books from their library. A school board had ordered removal of certain books because they were "anti-American, anti-Christian, anti-Sem[i]tic, and just plain filthy," holding "it is our duty, our moral obligation, to protect the children in our schools from this moral danger as surely as from physical and medical dangers" (457 U.S. 853: 857). The students sued for the books' return and ultimately won their case in the Supreme Court. However, the Supreme Court decision was very divided.

The plurality opinion, favoring the students, was written by Justice Brennan and joined by Justices Marshall and Stevens and mostly joined by Justice Blackmun. Brennan first reviewed the history of the proceedings and then noted the question at hand, holding that this was not a question of curriculum but only of the availability of books in the school library for optional reading. He summarized the questions here as "first, does the First Amendment impose any limitations upon the discretion of petitioners to remove library books from the Island Trees High School and Junior High School? Second, if so, do the affidavits and other evidentiary materials before the District Court, construed most favorably to respondents, raise a genuine issue of fact whether petitioners might have exceeded those limitations?" (457 U.S. 853: 863). Brennan, for himself, Marshall, and Stevens, noted the limitations placed on school boards by the First Amendment and the importance of ideas being available for students. He then turned to the specific limitations of the First Amendment here, ruling for the Court.

While school boards had discretion, the use of that discretion could not violate the First Amendment, as Brennan held that "our Constitution does not permit the official suppression of ideas" (457 U.S. 853: 871). He summarized the Court's holding as saying "that local school boards may not remove books from school library shelves simply because they dislike the ideas contained in those books and seek by their removal to prescribe what shall be orthodox in politics, nationalism, religion, or other matters of opinion" (457 U.S. 853: 872). Justice Blackmun concurred, arguing that schools could not decide between ideas in an unconstitutional manner, which he saw happening here.

Justice White also concurred, but only in the judgment, holding that the plurality had gone too far. Summary judgment should not have been issued by the district court, in his opinion, as there were still issues to be resolved, and he would have merely stated that and returned the case.

Chief Justice Burger, joined by Justices O'Connor, Rehnquist, and Powell, dissented. Burger accused the plurality of becoming their own school board, establishing a right to certain books in the school library. He argued that just because there needs to be access to ideas does not mean that the school board must aid in providing that access, and that "schools in particular ought not be made a slavish courier of the material of third parties" (457 U.S. 853: 889). Burger argued that the court had overstepped its bounds and provided no workable standards for regulating school boards or for

helping school boards to work. Justice Powell also dissented separately, arguing that this decision destroyed the system of school boards in place by encouraging litigation over every little decision. He also argued that by destroying the democratic system of school boards, the Court was not allowing the school board to model the democracy the school boards were supposed to be teaching.

Justice Rehnquist also dissented, in an opinion joined by Justice Powell and Chief Justice Burger. He argued that Justice Brennan decided a hypothetical question and noted that the Supreme Court was not supposed to decide such questions. He then argued that Brennan should not have been concerned about the school board's suppressing ideas, as the schoolchildren could still discuss the books, even though they could not have checked them out of the school library. Rehnquist then argued that the school board here was acting as an educator, not as an agent of the state, and that, as an educator, the board should have been given more leeway than if it had been the state prohibiting the selling of such books. He went on to argue that Brennan had created a new constitutional right in the right to receive ideas. Freedom of speech, Rehnquist argued, did not guarantee "a right of access to certain information in school" (457 U.S. 853: 911). He went on to argue that censorship was necessary to education, holding that "education consists of the selective presentation and explanation of ideas. The effective acquisition of knowledge depends upon an orderly exposure to relevant information" (457 U.S. 853: 914). How this squared with his comment above, that the students still had access to the books even if they are not in the school library, is not explained. For Rehnquist, the fact that the government was educating controlled everything here, as he held, "I think the Court will far better serve the cause of First Amendment jurisprudence by candidly recognizing that the role of government as sovereign is subject to more stringent limitations than is the role of government as employer, property owner, or educator" (457 U.S. 853: 919).

Justice O'Connor wrote a short opinion allowing that the school board had the power to remove the books from the library, but only if it stopped there. "If the school board can set the curriculum, select teachers, and determine initially what books to purchase for the school library, it surely can decide which books to discontinue or remove from the school library so long as it does not also interfere with the right of students to read the material and to discuss it" (457 U.S. 853: 921).

This opinion, like that in the case of *Des Moines* v. *Tinker,* which held that a school board cannot remove students from the classroom just because it disagrees with the political message of their clothing, holds that there are constitutional limitations on school boards. However, the fractured nature of this opinion, along with the fact that the removals would have been allowable had the school board not come directly out and stated that they were censoring the books for their political and religious views, means that the practical limitations on school boards are few and far between. The religious implications of this case were not directly touched on by many of the justices, but the same message holds as to the political cause for removing some of the books—a school board cannot remove books just because it views them as un-Christian.

See also *Bronx Household of Faith* v. *Community School District No. 10; Good News Club* v. *Milford Central School; Roberts* v. *Madigan;* Saluting the flag; *Smith* v. *Board of School Commissioners of Mobile County; Wiley* v. *Franklin; Wisconsin* v. *Yoder*

For further reading

Covey, Denise Troll. 2002. *Usage and Usability Assessment: Library Practices and Concerns.* Washington, DC: Digital Library Federation.
Epstein, Noel, ed. 2004. *Who's in Charge Here? The Tangled Web of School Governance and Policy.* Denver, CO: Education Commission of the States.
Flinchbaugh, Robert W. 1993. *The 21st Century Board of Education: Planning, Leading, Transforming.* Lancaster, PA: Technomic.
Hayes, William. 2001. *So You Want to Be a School Board Member?* Lanham, MD: Scarecrow Education.

Board of Regents of the University of Wisconsin System v. Southworth et al.

529 U.S. 217 (2000)

The case at issue here dealt with a general fee that University of Wisconsin students were required to pay. A variety of student organizations received this money, with the aim of creating a variety of viewpoints on campus. Those suing claimed they were being forced to support views they did not agree with, but the Supreme Court disagreed.

Justice Kennedy wrote the opinion for the Court. He first surveyed the history of the university and the program. He noted the ways that groups are funded and that the university admitted that some groups "engage in political and ideological expression" (529 U.S. 217: 224). Both sides in the dispute agreed that the program was administered "in a viewpoint-neutral fashion" (529 U.S. 217: 224). The student body could also vote to approve or disapprove the funding for any group. Also, only certain expenses were allowed, and those that were "politically partisan or religious in nature" were not allowed (529 U.S. 217: 225). Those opposed to the general fee had argued that the program "violated their rights of free speech, free association, and free exercise under the First Amendment. They contended the University must grant them the choice not to fund those RSO's [student organizations] that engage in political and ideological expression offensive to their personal beliefs" (529 U.S. 217: 227).

Kennedy first noted that the actor was the university, not a government, and that an open public forum existed here. He held that the students could demand safeguards. Kennedy then differentiated this from mandatory membership in an association, as members in a mandatory membership setting (such as in a union) had been held to be able to object to supporting objectionable (in their view) speech that was not central to the purpose of the association. The university setting was different, as the university wanted, as part of its mission, to broaden the range of speech available, so the previous test would not work. Kennedy concluded that "the University may determine that its mission is well served if students have the means to engage in dynamic discussions of philosophical, religious, scientific, social, and political subjects in their extracurricular campus life outside the lecture hall. If the University reaches this conclusion, it is entitled to impose a mandatory fee to sustain an open dialogue to these ends" (529 U.S. 217: 233). Justice Kennedy did state that viewpoint neutrality was necessary.

Justice Souter concurred, along with Stevens and Breyer. He did not think that government neutrality in administration was the key issue, but a weighing of the issues of the students' rights versus the program. He held that it was a proper government interest (Souter viewed the university as part of the government) and that the students were not being forced to support speech they did not like, just to contribute to a fund that distributed monies to groups.

Religion was not directly mentioned here, other than being one of the reasons given as an objection to the program. Groups supporting religious views might very well qualify for funding, as long as religious expenses were not reimbursed. Indeed, religious views might very well be supported by certain groups (or views against certain religions). This would cause some to feel that they were being forced to support groups opposed to their religion, denying them their free exercise, and supporting, arguably, a government infringement on certain religions. The Court, however, similar to their stance on the free speech claims here, probably would not have agreed with those views, as the whole point of the program was not to create a program agreeable to all, but to encourage a wide diversity of views, which by its very nature would have views disagreeable to some. Thus, a university is allowed to mandate a fee that might dispense funds to groups disagreeable to some, as long as this fee is administered in a way that is viewpoint neutral.

See also *Chapman* v. *Thomas; Good News Club* v. *Milford Central School; Police Department of City of Chicago* v. *Mosley; Rosenberger* v. *Rector and Visitors of the University of Virginia; Widmar* v. *Vincent*

For further reading

Gibbs, Annette. 1992. *Reconciling Rights and Responsibilities of Colleges and Students: Offensive Speech, Assembly, Drug Testing, and Safety.* Washington, DC: George Washington University.

Kaplan, William A., and Barbara A. Lee. 1997. *A Legal Guide for Student Affairs Professionals: Adapted from* The Law of Higher Education, *Third Edition.* San Francisco: Jossey-Bass.

Stevens, Ed. 1999. *Due Process and Higher Education: A Systemic Approach to Fair Decision Making.* Washington, DC: George Washington University.

Toma, J. Douglas, and Richard L. Palm. 1999. *The Academic Administrator and the Law: What Every Dean and Department Chair Needs to Know.* Washington, DC: George Washington University.

Bob Jones University v. United States
461 U.S. 574 (1983)

Most foundations and universities have tax-exempt status, a condition that allows them to avoid a variety of taxes and to receive money from donors who then get tax breaks for their gifts. However, gaining this status is dependent upon preconditions. When a religious group is

Bob Jones University in Greenville, South Carolina, is a fundamentalist Christian institution founded in 1926 by Bob Jones, Sr. The university has served as a training ground for some of today's leading members of the religious right. (Wikipedia)

granted nonprofit status, or that status is removed, the question of whether that grant (or removal) has any element of religion involved in it is also put into the mix. Such a query was at the heart of this case.

Bob Jones University is a private South Carolina university that also had kindergarten through high school classes. It had racially discriminatory policies. Specifically, it prohibited the admission or reenrollment of any student who dated interracially or advocated such dating, even while the university admitted African American students. In 1970, the Internal Revenue Service (IRS) moved to deny tax-exempt status to any university that practiced racial discrimination and also to deny this status to gifts given to such a university. That policy resulted, eventually, in this case. Bob Jones's case was combined with that of a kindergarten

through high school educational group from North Carolina that generally did not admit African Americans.

Chief Justice Burger wrote the opinion for the Court. He first surveyed the history of the policy, noting that a past court had approved it. He then surveyed the history of the two cases and turned to examining the history of the tax exemption policy of the IRS. The Court concluded that the government had intended for only charitable groups to receive the exemption and that being religious alone was not enough for a group to qualify for such status. Burger then noted that racial discrimination existed in opposition to government policy and that encouraging such in a school was enough to allow the government to remove the school's tax-exempt status. The opinion next examined the IRS and determined that the agency had enough constitutional authority to remove Bob Jones's tax-exempt status without a separate action by Congress. The IRS had the authority and had removed other organizations' tax-exempt status. As Congress had not acted to correct those removals, its approval of the policy was implied, meaning the IRS acted appropriately.

Burger next turned to the issue of religion, examining whether the IRS's change in tax status improperly burdened religion, which would be forbidden under the First Amendment. He first noted that not all burdens were unconstitutional, but only those not justified by a compelling government interest, and, Burger commented, preventing discrimination is such an interest. Bob Jones, however, claimed the university was racially neutral in admissions and was only following religion in their ban on interracial dating. The Court, however, did not agree, holding that controls on one's freedom of association, based on race, were also racial discrimination. Thus, the Court, in an 8–1 vote, found for the IRS.

Justice Powell wrote a concurrence, agreeing with most of the Court's opinion. He argued that the issue of whether a group created a public benefit, which the majority holds to be one of the crucial tests for tax-exempt status, is incorrect. He had some difficulty accepting the denial for racially discriminatory admissions, but ultimately went along with it. However, he felt forced to comment on the public benefit issue. He saw the Court as arguing that tax-exempt organizations must be in harmony with overall governmental views, and he disagreed, holding this to mean that charities should carry out government policy, which he thought to be clearly at odds with what charities should do. He also thought that Congress, not the IRS, should be the one to make the decisions in general on whether groups were tax exempt. Thus, although Powell thought there was enough reason for the IRS to act in the *Bob Jones* case, he also thought that the larger insinuations suggested by the opinion were troubling.

Justice Rehnquist dissented, thinking that the Court had gone beyond the wishes of Congress. While the majority argued that the lack of action by Congress to reverse the policies of the IRS since 1970 meant that it agreed with them, Rehnquist held that Congress knew how to modify tax policy and if it had wanted racially discriminatory schools to be removed it would have acted. Rehnquist held that "this Court continuously has been hesitant to find ratification through inaction" (461 U.S. 574: 622). Until Congress acted, Rehnquist would have allowed the tax-exempt policy to continue for Bob Jones and other racially discriminatory institutions.

The general denial of tax-exempt status has continued for schools that practice racial discrimination, whether the discrimination is justified on religious or other grounds. Bob Jones continues to exist, and some schools today even proudly proclaim their independence from government mandate, which they believe includes not falling under the government's tax-exempt status and not receiving any government money in any form. Thus, while the case of *Bob Jones University* v. *United States* may have satisfied the issue of whether schools can be funded in a tax-exempt status when their policies run counter to compelling government goals, it did not force all such schools to quit operating, change their policies, or cause them to run out of money in short order.

See also *Boerne* v. *Flores; Employment Division* v. *Smith; Fairfax Covenant Church* v. *Fairfax City School Board; Hibbs* v. *Winn; Mueller* v. *Allen; Public Funds for Public Schools of New Jersey* v. *Byrne; Swaggart Ministries* v. *California Board of Equalization; Walz* v. *Tax Commission of the City of New York*

For further reading

Dalhouse, Mark Taylor. 1996. *An Island in the Lake of Fire: Bob Jones University, Fundamentalism, and the Separatist Movement.* Athens: University of Georgia Press.

Hopkins, Bruce R. 2003. *The Law of Tax-Exempt Organizations.* Hoboken, NJ: John Wiley.

Patrick, John J., and Gerald P. Long, eds. 1999. *Constitutional Debates on Freedom of Religion: A*

Documentary History. Westport, CT: Greenwood Press.

Turner, Daniel L. 1997. *Standing without Apology: The History of Bob Jones University.* Greenville, SC: Bob Jones University Press.

Boerne v. *Flores*

521 U.S. 507 (1997)

In 1990, the Supreme Court decided *Employment Division* v. *Smith* (also sometimes called *Oregon* v. *Smith*), a case dealing with the use of peyote by Native Americans in a ceremony. Two Native Americans had used peyote and were fired from their jobs at a drug rehabilitation unit. These Native Americans then requested unemployment compensation, which was denied because the peyote use was held to be "misconduct" related to their work. They took the case all the way to the Supreme Court, which then asked the Oregon courts whether peyote use in religion was supposed to be illegal under state law. The Oregon Supreme Court held that yes, it was technically illegal, but the law violated the First Amendment, and the state of Oregon then appealed that decision to the Supreme Court. The Supreme Court then held that the state could deny the two individuals their benefits. Justice Scalia spoke for the majority, writing that one's beliefs do not excuse them from state laws, as long as those state laws are valid and neutral with regard to religion. Scalia went against the balancing test of *Sherbert* v. *Verner* (1963), which suggested that laws restricting religious practice must be prompted by a compelling state interest. Even though many states do have exemptions for religious use of peyote, Scalia did not find this convincing enough to hold that such exemptions were required under the First Amendment.

This decision prompted the Religious Freedom Restoration Act (RFRA) of 1993, which restored *Sherbert*'s compelling interest test and held it to be applicable in all cases where the "free exercise of religion is substantially burdened" and also provided an affirmative defense to those whose freedom of religion was so burdened.

However, this act was not without its own set of controversies, one of which resulted in *Boerne* v. *Flores.* This case did not arise out of a typical freedom of religion question but out of a zoning issue. In Texas, one archbishop wanted to expand a church in the city of Boerne. He applied for the permit, but the church was covered under a historic landmark designation and the applicable commission, along with the city leaders, denied the application. The archbishop sued, claiming in part that the Religious Freedom Restoration Act would exempt him from such regulations. The district court held that this act had gone beyond Congress's powers, and the case went all the way to the Supreme Court.

The Supreme Court struck down the Religious Freedom Restoration Act, holding it to be an overstepping of Congress's power under the Fourteenth Amendment. The Court agreed that Congress did have power under that amendment, but only power to restore rights or prevent future abuses, not the power to change what rights were given. The Court also held that Congress was stepping into the area that was more properly the Supreme Court's, as the law restricted the states in areas that the Fourteenth Amendment did not reach.

Justice Kennedy wrote the majority opinion. He first reviewed the history of the controversy, and then examined what powers the Supreme Court had under the Fourteenth Amendment. Kennedy first noted that the purpose of section five of the Fourteenth Amendment, which is what gives Congress power to enforce the Amendment, is to prevent future abuses or to remedy current abuses, and then he noted that this power can allow Congress to ban behavior that might not be directly related to abuses, if that ban is part of a wider constitutionally valid law. He then noted that this power was not unlimited and examined the history behind section 5, detailing how a broader grant had been at first suggested, and how it had then been limited. Kennedy then turned and examined the act, arguing that the ban enacted went much further than was justified in order to protect those rights that arguably had been restricted in *Smith*. On the whole, the majority held, there was no connection "between the means adopted and the legitimate end to be achieved" (521 U.S. 507: 533).

Justice Stevens wrote a short concurrence, arguing that since the RFRA gives the Catholic Church (in this case) a right that no nonreligious body would have to contest a zoning decision, it is a preference for religion over non-religion and thus violates the First Amendment, which does not allow government to advance religion.

Justice Scalia wrote a lengthy concurrence, arguing against the dissent, which was criticizing *Smith*. He first argued that the historical record supported *Smith,* and, even if it did not, the historical record still supported laws that banned certain conduct as "every breach of law is against the peace" (521 U.S. 507: 540), and peace was always the goal of the law. He also argued that the framers of the Constitution were not in support of allowing religious exceptions from the law, and that the historical record as a whole supported *Smith.*

Justice O'Connor dissented, not because she disagreed with the Court's reading of the Fourteenth Amendment but because she disagreed with *Smith*. She pointed out that *Smith* could and should be reconsidered and that the Court should force a return to a standard "that requires government to justify any substantial burden on religiously motivated conduct by a compelling state interest and to impose that burden only by means narrowly tailored to achieve that interest" (521 U.S. 507: 548). O'Connor then considered the historical evidence, both from before the Constitution and from the framers of the Constitution and suggested that this evidence was more in agreement with her dissent than with *Smith*.

Justice Souter also dissented, holding that the writ of certiorari should not have been granted, and the case should be sent back to the lower courts for a full discussion and briefing of the issues of *Smith*.

Justice Breyer issued his own dissent, arguing that *Smith* needed to be reexamined, and thus agreed with O'Connor, except that the whole issue of the Fourteenth Amendment needed to be considered in this case. Breyer thus wanted *Smith* to be reconsidered without examination of whether the Religious Freedom Restoration Act was allowable under the Fourteenth Amendment.

Congress attempted to increase protection for religious practices in the Religious Freedom Restoration Act, but the Court here held that Congress had overstepped its bounds. Note that this decision applied only to the states, as Congress was held to be able to limit its own power. Since 1997, Congress has been unable to enact a direct follow-up law, even though several members of Congress did speak against *Boerne* when it was announced. *Boerne* (and *Smith*) are thus still good law, holding that *Sherbert*'s compelling interest test does not have to be used. Congress did, however, enact the Religious Land Use and Institutionalized Persons Act, which increased the protections for churches in issues of zoning, as well as for prisoners, and that act has been upheld in *Cutter* v. *Wilkinson*.

See also *Church of the Lukumi Babalu Aye* v. *City of Hialeah; Employment Division* v. *Smith; Farrington* v. *Tokushige; Lamb's Chapel* v. *Center Moriches School District; Lyng* v. *Northwest Indian CPA;* Religious Freedom Restoration Act of 1993; *Reynolds* v. *United States; Sherbert* v. *Verner*

For further reading

Brisbin, Richard A. 1997. *Justice Antonin Scalia and the Conservative Revival.* Baltimore, MD: Johns Hopkins University Press.

Long, Carolyn Nestor. 2000. *Religious Freedom and Indian Rights: The Case of Oregon v. Smith.* Lawrence: University Press of Kansas.

Maltz, Earl M., ed. 2003. *Rehnquist Justice: Understanding the Court Dynamic.* Lawrence: University Press of Kansas.

Mauro, Tony. 2000. *Illustrated Great Decisions of the Supreme Court.* Washington, DC: CQ Press.

Schultz, David A., and Christopher E. Smith. 1996. *The Jurisprudential Vision of Justice Antonin Scalia.* Lanham, MD: Rowman & Littlefield.

Van Sickel, Robert W. 1998. *Not a Particularly Different Voice: The Jurisprudence of Sandra Day O'Connor.* New York: P. Lang.

Bowers v. Hardwick

478 U.S. 186 (1986)

This case dealt with a Georgia law penalizing sodomy, whether heterosexual or homosexual. The police investigation that eventually resulted in this case began with a citation written for an open container. The day after the fine was paid, an officer entered the home of Michael Hardwick and found him and a male companion engaged in sodomy when the door to his bedroom was open. Hardwick was then arrested for sodomy, but formal charges were never presented to a grand jury. Hardwick, however, decided to use this as a test case and attempt to have the state's sodomy law invalidated. The case eventually went all the way to the Supreme Court, which supported the law. Ultimately, however, and over a decade later, the court overturned the decision made in *Bowers* with *Lawrence and Garner* v. *Texas,* which supported the right to privacy of the individual and struck down laws against consensual sodomy.

Justice White delivered the opinion of the Court. He first reviewed the history of the case, noting that the Court was not going to create a "fundamental right to engage in homosexual sodomy" (478 U.S. 186: 192). He noted the "ancient roots" of Georgia's antisodomy laws and stated that the Court should not create new rights. White also noted that while the home creates additional rights, it does not prevent all conduct in the home from being criminalized, which meant the state could still criminalize sodomy. He concluded by stating that the law had a rational basis in morality and that morality was enough to sustain this statute.

Burger concurred "separately to underscore my view that in constitutional terms there is no such thing as a fundamental right to commit homosexual sodomy" (478 U.S. 186: 196). He went further, noting that "condemnation of those practices is firmly rooted in Judeo-Christian moral and ethical standards" (478 U.S. 186: 196). This perspective, in particular, incurred opposition from gay rights groups who held the view was prejudicial.

Powell concurred, holding that no fundamental right was violated, but noting that the twenty-year jail sentence associated with the law (Hardwick had not been so sentenced) seemed harsh and might, in his view, violate the Eighth Amendment, which prohibited cruel and unusual punishment. However, since the defendant was not even charged here, much less sentenced to twenty years, that issue could not be raised, meaning Powell voted to uphold the statute.

One dissent was filed by Justice Blackmun, and it was joined by Justices Brennan, Marshall, and Stevens. They first noted that this case was really about "the right to be let alone" (478 U.S. 186: 199). They argued that a tradition of condemnation did not justify its continued practice. They also commented that the statute at hand prohibited all sodomy, not just the homosexual sodomy focused on by the majority. The dissenters stated that there should be a right to privacy in the area of sexual intimacy, and that the majority ignored this for those who were not in typical families. The fact that it occurred in private homes also made the decision noxious to the dissent.

Justice Stevens also dissented and was joined by Justices Brennan and Marshall. They first noted that the law, as written, invaded heterosexual married people's bedrooms and that past cases could not be reconciled with this, meaning the law should have been struck down as written. They then considered the law if it was only applied to homosexuals. They argued that homosexuals should have the same liberty in private as heterosexuals and that there was no neutral and legitimate interest to justify the selective prosecution.

Even though the Georgia sodomy law was upheld here, the days of sodomy laws were numbered. In 2003, or seventeen years after *Bowers,* the Supreme Court heard *Lawrence and Garner* v. *Texas,* which dealt with a Texas law that criminalized only homosexual sodomy. The 2003 Supreme Court struck down the law as an invasion of privacy and specifically overruled *Bowers* v. *Hardwick.* The Supreme Court, however, was also careful to say that this ruling applied only to sodomy and did not go as far as creating a right for gays and lesbians to marry. Thus, even though sodomy laws are outlawed, the debate over gay and lesbian rights continues.

See also *Baehr* v. *Lewin; Employment Division* v. *Smith;* Gay marriage; *Lawrence and Garner* v. *Texas; Reynolds* v. *United States; Roe* v. *Wade*

For further reading

Cohen, Jean L. 2002. *Regulating Intimacy: A New Legal Paradigm.* Princeton, NJ: Princeton University Press.

Glenn, Richard A. 2003. *The Right to Privacy: Rights and Liberties under the Law.* Santa Barbara, CA: ABC-CLIO.

Irons, Peter H. 1990. *The Courage of their Convictions: Sixteen Americans Who Fought Their Way to the Supreme Court.* New York: Penguin.

Signorile, Michelangelo. 2003. *Queer in America: Sex, the Media, and the Closets of Power.* Madison: University of Wisconsin Press.

Boy Scouts of America v. *Dale*

530 U.S. 640 (2000)

This case examined whether the Boy Scouts of America can exclude leaders because they are gay. The criteria used by the Boy Scouts to exclude gay leaders had religious origins, but the Supreme Court still held that the Boy Scouts could exclude gays, as the right to association here was held to be more important than New Jersey's law banning discrimination against homosexuals.

The Boy Scouts have long been in America; they support a code of values, among which are being "morally straight" and "clean."

Demonstrators outside the National Council Conference for the Boy Scouts of America (BSA) protest the BSA's intolerance of homosexuality among its members in Philadelphia, Pennsylvania, on May 29, 2003. In the case Boy Scouts of America *v.* Dale *(2000), the U.S. Supreme Court ruled that, as a private organization, the BSA has the constitutional right to exclude homosexuals. (AP/Wide World Photos)*

They argued that admitting a homosexual leader would violate those values. In New Jersey, where the suit originated, laws existed requiring groups that use places of public accommodation not to discriminate on the basis of sexuality, and the assistant scoutmaster who was excluded sued under these laws.

In a 5–4 decision the Supreme Court upheld the right of the Boy Scouts to exclude.

Rehnquist, writing the opinion, discussed some of the past cases dealing with private groups. The Supreme Court had recognized a right to "expressive association," in which a group has the right to pick its own members when engaged in the public expression of ideas. The reasoning is that if the government mandates who must be admitted to a group, then the group may lose its opportunity to express its ideas, which may be minority views. Thus, if the majority could force itself in, the group would cease to have a purpose. This right is not absolute, as the government can force admission if it has a compelling state interest.

Rehnquist first turned to see if the Boy Scouts were engaged in expressive association. He looked at the Scouts, noting that they aimed to inculcate values in boys, thus finding that they participated in expressive activity. He then examined the lower court's assertion that the Boy Scouts' had a cap commitment to accept all young men, stating that it was not the Court's goal to decide whether a group was contradicting its own principles. He did examine the history of the Boy Scouts' views on homosexuality to determine whether the Scouts had been consistent, so as to examine the sincerity of the belief, and he found out that they had been. The Scouts as a whole took a position on homosexual leaders, and this view was allowed under the First Amendment's right to expressive association. He then turned and weighed the Scouts' right to expressive association versus the governmental interest articulated in the public accommodations statute. In the past, women had been ordered admitted to certain associations, such as the Jaycees, but the Court held in those cases that the group's right to expressive association had not been affected. On the whole, in this case, the Court held that "the state interests embodied in New Jersey's public accommodations law do not justify such a severe intrusion on the Boy Scouts' rights to freedom of expressive association" (530 U.S. 640: 659). Rehnquist then responded to the dissent's argument that homosexuality was

gaining acceptance, holding that the popularity of an idea does not allow the government to mandate that a group accept it.

The dissent written by Justice Stevens argued that the Boy Scouts' right to expressive association was not being restricted by New Jersey's law. He first examined the teachings of the Boy Scouts, stating that nowhere did they say that homosexuality was wrong; instead, for the most part, they avoided the issue of sex, telling leaders to have others counsel Scouts on the issue. He further stated that the principles of morally straight and clean were not connected to a view of homosexuality as immoral. The dissent also noted, in an issue ignored by the majority, that the Boy Scouts do not espouse a particular religious view and so do not put themselves in the religious camp of those who view homosexuality as immoral. The dissent further stated that there was a Boy Scout policy of not accepting homosexuals, but that it was a quiet policy, only circulated among the top leaders. It also argued that the Boy Scouts, before this case, had never connected the morally straight and clean teachings to a ban on homosexuals in their leadership. The dissent agreed with the majority that the test should be whether a significant burden would be created with exclusion, but as the policy of the Boy Scouts had never been publicly announced or linked to its values, the dissent felt that no such burden would be created. The dissent also noted that the Boy Scouts could ban Dale from addressing homosexuality, were he a member, and still be within the New Jersey law and their own right of expressive association. Stevens argued against homophobia, pointing out the ancient roots of it, and noted the religious basis for the hatred, stating that the time had come to reject such attitudes and expressing his desire for the Supreme Court to do so.

Justice Souter also dissented. He argued that the Boy Scouts had not taken a strong stand on homosexuality and thus could not use that standard to exclude gays from membership. These arguments did not carry the day, however. Rehnquist was able to carry a bare majority of the Court, and the Boy Scouts were permitted to exclude homosexuals. The Supreme Court has not heard another case on this issue since 2000, and thus troops are still allowed to exclude homosexual leaders. The policy has religious roots, as much homophobia is rooted in religious precepts, but the Scouts never used religion as a justification.

See also *Baehr* v. *Lewin; Good News/Good Sports Club* v. *School District of the City of Ladue; Maguire* v. *Marquette University*

For further reading

Macleod, David I. 1983. *Building Character in the American Boy: The Boy Scouts, YMCA, and Their Forerunners, 1870–1920.* Madison: University of Wisconsin Press.

Mechling, Jay. 2001. *On My Honor: Boy Scouts and the Making of American Youth.* Chicago: University of Chicago Press.

Rosenthal, Michael. 1986. *The Character Factory: Baden-Powell and the Origins of the Boy Scout Movement.* New York: Pantheon Books.

Louis Brandeis, the first Jewish member of the Supreme Court, became famous for his dissenting opinions in support of liberal causes. (Library of Congress)

Brandeis nomination and service on the Supreme Court

Louis D. Brandeis (1856–1941) grew up in Louisville, Kentucky, and was educated at Harvard Law School, graduating at the age of twenty and earning the highest average in school history. After law school he moved to Boston where he received recognition as a leading Progressive lawyer through his work in helping groups he thought would benefit society. He developed, with the help of others, the "Brandeis brief," which used sociological and medical evidence to help document industrial conditions to justify regulations that had been passed. This brief had its first success in *Muller* v. *Oregon* (1907) in which the Supreme Court upheld an Oregon law limiting women to ten working hours per day. Brandeis also opposed the efforts of J. P. Morgan to monopolize the rail lines around Boston.

Besides being a Progressive, Brandeis was also a leading Zionist, and he argued for the establishment of a Jewish homeland. He was visibly active in the worldwide Zionist movement to promote Palestine as a Jewish homeland, chairing the Provisional Committee for General Zionist Affairs. Once he became a Supreme Court justice in 1916, he worked mostly behind the scenes of the group.

Religious hostility greatly marked Brandeis's nomination and his service on the Supreme Court. His nomination by Woodrow Wilson touched off a firestorm of controversy. People opposed Brandeis for two reasons, first because he was a Progressive and second because he was a Jew. William Howard Taft, along with other past presidents of the American Bar Association, claimed that Brandeis was unfit to be a Supreme Court justice, a view based mostly in anti-Semitism.

While on the Court, Brandeis was not always treated with respect by his colleagues. At one time, Chief Justice Taft attempted to organize a group dinner for all the members of the Court. This ran into personal prejudices, however, as Justice McReynolds remarked, "I do not expect to attend, as I find it hard to dine with the Orient [by which he was referring to Brandeis]" (Polenberg, 1987: 205). McReynolds also would leave the room when Brandeis spoke in conference. McReynolds's final insult to Brandeis was his refusal to sign the farewell letter upon Brandeis's resignation from the Court. McReynolds later extended the same general treatment to Felix Frankfurter, the Court's next Jewish member.

See also Felix Frankfurter; Jewish Seat on the Supreme Court

For further reading
Baker, Leonard. 1984. *Brandeis and Frankfurter: A Dual Biography.* New York: Harper & Row.
Burt, Robert. 1988. *Two Jewish Justices: Outcasts in the Promised Land.* Berkeley: University of California Press.
Dawson, Nelson L., ed. 1989. *Brandeis and America.* Lexington: University Press of Kentucky.

Braunfeld v. *Brown*

366 U.S. 599 (1961)

Braunfeld dealt with a Sunday closing law. Many states had passed laws that forbade working on Sundays, and the original basis of these laws was in the Bible. The Ten Commandments required observance of the "Sabbath," which most Christians took to be Sunday, and Sunday closing laws came from this. Along with laws that forced most things to be closed on Sundays were laws that prohibited alcohol sales or Bingo games.

This law had been passed relatively recently (at least in its last formulation) and it required businesses selling clothing, among other businesses, to close on Sunday. Those suing were Orthodox Jews, who, by their religion, were obliged to close from Friday night to Saturday night, and thus, between their religion and the law, were forced to take two days off. The plurality opinion was written by Chief Justice

Warren and was joined by Justices Clark, Black, and Whitaker.

The Court first looked at the history of Sunday closing laws, noting that they were at first religious, but now seem more aimed at making Sunday a day of rest to improve the "health, safety, morals and general well-being of our citizens" (366 U.S. 599: 603). It also noted that even after the passage of the Virginia (which is where the law was) Declaration of Rights, Sunday closing laws were still kept. The Court then carefully differentiated between belief and practice. It stated that a state cannot ban a religious belief, but that religious practices could be restricted. However, here, in the opinion of the plurality, religious practices of the defendants were not prohibited but simply made their religion more expensive. Also, only those who want to work on Sunday were hurt, said the Court. The Court held thus that this law was acceptable. However, it did not say the same applied for all such laws: "if the purpose or effect of a law is to impede the observance of one or all religions or is to discriminate invidiously between religions, that law is constitutionally invalid even though the burden may be characterized as being only indirect. But if the State regulates conduct by enacting a general law within its power, the purpose and effect of which is to advance the State's secular goals, the statute is valid despite its indirect burden on religious observance unless the State may accomplish its purpose by means which do not impose such a burden" (366 U.S. 599: 607). Those suing had suggested that the state should be required to allow them an exemption from the law, but the Court held that even though an exemption was constitutionally allowable, and done in other states, it was not required.

Justices Brennan and Stewart dissented. Brennan agreed with Warren that parts of the case had no merit, but Brennan, unlike Warren, did find merit in the religion claim. Brennan held that the state was forcing the Orthodox Jew to choose "between his business and his religion" (366 U.S. 599: 611). Brennan also suggested that there needed to be a "compelling state interest" before the freedom of religion could be restricted and that the state had no such interest here, but only the interest of "the mere convenience of having everyone rest on the same day" (366 U.S. 599: 614). The justice argued that this in no way justified a restriction of the freedom of religion. Justice Stewart filed a short statement agreeing with Brennan.

Justices Harlan and Frankfurter filed an opinion in *McGowan v. Maryland,* decided the same day, which also covered this case. Frankfurter first reviewed the history behind the First Amendment, suggesting that the ban on a government establishing a church embodied in that amendment was due largely to the dislike many had for the established church of that day and the taxes that were paid to support it. Frankfurter made a very sweeping statement in his opinion: "The Establishment Clause withdrew from the sphere of legitimate legislative concern and competence a specific, but comprehensive, area of human conduct: man's belief or disbelief in the verity of some transcendental idea and man's expression in action of that belief or disbelief. Congress may not make these matters, as such, the subject of legislation, nor, now, may any legislature in this country" (366 U.S. 420: 465–466). Frankfurter held that those suing against the Sunday laws could prevail only if the Sunday laws did not have a secular purpose. He then examined the laws, granting that many started with a religious purpose but have come to have a secular purpose. He also held that even though many of the statutes refer to the day taken off as "the Lord's day," this did not make the statute religious. Frankfurter also noted that many of the statutes had been recently reconsidered and so the question was not one that old attitudes still prevailed on. He also noted that even though the laws were complex, this did not make them irrational, which would have voided them under the due process clause of the Fourteenth Amendment. Thus, Frankfurter in general gave wide latitude to the legislature and seemed to need almost a prayer in the current statute to acknowledge the religious elements. Frankfurter, though, would have remanded this case to allow the Orthodox Jews a chance to argue it (the case came to the Supreme Court as an appeal of a dismissed case). Justice Harlan mostly agreed with Frankfurter but concurred in the dismissal of this case.

Justice Douglas dissented, arguing that the First Amendment deserved a much more protective treatment than that given by Frankfurter and Warren. Douglas stated that "the First Amendment commands government to have no interest in theology or ritual" (366 U.S. 420: 564). Douglas rebukes Frankfurter by noting that even though modern regulations phrased the questions in terms of what helped society, "no matter how much is written, no matter what is said, the parentage of these laws is the Fourth Commandment; and they serve and satisfy the religious predispositions of our Christian communities" (366 U.S. 420: 572–573). Douglas suggested that only criminal activities could be banned in the area of religion. "There is in this realm no room for balancing. I see no place for it in the constitutional scheme. A legislature of Christians can no more make minorities conform to their weekly regime than a legislature of Moslems, or a legislature of Hindus. The religious regime of every group must be respected—unless it crosses the line of criminal conduct" (366 U.S. 420: 575). While the state could require a day of rest in seven, it could not pick the one, in Douglas's view.

The Court as a whole allowed Sunday closing laws, holding that the secular purpose outweighed the disproportionate impact on people of certain religions, and that laws that had originated in a religious forum could, over time, become secular. However, laws originating in religion and having a religious purpose still today were not allowed. Thus, "blue laws," as these laws are sometimes known, are still allowed, and religion is still allowed to have an impact on our work schedule, even while fewer and fewer businesses are wholly closed on Sunday.

See also *Estate of Thornton* v. *Caldor; McGowan* v. *Maryland; Metzl* v. *Leininger;* Influence of religion on Eighteenth Amendment; *Loving* v. *United States; Sherbert* v. *Verner; Swaggart Ministries* v. *California Board of Equalization*

For further reading

Goldman, Roger L. *Justice William J. Brennan, Jr.: Freedom First.* New York: Carroll and Graf.

Johnson, Alvin Walter, and Frank H. Yost. 1969. *Separation of Church and State in the United States.* New York: Greenwood Press.

Laband, David N., and Deborah Hendry Heinbuch. 1987. *Blue Laws: The History, Economics, and Politics of Sunday-Closing Laws.* Lexington, MA: Lexington Books.

Lewis, Abram Herbert. 1997. *A Critical History of Sunday Legislation from 321 to 1888 A.D.* Buffalo, NY: Hein.

Schwartz, Bernard. 1983. *Super Chief, Earl Warren and His Supreme Court: A Judicial Biography.* New York: New York University Press.

Urofsky, Melvin I. *Felix Frankfurter: Judicial Restraint and Individual Liberties.* Boston: Twayne.

Wasby, Stephen L., ed. 1990. *"He Shall Not Pass This Way Again": The Legacy of Justice William O. Douglas.* Pittsburgh: University of Pittsburgh Press for the William O. Douglas Institute.

Bronx Household of Faith v. Community School District No. 10
127 F.3d 207 (2d Cir. 1997)

Bronx Household of Faith dealt with whether a public building could prevent its use by a church. Many schools do not want their buildings used by others for a variety of reasons, and when religious organizations want to use the facilities, the issue of promoting religion also comes into play. School boards, for obvious constitutional reasons, do not want to promote religion and so many deny use. Religious organizations, however, have a need for facilities and so often complain against these restrictions. It was this sort of conflict that brought about this case in the Second Circuit Court of Appeals.

The facts of the case were that the church wanted to use the school auditorium for services, and the school refused and so the church sued. A summary judgment had been issued in favor of the school, and the church appealed. The decision was upheld on appeal. Circuit Judge Miner wrote the opinion. The school district had set up a policy to determine what the building could be used for, and the policy specifically stated that "no outside organization or group may be allowed to conduct religious services or religious instruction on school premises after school" (127 F.3d 207: 210). However, the school district did allow some religious activities, as that same policy held that "the use of school premises by outside organizations or groups after school for the purposes of discussing religious material or material which contains a religious viewpoint or for distributing such material is permissible" (127 F.3d 207: 210). The school had been used for a variety of purposes by several different groups over the years and the Bronx Household of Faith had even used it for various things, including a banquet. However, requests for a service were denied.

The opinion then examines the objections of the church to the school board's ruling. The first claim considered is that of freedom of speech, and the court ruled first on the type of forum that the school had created, in whether it was a limited or open public forum. The opinion first held that this was a limited public forum, differentiating it from *Lamb's Chapel* as that decision dealt with a film series while this case was clearly a religious service. The court also stated that as the school had consistently maintained a limited public forum, the church's citation of cases dealing with open public forums was irrelevant. The court held that these regulations were reasonable and were viewpoint neutral, as the school had always maintained a ban on religious services. The court also examined the case and determined that the school board's regulation did not interfere with the free exercise of the church's religion, as the school board was simply saying that the church needed to find somewhere else to practice its religion.

Judge Cabranes agreed with the majority in part and dissented in part. He agreed that the school was a limited public forum and agreed that the ban on religious services was allowable as it was reasonable and viewpoint neutral. However, he disagreed with the ban on religious instruction, as he found it to be not viewpoint neutral. Cabranes read the *Lamb's Chapel* case differently from the majority. He read it to mean that one could not discriminate on viewpoint, and that banning religion while allowing secular instruction did just that, stating that "the District's policy banning religious instruction, while at the same time allowing instruction on any subject of learning from a secular viewpoint, is an impermissible form of viewpoint discrimination" (127 F.3d 207: 220). Thus, even though bothered by the ban on religious services, Cabranes would go along with the majority's ban on such services, even while desiring to reverse their ruling upholding the ban on religious instruction; he saw this ban on instruction as discriminating on the basis of viewpoint, which was not allowable in a limited public forum. Thus, Cabranes would allow a ban on services even while striking down a ban on religious instruction. One can ban a subject, but once allowing a subject, one cannot discriminate on the basis of viewpoint.

A school board can ban religious services from its facilities as long as that ban extends to all religious services. The dissent suggested that a ban on religious instruction might not be constitutional, but that did not carry the day. One cannot ban all religious items, though, unless one bans all outside groups, and this case continues the view announced by the Supreme Court in *Lamb's Chapel* in that one cannot ban religious groups from using the facilities for uses other than instruction and services if it allows other groups to use the facilities for such purposes. Religious groups are therefore allowed equal opportunity with secular groups to use the facilities.

See also *Employment Division* v. *Smith; Good News Club* v. *Milford Central School; Lamb's Chapel* v. *Center Moriches School District; Rosenberger* v. *Rector and Visitors of the University of Virginia; Tipton* v. *University of Hawaii*

For further reading

Fraser, James W. 1999. *Between Church and State: Religion and Public Education in a Multicultural America.* New York: St. Martin's Press.

Haynes, Charles C., et al. 2003. *The First Amendment in Schools: A Guide from the First Amendment Center.* Alexandria, VA: Association for Supervision and Curriculum Development.

Jurinski, James. 1998. *Religion in the Schools: A Reference Handbook.* Santa Barbara, CA: ABC-CLIO.

C

Cantwell v. Connecticut

310 U.S. 296 (1940)

This case dealt with a group of Jehovah's Witnesses, a father and two sons, who went around New Haven, Connecticut, visiting homes. They asked, upon knocking at a door, if they could play a record, and played the record if allowed to. They also offered for sale books and pamphlets, and, if the attempt to sell was unsuccessful, respectfully asked for donations. If asked to leave, they did so. They were convicted of a breach of the peace and the father was also convicted of failing to have a license to solicit. The case came before the Supreme Court in 1940. It was one of the first times that the Court had had to deal with the issue of freedom of religion after *Gitlow* v. *New York*. *Gitlow* is significant here, as it extended the protection of parts of the First Amendment against the states, in addition to the federal government, and it was the first case to do this.

Justice Roberts wrote the Court's opinion in *Cantwell*. He surveyed the facts of the case, and then quickly held "that the statute, as construed and applied to the appellants, deprives them of their liberty without due process of law in contravention of the Fourteenth Amendment" (310 U.S. 296: 303). He surveyed how the Fourteenth Amendment applied the First against the states, noting that the freedom of religion "embraces two concepts—freedom to believe and freedom to act" and that "the first is absolute but, in the nature of things, the second cannot be" (310 U.S. 296: 303–304). Roberts then held that legislation may restrict the time, place, and manner of solicitation, but that the regulation here did not do that. The Supreme Court granted that a regulation similar to the one here where registration was required might be permissible, but this regulation worked through a state official who had the power to grant or deny the license to solicit. This was found to be unacceptable, as the Court held that "such a censorship of religion as the means of determining its right to survive is a denial of liberty protected by the First Amendment and included in the liberty which is within the protection of the Fourteenth" (310 U.S. 296: 305). The court reviewed the safeguards in place and concluded that "to condition the solicitation of aid for the perpetuation of religious views or systems upon a license, the grant of which rests in the exercise of a determination by state authority as to what is a religious cause, is to lay a forbidden burden upon the exercise of liberty protected by the Constitution" (310 U.S. 296: 307). Thus, the requirement of a license that could be granted or denied by a state official was struck down as an infringement of the First Amendment.

The Court went on to examine the issue of the conviction for "breach of the peace." The Court noted the calm and nonoffensive demeanor of Jesse Cantwell, who played a record for two men and then left after the two men were offended and asked him to leave. Roberts stated, "We find in the instant case no assault or threatening of bodily harm, no truculent bearing, no intentional discourtesy, no personal abuse. On the contrary, we find only an effort to persuade a willing listener to buy a book or to contribute money in the interest of what Cantwell, however misguided others may think him, conceived to be true religion" (310 U.S. 296: 310). The Court thought Cantwell's solicitation was, under the circumstances, acceptable, as it was also deemed an exercise of his freedom of religion. The Court found, about religion in general, that "in the realm of religious faith, and in that of political belief, sharp differences arise. In both fields the tenets of one man may seem the rankest error to his neighbor. To persuade others to his own point of view, the pleader, as we know, at times, resorts to exaggeration, to vilification of men who have been, or are, prominent in church or state, and even to false statement. But the people of this nation have ordained in the light of history, that, in spite of the probability of excesses and abuses, these liberties are, in the long view, essential to enlightened opinion and right conduct on the part of the citizens of a democracy" (310 U.S. 296: 310).

Thus, the convictions for breach of the peace and for soliciting without a license were overturned. This case established two different principles that have largely lasted until today. First, time, place, and manner restrictions can be placed upon those who go door to door or solicit, but these regulations must be applied generally and cannot single out those who are going door to door for religion. Second, while the probable effect of a communication upon the receiver is allowed to be considered, a common law offense (i.e., one that is based upon custom and not upon a specific statute) is not going to be generally upheld if the person starting the communication is peaceful. Laws, not surprisingly, that do aim to create codified versions of things similar to "breach of the peace" have generally been carefully scrutinized to make sure that they were not targeted against religion. A heckler's veto, where those opposed to speech are allowed to force it to end, has generally not been upheld, and here, where the heckler's veto was attempted to be turned into a heckler's indictment, was, not surprisingly, not upheld either. One may not like door-to-door religious solicitation, but the Supreme Court here says that one person's annoyance is another's liberty and the First Amendment sides with the liberty, particularly when the religious observant is faithfully polite about it.

See also Chapman v. Thomas; Church of the Lukumi Babalu Aye v. City of Hialeah; Employment Divi-

sion v. Smith; Heffron v. International Society for Krishna Consciousness, Inc.; International Society for Krishna Consciousness v. Lee; Saluting the flag

For further reading

Newton, Merlin Owen. 1995. *Armed with the Constitution: Jehovah's Witnesses in Alabama and the U.S. Supreme Court, 1939–1946*. Tuscaloosa: University of Alabama Press.

Noonan, John Thomas. 1998. *The Lustre of Our Country: The American Experience of Religious Freedom*. Berkeley: University of California Press.

Peters, Shawn Francis. 2000. *Judging Jehovah's Witnesses: Religious Persecution and the Dawn of the Rights Revolution*. Lawrence: University Press of Kansas.

Urofsky, Melvin I. 2002. *Religious Freedom: Rights and Liberties under the Law*. Santa Barbara, CA: ABC-CLIO.

Capital punishment and religious-based opposition to it

Many religions are opposed to the death penalty, others allow their individual members to choose a position on this issue, and still others clearly permit capital punishment. Hindu worshipers can choose how to follow the right path, and there is a plurality of opinion about capital punishment in the religion. However, by and large, its use is discouraged, as criminals are supposed to have the chance to fix the problems they have created with the social order. Buddhism focuses on behaving correctly to achieve enlightenment, and its followers are forbidden from taking life. Islamic law allows for the death penalty, but ideas of capital punishment vary from one Islamic country to another, and the focus of laws is generally on keeping a society functioning. Similarly, Judaism and Christianity allow for a plurality of belief about the death penalty among their followers.

One Christian religion clearly identified with opposition to capital punishment in recent years is the Catholic Church. The Catholic Church has not always opposed the

Sister Helen Prejean, an anti–death penalty activist, outside the Texas capitol in Austin in January 1998. She wrote the popular novel Dead Man Walking *(1994), about her experiences as the spiritual advisor to death row inmate Patrick Sonnier in 1982. The cross she wears was a gift from a condemned prisoner who was later executed. (Andrew Lichtenstein/Corbis Sygma)*

death penalty, but moved, since the 1950s, and really since the 1970s, into opposition. Christian Brugger argues that the death penalty, in current Catholic doctrine, is only acceptable "if and only if the need to defend people's lives and safety against the attacks of an unjust aggressor can be met by *no other means*" (Brugger, 2003: 20, emphasis in original). The official pronouncements of the Catholic Church support this view. Catholic catechisms only allow killing in self-defense and hold that "any killing that results (and any harm, for that matter) must not be willed for its own sake or as a means to some future end, but rather must be accepted as a side effect, perhaps foreseen, of an act of force intended to render an aggressor incapable of causing harm" (Brugger, 2003: 3). Rehabilitation, even for those who have com-

mitted crimes that might bring the death penalty, is still an important goal for criminal justice in the eyes of the Catholic Church. The 1997 catechism directly stated that the death penalty is not an exception to the commandment not to kill.

Several of the best-known opponents of the death penalty are Catholic figures. These include Sister Helen Prejean, who wrote *Dead Man Walking,* later made into a movie. She noted that "the paths of history are stained with the blood of those who have fallen victim to 'God's Avengers.' Kings and Popes and military generals and heads of state have killed, claiming God's authority and God's blessing. I do not believe in such a God" (Prejean, 1994: 21).

In addition, Quakers also oppose the death penalty, and some as early as the eighteenth century, argued for abolition. Pennsylvania, under their influence, eliminated the death penalty for a time except for the crime of murder. While those Quakers and Catholics who opposed the death penalty have not been wholly successful, they have managed to help the effort to abolish it in some states and to create a religious answer to those who justify the death penalty with biblical invocations that seem to call for equal retribution. It should be noted that there is also a vigorous debate over whether the biblical passages really justify the death penalty and whether, for Christians, Jesus' teachings in the New Testament arguing for forgiveness trump the Old Testament readings and thus forbid the death penalty.

See also Influence of religion on Eighteenth Amendment; Witchcraft and the law—past and present

For further reading

Banner, Stuart. 2002. *The Death Penalty: An American History.* Cambridge, MA: Harvard University Press.

Brugger, E. Christian. 2003. *Capital Punishment and Roman Catholic Moral Tradition.* Notre Dame, IN: University of Notre Dame Press.

Prejean, Helen. 1994. *Dead Man Walking: An Eyewitness Account of the Death Penalty in the United States.* New York: Vintage Books.

Prejean, Helen. 2005. *The Death of Innocents: An Eyewitness Account of Wrongful Executions.* New York: Random House.

Capitol Square Review and Advisory Board v. *Pinette*

515 U.S. 753 (1995)

The First Amendment guarantees freedom of religion, and religious symbols are not supposed to be, generally, regulated by the government. However, when religious symbols are used by a group for either a nonreligious purpose, or at best a purpose with both religious and nonreligious elements, the question arises as to whether a government can regulate that use. Also, if a group wants to use a public area to erect a religious symbol, can they be pre-

vented on the grounds that the government is not supposed to support religion? The group was, in this case, the Ku Klux Klan (KKK), who wanted to set up a cross in the public square. The government denied this use on the grounds that it did not want to violate the establishment clause, claiming that if it allowed a cross it would be establishing religion; but the KKK claimed the denial was because of hatred of the Klan's ideas.

The Supreme Court looked only at the establishment issue, with most of the opinion written by Justice Scalia. The Court first held that this was private expression, saying "respondents' religious display in Capitol Square was private expression. Our precedent establishes that private religious speech, far from being a First Amendment orphan, is as fully protected under the Free Speech Clause as secular private expression" (515 U.S. 753: 760). The Court stated that since "the State did not sponsor respondents' expression, the expression was made on government property that had been opened to the public for speech, and permission was requested through the same application process and on the same terms required of other private groups" (515 U.S. 753: 763), then the state should treat their petition the same as the other private groups. There ended Scalia's portion of the opinion that held for the entire Court.

Speaking for four justices, Scalia further wrote that the government's claim that some might misinterpret the Klan's cross, since it was in a square very close to the seat of government, as endorsed by the government, was fallacious. He argued that as the square was traditionally open, all those familiar with it should know that the government does not control it in terms of content and that the opinions of those unfamiliar with this policy did not matter. Scalia further suggested that Ohio could require each display to be identified with its sponsor, and thus people would know that the Klan had erected the cross, but the government could not ban its display. The overall opinion of the Court held that the restriction was unconstitutional as it misused the establishment clause.

Justice Thomas filed a concurrence, noting that the establishment clause could not be used to deny the petition, but that the Klan used the cross as a political symbol, not a religious one, and thus the establishment clause should not have been at issue at all.

Justice O'Connor wrote a concurrence, which was joined by Justices Souter and Breyer, and she agreed that the petition asking for the right to put up the cross had been wrongly denied but did not give as much leeway to the side of those wanting to use the traditional public forum as Scalia had done. O'Connor held that "the endorsement test necessarily focuses upon the perception of a reasonable, informed observer" (515 U.S. 753: 773). For that informed observer, the establishment clause should step in sometimes, O'Connor argued, even when the state was acting only by allowing a private group to speak. "When the reasonable observer would view a government practice as endorsing religion, I believe that it is our duty to hold the practice invalid" (515 U.S. 753: 777). O'Connor went on to argue that "where the government's operation of a public forum has the effect of endorsing religion, even if the governmental actor neither intends nor actively encourages that result, . . . the Establishment Clause is violated. This is so . . . because the State's own actions (operating the forum in a particular manner and permitting the religious expression to take place therein), and their relationship to the private speech at issue, actually convey a message of endorsement" (515 U.S. 753: 777). By using the "reasonable observer" standard, O'Connor would still allow the display as that observer would know that historically many different groups have used the area.

Justice Souter concurred separately, noting that a reasonable observer could have held that endorsement occurred and that the plurality gave too much power to the state, which it could use to endorse religion. He voted with the judgment, however, as he felt that the board did not use its "most narrowly drawn" option to prevent this observer from wrongfully receiving the impression of a government endorsement of religion.

Justice Stevens dissented, holding that this unattended symbol was a religious symbol and needed to be considered as such. Stevens suggested that the standard used should be the image understood by a "reasonable observer," and he argued that such an observer would, with a cross right next to the seat of Ohio's government, view it as an endorsement. Stevens made much of the fact that the display was unattended and thus allowed observers to put their own understanding on the display. Stevens then suggested that the Court should have held that the "Constitution generally forbids the placement of a symbol of a religious character in, on, or before a seat of government" (515 U.S. 753: 806–807). In the end, Stevens noted that "the Court's decision today is unprecedented. It entangles two sovereigns in the propagation of religion, and it disserves the principle of tolerance that underlies the prohibition against state action 'respecting an establishment of religion'" (515 U.S. 753: 815).

Justice Ginsberg wrote a short dissent, noting that the state had not required a disclaimer on the cross, and thus the decision must be made with the cross having no identifying marks, and thus should not be allowed.

Discrimination against speech is not allowed by government just because the government disagrees with the viewpoint expressed in the speech, and that is one complicating factor here. The government of Ohio may have disliked the Klan and wished to ban their cross, and also may have been worried about establishment issues, as the cross was to be constructed near the seat of government. Neither reason for the ban was upheld by the Supreme Court, though, as the first reason was not considered and the ban was far too wide to be justified by fears of observers believing that Ohio was creating an establishment of religion. Some of the Court, however, allowed that Ohio could have regulated the cross by requiring a disclaimer, but the Court's opinion was silent on this issue, as four justices thought that the mere presence of a traditionally open forum in the square removed the need for a disclaimer. Thus, Ohio's desire to prevent the cross on political grounds, as suspected, would have to continue unabated and concerns about establishment issues would have to wait for another attempt by the Klan to erect a cross. The battle between the Klan, which stands for freedom of religion here, and the state, using concerns over the establishment clause to fight against what it sees as racism, still rages on until the present.

> **See also** *Airport Commissioners* v. *Jews for Jesus;* Celebration of Halloween and singing Christmas carols; *County of Allegheny v. Greater Pittsburgh ACLU; Employment Division* v. *Smith; Lamb's Chapel* v. *Center Moriches School District*

For further reading

Ahdar, Rex J., ed. 2000. *Law and Religion.* Burlington, VT: Ashgate/Dartmouth.

Brisbin, Richard A. 1997. *Justice Antonin Scalia and the Conservative Revival.* Baltimore, MD: Johns Hopkins University Press.

Chalmers, David Mark. 1981. *Hooded Americanism: The History of the Ku Klux Klan.* Durham, NC: Duke University Press.

Wade, Wyn Craig. 1987. *The Fiery Cross: The Ku Klux Klan in America.* New York: Simon and Schuster.

Celebration of Halloween and singing Christmas carols

Even the questions of what holidays can be celebrated in public schools turn on the question of how religion interacts with the law. Celebration of Halloween has generally been allowed, whereas the question of whether Christmas carols can be sung is a more complex one.

One of the leading cases in the area of Halloween is *Guyer* v. *School Board of Alachua County,* which was decided by the court of appeals of Florida in 1994. In that case, a parent

of two students sued the school board, arguing that the Halloween observances created an establishment of religion. In particular the parent was opposed to the "depiction of witches, cauldrons, and brooms included in decorations placed in the public elementary schools in Alachua County, . . . [and to] teachers dressing up as witches in black dresses and pointed hats" (634 So. 2d 806: 806–807). The parent argued that the use of these symbols created an establishment of the Wicca religion. The trial court had granted summary judgment to the school board and the parent appealed. The court of appeals held that under the *Lemon* test, there was a secular purpose to the decorations and costumes, that of having fun, and that the wide variety of costumes, along with the fact that witches and cauldrons were in the context of Halloween, assured that the parties would be viewed secularly. Thus, it ruled no establishment existed and allowed the celebrations.

Christmas carols are a much murkier issue, however. A school can prohibit the singing of Christmas carols in its policy. In New York, a school board had banned the singing of Christmas carols, and the supreme court of New York upheld this ban. Other states, however, have allowed schools to choose to sing Christmas carols. In one district in South Dakota, a Christmas celebration sparked concerns, and so the school district formulated a new policy, which was challenged. The challenge came, eventually, in front of the Eighth Circuit Court of Appeals, who decided the case in 1980 (*Florey* v. *Sioux Falls School District 49–5*). The court noted that the *Lemon* test controlled this case.

The court turned first to the purpose of the new policy, examining both its stated purpose and its actual restrictions. It held that the policy's aim "was simply to ensure that no religious exercise was a part of officially sanctioned school activities" (619 F.2d 1311: 1314). It then turned to the second part of the *Lemon* test, the effect of the policy. The appeals court commented that "the rules guarantee that all material used has secular or cultural significance" (619 F.2d 1311: 1316–1317). From this, and from a general review of the program's effect, the appeals court found that "since all programs and materials authorized by the rules must deal with the secular or cultural basis or heritage of the holidays and since the materials must be presented in a prudent and objective manner and symbols used as a teaching aid, the advancement of a 'secular program of education,' and not of religion, is the primary effect of the rules" (619 F.2d 1311: 1317). In terms of Christmas carols, the court concluded, in a footnote, that it was acceptable, "it being entirely clear to us that carols have achieved a cultural significance that justifies their being sung in the public schools of Sioux Falls, South Dakota, if done in accordance with the policy and rules adopted by that school district" (619 F.2d 1311: 1316).

The court finally turned to the issue of entanglement, holding that the new rules were intended to reduce entanglement and that they had that effect, meaning they passed the third prong of the *Lemon* test as well. On whether school celebrations violate the free exercise of religion, as forcing one to participate in an activity that would violate his or her religion might do, the court noted that the school board rules expressly required students to be allowed to be excused.

One judge did dissent. He argued that, first, there was not a clear secular purpose to the rules. In particular, he held that "to the extent the policy and rules focus only on religious holidays, I would find the policy and rules unconstitutionally operate as a preference of religion" (619 F.2d 1311: 1324). The dissent further argued that the secular purpose of increasing knowledge about holidays might be better served by focusing on holidays less well known, such as Hindu and Muslim holidays rather than the better-known ones, like Christmas, which were also the ones studied. As far as the effect went, the dissent held that "Christmas assemblies have a substantial im-

pact, both in favor of one religion and against other religions and nonbelief, on the school district employees, the students, the parents and relatives of the students and the community" (619 F.2d 1311: 1327). The dissent also found that the policy increased controversy, violating the entanglement clause and that even though excusal was allowed, peer pressure at the school level might prevent those opposing religion from being excused, thus violating the freedom of religion.

The Eighth Circuit found that singing of Christmas carols was allowed, but the whole question is a more closely divided one than that of Halloween. Courts have generally allowed Halloween celebrations, as there was no credible evidence of school boards promoting any religion. However, Christmas celebration and Christmas carol rulings have varied from state to state.

> **See also** *County of Allegheny* v. *Greater Pittsburgh ACLU; Engel* v. *Vitale; Lee* v. *Weisman; Lemon* v. *Kurtzman; Metzl* v. *Leininger*

For further reading

Connelly, Mark. 1999. *Christmas: A Social History.* New York: I. B. Tauris.

Johnston, Aaron Montgomery. 1979. *School Celebrations: Teaching Practices Related to Celebration of Special Events, Grades K–6, in the United States.* Knoxville: Bureau of Educational Research and Service, College of Education, University of Tennessee.

Rogers, Nicholas. 2002. *Halloween: From Pagan Ritual to Party Night.* Oxford: Oxford University Press.

Center for Law and Religious Freedom

The Center for Law and Religious Freedom is one of the leading litigation groups arguing for allowing the government a role in religion. This group describes its mission as an effort to use the court and educational systems to protect the sacredness and liberty of human lives.

The group has filed amicus briefs in many recent cases, including *Elk Grove Unified School*

District v. *Newdow,* where the Center argued on the side of Elk Grove, suggesting that the phrase "under God" did not violate the First Amendment but rather admitted that a Creator was the source of the rights of humanity and supported the idea that the U.S. government had limits. The group considered the Supreme Court's throwing the case out on a technicality as a total victory for the phrase. This is overstating its case a bit, of course, as the Court did not rule on the issue of "under God" being in the pledge directly but instead decided that case on the basis of the issue of standing, as it held that Newdow did not have standing to challenge the pledge. (Three justices in their rulings affirmed that Newdow did have standing and ruled that the pledge should have been upheld.)

The Center has recently worked in a variety of areas in several different ways, including litigation, filing friends of the courts briefs in litigation started by other parties, and working to gain its objective through prelitigation negotiation. One case that the Center has litigated recently is against a Maryland school district: the district refused to distribute flyers from a group wanting to hold after-school meetings (the case is still in the courts and the Center argues that the denial was discriminatory). Another case was filed against Ohio State University (OSU) because the university wanted to "de-recognize" a student religious group because that group did not follow OSU's nondiscrimination policy. (After the lawsuit OSU agreed to continue recognizing the group and not to force them to follow the policy.)

The Center filed an amicus curiae (friend of the court) brief in a case in which the Boy Scouts were denied aid by the Connecticut State Employee Charitable Campaign because they chose not to use homosexuals as leaders. (The Center argued that since the Supreme Court had held this practice of denying leadership roles to homosexuals to be legal, the denial of aid violated the First Amendment.) It also filed a brief in a case in which a Catholic char-

ity had asked the Supreme Court to reconsider a lower court ruling forcing those groups that offered health coverage to cover prescription contraceptives. (The charity argued that the forced coverage violated the First Amendment.) It also filed a brief in *Locke* v. *Davey,* in which Washington State had set up a scholarship program for certain people but refused to fund students who went to a religious school and majored in theology. (The Center argued that the program was not neutral in respect to religion and that the Constitution merely required neutrality, not avoidance of any aid to religion.) In *Locke,* the Supreme Court ruled that while the denial of funding was not required by law, it was allowed.

The Center has also worked to achieve its goals through prelitigation negotiation. One negotiated situation involved a religious group at the University of Virginia. The group was denied funding to attend a conference the university believed would give religious training, and the religious group thought that the denial was religious discrimination. After an appeal, the funding was still denied. In another situation, a church was renting space in the community center and someone protested the use. After a letter from the Center, the group was allowed to continue to rent space.

The Center previously has worked for laws that they see as beneficial, including the Religious Freedom Restoration Act (RFRA, passed in 1993) and the Equal Access Act (EAA, passed in 1984). The RFRA aimed to overturn the *Employment Division* v. *Smith* case and required that the government not overburden the free exercise of religion unless that burden was proven necessary to advance a compelling government interest and was imposed in a manner using the least possible restrictions. The EAA required, as the name suggests, equal access to school facilities by religious non-school groups if nonreligious groups were allowed. It also required the school to give equal access to religious and nonreligious clubs. The RFRA, however, and this is not mentioned directly on the Center's website, was struck down in 1997 by the Supreme Court as it held that Congress, by enacting this requirement, had expanded the First Amendment (or at least the free exercise portion of it) and so had encroached on the rights of the judiciary. The Center has some 4,500 attorneys who are members of the Christian Legal Society and has five attorneys on staff who participate in activities. Thus, this is a relatively small group that enlists many members across the country to advance its goals.

See also Americans United for Separation of Church and State; *Boy Scouts of America* v. *Dale; Elk Grove Unified School District* v. *Newdow; Employment Division* v. *Smith; Locke* v. *Davey;* Religious Freedom Restoration Act of 1993

For further reading

Center for Law and Religious Freedom. http://www.clsnet.org/clrfPages/index.phpx.

Gaustad, Edwin S. 2003. *Proclaim Liberty throughout All the Land: A History of Church and State in America.* New York: Oxford University Press.

Noll, Mark A., ed. 1990. *Religion and American Politics: From the Colonial Period to the 1980s.* New York: Oxford University Press.

Segers, Mary C., and Ted G. Jelen. 1998. *A Wall of Separation?: Debating the Public Role of Religion.* Lanham, MD: Rowman & Littlefield.

Witte, John. 2000. *Religion and the American Constitutional Experiment: Essential Rights and Liberties.* Boulder, CO: Westview Press.

Chapman v. Thomas

743 F.2d 1056 (1984)

This case dealt with a residence hall at a university and whether the university could create a rule forbidding distribution of religious materials. The particulars here were that Chapman was a student at North Carolina State University, a public university, and he felt that the rule was an interference with his First Amendment rights, so he sued. The case went as far as the Fourth Circuit Court of Appeals, which determined that the university could forbid religious solicitation.

The opinion first reviewed the facts of the case and then examined the nature of the venue being considered. The court of appeals quoted a previous case as saying the "character of the property at issue" played a large role in determining what types of rules were allowed (743 F.2d 1056: 1058). In traditional public forums, content-based regulations must be narrowly drawn and serve a compelling state interest, even though content-neutral time, place, and manner restrictions are allowed. If a forum is not a traditional public forum but is opened by the state to the freedom of expression, then the same rules apply. Public property that is not opened for the freedom of expression is considered a nonpublic forum. In those areas, the court quoted an earlier case as saying that the state "may [also] reserve the forum for its intended purposes, communicative or otherwise, as long as the regulation on speech is reasonable and not an effort to suppress expression merely because the public officials oppose the speaker's view" (743 F.2d 1056: 1058).

The court then considered the type of forum the university dorm was, holding that that this had not traditionally been a place for free expression and that regulations had existed on it prior to the lawsuit, making it a nonpublic forum. The court also held the regulations to be reasonable, as the university had the reasonable right to protect students from intrusion, and the university also could create an exception for the most important student government roles, as student government was an important and broadly aimed campuswide student group.

The nature of the forum was the controlling factor here. As campus dormitories have not been places for the freedom of expression, preventing religious solicitation there was quite reasonable, in the eyes of the court. Of course, had it been a building generally aimed at producing student discussion, like the student union, the court might very well have had a different reaction.

See also *Airport Commissioners* v. *Jews for Jesus; Board of Regents of the University of Wisconsin System* v. *Southworth et al.; Rosenberger* v. *Rector*

and Visitors of the University of Virginia; Widmar
v. *Vincent*

For further reading

Bryan, William A., and Richard H. Mullendore. 1992. *Rights, Freedoms, and Responsibilities of Students.* San Francisco: Jossey-Bass.

French, David A. 2002. *FIRE's Guide to Religious Liberty on Campus.* Philadelphia: Foundation for Individual Rights in Education.

Cheema v. Thompson

67 F.3d 883 (9th Cir. 1995)

The freedom to practice one's religion is guaranteed in the First Amendment, but that freedom is not absolute. Most people agree that one time the freedom of religion can be restricted is when it interferes with the rights of another. In this case, one group's interest in practicing their religion interfered with another group's right to safe schools.

This case dealt with schoolchildren who wanted to carry kirpans (sacred knives) that were required by their Sikh religion. In their policy the school district banned the carrying of such weapons, additionally citing two state laws in their defense. The district court denied an injunction allowing the students to carry the weapons and the children appealed. The Ninth Circuit Court of Appeals returned the case to the district court, ordering both sides to prepare a record and to try to negotiate a compromise. The negotiations failed, and the district court, as the appeals court had instructed, imposed a remedy. The case then returned to the appeals court.

The Ninth Circuit Court of Appeals upheld the district court, and Judge Hall wrote the opinion. The main issue on this appeal, legally, was whether the district court had abused its authority, and the appeals court held that it had not. The solution the district court imposed weighed the issues of religious freedom against the issue of safety on the part of the school district, as required under the 1993 Religious Freedom Restoration Act, and tried to work out a compromise. The kirpans were allowed, but they had to be dull, "sewn tightly to its [their] sheath" (67 F.3d 883: 886), worn under the clothing of the student, and district officials were allowed to inspect the student to make sure that these regulations were followed. The district, for its part, had to make sure that the Sikh students were not harassed. The total ban was not allowed as the district had not shown, and never claimed to be able to show, that the ban was the least restrictive alternative available to the district, which still guaranteed the safety of the other students.

One judge dissented, holding that the school district was protecting "a compelling government interest" (which the Religious Freedom Restoration Act required). He stated two such interests, that of the "safety of [all] the students" and that of producing a "peaceful learning environment" (67 F.3d 883: 889, 892). The dissent went into the district court record and noted that one expert for the children admitted, basically, that the kirpans were still dangerous. The judge summarized the expert's findings by saying "his testimony, however, not only convinces that wearing the kirpan is an integral part of the Khalsa Sikh faith, but also that kirpans pose a threat to the safety of the District's classrooms" (67 F.3d 883: 890). The dissenting judge also believed that producing a "peaceful learning environment" was a fundamental interest, even though the majority of the court did not, and that the compromise reached was not the "least restrictive means" (which was required under the Religious Freedom Restoration Act). The judge suggested that riveting the knives into the sheaths would protect the fellow students, even though this was opposed by the children's parents as they believed it would violate their faith. He stated "the least restrictive means of furthering these admittedly compelling interests is to require that any knives in school be short and nonremovable" (67 F.3d 883: 893). In the end, the dissenting justice concluded, "It is axiomatic that we owe our children a safe, and effective, learning environment. The current plan of accommodation, however, does not allow the school district to provide either. I trust that a better decision will be reached at the conclusion of the pending trial. We simply cannot allow young children to carry long, wieldable knives to school. Period" (67 F.3d 883: 894).

Thus, the children who were part of the Sikh faith were allowed to carry their knives into school, and the total ban was not allowed. This was due to the Religious Freedom Restoration Act, which ordered that a compelling government interest be shown before religious freedoms be restricted and that the least restrictive means be used. However, in 1997, the Religious Freedom Restoration Act itself was overturned, and so it is unclear what result would be reached today, even though the interests of the school board would probably be given more weight in the absence of the act.

> **See also** *Boerne* v. *Flores; Church of the Lukumi Babalu Aye* v. *City of Hialeah; Employment Division* v. *Smith; Goldman* v. *Weinberger; Lamb's Chapel* v. *Center Moriches School District; Lyng* v. *Northwest Indian CPA; Reynolds* v. *United States; Sherbert* v. *Verner*

For further reading

Gibson, Margaret A. 1988. *Accommodation without Assimilation: Sikh Immigrants in an American High School.* Ithaca, NY: Cornell University Press.

Mann, Gurinder Singh. 2004. *Sikhism.* Upper Saddle River, NJ: Prentice-Hall.

Mann, Gurinder Singh, Paul David Numrich, and Raymond B. Williams. 2001. *Buddhists, Hindus, and Sikhs in America.* New York: Oxford University Press.

McLeod, W. H. 1999. *Sikhs and Sikhism.* New York: Oxford University Press.

Church of the Holy Trinity *v. United States*

143 U.S. 457 (1892)

This case dealt with U.S. immigration policy. At the time of this policy, there were not nearly the number of controls on immigration that there are today, but immigration still had restrictions. In the restriction being challenged here, non-U.S. citizens were not allowed to be brought to the United States to work under contracts. The Church of the Holy Trinity had brought a preacher into America from England, and the move was held to be illegal. The preacher and the church challenged the move, and the case went all the way to the Supreme Court, which held in their favor.

Justice Brewer wrote the opinion. He first reviewed the legislation and then held that he did not think Congress intended the policy to reach religious figures. The Court examined the title of the legislation, which aimed to prohibit imported labor, and Brewer commented that "obviously the thought expressed in this reaches only to the work of the manual laborer, as distinguished from that of the professional man. No one reading such a title would suppose that Congress had in its mind any purpose of staying the coming into this country of ministers of the gospel, or, indeed, of any class whose toil is that of the brain" (143 U.S. 457: 463). The Court also examined the intent of the program, and Brewer held that "it was this cheap unskilled labor which was making the trouble, and the influx of which Congress sought to prevent. It was never suggested that we had in this country a surplus of brain toilers" (143 U.S. 457: 464). Thus, for several reasons, the Court held that the legislation did not reach the preacher.

However, the Court also held that America could not have intended to oppose religion. Brewer wrote, "But beyond all these matters no purpose of action against religion can be imputed to any legislation, state or national, because this is a religious people" (143 U.S. 457: 465). Brewer cited a long litany of proclamations, grants, and state constitutions, all of which referred to God. He also stated that if a law had been proposed banning the import of religious talent, that law would not have passed, and this meant Congress could not have intended to ban such importation in the legislation challenged here.

Thus, Brewer felt that Congress did not intend to prevent ministers from coming to this country, and the Court overturned the conviction. The First Amendment was not directly addressed here, even though the decision limited the federal government. Brewer looked more at the United States as a religious country, which therefore could not have acted against religion. This opinion is a good snapshot of the public view of religion at this time and something of a view of the legal opinion of religion at the time. The reason for the First Amendment's omission is not clear. The decision is still sometimes cited today for its words on interpretation of a congressional statute, even though immigration policy has changed markedly.

> *See also* American Revolution's effect on religion; *Employment Division* v. *Smith;* Established churches in colonial America
>
> **For further reading**
> Brodhead, Michael J. 1994. *David J. Brewer: The Life of a Supreme Court Justice, 1837–1910.* Carbondale: Southern Illinois University Press.
> Daniels, Roger, and Otis L. Graham. 2001. *Debating American Immigration, 1882–Present.* Lanham, MD: Rowman & Littlefield.

Church of the Lukumi Babalu Aye v. City of Hialeah
508 U.S. 520 (1993)

This case dealt with the Santeria religion "which employs animal sacrifice as one of its principal forms of devotion" (508 U.S. 520). The city had passed regulations prohibiting animal sacrifice and had passed these laws as general laws rather than laws targeting the Santeria religion. The religion sued, and the district court and court of appeals upheld the regulations. The majority opinion at the Supreme Court level was written by Justice Kennedy.

Kennedy first went through a history of the Santeria religion, noting how it had been persecuted in Cuba, how it had been brought here, and its history and rationale for animal sacrifice. Kennedy next noted that the church had been planned in Hialeah and that the community had reacted by passing laws to ban

animal sacrifice. The opinion stated that the city did try to follow applicable state law. At the district court level, the district court had found that the state had four compelling state interests, including those of protecting health, protecting children from the harm of watching the animal sacrifice, preventing suffering of animals before sacrifice, and controlling the health risks of housing animals for sacrifice. The court of appeals then upheld the district court opinion, stating that the district court had employed a stricter test than that of *Employment Division* v. *Smith,* and so its opinion could still be upheld (*Smith* had been decided after the district court's decision).

The Supreme Court, after noting this history, examined the First Amendment, holding that the laws in question were not neutral with respect to religion and were not generally applicable and so "must be justified by a compelling governmental interest, and must be narrowly tailored to advance that interest" (508 U.S. 520: 531–532). The Court examined the laws, finding that although they were neutral on their face, their purpose was to ban the Santeria religion, both in terms of how they were applied and the city council's stated purpose for the legislation when it was passed. The opinion noted that killing animals for food purposes was allowed, as was the treatment of animals in a kosher plant, but that ritual sacrifice was banned, which, in the Court's eyes, meant that this law was aimed only at this one religion.

Justice Kennedy also observed that these regulations were passed and enforced only after the Santeria Church came into the picture, further proving their discriminatory intent, but this was the opinion of Kennedy alone and did not hold for the entire Court.

The Court as a whole then examined whether this law targeted religion only, and examined the claimed purposes of health and preventing cruelty to animals. After reviewing the laws and their scope, the Court concluded "that each of Hialeah's ordinances pursues the city's governmental interests only against conduct motivated by religious belief" (508 U.S. 520: 545). As this law specifically targeted religion, it could be allowed only if it "advance(d) 'interests of the highest order,' and must be narrowly tailored in pursuit of those interests" (508 U.S. 520: 546). The Court held that these laws did not, as they were not tightly drawn, and the state had not prohibited most other practices that threatened these same claimed interests. For these reasons the laws were struck down.

Justice Scalia and Chief Justice Rehnquist concurred in part and concurred in the judgment in a statement written by Scalia. His dispute was with the test used to strike down the law. He argued that the ideas of neutrality and general applicability that the Court held necessary were not as far different as the Court made them seem and disagreed with the Court when it tried to determine the reason the city council passed the law, holding this analysis to be impossible. He argued that an analysis of the effects was all that is proper.

Justice Souter agreed with the result but did not agree with the *Smith* decision, and wrote arguing against *Smith*. He stated that the rules here were not generally applicable, and so should be struck down on that basis, not on the basis of *Smith*. The decision in *Smith* held that selective laws burdening religion could not be enforced, even though generally applicable laws could: "If prohibiting the exercise of religion results from enforcing a 'neutral, generally applicable' law, the Free Exercise Clause has not been offended" (508 U.S. 520: 559). Souter suggested several problems with *Smith*, one of which was that it had not been subjected to a full discussion by the Court at the time of its adoption. Souter also suggested that the original intent of the First Amendment needed to be considered, and this was not done in *Smith*. Thus, Souter suggested several reasons to reexamine *Smith*.

Justices Blackmun and O'Connor also wrote to agree with the result but not the reasoning, and they also attacked *Smith*. Blackmun argued that the proper test was one that

had been present before *Smith,* and that "when the State enacts legislation that intentionally or unintentionally places a burden upon religiously motivated practice, it must justify that burden by 'showing that it is the least restrictive means of achieving some compelling state interest'" (508 U.S. 520: 578). He added that laws that were either underinclusive or overinclusive failed to be constitutional and that laws targeting religion were either underinclusive or overinclusive and would automatically fail the "strict scrutiny" they would justly face. The concurrence also hinted that if the law had been a general law covering all animal abuse and the church had wanted to be excused from it, which was different from the situation in this case, then Blackmun and O'Connor's votes might have been different. But as that was not the case here, that issue was not decided. In the end, Blackmun held, "Thus, unlike the majority, I do not believe that '[a] law burdening religious practice that is not neutral or not of general application must undergo the most rigorous of scrutiny.' In my view, regulation that targets religion in this way, ipso facto, fails strict scrutiny. It is for this reason that a statute that explicitly restricts religious practices violates the First Amendment. Otherwise, however, '[t]he First Amendment . . . does not distinguish between laws that are generally applicable and laws that target particular religious practices'" (508 U.S. 520: 579–580).

The city of Hialeah disliked the religion of Santeria and moved to use laws to ban it. The fact that the laws were, on their face, generally applicable, was not enough to save them at the Supreme Court level as the Court found that these laws were targeted against that religion. Laws that impact a fundamental freedom like religion should be both generally applicable and neutral, and this is what the *Smith* decision held. As this law was neither, it needed to advance a fundamental government interest, and the majority held that it did not. Not all of the Court agreed with the *Smith* decision, and some called for a reinvigoration of the prior standard, which held that laws that burdened religion and were not generally applicable were not allowed and that laws that were generally applicable required a substantial government interest to justify them. As neither of these tests was met, even those who disagreed with *Smith* voted to strike down this law.

See also *Berg* v. *Glen Cove City School District; Boerne* v. *Flores; Cheema* v. *Thompson; Employment Division* v. *Smith; Lyng* v. *Northwest Indian CPA; Police Department of City of Chicago* v. *Mosley; Reynolds* v. *United States*

For further reading

Ahdar, Rex J., ed. 2000. *Law and Religion.* Burlington, VT: Ashgate/Dartmouth.

Ayorinde, Christine. 2004. *Afro-Cuban Religiosity, Revolution, and National Identity.* Gainesville: University Press of Florida.

De La Torre, Miguel A. 2004. *Santería: The Beliefs and Rituals of a Growing Religion in America.* Grand Rapids, MI: William B. Eerdmans.

Haiman, Franklyn Saul. 2003. *Religious Expression and the American Constitution.* East Lansing: Michigan State University Press.

O'Brien, David M. 2004. *Animal Sacrifice and Religious Freedom: Church of the Lukumi Babalu Aye* v. *City of Hialeah.* Lawrence: University Press of Kansas.

Comity doctrine between states in the area of marriage and divorce

Comity, in all areas of the law, means basically that one state must generally recognize a final, binding judgment of another state on a given issue. The basis of comity is the full faith and credit clause of the Constitution that states "full faith and credit shall be given in each State to the public acts, records, and judicial proceedings of every other state" (U.S. Constitution, Article IV, section 1). The reason is that if one state did not respect another, people who commit a legal infraction could simply flee the jurisdiction with impunity and never have to worry about obeying laws they disliked, even if found. Comity is part of the larger question of how a court deals with conflicting laws.

There are three main points to conflicts between laws in different states: the choice of the law used, the question of which state has jurisdiction, and the question of how judgments are enforced. Each state uses its own procedures, and each state has a system of deciding which state's substantive law is used. Substantive law refers, among other things, to whether something can be the subject of a lawsuit. For instance, is it an injury if one is hit by a car? If it is in some states and not in others, then which law applies? It might seem that the full faith and credit clause means that each state has to follow the others' laws, but that would produce a circular judicial system, as Indiana would follow Ohio's law, and Ohio would follow Indiana's, and so on. In order for a law to be applicable, a state first has to have jurisdiction over a case. Once a court reaches a final judgment, if its state had jurisdiction, and if the procedural law of that state was followed, then every other state must follow that judgment and agree to enforce it.

Comity, in the area of marriage, has not always been practiced between the states and is not necessarily always practiced today. In the 1800s, many states did not recognize marriages or divorces from other states, so a couple might find themselves married in one state but not in another, or, more commonly, divorced in one state but not in another. These different standards existed largely for religious reasons. States' marriage and divorce laws often reflected the views of the largest religious group or groups in the state, and neither the states nor the religious groups wanted to accept the views of states whose religious groups held greatly different perspectives. This lack of acceptance of other states' laws eventually changed in the area of divorce and marriage.

Loving v. *United States* (1967) effectively extended racial equality in marriage to all fifty states. The case struck down antimiscegenation laws preventing people of different races from marrying in a state that allowed interracial marriage and then going as a married couple to a state that prohibited interracial marriages and would not recognize their marriage.

Indeed, for quite a long time most states used the "comity" doctrine between each other in the areas of marriage and divorce. This effectively meant that whatever minimum standard one state had for marriage and divorce now applied to all states, providing that the first state had jurisdiction over the marrying and divorcing couple. In fact, when the couple in question consists of a man and a woman, the comity doctrine is still generally in place. However, the comity doctrine was one of the factors behind the controversy over Hawaii's 1993 ruling that gays and lesbians could marry, because it could have meant that all states might have to respect marriages performed in Hawaii. However, such recognition did not happen for several reasons; for one, Hawaii's voters revised their state constitution to prohibit same-sex unions, and second, Congress enacted the Defense of Marriage Act (DOMA) in 1996, which held that states did not have to respect marriages that were not between one man and one woman. Other states have since moved to legalize gay marriages or to create civil unions for both heterosexual and homosexual couples. These civil unions are generally considered the legal equivalent of marriages, but all states are not required to accept those marriages and unions when the couple is homosexual.

Public policy sometimes negates the comity doctrine in marriage and divorce between men and women, as well. Some states have voided marriages for being between people who are too closely related, even though those marriages would have been legal in the state where they were contracted. This situation has occurred mostly between close relatives (uncle and niece, first cousins, etc.) and in cases in which the people returned to the more restrictive state soon after the wedding. It also depends on how long the marriage has existed without controversy, particularly if one of the parties to the marriage is seeking to have it de-

clared void. Divorces are generally accepted, and the state granting the divorce always uses its own standards for causes. Annulments, however, generally follow the law in the state where the marriage occurred. Because an annulment says essentially that the marriage never took place, the laws that established the union originally control the annulment.

A related area in which the states generally follow the full faith and credit clause is that of child custody. States now accept the ruling of a sister state that has jurisdiction so that a parent who has legal custody in California, for example, will still have custody in New York. Otherwise, when that parent came to New York, whose courts might have granted the other parent custody, the parent might be guilty of kidnapping a child in New York but would still have custody when the plane touched down in California. The full faith and credit clause holds that when the correct state rules, the other states need to respect their rulings in the custody area.

Thus, the whole idea of the full faith and credit clause is that each state should respect the judgments of its sister states, and the recognition of those judgments is called comity. Each state generally respects another state's judgments, important to the issue of religion and the law in the area of divorce and marriage, among others, and only inquires as to whether the state issuing the decree had jurisdiction. This prevents problems of being married in one state and not in another, at least for heterosexual couples. As more states enable gay marriages and civil unions, DOMA is likely to come into question at the Supreme Court level, meaning the comity doctrine will likely appear in the news again before long.

See also Custody battles; Divorce, marriage, and religion; Gay marriage; Marriage—right to conduct; State constitutions and the federal First Amendment

For further reading

Richman, William M., and William L. Reynolds. 2003. *Understanding Conflict of Laws.* Newark, NJ: LexisNexis.

Scoles, Eugene F., and Peter Hay. 1992. *Conflict of Laws.* St. Paul, MN: West.

Siegel, David D. 1994. *Conflicts in a Nutshell.* St. Paul, MN: West.

Common law marriage

Common law marriage exists when a man and woman cohabit for a specific period of time, presenting themselves, for all practical purposes, as married, but no formal wedding vows are ever taken. Some eleven states and the District of Columbia still recognize this type of marriage, with another four acknowledging those created before the state stopped recognizing them, but this number is fewer today than it was in the past.

Common law marriage is not only important in studying marriage but is also important in studying the interaction of religion and the law. The reason is this: marriage in the United States has often been viewed as a contract between a man and a woman, a legal state, and a binding covenant. In a common law marriage, however, a man and a woman can create a marriage merely by agreeing to it, with little state intervention, so long as both abide by the agreement for a specific period of time. Religion played more of a role in common law marriages in the early American West, where traveling preachers covered large territories and rarely reached the more distant communities on their circuits. In these towns, it was considered acceptable for a couple to announce their wedding with no formal vows so they could begin their married lives, rather than having to wait the three or four months it might take for the minister to return to the area. The couple would generally receive the minister's blessing on his next visit.

More recently, with weddings performed by justices of the peace and with religious facilities readily available to those of nearly all faiths, this justification (and need) for common law marriage has decreased. Now, these marriages serve a different role in society, and religion's part in that role has changed drastically. After all, many gay and lesbian couples have long since fulfilled the requirements for a common law marriage in the states where they reside, but their relationships are not formally recognized. Indeed, many have even had their unions blessed by religious officials, but most U.S. states still will not issue them a marriage license. Opponents of gay marriage often base their views on religious precepts. Massachusetts, the one state that recognizes same-gender marriages as of this writing, is not one of the states that has a common law marriage. Similarly, New Jersey and Vermont, which allow same-gender civil unions, do not allow common law marriages.

The requirements for a common law marriage vary, but they generally include living together for a specific and significant period of time and for the pair to present themselves as

---

Which States Recognize Common Law Marriage?

Alabama	Colorado
District of Columbia	Georgia (if created before 1/1/97)
Idaho (if created before 1/1/96)	Iowa
Kansas	Montana
New Hampshire (for inheritance purposes only)	Ohio (if created before 10/10/91)
Oklahoma	Pennsylvania (if created before 1/1/05)
Rhode Island	South Carolina
Texas	Utah

a married couple. Although common law marriages are not possible in all states, a common law marriage in one state must be recognized in another, generally. One other note on common law marriages—there is no such thing as a common law divorce in any state. If considered married in a common law marriage, a couple wishing to part must go through a legal divorce through the courts, just like any other married pair.

See also Comity doctrine between states in the area of marriage and divorce; Divorce, marriage, and religion; Gay marriage; Marriage—right to conduct

For further reading

Bernstein, Anita, ed. 2006. *Marriage Proposals: Questioning a Legal Status.* New York: New York University Press.

Jasper, Margaret C. 2003. *Living Together: Practical Legal Issues.* Dobbs Ferry, NY: Oceana Publications.

Krause, Harry D., and David D. Meyer. 2004. *Family Law.* 3rd ed. St. Paul, MN: Thomson/West.

Confidentiality for religious figures

Confessions to clergy and other religious parties, particularly secrets revealed to priests in confessionals, are supposed to be held in strict confidence, even when crimes are discussed. However, the law obviously has an interest in criminal details, and so one question in religion and the law is whether the court system can have access to conversations between criminals and their religious confessors. Generally the court system has said no, and the religious system has definitely said no. For a variety of reasons, courts have granted specific individuals the privilege of keeping secret any information given in confidence. The privilege granted to religious conversations has been based in the First Amendment, while other privileges are based in societal considerations. The case *Jaffee v. Redmond* (518 U.S. 1), decided by the U.S. Supreme Court in 1996, extended the privilege to a social worker, and the federal rules of evidence also generally extend the privilege to a psychotherapist. The Supreme Court upheld a lower court's decision in this case, stating that the privilege of privacy is necessary to build the patient-therapist trust needed for a successful treatment and cure. The Court also noted that all of the states give a psychotherapist this privilege, although it varies in extent.

For religious figures, a privilege has generally been granted. Churches, of course, support this privilege, and the Episcopal Church greatly supports it. It holds that the sanctity of the confessional cannot be violated, and that priests should not testify to what is said in the confessional, even if the person who confessed has now waived that privilege. A more complicated question occurs when a figure in a court trial is working with someone who is both a clergy member and a social worker (or a psychiatrist, etc.). The conversations then may not be privileged, depending upon state regulations. The central question becomes the nature of the meeting between the figures: if the meeting is religious, the conversations will probably be protected; if the nature of the meeting is more psychiatric, the conversations may not be protected and the clergy member will then be treated like any other psychiatrist or social worker. On a very few occasions, taped confessions to clergy have appeared in the courtroom, but courts have almost universally not allowed their use. In general, the law and religion agree in this situation: even criminals have the right to confide in private religious figures whose lives revolve around issues of sin and salvation.

See also Nally v. Grace Community Church of the Valley; Ohio Civil Rights Commission v. Dayton Schools

For further reading

Bush, John C., and William Harold Tiemann. 1989. *The Right to Silence: Privileged Clergy Communication and the Law.* Nashville, TN: Abingdon Press.

Slovenko, Ralph. 1998. *Psychotherapy and Confidentiality: Testimonial Privileged Communication,*

Breach of Confidentiality, and Reporting Duties.
Springfield, IL: Charles C. Thomas.

Corporation of Presiding Bishop v. Amos

483 U.S. 327 (1987)

Pime v. *Loyola*

(803 F.2d 351) (1986)

Most corporations and organizations are not allowed to discriminate on the basis of religion. The main exceptions to this law involve religious corporations or organizations. Of course, one would not expect a church to have to give equal standing for a member of its own faith and a member of a different faith when considering which minister to hire. The question, of course, is how far does that exception go, and the *Pime* v. *Loyola* and *Corporation of Presiding Bishop* v. *Amos* cases partially answer that question. Both were filed under Title VII of the 1964 Civil Rights Act, which generally forbade any discrimination on the basis of religion. One exception was that it allowed religious organizations to discriminate on the basis of religion, and in 1972, the exception had been broadened from religious activities in those organizations to all activities in those organizations.

Pime v. *Loyola,* decided in 1986 by the Seventh Circuit Court of Appeals, came about when Loyola University decided to hire Jesuits as the next three members of one university department and Professor Pime sued. Loyola claimed that part of the 1964 Civil Rights Act allowed religious discrimination when the institution was controlled by a religion and also allowed discrimination when the religion was a "bona fide occupational qualification reasonably necessary to the normal operation of that particular business or enterprise" (803 F.2d 351). The court noted that though Loyola had long been controlled by Jesuits, most of its faculty were not Jesuits and that the school had taken steps, including the one challenged here, to increase the number of Jesuits. The court then reviewed Pime's history and held that

even if Pime had been discriminated against on the basis of his religion, being Jesuit was a bona fide occupational qualification and so establishing this as a requirement was acceptable.

Judge Posner concurred, and he examined what was required to make a case under this part of the 1964 Civil Rights Act. He held that because a specific religious order was required here "casts doubt on my brethren's assumption that the mere fact of reserving one or more slots for members of a religious order establishes a prima facie case" (803 F.2d 351: 354–355). Posner claimed that neither a disparate impact on one religion nor intentional discrimination had been argued, and so a prima facie case of discrimination had not been proven. Posner would have stopped the court there, as he also argued that being Jesuit should not have been characterized as a bona fide occupational qualification. Posner also cast doubt on whether Loyola could be described as being controlled by the Jesuits. Posner, though, held that Pime had not proven his case of discrimination, meaning it was not necessary to address the issues of the 1964 Civil Rights Act.

Corporation of Presiding Bishop v. *Amos,* decided by the Supreme Court in 1987, was also filed under Title VII of the 1964 Civil Rights Act. The facility in this case was a gymnasium, run by the Latter-day Saints but open to the general public. The person in question had worked at the gymnasium for over a decade as an engineer and then was fired for not being a Mormon. Ultimately, the court determined that the firing was legal.

Justice White delivered the opinion of the Court, in which four other justices fully joined. First, the Court determined that the engineer's work was not religious in nature and then looked at the section of the Civil Rights Act relating to nonreligious activities in religious organizations. He determined that the law as worded in the Civil Rights Act was constitutional, as it met all of the provisions of the *Lemon* test. First, it had a secular purpose, that of minimizing government interference with religion. Without the enlarged exemption, there would always be the question of whether an activity was religious, and without the original exemption, churches' activities would be greatly interfered with. The Court also held that the government itself had not advanced religion through this statute, even though religion might have benefited. White concluded that the equal protection statute was not offended, as it treated all religions equally and that the statute did not impermissibly entangle the government and religion.

Justice Brennan authored a concurrence, joined by Justice Marshall. They focused on the nonprofit nature of the gymnasium, holding that a blanket exception could be allowed. Having an exemption only for religious activities would, Brennan believed, cause excessive entanglement. Implied but not stated is the condition that were a religious group to organize a for-profit venture, then in only those things that were religious could discrimination be allowed.

Justice Blackmun issued a short concurrence but mostly joined in one by Justice O'Connor. O'Connor concurred but mostly wanted to note problems with the *Lemon* test. She argued that the effect of a government law, in the characterization the Court puts on it, will almost always be to allow a church to advance religion, rather than the government advancing it. Because of this, she would have desired to see the whole *Lemon* test reevaluated rather than simply being used as precedent. She argued that rather than examining the effect, justices should examine what a "rational observer" would see—whether the observer would see the government as advancing religion (not allowed) or as accommodating the free exercise of religion (allowed).

Thus, organizations, when held to be religiously controlled, or religiously enough controlled, and churches, even when doing things outside what many think of as religious, are allowed to discriminate in the hiring of their employees. This is one of the few general exceptions allowed to the 1964 Civil Rights Act, which generally forbade discrimination on the basis of religion.

See also *Ansonia Board of Education* v. *Philbrook; Farrington* v. *Tokushige; Lemon* v. *Kurtzman; Ohio Civil Rights Commission* v. *Dayton Schools*

For further reading

Epstein, Richard Allen. 1992. *Forbidden Grounds: The Case against Employment Discrimination Laws.* Cambridge, MA: Harvard University Press.

Hauck, Vern E. 1997. *Arbitrating Race, Religion, and National Origin Discrimination Grievances.* Westport, CT: Quorum Books.

Sandin, Robert T. 1990. *Autonomy and Faith: Religious Preference in Employment Decisions in Religiously Affiliated Higher Education.* Atlanta: Omega.

County of Allegheny v. Greater Pittsburgh ACLU

492 U.S. 573 (1989)

This case dealt with the construction, with state permission, of a crèche (manger scene) inside a city building and a menorah just outside a city building in Allegheny County, Pennsylvania. Some members of the community considered this an unconstitutional violation of the separation of church and state, as the state might very well be saying that some version of Judeo-Christian teaching was favored by the state. Thus, establishment of a religious icon in a city building would naturally be controversial, as it was here, and this case made it all the way to the Supreme Court.

Justice Blackmun wrote the opinion of the Court. He concluded that the crèche was not permissible while the menorah was, both based largely on their physical settings and surroundings. Blackmun first surveyed the physical settings of both items. The manger scene was largely isolated whereas the menorah was near a larger Christmas tree and a sign describing the lights on the Christmas tree as a sign of liberty around the world. Blackmun then recounted the history of the legislation. The Court noted the First Amendment and the history of cases and ideas leading up to the three-pronged *Lemon* test. Blackmun stated that the key here was the second prong, which he concluded as holding, in issues like this one, that "the Establishment Clause, at the very least, prohibits government from appearing to take a position on questions of religious belief" (492 U.S. 573: 593–594). He then looked at past decisions, and at the crèche itself, holding that the crèche was the only thing on the staircase and that the sign stating "glory to God in the highest" clearly endorsed religion. He disagreed with the dissent, which would have allowed the crèche, stating that there was a distinct difference between the reference to God on our money, the allowing of chaplains in our legislature, and this display, as the display endorsed one specific religion. Blackmun also disagreed with the dissent, which painted the majority as antireligious, and Blackmun noted that in order to be fair to all, the government must promote no single religion.

Blackmun then turned to the menorah. He noted that the menorah is a clear symbol for Hanukah, but he also noted that Hanukah was both secular and religious. He also noted "moreover, the menorah here stands next to a Christmas tree and a sign saluting liberty" (492 U.S. 573: 614). The Christmas tree was important, in Blackmun's analysis, as it was wholly secular, and the three things combined together made the overall display simply a note of the "winter-holiday season" and so were allowable (492 U.S. 573: 616). The tree was also significantly taller than the menorah, decreasing the menorah's religious message.

O'Connor, with whom Brennan and Stevens agreed in part, concurred. She first discussed the *Lynch* case, in which the Supreme Court had, some five years before, allowed a crèche that was mixed with a large number of secular symbols and was placed in a private park. The crèche in the *Allegheny* case was in the county courthouse and was alone, and this

was enough to fatally condemn it for O'Connor. She also argued against the dissent, which wished to rework or drop the endorsement part of the *Lemon* test. O'Connor also invoked the idea of "ceremonial deism," which she held as meaning practices whose purpose was "solemnizing public occasions" and "expressing confidence in the future" (492 U.S. 573: 630). Those practices, which she held as including chaplains in legislatures and "In God We Trust" on the currency, were acceptable. The crèche, however, went far beyond that. She also agreed with the majority that there was no hostility to religion here. As far as the menorah went, O'Connor saw the three symbols combined as more of a sign of respect for "pluralism and freedom" than any endorsement of religion or a totally secular message, which is how Blackmun had painted it (492 U.S. 573: 635).

Justice Brennan wrote a partial concurrence, joined by Marshall and Stevens. They would have disallowed both the crèche and the menorah. They did not think that you could divorce the Christmas tree from Christmas, which they thought was necessary to allow it to continue, nor could they divorce the menorah from Judaism.

Justice Stevens also wrote a concurrence, joined by Marshall and Brennan. Stevens surveyed the history of the First Amendment, arguing that there should be a "presumption" against any religious symbols on government land and agreeing with Justice Brennan on the incorrectness of the menorah and crèche.

Justice Kennedy dissented in part and concurred in part and was joined by Justices White and Scalia and Chief Justice Rehnquist. He held that Justice Blackmun's opinion regarding the crèche, and the ideas behind it, "reflects an unjustified hostility toward religion, a hostility inconsistent with our history and our precedents" (492 U.S. 573: 655). Kennedy would have liked to discard *Lemon* but thought that working within it, the county could still have a crèche. He argued that past decisions allowed a government to recognize the "central role religion plays in our society," and he saw the crèche as this (492 U.S. 573: 657). Kennedy certainly wanted to ban coercion, but he wanted to allow "accommodation." Kennedy also argued that banning any recognition of the religious elements of Christmas was hostile toward Christianity. Those who disliked the religious displays, he suggested, could "ignore them, or even . . . turn their backs" (492 U.S. 573: 664). Kennedy stated that a temporary crèche could not be coercion and so was allowable, and he did not think that the placement of the crèche by itself or on city property was important. He also argued that how a reasonable observer would view the display was the most important thing, and he did not think that such an observer would object. He then cited numerous religious elements in public life, like "In God We Trust" on our money and stated that the majority was rejecting these and thus moving to invalidate them or ignoring them. He argued that the state should be allowed to accommodate religious elements of holidays without running afoul of the First Amendment, and failure to allow this was hostility to religion. Of course, with all of this, the four dissenters on the crèche also agreed the menorah should be allowed.

Thus, the crèche was struck down as too religious while the menorah, in its setting along with the Christmas tree and the sign recognizing liberty, was allowed. This decision, while straddling the fence, did not satisfy either side of the debate. It neither outlawed nor allowed all religious symbols but continued the need for a case-by-case adjudication that was begun in *Lynch*.

See also *ACLU of Kentucky v. McCreary County; Capitol Square Review and Advisory Board v. Pinette; Elk Grove Unified School District v. Newdow; Marsh v. Chambers; McCreary County v. ACLU; Metzl v. Leininger*

For further reading
Miller, William Lee. 1986. *The First Liberty: Religion and the American Republic.* New York: Knopf.

Patrick, John J., and Gerald P. Long, eds. 1999. *Constitutional Debates on Freedom of Religion: A Documentary History.* Westport, CT: Greenwood Press.
Swanson, Wayne R. 1990. *The Christ Child Goes to Court.* Philadelphia: Temple University Press.

Creation Research Society

The Creation Research Society (CRS) is among a growing number of groups who aim to demonstrate scientific proof behind theories claiming the earth's creation by God. Generally backed by fundamentalist Christians, these groups have grown increasingly popular in the current wave of backlash against teaching evolution in public schools. CRS was founded in Michigan as a tax-exempt charity, its membership secretary is in Missouri, it has a research center in Arizona, and thus it exists throughout the middle of America. It makes several statements about what its members must believe. Particularly, they must believe in biblical creation of the universe and earth, as opposed to evolution being responsible for either. The group emphasizes that its membership includes research scientists.

Like other such groups, CRS believes the earth and its inhabitants were created during the week of creation described in the book of Genesis. Members also believe that while change within one type of animal is possible, no new animals have evolved. The group founded its own journal after established scientific journals refused to publish their work. CRS now publishes a variety of periodicals, including a newsletter and a quarterly journal. The quarterly journal includes articles it terms scholarly that support intelligent design theory, one current popular belief designed to oppose evolution. Some of the articles in this journal are, indeed, extremely technical in nature. Published every other month, the journal includes letters, some articles, and short subjects. It has printed articles written by a medical doctor who specializes in pathology, a podiatrist, and a physicist.

The group has also produced a number of books on the topic of intelligent design, including a rhyming book for children about the creation, a copy of Ussher's chronology of the earth, a defense of the creationist position about the lack of ice ages, and an astronomy designed to introduce students to the heavens without causing them to doubt the Bible. Videos are also available for sale on the group's website, and their topics range from plate tectonics, to how the Grand Canyon proves the great flood actually occurred, to evidence in the fossil record that the group believes supports a creationist viewpoint. The society includes scientists from a wide variety of fields. Its board includes four physicists, a physical geographer, a botanist, an anatomist, a computer scientist, a geologist, and an animal scientist, all with Ph.D.s. All members of the board of directors appear to be white males.

Like other creationist groups, CRS supports the teaching of intelligent design in public schools and opposes evolution theory, considering it harmful and un-Christian. Groups like these have gained in popularity in attempts to prove that those who oppose evolution are not stupid and backward. That the group must currently overcome such public perceptions demonstrates the lasting power of the Scopes Trial, in which those in Tennessee who opposed evolution were presented as backward in a highly publicized manner. However, as national lawmakers become increasingly involved in determining the content of science classrooms, these groups will represent a force with which those who favor evolution will have to contend.

See also Answers in Genesis; Avoidance of the issue of evolution in many teaching standards; Creation Science Research Center; *Scopes* v. *Tennessee*/Scopes Monkey Trial
For further reading
Creation Research Society. http://www.creation research.org/ (accessed July 9, 2005).

Montagu, Ashley, ed. 1984. *Science and Creationism.* New York: Oxford University Press.
Numbers, Ronald L. 1992. *The Creationists.* New York: Knopf.
Understanding Evolution. http://evolution .berkeley.edu/ (accessed June 15, 2005).

Creation Science Research Center

The Creation Science Research Center is based in San Diego, California, and aims to fight against the teaching of evolution in public elementary and high schools. Its self-stated guiding principle is to protect Christian children from having their faith in God as Creator threatened. The group has existed since 1967 and it began to achieve some level of notoriety in 1980, when it sued California for teaching evolution. One of its main aims is to produce material that reconciles science with a belief in creationism, and then to provide those materials to home schools, to public and private schools to be adopted in the curriculum (the Center's hope), and to individuals who wish to do private faith-based investigation. The Center's ultimate goal is to have creation science prevail over evolution. Their materials are designed specifically to connect the biblical creation record with scientific data. The group believes it is acting on God's commission to bring the country to a decision for or against creationism.

The Creation Science Research Center puts out a variety of publications. Some of these are books, including *The Handy Dandy Evolution Refuter* and *The Creation Explanation,* and some are multimedia, set up as "Little Talkers." These are animal stories relating a biblical message. The series includes a whole host of materials, including coloring books, videos, MP3s, parent guides, and quizzes. The Center also produces student kits aimed at helping public school students refute the school's teaching of evolution. It should be noted that not all Christian religions are accepted by the Center. The Center does not believe that either Roman Catholicism or many of the major Protestant denominations are true Christian religions. Thus, the Center's message should not be considered to represent, by far, the whole Christian population.

The Center is run by a group called the Parent Company, whose aim seems to be to produce sales materials for companies. And in spite of its rejection of most of the majority Christian religions, the Creation Science Research Center is one of the best-known groups fighting evolution in the public schools and producing materials to help students (and their parents, of course) in this battle.

> **See also** Edwards v. Aguillard; Kitzmiller v. Dover Area School District; National Center for Science Education; Scopes v. Tennessee/Scopes Monkey Trial

> **For further reading**
> Creation Science Research Center website. http://www.parentcompany.com/csrc/csrcinfo.htm.
> Larson, Edward J. 2003. Trial and Error: The American Controversy over Creation and Evolution. New York: Oxford University Press.
> Moore, Randy. 2002. Evolution in the Courtroom: A Reference Guide. Santa Barbara, CA: ABC-CLIO.

Crowley v. Smithsonian Institution
636 F.2d 738 (D.C. Cir. 1980)

Crowley, along with a case from South Dakota, dealt with a challenge to evolution. A person filed a legal challenge to a Smithsonian exhibit that was titled The Emergence of Man. The exhibit supported evolution and Crowley opposed this, claiming the government support for the Smithsonian and such an exhibit created secular humanism, or a secular religion.

The exhibit in question demonstrated adaptation of things to the environment and used them as support of evolution. It did not, however, criticize religion or support evolution as the only answer. The D.C. Circuit Court of Appeals held that even if evolution could not be proven and had to be accepted as a thoroughly tested scientific theory, this did not mean that such acceptance created a reli-

gion. The court said that the Smithsonian had the right under its charter to set up this exhibit. On the issue of religion, the decision stated that a balance needed to be made between freedom of religion and the right to learn. "This balance was long ago struck in favor of diffusion of knowledge based on responsible scientific foundations, and against special constitutional protection of religious believers from the competition generated by such knowledge diffusion" (636 F.2d 738: 744). Thus, the district court's decision was upheld and the challenge was struck down.

Besides the government's right to create exhibits concerning evolution, there has long been a concern about how much evolution is required in the classroom. One question is how much time a teacher can spend on the whole question of evolution versus creationism. This issue was resolved in Dale v. Board of Education, Lemmon Independent School District (1982). There, the supreme court of South Dakota upheld Lloyd Dale's firing for teaching creation science. The local school board had established teaching guidelines for Dale, who was given "up to one week of class time to teach the theories of evolution or creation" (316 N.W. 2d 108: 110). Thus, he could still teach some creationism. However, he spent too much time on creationism as opposed to evolution, and so the school district fired him. The court found that the appeals court's rulings were not erroneous and so did not have to be overturned. Perhaps the best comment on Dale's case came in a concurrence, which held "essentially, Mr. Dale wanted to be a preacher, not a teacher. This is intolerable in a classroom under our state law, state constitution, and federal constitution" (316 N.W. 2d 108: 115).

Thus, the court's decisions reflected the government tendency to uphold religious freedom. It determined, in Crowley, that the Smithsonian was not establishing a state religion when it created an evolution exhibit. It determined, in Dale, that when teachers were permitted to teach creationism, they had to

Smithsonian Institution's old administration building, built in 1854. The Smithsonian Institution in Washington, D.C., is the official museum of the United States. The institution was created from an inheritance given to the United States by British scientist James Smithson to increase and diffuse knowledge of science, technology, and the arts. (PhotoDisc, Inc.)

balance their teaching with evolution, as dictated by the local school board. These decisions, particularly *Dale,* reflect the government mandate to maintain a separation of church and state, which prohibits the government from favoring any one religion over another.

See also *Edwards* v. *Aguillard; Epperson* v. *Arkansas; Scopes* v. *Tennessee*/Scopes Monkey Trial; *Tilton* v. *Richardson*

For further reading

Campbell, John Angus, and Stephen C. Meyer, eds. 2003. *Darwinism, Design, and Public Education.* East Lansing: Michigan State University Press.

Webb, George Ernest. 1994. *The Evolution Controversy in America.* Lexington: University Press of Kentucky.

Cults, law's treatment of people in

The very word "cult," it should be noted, is a loaded term. After all, one person's cult may be another's religion. However, cult will be used here in the sense of a religious sect whose general philosophies are widely considered extremist or false. And the concept of cults suggests groups of people, often with charismatic leaders, who follow an idea obsessively and carry out extreme behaviors with what they claim are religious justifications. Jim Jones, for instance, led his cult to Guyana in South America where they founded Jonestown and committed mass suicide. David Koresh holed up with his Branch

Fire engulfs the Branch Davidian compound near Waco, Texas, on April 19, 1993. Eighty-two Davidians, including leader David Koresh, perished as federal agents tried to drive them out of the compound. (AP Photo/Ron Heflin)

Davidians in their group compound in Waco, Texas. The group engaged in a tense standoff with government officials over weapons possession, ending in a fire that destroyed the compound, causing many deaths.

The law interacts with cults in a number of different ways. To begin with, laws are sometimes used to try to shut down religious minorities. Very often those religious groups fight the laws in court. A relatively recent lawsuit of this type was in Florida. The case went all the way to the Supreme Court in *Church of the Lukumi Babalu Aye* v. *City of Hialeah* (1993). There, a city had tried to shut down the Santeria religion, which practiced animal sacrifice. The city council passed a law regulating all animal sacrifice, justifying the law with its intent to protect animals and health, not any attempt to prevent the practice of Santeria. However, it was widely recognized that the city council considered the Santeria religion to be a cult

and wanted their activities halted. The Supreme Court ruled in favor of the Lukumi Babalu Aye, stating that laws that were not neutral in the area of religion needed a compelling government interest and needed to be narrowly written, and the city of Hialeah's law failed these tests.

Cults and the people in them hit the newswires heavily in the 1960s and 1970s. The Symbionese Liberation Army kidnapped and brainwashed heiress Patty Hearst into participating in its bank heists. Charles Manson brainwashed a group of people who called itself The Family. Members of that cult went to the home of actress Sharon Tate, killed her and several of her guests on Manson's orders, and also murdered another couple.

Beginning in that era and continuing to the present are the efforts of parents to retrieve their children from cults. Specifically, and less well known than famous cases but still heavily reported from time to time, are parents' attempts to kidnap their children and have them deprogrammed. There is a more direct legal connection when it is believed that a cult has entrapped someone into it, or when the parents of a young member kidnap that person out of the cult. Parental kidnappings are often based strongly on three ideas. First, of course, is the belief that the young person did not go willingly or was lured under false pretenses and that the cult presents a danger. Second is the belief that a bit of persuasion, or, to use the term that was bandied about in the 1970s, deprogramming, will remove the cult's influence and the young person will be well again. Third is the hope that true religion or faith will resist deprogramming, while false religion or the religion of cults will not. A cottage industry of deprogrammers grew up in the 1970s.

In court cases stemming from such deprogrammings, questions have included the level of honesty required of cult leaders. However, similar to all other religions, there are really few regulations on the leaders of cult movements. Leaders and recruiters for any religion do not have to inform their potential recruits of their goals. Those who dislike a group after they leave it generally cannot sue but can, instead, campaign against it, try to get the government to go after it, or become deprogrammers themselves.

A second legal question is what actions can be brought against parents for their actions in taking their children out of cults. Civil actions by the people who were kidnap-rescued have sometimes been successful, but those placing the suits must have generally been adults at the time of the deprogramming efforts and resisted deprogramming throughout. It is generally not acceptable for them to be successfully deprogrammed, remain with their parents or deprogrammers, and then sue. Even when a kidnap-rescue victim recovers monetary damages, these damages are generally small. It is also difficult to compare the behavior of parents kidnapping their children out of what they considered a cult against the behavior of parents who merely object to a child's religious choices. Most parents would be aghast if someone broke into a monastery and stole their adult child who had decided to become a priest, even if they disagreed with their son's decision. However, the same parents might initiate the kidnapping if they felt their children were in danger from a cult. Parents are given more legal control until children reach the age of majority, which is generally eighteen, and there is also natural sympathy with the parents who want to be able to protect their children against cult recruiters. But danger is often in the eye of the beholder, and the law must balance the religion's right to exist against the parents' rights to protect their child. In the area of kidnapping, the criminal law and the civil law often side with the parents, as noted, even of adult children.

A related question is what level of honesty religious groups have to have in selling things. In one case, a religious group was allowed to sell scientific equipment which had allegedly been mislabeled, as long as the group made only religious and not scientific claims about the equipment. On the other hand, deceptive practices such as lying about what use will be made of donated money have been found to be illegal, even for religious causes. Courts cannot investigate the truth of religious beliefs, but they can investigate the sincerity of them, or how fully and strongly they are held. Courts have also considered whether groups can be held responsible for promising to perform miracles (for money, generally, in the cases that came into the courts) and then failing. Judges have generally focused more on the sincerity of the belief than in the actual ability to perform miracles.

Another of the most famous cults in the twentieth century, the Branch Davidians, made headlines as much for perceived government interference as for their extremist beliefs and practices. Led by the charismatic David Koresh, the cult had hoarded a large number of weapons at its compound in Waco, Texas. The weapons cache was declared illegal, and law enforcement officials attempted to seize the weapons and arrest cult leaders. However, the group turned its compound into a fortress, refusing the government entry and threatening to burn themselves to the ground. Eventually, the compound was burned, and eighty-two lives were lost. As the compound was on private property and some of the dead were children, the government's need for involvement came under heavy question after the fact. Indeed, this situation highlights the crux of the relationship between cults and the law. A careful balance between public safety and religious freedom must be preserved. When the balance shifts in either direction, lives are generally lost. The Manson Family killed others, and Jim Jones and his followers, along with groups like the Heaven's Gate cult, committed mass suicide due to their extremist beliefs. However, the Branch Davidians may have died as much because of the government's strong-handed tactics as because of their nonstandard practices.

The interaction of religious cults and the law thus raises a number of difficult issues. The courts generally side with religious groups in allowing them a relatively wide latitude to advertise themselves and to raise monies. However, the law often sides with parents who rescue their children, even if adults, from those same cults. The law is on the side of the federal government when it wants to corral groups who are extremist and possess weapons, but public opinion is not, if the raids are not successful. In a dicey pinch, however, if the raids are not carried out, and harm results, public opinion is not on the side of government then either, even though the law technically is. As new cults form and come under legal scrutiny, legal officials will have to continually balance these factors to achieve even a semblance of justice in such murky ground.

See also *Airport Commissioners* v. *Jews for Jesus; Church of the Lukumi Babalu Aye* v. *City of Hialeah; Heffron* v. *International Society for Krishna Consciousness, Inc.; Jones* v. *Opelika*

For further reading

Burstein, Abraham. 1980. *Religion, Cults, and the Law.* Dobbs Ferry, NY: Oceana Publications.
Lewis, James R. 1998. *Cults in America: A Reference Handbook.* Santa Barbara, CA: ABC-CLIO.
Melton, J. Gordon. 1992. *Encyclopedic Handbook of Cults in America.* New York: Garland.
Shupe, Anson D., Jr., David G. Bromley, and Donna L. Oliver. 1984. *The Anti-Cult Movement in America: A Bibliography and Historical Survey.* New York: Garland.
Tabor, James D. 1995. *Why Waco? Cults and the Battle for Religious Freedom in America.* Berkeley: University of California Press.

Curriculum of home schools and reporting

For a number of reasons, parents choose to home school their children rather than send them to traditional classrooms. Many parents simply feel public and private schools are inadequate to the task of educating a child. However, others choose to home school for religious reasons, desiring to incorporate religion into their children's curriculum in their own ways. The stereotypical portrait of this second type of home-school parent depicts a backward fundamentalist who believes there is too little God in public school, or too much secular humanism. However, parents who choose to home school for religious reasons actually come from a broad variety of perspectives, and most feel strongly that they can control their children's educations better than the state. Thus, it is easy to see why some parents who choose to home school for religious reasons feel that a state-controlled reporting system or a state-guided curriculum might represent a breach of the wall between church and state. Several cases in the last two decades have set guidelines for what reporting and curriculum guidelines the state can legally establish for home schools.

One of the leading cases testing the constitutionality of such requirements is *Mazanec* v. *North Judson-San Pierre School Corporation*, decided by the Seventh Circuit Court of Appeals

Diane Toler, director of the Catholic Homeschoolers of New Jersey, plays a game to help improve the math and writing skills of her children at their home in Cherry Hill, New Jersey, in May 2004. (AP Photo/Daniel Hulshizer)

in 1987. There the court found that mandatory attendance and reports can be required. States can prosecute for failure to file such reports, and a prosecution, even if against a home school whose creation was religion based, cannot be, absent of proof, assumed to be motivated by religion. The court held that the parents in this case had not cooperated and so deserved any prosecution they received. The court held "thus, even in a state with a constitutionally perfect education law and system, people like the plaintiffs who frustrate state officials in enforcing the compulsory education law will be prosecuted" (798 F.2d 230: 236). Also, the court held that cooperation was necessary at the most basic level before the parents could argue that a less restrictive method of reporting should have been used.

Another question is whether states can force home schoolers to file reports if parents think they have to report only to God. This issue was addressed by the Supreme Court of Iowa in 1993 in *State* v. *Rivera*. The state there had a rather common requirement that forced each parent who home schooled to file a copy of the curriculum with the state. This regulation was challenged as a violation of the free exercise of religion. The parents in that case argued "that their religious beliefs mandate a course of action wherein a Supreme Being must be accorded exclusive authority over their children's home education program. Any requirement for reporting the details of that program to the state, defendants urge, impedes upon the free exercise of that belief" (497 N.W. 2d 878: 880). The court, though, held that the reporting requirements were necessary to assure a minimal standard of education, and that the burden upon the parents' religion was acceptable in order to achieve this goal.

Two final questions are about the ability of the state to require certain elements of a curriculum, and whether a state can impose a curriculum when that action would lower the amount of religion taught in a home school. This issue was considered by the U.S. District Court for Maryland in 1995 in *Battles v. Anne Arundel County Board of Education*. The state there required "instruction in English, mathematics, science, social studies, art, music, health, and physical education" and that "the parent must maintain a portfolio of instructional materials and examples of the child's work to demonstrate that the child is receiving regular and thorough instruction in those areas, and must permit a representative to observe the teaching provided and review the portfolio at a mutually agreeable time and place not more than three times a year" (904 F. Supp 471: 473). The suing parent, however, objected to any government-dictated oversight, believing this same agency, in the public schools, created "atheistic, antichristian education" (904 F. Supp 471: 473). The court held that the parent did not prove that Maryland had substantially infringed upon her education merely by making her teach certain subjects and follow reporting requirements. Thus, the state was allowed to maintain the reporting and curriculum requirements.

States cannot force students to go to public schools, and that has been established law since 1925. However, states can force private and parochial schools, and those who are home schooled, to learn certain subjects and to have their curriculum monitored. Parents are also required to cooperate with these restrictions, even if they feel that their religion is being infringed upon.

See also New Jersey v. Massa; Null v. Board of Education; Paying for tests and other aid for private schools

For further reading

Bauman, Kurt. 2001. *Home Schooling in the United States: Trends and Characteristics.* Washington, DC: U.S. Census Bureau.

Klicka, Christopher J. 2002. *The Right to Home School: A Guide to the Law on Parents' Rights in Education.* Durham, NC: Carolina Academic Press.

Van Galen, Jane, and Mary Anne Pitman. 1991. *Home Schooling: Political, Historical, and Pedagogical Perspectives.* Norwood, NJ: Ablex.

Custody battles

Custody battles often hinge on religious issues, as one parent feels the other will corrupt their mutual children against a particular religion, or that the other parent will corrupt the children *with* that religion. As in other areas, the courts here have differentiated between belief and action. The courts are not allowed to consider the validity of a belief and thus cannot rule on whether they think a child is being raised in a good religion, or whether the child would be better off being raised in a home with no religion. However, the court may consider the actions that parents take that are influenced or directed by religion and how those actions affect the child, as part of the overall consideration of the child's best interests, which is the current generally applicable standard in most jurisdictions. One threshold that must be reached first is making sure that both parents can provide for the child. If one parent cannot, religion is never an issue. In one of the earliest cases, in California, the court would have placed a child with its mother, but the mother belonged to a religion that would have detached the child from society. The court therefore held that the damage to the child's social development from this isolation required the court to place the child with the father instead.

Other courts have developed this idea to require that an alleged harm have a high probability of occurring—a potential harm was not enough. Religion has generally been held to only be one element affecting the child's best interests and not to bear any more weight than any other factor influencing those interests. Appellate courts have also been reluctant to reverse awards of custody when the losing parent complained that issues of religion would damage the child's best interests. Generally, the appeals court has upheld the lower court, if the lower court had a reasonable basis for awarding the child's custody.

The courts, conversely, have also generally not enforced divorce agreements on religious matters. For instance, if the parents agree to raise the child in one faith at the time of the divorce and sign an agreement to that effect, but the custodial parent later changes his or her mind and stops raising the child in that faith, courts will not generally force the custodial parent to follow that original agreement. The controlling standard here again is the best interests of the child. The custodial parent is generally left alone to make those decisions.

Religious practices may be taken into account when awarding custody. However, the courts are expected to abstain from ruling on the validity of a religion's beliefs. Moreover, religion is only one element involved in the contemplation of a child's best interests, and those best interests are the overriding legal concern.

See also Divorce, marriage, and religion; Religion and attitudes toward marriage historically in the United States

For further reading

Douglas, Gillian. 2001. *An Introduction to Family Law.* New York: Oxford University Press.

Luepnitz, Deborah Anna. 1981. *Child Custody: A Study of Families after Divorce.* Lexington, MA: Lexington Books.

Cutter v. Wilkinson

544 U.S. 709 (2005)

This case was one of the first to reach the Supreme Court dealing with the 2000 Religious Land Use and Institutionalized Persons Act (RLUIPA). That act had required the states and the federal government to not substantially burden a church's land use or a prisoner's religious rights unless a compelling government interest was advanced and the means used were the least restrictive necessary, when the prison received federal funds or the church was connected with commerce. Nearly all prisons and churches fall under these umbrellas, but they are necessary to give the federal government jurisdiction over the areas. The cases here dealt with the prisoner aspect of the legislation.

This legislation returned to the issue of when a government can burden the free exercise of religion. From 1963, in *Sherbert v. Verner,* until 1990, the Supreme Court had required the government to have a compelling government interest to pass a restriction of the free exercise of religion. However, in 1990, the Supreme Court, in *Employment Division v. Smith,* ruled that the government can restrict religious liberty through legislation in other areas when it has a rational basis to do so and when done in a way that is neutral with respect to the type of religion regulated, without needing the compelling government interest. This decision provoked considerable controversy because it set the precedent that the government can restrict religious freedom through regulations in other areas. In the 1993 Religious Freedom Restoration Act (RFRA), Congress attempted to force a return to the 1963 *Sherbert* standard. The Supreme Court held firm, though, and in 1997 struck down that part of RFRA that applied to the states, arguing that Congress was creating new rights, a function outside its province. This was a large part of the reason for Congress's creation of RLUIPA in 2000. The purpose of the act, just like that of RFRA, was to require the government to abide by the compelling government interest standard. This time, however, Congress tied its legislation to the commerce and spending clauses of the Constitution, among other areas, to indicate that it was not creating new laws.

Here, several Ohio prisoners, including Jon B. Cutter, sued for violation of their religious rights. The state had two basic arguments, and the nature of their arguments, as well as the court's response, show that the real question was RLUIPA's constitutionality rather than whether the prisoners' rights had been infringed upon. First, the state argued that RLUIPA established a religion, and second, it insisted that using RLUIPA guidelines would endanger the security of the prison institutions. However, the Supreme Court unanimously struck down these objections, finding for the prisoners and upholding RLUIPA. Justice Ruth Bader Ginsburg wrote for the Court. She first addressed the controversy, including the fact that the suing prisoners were of minority religions, including Wicca and Satanist, and that they believed they had experienced discrimination. In supporting RLUIPA, Ginsburg first turned to the establishment clause issue. She stated that the law preserved the free exercise rights of the prisoners but did not create an establishment of religion, that the law required neutrality among religions, and that it also required that those who were of no religion could not be discriminated against. Thus, she explained, there was no establishment clause violation.

She then turned to the issue of safety. She noted that RLUIPA did not try to suggest that safety was a lesser concern, only that safety had to be examined alongside the religious rights at issue to reach a balance. Safety could not be used as a blanket excuse to deny prisoners their rights. She stated that religious rights could be given more protection than other rights, as speech restrictions were maintained in prison even while religion was somewhat protected under this law. She also noted—and this was one of the points most clearly illustrating that the case was more about RLUIPA generally than it was about

the rights of the specific individual prisoners suing—that Ohio was free to return to Court and try to prove that prison safety was indeed threatened by the requests of these prisoners, since RLUIPA allowed the denial of religious rights when prison security was significantly compromised.

Justice Thomas wrote a concurrence, noting that this law and federalism—or the idea that states have areas of jurisdiction and power all their own separate from those of Congress—concurred in the result. He argued that Ohio's position had no historical grounding in its argument that the First Amendment kept Congress wholly out of the field of religion at all. He also observed that the whole law was tied to federal funding, and that the states were willingly accepting the restrictions by accepting federal funding. No federalism issue existed here, in Thomas's opinion, and he did not address the crux of the federal funding problem, that most institutions receiving federal funds could not exist without them and that many, like prisons, serve an essential public function. However, this case was clearly not the place for such an argument. His point was to keep alive his idea that the First Amendment allowed government action in the area of religion (remember that Thomas would have allowed more action than previously had been accepted, as, for instance, he would have allowed prayer at graduations), and to answer the charge that federalism, an idea dear to him, conflicted with RLUIPA.

Thus, Congress's approximately ten-year-long public campaign to protect religious freedom finally met with Court approval with RLUIPA. For those not impacted with land use regulations of their religion and who are not institutionalized, this case may seem to offer little protection, but it does show that the federal government can, when the legislation is crafted carefully and is directly connected with approved government functions, like the commerce and spending clauses, protect religious liberty from state infringement. The complete list of areas in which this power is used, of course, has yet to be seen, and it is always possible that courts will not continue to uphold the legislation.

See also *Boerne* v. *Flores; Braunfeld* v. *Brown; Cheema* v. *Thompson; Employment Division* v. *Smith; Gonzales* v. *O Centro Espirita Beneficiente Uniao Do Vegetal;* Religion and prisons; Religious Freedom Restoration Act of 1993; *Sherbert* v. *Verner*

For further reading

Branham, Lynn S. 1994. *Sentencing, Corrections, and Prisoners' Rights in a Nutshell.* St. Paul, MN: West.

Carter, Lief H. 1991. *An Introduction to Constitutional Interpretation: Cases in Law and Religion.* New York: Longman.

Mandelker, Daniel R., and Rebecca L. Rubin, eds. 2001. *Protecting Free Speech and Expression: The First Amendment and Land Use Law.* Chicago: American Bar Association.

Mushlin, Michael B. 2002. *Rights of Prisoners.* St. Paul, MN: Thomson West.

Rafter, Nicole Hahn. 1999. *Prisons in America: A Reference Handbook.* Santa Barbara, CA: ABC-CLIO.

Urofsky, Melvin I. 2002. *Religious Freedom: Rights and Liberties under the Law.* Santa Barbara, CA: ABC-CLIO.

D

Dawes Severalty Act and the banning of Native American religions

Europeans long mistrusted Native Americans and their religion. One of the conquistadores' three Gs was "God," meaning the Spaniards meant to convert the inhabitants of any land they found to some form of Christianity. (The other two Gs were "Gold" and "Glory.") Soon after the Pilgrims landed as the first English presence in New England, they launched attempts to convert Native Americans. By the 1640s in Massachusetts, Native Americans, decimated by disease, were moved into praying towns, and missionaries took it upon themselves to convert them. Such was the story throughout colonial America, especially in the North.

With the push of white Americans westward, however, the aim soon became more one of conquest than conversion. This goal continued throughout most of the nineteenth century. The U.S. government accomplished its conquering goals by the 1880s, as the last rebelling groups were surrounded and put on reservations in the West. Now the question of what was to happen to the Native Americans arose again, as the question up to this point had been how the United States gained control of their land. As in the colonial period, the answer soon became one of conversion, albeit one

Omaha boys in cadet uniforms at the Carlisle Indian School in Carlisle, Pennsylvania, ca. 1880. The boys, who attended the nation's first off-reservation boarding school, were required to abandon their native clothing and hairstyles in an attempt to assimilate them into white culture. (National Archives)

combined now with the idea of racial amalga-mation. The idea was to make good white Christians out of the Native Americans, whose skin color and religion doomed them to what the government and settlers considered savage behaviors. The main act that helped this along was the Dawes Severalty Act (1887).

This act combined a number of goals. In addition to the belief that Native Americans could not continue to live on their own lands, it also picked up on the unfair treatment Na-tive Americans had received in the past. The federal government had not lived up to its promises, but the Dawes Severalty Act's solu-tion to this problem actually exacerbated the situation. Its answer to the question of what was to be done with the Native Americans was to assign them white Christian values and de-sires, giving each family 160 acres of land and allowing them to become farmers. This dif-fered from the practice of most Native Amer-icans before this in that they had owned land, when they had that idea, on a tribal basis. Many of those in favor of the act also wanted to eliminate Native American culture, includ-ing their religion. By giving them land owned individually, which all whites wanted, and by wiping out their "savage" religion and replac-ing it with Christianity (preferably Protestant Christianity), a new white race would be born. The act itself was a failure. Much of the best land was taken by speculators, as not all of the reservation land was set aside for Native American families, but only as much as was needed for those families who agreed to come under the terms of the act. Native American culture also ran contrary to this act, as Native Americans generally organized in tribes, but the act dealt with them as family units.

The act resulted in the loss of much of Na-tive American land, as, in addition to empha-sizing their confinement to the reservations, it did not even allow enough land in those reser-vations to meet its own promises. Almost two-thirds of the land originally in the reservations had been taken by whites by the 1930s. This

seizure was accomplished in two ways. First, when land set aside for Native Americans was not given to families as not enough families signed up under the act, speculators would buy the unassigned land (and often finagled the system so that the worst land was given to Na-tive Americans and the best left for specula-tors). Second, many financiers loaned money to Native American families, knowing that their farms would fail and that the land that they had been given would then be sold to pay the debt.

Another effect of the act was to allow well-meaning reformers to try to eliminate the Na-tive American religion. With the Native Amer-icans concentrated on reservations, many whites established boarding schools for Native American children, with the intent of Chris-tianizing them. Richard Henry Pratt sloga-nized his goal as "kill the Indian in Him and Save the man" (Witmer, 2002: 50). Pratt estab-lished his school in Carlisle, Pennsylvania, per-haps best known for Jim Thorpe, the Olympic and early football star. Native Americans were manipulated and coerced to go to these schools, and at the schools, they were given Christian names, forbidden to use their own names, and taught to be Christians and say prayers. Also, once the students had learned skills, they were farmed out to local families. By the turn of the century thousands of Na-tive Americans were going to these schools, and some did assimilate into white culture, which often meant the death of their religion. Some of the children who were forced into the Indian schools returned home and made a point of learning their own cultures, but it was not an easy return. As noted, one of the whole ideas behind the Dawes Act was to extermi-nate Native American culture, including their religion, for their own good (even if, as the act's authors surmised, they were too uncivi-lized to know it), and this goal was not re-versed at all until the 1930s.

By the 1930s, much of Native American land set aside on the reservations had been taken by white people. John Collier, a white reformer sympathetic to the Native Americans, argued for an abandonment of the Dawes Act. He managed to get the New Deal to fund improvements on the reservations and tried to strengthen Native American culture by restoring the tribal structure. The tribes were restored and land loss was halted, but there was no great push for a rebirth of Native American culture in federal policy. Not until the 1960s and 1970s and protests such as those at Alcatraz and at Wounded Knee did the issues reemerge. Only later, in the 1980s and 1990s, did Native Americans finally have some successes with lawsuits. However, very often the primary venture tribes could undertake in the wake of a successful lawsuit settlement was to build a reservation casino to attract white tourists. These were often only allowed to tribes as tribes, in a policy harkening back to the 1831 *Cherokee Nation* v. *Georgia* decision, ruled by federal law, not state law. Therefore, the lawsuits of the late twentieth century did little to revive Native American religion or culture. It is now estimated that only a very few languages are currently spoken among Native Americans, and in the last census, only a fraction of the population self-identified as Native American now claim Native American religions. Some change came from a movement to revive Native American cultures and desire of some modern Native Americans who were not raised in their native tribal cultures to learn their history before it was lost completely. However, such actions occurred so long after the initial attacks from white culture that their reparative impact has been minimal.

See also American Indian Religious Freedom Act; *Lyng* v. *Northwest Indian CPA*

For further reading

Allen, Paula Gunn. 1991. *Grandmothers of the Light.* Boston: Beacon Press.

Arden, Harvey, Steve Wall, and White Deer of Autumn. 1990. *Wisdomkeepers.* Hillsboro, OR: Beyond Words.

Treat, James. 2003. *Around the Sacred Fire.* New York: Palgrave Macmillan.

Witmer, Linda F. 2002. *The Indian Industrial School.* Carlisle, PA: Cumberland County Historical Society.

Discovery Institute

The Discovery Institute is one of the leading groups involved in the battle over intelligent design (ID). The Institute is based in Seattle, Washington, and receives funding from a wide variety of sources, most of whom lean toward the conservative side of the spectrum. The Institute's interests, in the area of religion and the law, mostly focus on how to have ID introduced into public school classrooms.

The Institute was established in 1990. It was founded by George Gilder, a conservative antifeminist writer; Stephen Meyer, a philosopher of science; and Bruce Chapman, a politician and writer. The three received money from individuals and foundations, including Howard Ahmanson, Jr., Richard Scaife, and the MacLellan Foundation. Ahmanson is a believer in bringing the Bible back into public life and supports a philosophy known as Christian Reconstructionism, which holds that if the Bible is not brought back, society will collapse. To avoid this collapse, the movement argues for a return to biblical punishments and a strong condemnation of homosexuality and blasphemy. (Ahmanson also funded publications that called for the stoning of gays and lesbians.) Scaife has contributed to a wider variety of causes, most of them conservative but some liberal, including Planned Parenthood. The MacLellan Foundation believes that the Bible is literally correct as written and thus supports the six days of creation argument.

The ID efforts were promoted by the 1987 Supreme Court decision in *Edwards* v. *Aguillard,* which held that a legislature could not mandate the teaching of evolution and creation science on an equal basis, as this promoted religion. Many creation scientists turned to favor intelligent design, and the main textbook for intelligent design, *Of Pandas and People,* may have been originally written for creation science and altered by replacing the term "creation science" with "intelligent design" with no other alterations. The Discovery Institute gave support to something that came to be known as the Wedge Theory. This argued that the first step that needed to be taken was to have the teaching of ID brought into schools under the idea that ID was another scientific answer to the world's origin, and that evolution had too many holes to be the only explanation. Supporters felt this would decrease evolution's image, which, in turn would eventually allow intelligent design to be taught. The goal of many ID supporters now is to "teach the controversy," arguing that both sides of the evolution/anti-evolution argument should be presented, in the name of academic freedom. They also want to keep evolution in question long enough for ID to find all the answers.

Since its inception, the Discovery Institute has spent a lot of money publicizing their perspective. They have produced a wide variety of publications and also do a great deal of research into the public side of the issue, taking polls and producing pieces intended to convince the wider public of ID's validity. They also have given fellowships to some of the leading ID writers, allowing them time to write about the issues. One of the leading ID writers supported by the Discovery Institute, William Dembski, was just hired by the Southern Baptist Theological Seminary, which demonstrates the connection between the religious issues and the Discovery Institute at times. The Discovery Institute has had a measured amount of success on the issue. At least three states have passed legislation allowing teachers to challenge evolution in the classroom, and many other states have seen school boards considering measures on the question. The Discovery Institute responds to requests for information and offers legal advice on the issue when questioned.

The Discovery Institute maintains that ID is agnostic, with no sacred text to defend, unlike creation science, which was wholly based in the account of Genesis found in the Bible. However, some critics have charged that this is the group's public attitude, which is belied by their alleged comments to religious groups suggesting that God is definitely part of the ID equation.

The Discovery Institute is also interested in other issues that do not receive as much publicity. Among those are cooperation between Canada and the United States in the region around Seattle, and transportation. The Bill and Melinda Gates Foundation has given a large amount of money to support the transportation initiative, but they have specified clearly that the money may be spent *only* on that issue.

In an interesting twist, Edward Larson, one of the leading scholars on the Scopes Trial, which dealt with one of the early efforts to ban the teaching of evolution, received support in the early and mid-1990s from the Discovery Institute. He, however, takes great pains to point out that he was affiliated with that group before they became as interested in intelligent design as they now are.

The Discovery Institute thus mixes support from those who favor a religious revival with those more interested in the scientific end of the ID equation. While publicly noting support for increased scientific inquiry, the Institute still privately notes a desire to implement an ID-only curriculum. Regardless of one's personal opinion of the Institute, it clearly has had, and will continue to have, an important impact on the whole debate over the teaching of evolution.

See also Edwards v. Aguillard; Kitzmiller v. Dover Area School District; Scopes v. Tennessee/Scopes Monkey Trial

For further reading

Davis, P. William, and Dean H. Kenyon. 1989. *Of Pandas and People: The Central Questions of Biological Origins.* Dallas, TX: Haughton.

Larson, Edward J. 2003. *Trial and Error: The American Controversy over Creation and Evolution.* Oxford: Oxford University Press.

Pennock, Robert T., ed. 2001. *Intelligent Design Creationism and Its Critics: Philosophical, Theological, and Scientific Perspectives.* Cambridge, MA: MIT Press.

Rich, Andrew. 2004. *Think Tanks, Public Policy, and the Politics of Expertise.* New York: Cambridge University Press.

Robbins, Thomas, and Susan J. Palmer, eds. 1997. *Millennium, Messiahs, and Mayhem: Contemporary Apocalyptic Movements.* New York: Routledge.

Divorce, marriage, and religion

Divorce and marriage were originally seen largely as religious events with some intersection with the state. For this reason, marriage licenses were granted by the state from early in the life of the country, but most marriages were performed by churches. Marriage and divorce standards greatly differed from state to state, and these differences often had to do with which religion was prevalent in the state. People sometimes tried to go to a different state for divorce from the one in which they lived or were married. Sometimes, these out-of-state divorces were not recognized in their home states when the individuals returned. Thus, if both parties were not amicable to a divorce, or if notice was not given, the divorce might not be recognized by the state.

One of the more famous and tragic cases in the nineteenth century was that of Abby Mc-Farland, who lived in New York City. Though legally married to Daniel McFarland, she had separated from him and had begun to see Albert Richardson. Daniel McFarland in 1867 shot Richardson, who survived. In 1868 Abby moved to Indiana and divorced McFarland in 1869 under Indiana state laws. Abby later returned to New York, and Daniel McFarland and Albert Richardson exchanged mudslinging letters about the 1867 shooting. In November 1869, Daniel again shot Albert, who died, but not before marrying Abby. In the trial, Abby could not testify against Daniel as she was, in the eyes of New York, probably still his wife. Daniel had never been given notice of the Indiana proceedings and so they were, in New York, probably not valid. While out-of-state divorces were respected in New York, notice had to be given to the party remaining in state.

Daniel, in the end, was acquitted, as his lawyers depicted him as a defender of his family, both threatened by Albert and driven insane by the thought of losing his wife to the seducer.

Divorce itself was generally disfavored by the state, largely due to the dislike of divorce by the church. Originally in England at that same time, the only form of divorce was *divortium semiplenum.* The Crown had to grant a separation order and both parties had to live apart; however, neither could remarry, and they still were married in the eyes of the law as far as property and children were concerned. In early America, after the Revolution, courts could not grant divorces, and the legislature had to act. (This is not as unusual as it sounds, as the legislatures did many things then that they do not do now. For instance, charters incorporating businesses had to be passed specifically by the legislature.) It was not until the 1820s that the first state allowed courts to grant divorces. States started out allowing them on relatively wide grounds but narrowed those eventually to desertion, cruelty, adultery, and a jail term of over five years. If the defendant issued any defense whatsoever, some states would still not allow the divorce. The standards for proving these grounds were also strict. For instance, to prove adultery, one had to prove vaginal intercourse. Not until the early twentieth century did New York adopt a looser standard allowing the assumption that a man and a woman who were not married and were in the same bedroom had committed adultery. Some states still required suspicious circumstances in addition to opportunity. Only in the 1960s did laws change to allow easier grounds again for divorce. It should be noted that the rise in the divorce rate started in the 1930s, well before this last change.

Another issue to be considered is that of annulments. Annulments were generally favored over divorces in church law, including in the Roman Catholic Church. In the Catholic Church, divorced people were not supposed to receive the sacraments. Laws also sometimes penalized those with annulments less harshly.

Annulments were originally allowed in England for only a few reasons, including that the parties were closely related, that one party was impotent, or that one person had married before.

Law, directly, issues annulments only rarely. The principal circumstances are for two people to be married in a civil ceremony with one promising the other that later they will be married in the second person's church or synagogue, then refusing to carry out that promise. A few states have granted annulments, however, when the marriage itself was never consummated due to failure to go through the religious ceremony.

Religion also enters into law in the state of families after divorce. Courts have generally been unwilling to enforce parts of private divorce decrees that control the religion in which a child will be raised. The parent who has custody is normally allowed total control over the religion of the child, even if the parent had signed documents stating that he or she would raise the child in a certain religion.

Thus, religious attitudes and holdovers from religious law have greatly affected how divorce law still is carried on today, even though this is less true than it was fifty years ago.

See also Gay marriage; Marriage—right to conduct; Religion and attitudes toward marriage historically in the United States

For further reading

Coontz, Stephanie. 2005. *Marriage, a History: From Obedience to Intimacy, or How Love Conquered Marriage.* New York: Viking.

Gregory, John DeWitt, Peter N. Swisher, and Sheryl L. Wolf. 2001. *Understanding Family Law.* Newark, NJ: LexisNexis.

Outhwaite, R. B., ed. 1982. *Marriage and Society: Studies in the Social History of Marriage.* New York: St. Martin's Press.

Donahoe v. Richards

38 Me. 379 (1854)

Bible reading was very often a part of the American school day in the nineteenth century. Many Catholics opposed this policy, as the Bible used was generally the King James Bible, not the Douay Bible approved by the Catholic Church. Sometimes riots broke out over the practice, and sometimes the protests were more quiet. In Maine in the early 1850s, one student protested against reading the King James Bible and was expelled from school.

Her father sued on this student's behalf, as did the student. The father's suit was dismissed as the father had no rights, and while the student was able to proceed further, she lost as well. The reasoning used by the Maine Supreme Court was that it was not illegal for the school board to order the reading of the Bible and to expel any student who refused to read from the Bible. It held that this situation was the same as with any student who refused to read a book on the grounds of conscience. The court first held that as the school board was acting in good faith when it set up the laws and expelled the student, the school board could not be held liable as public officials were, at the time, generally given immunity. The court also examined the right of the school board to establish policy and held it to be generally unlimited. If bad books or policies were adopted, said the court, the people had the right to dismiss the board at the next election, and this was the people's sole remedy. The school board's power to force students to follow its orders by threatening penalties up to expulsion for not following the rules was also held to be necessary.

The court was a bit more circuitous in dealing with the religion issue. It first held that no sect was allowed to be promoted, and then held that no sect had been promoted by the selection of the Bible, apparently ignoring the fact that the selection of the version of the Bible supported by Protestants, by its nature, favored Protestantism over Catholicism. The court further stated that other religious texts could also be used, ignoring that only this one was used, and held that since no one was forced to believe in the Bible, no faith was promoted. Also, this decision stated that allowing this one book to be challenged would open all to challenge, without considering that no other books were likely to be challenged. This endless series of challenges, the court suggested, would   interfere with education. Finally, Sunday closing laws and the rejection of witnesses who would not swear oaths was, in the eyes of the Maine Supreme Court, acceptable; therefore, this choice of requiring the King James Version of the Bible to be read was acceptable as well. The court closed by noting that the student was the one favoring one religion over another, not the school, as her faith, in her eyes, gave her the right to challenge books in the schools.

Finally, the Maine Supreme Court viewed education as a huge benefit and one necessary for dealing with the masses of immigrants. Only through the schools could the immigrants be Americanized, and so the schools needed to be supported in their attempts and not restricted, as the court saw the plaintiff doing. This reflected the common anti-Catholic, anti-immigration bias of the day, as large numbers of Irish Catholic immigrants were wrongly stereotyped by the established populations of the country, who often equated their perception of the taint of immigrant poverty directly with Catholicism. The court noted, near the end of its opinion, "large masses of foreign population are among us, weak in the midst of our strength. Mere citizenship is of no avail, unless they imbibe the liberal spirit of our laws and institutions, unless they become citizens in fact as well as in name. In no other way can the process of assimilation be so readily and thoroughly accomplished as through the medium of the public schools, which are alike open to the children of the rich and the poor, of the stranger and the citizen. It is the duty of those to whom this sacred trust is confided, to discharge it with magnanimous liberality and Christian kindness" (38 Me. 379: 413). Apparently, though, Christian kindness did not extend to admitting

that Catholics might have a point in objecting to being told that their Bible, the core of their beliefs, was the wrong one to use.

See also Board of Education of Cincinnati v. *Minor; Lee v. Weisman; McCreary County v. ACLU; School District of Abington Township v. Schempp*

For further reading

Fraser, James W. 1999. *Between Church and State: Religion and Public Education in a Multicultural America.* New York: St. Martin's Press.

Gillis, Chester. 1999. *Roman Catholicism in America.* New York: Columbia University Press.

Ravitch, Frank S. 1999. *School Prayer and Discrimination: The Civil Rights of Religious Minorities and Dissenters.* Boston: Northeastern University Press.

Doremus v. *Board of Education*
342 U.S. 429 (1952)

This case dealt with what was needed before a person could sue over a separation of church and state. If something was occurring in a school that an individual believed was unconstitutional, could that person sue if he or she had no direct involvement with that school? *Doremus* v. *Board of Education* answered the question in the negative.

This case was brought by a parent and another taxpayer (the parent was also a taxpayer) who objected to Bible reading in the public schools. The parent's child, however, had graduated, and so the court, in an opinion written by Justice Jackson, noted that the case was moot. The Court also noted that as the Bible reading could be objected to and the students excused, no injury was proven. As far as the taxpayer's case existed, no injury was stated by those paying taxes, and taxes were not shown to be directly affected by the Bible reading. The Court seemed to be saying that unless the Bible reading cost money that would change the tax levels, taxpayers could not bring suits against the schools for Bible reading. The Court differentiated this case from that of *Everson,* stating "it is true that this Court found a justifiable

Robert H. Jackson was an associate justice of the U.S. Supreme Court from 1941 to 1954. (Library of Congress)

mismanagement of the school system that is alleged is clear and plain" (342 U.S. 429: 435). He then stated that if New Jersey wanted, they could allow the taxpayers to sue, even if in federal court the suit would not be allowed.

This case, in the area of Bible reading, upheld the right of schools to order Bible readings by default as it prevented the challenge that the parent wanted to bring. It, however, did not rule directly on the correctness of that practice. Not until 1963 would the Supreme Court strike down that practice as creating a violation of the First Amendment.

> *See also* Bible controversy and riots; *Engel* v. *Vitale; People ex rel. Ring* v. *Board of Education; Roberts* v. *Madigan; School District of Abington Township* v. *Schempp; Tudor* v. *Board of Education of Borough of Rutherford*

For further reading

Ackerman, David M., ed. 2001. *Prayer and Religion in the Public Schools.* New York: Novinka Books.

Greenawalt, Kent. 2005. *Does God Belong in Public Schools?* Princeton, NJ: Princeton University Press.

Hockett, Jeffrey D. 1996. *New Deal Justice: The Constitutional Jurisprudence of Hugo L. Black, Felix Frankfurter, and Robert H. Jackson.* Lanham, MD: Rowman & Littlefield.

Wasby, Stephen L., ed. 1990. *"He Shall Not Pass This Way Again": The Legacy of Justice William O. Douglas.* Pittsburgh, PA: University of Pittsburgh Press for the William O. Douglas Institute.

controversy in *Everson* v. *Board of Education*. But *Everson* showed a measurable appropriation or disbursement of school-district funds occasioned solely by the activities complained of. This complaint does not" (342 U.S. 429: 434). Taxpayers were thus allowed to sue the school only when a direct financial interest was shown.

Justices Douglas, Reed, and Burton dissented, in an opinion written by Justice Douglas. Douglas held that these taxpayers and the parents together had enough of an interest for the lawsuit to be decided on its merits. (This Supreme Court case was only a dispute over whether the lawsuit should be dismissed as not stating a controversy.) Since all of the taxpayers could sue, why not a few, asked Douglas, holding "if all can do it, there is no apparent reason why less than all may not, the interest being the same. In the present case the issues are not feigned; the suit is not collusive; the

Duro v. *District Attorney, Second Judicial District of North Carolina*

712 F.2d 96 (4th Cir. 1983)

In re McMillan

226 S.E. 2d 693 (Court of Appeals of N.C., 1976)

Since the mid-nineteenth century in America there have been compulsory school laws. The laws originally encountered parental objections in the area of religion, in that students were forced to read from a Protestant Bible, even if the student was Catholic, some other non-Christian religion, or not religious at all. Some court challenges in this area were successful (and others were not), and many Catholics responded by setting up their own schools. In the twentieth century, attempts to force students to attend public schools included such radical acts as the banning of private schools, and these challenges failed. Some parents did not want to send their children to public schools for a variety of reasons. In the *Duro* case, parents objected to the compulsory school laws because of the values they saw being imposed on their children by the schools.

The Fourth Circuit Court of Appeals held for the state and the compulsory school law. Duro claimed that the mandatory attendance law violated his freedom of religion in three different areas. He was opposed to what he called the "unisex movement" that he saw in public schools, as he objected on religious grounds to any movement that made all the boys and girls the same. He also felt the public schools promoted secular humanism (or a secular religion). Finally, he did not want his children to have to interact with the different beliefs that people brought to public school. The district court initially found for Duro on a motion for summary judgment. The district court had used the *Yoder* test, which looked at two things: "(1) whether a sincere religious belief exists, and (2) whether the state's interest in compulsory education is of sufficient magnitude to override the interest claimed by the parents under the Free Exercise Clause of the First Amendment" (712 F.2d 96: 97).

The Circuit Court of Appeals agreed that the test was correct but felt that it was wrongly applied. The higher court argued that Duro, a Pentecostal, was different from the Amish in *Yoder* in that the Amish lived as a separate society and had been doing so in different societies for three centuries. The Amish also allowed their children to be educated in public schools through grade eight, whereas Duro did not want his children to attend any school at all. Duro also was unwilling to enroll his children in any type of an accredited school, and his wife, who had home schooled the children,

had not been certified. "Duro has not demonstrated that home instruction will prepare his children to be self-sufficient participants in our modern society or enable them to participate intelligently in our political system, which, as the Supreme Court stated, is a compelling interest of the state" (712 F. 2d 96: 99). Thus, the district court decision was reversed, and the Duro children were required to attend school. A concurrence by Judge Sprouse held that the interest of the state in educating, no matter how stated, did not increase the state's interest in this case and that the state's right to educate needed to be weighed within the First Amendment. Sprouse also noted that the children's rights were not in question here. Thus, Duro had no right to keep his children at home and to home school them in a setting with a teacher of unproven competency, and the compulsory attendance law was upheld.

Besides challenges to the overall effect of public schools, there have also been challenges to what the schools taught. In North Carolina there was a charge of neglect against parents who had kept their children out of school on the basis that the schools did not teach enough Native American heritage. That case was *In re McMillan,* or in the matter of McMillan. The parents were keeping their children out of school because "they were not taught about Indians and Indian heritage and culture" (226 S.E. 2d 693: 105). The children had no other issues of neglect other than being kept out of school, but the court of appeals of North Carolina held this to be enough to create neglect. The parent's rights were said to be different from those in *Yoder,* as a concern for one's heritage was not said to be equal with a religion. Also, "there is no showing that Shelby and Abe McMillan receive any mode of educational programs alternative to those in the public school. There is also no showing that the Indian heritage or culture of these children will be endangered or threatened in any way by their attending school" (226 S.E. 2d 693: 695). On the whole, the court concluded that "it is fundamental that a child who receives proper care and supervision in modern times is provided a basic education. A child does not receive 'proper care' and lives in an 'environment injurious to his welfare' when he is deliberately refused this education" (226 S.E. 2d 693: 695). Thus, the court found for the state and upheld the charge of neglect.

One might have thought that the Amish's victory in *Yoder* signified a retreat of the states' power in the area of compulsory education. However, these two cases show that the retreat, if any, was minor, in that one had to be of a separate society, similar to the Amish, or had to be willing to educate the children in a home school with a competent teacher or an accredited private school. Thus, the state still had a strong right in the area of forcing children to be properly educated.

See also *Berg* v. *Glen Cove City School District; Cheema* v. *Thompson; Farrington* v. *Tokushige; New Jersey* v. *Massa; Wisconsin* v. *Yoder*

For further reading

Adams, David Wallace. 1995. *Education for Extinction: American Indians and the Boarding School Experience, 1875–1928.* Lawrence: University Press of Kansas.

Lines, Patricia M. 1984. *Education Reform and Education Choice: Conflict and Accommodation.* Washington, DC: National Institute of Education.

Machan, Tibor R., ed. 2000. *Education in a Free Society.* Stanford, CA: Hoover Institution Press.

Stevens, Mitchell L. 2001. *Kingdom of Children: Culture and Controversy in the Homeschooling Movement.* Princeton, NJ: Princeton University Press.

E

Edwards v. Aguillard
482 U.S. 578 (1987)

Ever since the Scopes Monkey Trial in 1925, the question of whether a state can ban the teaching of evolution has been answered the same way: no. The Scopes Trial was not a Supreme Court case, and, legally, did not even overturn Tennessee's law banning the teaching of evolution. It was not until 1968 and *Epperson* v. *Arkansas* that the Supreme Court weighed in on the matter, holding that the Arkansas law violated the First Amendment. However, even this ruling has not stopped those opposed to the teaching of evolution, as they have changed tactics. Opponents of evolution have also been helped by the emergence of creation science and intelligent design advocates; the first group argues that science proves the creation story of Genesis and the second group claims that science indicates there must be an intelligent being behind the formation of the world, as it is too complex to have emerged just by chance. Those opposing the teaching of evolution have seized upon these groups and argued that their theories should be given equal time as that of evolution. In 1982, Louisiana passed a law requiring that if evolution were to be taught, creation science must be given equal time and that law was at issue in *Edwards* v. *Aguillard*.

Justice Brennan wrote the opinion for the Court, which was fully joined by four other justices and partially joined by Justice O'Connor. Brennan first surveyed the history of the law in question, the "Creationism Act," and noted that "no school is required to teach evolution or creation science. If either is taught, however, the other must also be taught" (482 U.S. 578, 581). He then held that the three-part *Lemon* test applied, and he defined this test

William Brennan was an associate justice of the U.S. Supreme Court from 1956 to 1990 and established a liberal reputation as a defender of individual rights. (Heinen/Collection of the Supreme Court of the United States)

as "first, the legislature must have adopted the law with a secular purpose. Second, the statute's principal or primary effect must be one that neither advances nor inhibits religion. Third, the statute must not result in an excessive entanglement of government with religion" (482 U.S. 578: 583). While school boards and states are generally given leeway in the area of curriculum and instruction, this is much less true where the First Amendment is concerned.

Brennan then turned to the *Lemon* test and its first prong, the law's purpose. He held that there it had no clear secular purpose, as it did not advance academic freedom nor did it create a more comprehensive curriculum. The state, however, argued, both in court and in the hearings, that it did have these purposes. Normally a court will defer to a state, so Brennan's decision that the law had no clear secular purpose was controversial. Brennan did look to what the bill's supporters stated and held that "it is clear from the legislative history that the purpose of the legislative sponsor, Senator Bill Keith, was to narrow the science curriculum," as Keith wanted evolution to cease being taught (482 U.S. 578: 587). He also noted that teachers' academic freedom was not advanced. The Supreme Court concluded "thus we agree with the Court of Appeals' conclusion that the Act does not serve to protect academic freedom, but has the distinctly different purpose of discrediting 'evolution by counterbalancing its teaching at every turn with the teaching of creationism'" (482 U.S. 578: 589).

After disagreeing with the legislature's description of what the purpose of the law was, the Supreme Court then looked at the actual purpose of the law. It first noted "there is a historic and contemporaneous link between the teachings of certain religious denominations and the teaching of evolution" (482 U.S. 578: 590). From this, and from looking at past cases, the Court determined that "the preeminent purpose of the Louisiana Legislature was clearly to advance the religious viewpoint that a supernatural being created humankind" (482 U.S. 578: 591). To support this conclusion, they examined testimony from the legislature's hearings and concluded that "the term 'creation science,' as contemplated by the legislature that adopted this Act, embodies the religious belief that a supernatural creator was responsible for the creation of humankind" (482 U.S. 578: 592). Thus, the very curriculum that was required, if one taught evolution, had a religious viewpoint. The Court held that "because the primary purpose of the Creationism Act is to advance a particular religious belief, the Act endorses religion in violation of the First Amend-

ment" (482 U.S. 578: 593). The Court also held that summary judgment had been correctly granted at the district court level and so upheld the order of the lower court that this act was unconstitutional.

Justice Powell concurred, joined by Justice O'Connor. Powell first noted the terms of the act and that the legislature did not define either evolution or creation science. Then, by turning to the legislative history, he stated that creation science implies a religious purpose. Powell examined the two main institutions behind creation science, at least as presented to the Louisiana legislature, and noted that both were religious. He concluded that "here, it is clear that religious belief is the Balanced Treatment Act's 'reason for existence'" (482 U.S. 578: 603). Powell then affirmed the general leeway given local school boards to set policy, noting that schools could teach the religious heritage of America, but he also cautioned that religious doctrine could not be advanced, which he believed was happening in Louisiana.

Justice White concurred in the judgment. He noted that lower court's interpretation of statutes was normally accepted and that there was no strong reason here to reconsider the decisions. As this was true, he affirmed the lower court's judgment. He hints that he might have a different reading of the statute's purpose, but that with the lower court's ruling as it did, he had to agree with them.

Justice Scalia dissented, joined by Chief Justice Rehnquist. He held that the Court was ignoring the true purpose of the act and substituting its own beliefs for the claimed purpose of the act as stated by the legislature. He commented that "the question of its constitutionality cannot rightly be disposed of on the gallop, by impugning the motives of its supporters" (482 U.S. 578: 611). Scalia then turned to what some scientists said, and held that only science was being discussed here, at least arguably, and so "at this point, then, we must assume that the Balanced Treatment Act does not require the presentation of religious doctrine" (482 U.S.

578: 612). Scalia argued that for a law to be struck down under the first part of the *Lemon* test, its "sole motive" must have been "to promote religion" (482 U.S. 578: 614). Scalia also held that acting on religious motives was acceptable as long as the goal was not to advance religion. He held that acting according to religion was sometimes needed as "today's religious activism may give us the Balanced Treatment Act, but yesterday's resulted in the abolition of slavery, and tomorrow's may bring relief for famine victims" (482 U.S. 578: 615). Scalia also held that neutrality with regard to religion was needed and that the government could act to bring this about.

Scalia then turned to the purposes, as he saw them, of this act. About the legislature, he noted "the vast majority of them voted to approve a bill which explicitly stated a secular purpose; what is crucial is not their wisdom in believing that purpose would be achieved by the bill, but their sincerity in believing it would be" (482 U.S. 578: 621). He then commented how reputable witnesses testified as to the two different "origins of life" and how "both posit a theory of the origin of life and subject that theory to empirical testing" (482 U.S. 578: 622). As both had science behind them, and as, according to the witnesses heard in the legislature, "creation science is educationally valuable" (and not being taught then), the legislature had an educational goal in this bill (482 U.S. 578: 623). Scalia accepted (or at least argued that the Court should accept) at face value the bill's supporters' statement that religion was not the purpose of this act. He therefore would have allowed it. He also surveyed the evidence on academic freedom and found enough evidence there to support it as a purpose of the bill. Scalia even held that if most legislators wanted to advance religion, that might be acceptable. "In sum, even if one concedes, for the sake of argument, that a majority of the Louisiana Legislature voted for the Balanced Treatment Act partly in order to foster (rather than merely eliminate discrimination against) Christian fundamentalist beliefs, our cases establish that that alone would not suffice to invalidate the Act, so long as there was a genuine secular purpose as well" (482 U.S. 578: 633–634).

Scalia also had a direct attack on the whole "purpose" part of the *Lemon* test. He noted that the purpose part has produced a "maze" of conflicting rulings. He also said "to look for the sole purpose of even a single legislator is probably to look for something that does not exist," and so to determine the purpose of the overall legislature is truly impossible (482 U.S. 578: 637). Scalia went back to the First Amendment and held that the purpose test was not necessary as it was not supported by the text of that amendment. In closing, he commented that "abandoning *Lemon*'s purpose test—a test which exacerbates the tension between the Free Exercise and Establishment Clauses, has no basis in the language or history of the Amendment, and, as today's decision shows, has wonderfully flexible consequences—would be a good place to start" (482 U.S. 578: 640).

The attempt of the Louisiana legislature to require equal treatment for the teaching of creation science, for whatever purpose it was attempted, was struck down by the Supreme Court. Since that time, few legislatures have tried to ban the teaching of evolution or to require equal treatment. This has not stopped those arguing for a teaching of creation science, or for those advocating intelligent design, which does not hold for a scenario, however well scientifically supported it might be, that mirrors the first chapter of Genesis in the Bible. Intelligent design instead argues and posits scientific evidence for the existence of higher intelligence in the universe's creation. It contends the world is too complex for that intelligence not to exist and various things are complex enough, or designed enough, to demonstrate that. School boards and state curriculum committees have sometimes required some treatment of these and, more often, particularly with the increased need for testing after President George W. Bush's No Child Left

Behind program, have often left the issue of evolution out of the state-mandated list of subjects that must be taught. Thus, the battle between those opposed to, and those favoring, the teaching of evolution continues to itself evolve, even while direct statewide laws like the one in *Edwards* v. *Aguillard* are less common.

> **See also** Avoidance of the issue of evolution in many teaching standards; *Crowley* v. *Smithsonian Institution; Epperson* v. *Arkansas; Peloza* v. *Capistrano Unified School District; Scopes* v. *Tennessee/Scopes Monkey Trial*
>
> **For further reading**
>
> Barlow, Connie, ed. 1994. *Evolution Extended: Biological Debates on the Meaning of Life.* Cambridge, MA: MIT Press.
>
> Dembski, William A., and Michael Ruse, eds. 2004. *Debating Design: From Darwin to DNA.* New York: Cambridge University Press.
>
> Israel, Charles A. 2004. *Before Scopes: Evangelicalism, Education, and Evolution in Tennessee, 1870–1925.* Athens: University of Georgia Press.
>
> Larson, Edward J. 1997. *Summer for the Gods: The Scopes Trial and America's Continuing Debate over Science and Religion.* New York: Basic Books.
>
> Larson, Edward J. 2003. *Trial and Error: The American Controversy over Creation and Evolution.* Oxford: Oxford University Press.
>
> Livingstone, David N. 1987. *Darwin's Forgotten Defenders: The Encounter between Evangelical Theology and Evolutionary Thought.* Grand Rapids, MI: W. B. Eerdmans.
>
> Numbers, Ronald L. 1992. *The Creationists.* New York: Knopf.

EEOC v. *Kamehameha Schools/Bishop's Estate*

990 F.2d 458 (9th Cir. 1993)

This decision dealt with whether a private school could require that all of its teachers be Protestant. Title VII of the 1964 Civil Rights Act generally prohibited this. Bishop had been a member of the Hawaiian royal family and had left part of her estate to form two schools, the Kamehameha schools. One stipulation was that the schools employ only Protestant teachers. A non-Protestant teacher applied and was in-

formed of the requirement. He contacted the Equal Employment Opportunity Commission (EEOC), who sued. The case reached the Ninth Circuit Court of Appeals, which found for the EEOC.

Judge Browning wrote the decision. The schools had claimed exemption on three grounds, all of which had been granted by the district court. The grounds were that this was a "religious . . . educational institution," that being Protestant was a "bona fide occupational qualification" for the position, and that the curriculum of the school was directed at Protestants and so hiring Protestants only was allowed (990 F.2d 458: 459).

The Ninth Circuit reviewed each of these in turn. They first held that the school was mostly secular and was not sufficiently affiliated with the Protestant religion. No particular Protestant denomination had ever owned the school, and the estate itself was mostly secular. The purpose of the school was not to teach religion but to teach ethics, and the student body itself was not overly Protestant. The teachers were Protestant, as was required, but active Protestant membership was not required. The students were required to fulfill a "limited religious education requirement" (990 F.2d 458: 463). Reflecting all of these factors, the court held that "we conclude the Schools are an essentially secular institution operating within an historical tradition that includes Protestantism, and that the Schools' purpose and character is primarily secular, not primarily religious" (990 F.2d 458: 463–464).

The court then turned to the question of whether the school itself was aimed at increasing the Protestant religion, which would have justified an exemption. The court noted that there were few previous decisions on this point, so it was covering new ground. However, the court noted "the curriculum of the Schools has little to do with propagating Protestantism," and so held that the school did not qualify.

The court finally turned to the question of whether being a Protestant was a "bona fide occupational qualification. [BFOQ]." They first noted that in order for it to qualify as such, being Protestant must be essential for job performance. The court then surveyed the trial record, the job in question, and the general range of jobs done at the school and concluded, "Except for the Schools' religious education teachers (as to whom Protestant affiliation is conceded to be a BFOQ), teachers at the Schools provide instruction in traditional secular subjects in the traditional secular way. There is nothing to suggest that adherence to the Protestant faith is essential to the performance of this job" (990 F.2d 458: 466). Thus, Protestantism was not held to be a bona fide occupational qualification. It was suggested that keeping the teachers Protestant was required to abide by the wishes of the will, but the court held that "the fact that the Protestant-only requirement appears in Mrs. Bishop's will cannot in itself alter the result" (990 F.2d 458: 466).

For all these reasons, the court held that the school could not require that its teachers be Protestant. The law since has largely continued this trend, but few schools have such an explicit statement in their charter that are not also religious schools aimed at increasing, or at least limited to, their faith. The basic point of this case has continued, though, that mere preference, however forcefully stated, for people of one religion does not create a right to hire only those of that religion, and prior practice does not make discrimination legal. While there are exemptions, the exemptions are narrowly drawn and past practice does not make one fit into those exemptions.

See also *Corporation of Presiding Bishop* v. *Amos;*
Farrington v. *Tokushige; Lemon* v. *Kurtzman;*
Ohio Civil Rights Commission v. *Dayton Schools*

For further reading

Dwyer, James G. 1998. *Religious Schools v. Children's Rights.* Ithaca, NY: Cornell University Press.

Jurinski, James. 1998. *Religion in the Schools: A Reference Handbook.* Santa Barbara, CA: ABC-CLIO.

La Morte, Michael W. 2001. *School Law: Cases and Concepts.* Boston: Allyn and Bacon.

Elk Grove Unified School District v. *Newdow*

542 U.S. 1 (2004)

The Pledge of Allegiance is something that most American schoolchildren have said at one time or another, but relatively few have thought much about it. Many students stop saying it at the elementary level, and many fewer elementary students question their teachers than at higher school levels. Students are also, in general, taught to conform, and all of these factors mean that few students question the pledge. However, legal challenges to the pledge nonetheless stretch back to World War II and before, as Jehovah's Witnesses challenged the pledge on the grounds that it forced them to salute a graven image, an action banned by their religion. In 1943, the Supreme Court reversed an earlier ruling and held for them. In 1954, Congress added "under God" to the pledge to differentiate the United States from the "godless communists" of the USSR. After the United States won the Cold War and the USSR dissolved, the phrase remained. A father, Michael Newdow, objected to his daughter saying the pledge, as he believed the phrase created an establishment of religion, which would be illegal under the First Amendment. The case made it all the way to the Supreme Court, but a technicality ultimately allowed the Court to defer judgment on this issue.

Justice Stevens wrote the opinion, which was joined by Justices Kennedy, Souter, Ginsburg, and Breyer (Justice Scalia did not participate in the case). Stevens first held that the Court "conclude[s] that Newdow lacks standing" (542 U.S. 1: 5). He reviewed the history of the pledge and California's requirement that it

Michael Newdow, plaintiff in Elk Grove Unified School District v. Newdow *(2004), enters the U.S. Supreme Court on March 24, 2004. Newdow challenged the constitutionality of the phrase "under God" in the Pledge of Allegiance. (Mannie Garcia/Getty Images)*

be recited in each elementary school. Note that "the School District permits students who object on religious grounds to abstain from the recitation" (542 U.S. 1: 9).

Stevens then turned to the issue of standing. He noted that the Supreme Court has long had a history of not deciding constitutional issues unless they must, and he defended this policy since "the command to guard jealously and exercise rarely our power to make constitutional pronouncements requires strictest adherence when matters of great national significance are at stake. Even in cases concededly within our jurisdiction under Article III, we abide by 'a se-

ries of rules under which [we have] avoided passing upon a large part of all the constitutional questions pressed upon [us] for decision'" (542 U.S. 1: 15). The Court then noted that the person suing must have suffered an injury, and that generally the whole issue of custody is left to the states. At issue here was whether Michael Newdow had enough of an interest, legally, in his child, as the child's mother had custody. Newdow claimed that even though he did not have custody, he still had the "right to inculcate in his daughter—free from governmental interference—the atheistic beliefs he finds persuasive" (542 U.S. 1:

22). The Court held that though Newdow had a right to discuss his religious beliefs with his daughter, he did not have a right to control what others said to her about religion, which in this case the custodial parent would have. This meant he did not have standing, and as the girl's mother was actively fighting her ex-husband's right to sue on their daughter's behalf, that ended the case for the majority.

Justices O'Connor and Thomas along with Chief Justice Rehnquist concurred in the judgment, which meant that they agreed with the Court's decision but not with the method by which the judgment was reached. Rehnquist wrote the opinion and first turned to the issue of standing. He held that the Court in the past had not gone into issues of family law only by disallowing standing in family law cases in very limited circumstances. (Rehnquist would have deferred to the Ninth Circuit, which he held as being more knowledgeable about California law, and which had granted standing to Newdow, and so Rehnquist would have granted standing.)

He turned to the issue of the pledge. Rehnquist made an interesting comment early in his discussion. "To the millions of people who regularly recite the Pledge, and who have no access to, or concern with, such legislation or legislative history, 'under God' might mean several different things: that God has guided the destiny of the United States, for example, or that the United States exists under God's authority. How much consideration anyone gives to the phrase probably varies, since the Pledge itself is a patriotic observance focused primarily on the flag and the Nation, and only secondarily on the description of the Nation" (542 U.S. 1: 41). Thus, Rehnquist admitted having an unclear grasp on what people think the phrase means. Rehnquist, though, was more concerned with the past than the present and cited many examples in which past presidents and other public figures had discussed and used "God" in public addresses and proclamations. From this he concluded, "All of these events strongly suggest that our national culture allows public recognition of our Nation's religious history and character" (542 U.S. 1: 47).

Rehnquist then turned to whether the pledge was constitutional. He held "I do not believe that the phrase 'under God' in the Pledge converts its recital into a 'religious exercise.' . . . Instead, it is a declaration of belief in allegiance and loyalty to the United States flag and the Republic that it represents. The phrase 'under God' is in no sense a prayer, nor an endorsement of a religion, but a simple recognition of the fact noted in [a House resolution]. . . . From the time of our earliest history our peoples and our institutions have reflected the traditional concept that our Nation was founded on a fundamental belief in God. Reciting the Pledge, or listening to others recite it, is a patriotic exercise, not a religious one; participants promise fidelity to our flag and our Nation, not to any particular God, faith, or church" (542 U.S. 1: 49–50). The difference between a religious exercise and a pledging of fidelity to a nation under God (and one that was "founded on a fundamental belief in God") is not discussed. Rehnquist also argues that it is patriotism that is encouraged here, not religion, and asks where the line will be drawn with people objecting to the pledge. He states, "There may be others who disagree, not with the phrase 'under God,' but with the phrase 'with liberty and justice for all'" (542 U.S. 1: 51). Rehnquist does not state what the objection would be and whether that objection would be based in religion, but feels that such an objection should not be acceptable. He concludes, "The Constitution only requires that schoolchildren be entitled to abstain from the ceremony if they choose to do so. To give the parent of such a child a sort of 'heckler's veto' over a patriotic ceremony willingly participated in by other students, simply because the Pledge of Allegiance contains the descriptive phrase 'under God,' is an unwarranted extension of the Establishment Clause, an extension which would have the unfortunate effect of prohibiting a commendable patriotic observance" (542 U.S. 1: 52).

Justice O'Connor also concurred in the judgment. She argued that often a reasonable observer standard was used in cases in which the issue being contested was whether a government action created an endorsement of religion. However, here she felt that such a standard was unworkable. She then argued that references to religion were acceptable in some circumstances. She reminded the Court of her past rulings, holding "I believe that although these references speak in the language of religious belief, they are more properly understood as employing the idiom for essentially secular purposes," and so are acceptable (542 U.S. 1: 56). She also held that such references are acceptable when they "can serve to solemnize an occasion instead of to invoke divine provenance" (542 U.S. 1: 58). O'Connor looked at four factors in allowing the phrase. First among these was its history. "Under God" had been in the pledge for fifty years and widely used and rarely challenged. Second, she argued that no prayer exists in the Pledge of Allegiance. Third, she argued that no particular religion (other than one favoring a god rather than anything else, and O'Connor notes this) is promoted. And fourth, she observed that only a small part of the pledge discusses God.

Justice Thomas also concurred and argued that this was the time to start rethinking the whole issue of the First Amendment's establishment clause. He argued that it should never have been used to limit the states. He wrote, "It makes little sense to incorporate the Establishment Clause" (542 U.S. 1: 81). The rationale he gave is "the text and history of the Establishment Clause strongly suggest that it is a federalism provision intended to prevent Congress from interfering with state establishments" (542 U.S. 1: 80–81). Thus, Thomas used this case to launch a call for a reconsideration of a doctrine settled for nearly a century. Since 1925, *Gitlow* v. *New York,* the establishment clause has been applicable to the states. Thomas, Rehnquist,

and O'Connor would have all allowed the case to be heard and would have voted in favor of the pledge.

The Supreme Court here, on a 5–3 decision, denied standing to Newdow. Five justices believed that Newdow did not have standing, and three more thought the pledge should be upheld. Thus, all eight justices agreed that the Ninth Circuit Court of Appeals ruling, striking down the pledge, needed to be reversed. With the narrow division of the Court, the issue is sure to remain in the press. After the *Newdow* ruling, other groups and Newdow himself, moved to file (and re-file) challenges to the law with clearer meetings of the standing issue. Thus, this is surely not the last that the nation will hear of the pledge and its relationship to the First Amendment.

> **See also** *Engel* v. *Vitale; Gitlow* v. *New York; Lee* v. *Weisman; Lemon* v. *Kurtzman;* Saluting the flag
> **For further reading**
> Bosmajian, Haig A. 1999. *The Freedom Not to Speak.* New York: New York University Press.
> Eastland, Terry, ed. 2000. *Freedom of Expression in the Supreme Court: The Defining Cases.* Lanham, MD: Rowman & Littlefield.
> Fisher, Leonard Everett. 1993. *Stars and Stripes: Our National Flag.* New York: Holiday House.
> Levinson, Nan. 2003. *Outspoken: Free Speech Stories.* Berkeley: University of California Press.
> Raskin, Jamin B. 2003. *We the Students: Supreme Court Decisions for and about Students.* Washington, DC: CQ Press.

Employment Division v. *Smith*
494 U.S. 872 (1990)

Laws that directly prohibit religious practices and only religious practices are clearly laws prohibiting the free exercise of religion. For instance, a law banning only Catholics (or any other religion) from drinking wine would result in an easy case for a court to decide. However, laws that are general in nature but ban practices integral to a religion make for harder court cases. Such a law was in question in the case of *Employment Division* v. *Smith.*

This case arose in Oregon and is sometimes referred to as *Oregon* v. *Smith*. Oregon law banned those who lost their jobs as a result of work-related misconduct in getting unemployment compensation. Two workers at a drug rehabilitation unit lost their jobs because of the use of peyote in a religious ceremony. Using peyote was banned under state law, even though ceremonial use of it was required by some Native American religions. Thus, while there were legal grounds for the dismissal, the workers felt they had had religious justification to sue for unemployment benefits. The case actually came before of the U.S. Supreme Court twice, once in 1988, when the Court returned the case to the state courts, and again in 1991, when the Supreme Court declared that the ban on peyote was acceptable and the workers were not due any unemployment benefits.

Originally, the state court of appeals reversed the ban on the unemployment compensation as a restriction of the men's First Amendment rights. The Supreme Court in 1988 sent the case back to the state supreme court (which had upheld the state court of appeals) in order for the state courts to determine whether state law banned the use of peyote in religious services. The state supreme court held that it did but also held that the law violated the First Amendment.

The final U.S. Supreme Court opinion was written by Justice Scalia. Scalia first surveyed the history of the case and then turned to previous Supreme Court decisions. He differentiated between religious belief, which cannot be controlled, and religious acts, which sometimes can. Scalia reminded the Court that, in general, "we have never held that an individual's religious beliefs excuse him from compliance with an otherwise valid law prohibiting conduct that the State is free to regulate" (494 U.S. 872: 878–879). He went further and held that general laws have been restricted only in specific circumstances. "The only decisions in which we have held that the First Amendment bars application of a neutral, generally applica-

ble law to religiously motivated action have involved not the Free Exercise Clause alone, but the Free Exercise Clause in conjunction with other constitutional protections" (494 U.S. 872: 881).

Scalia then addressed the issue of what test to use in order to evaluate the law banning peyote, including its religious use, since such laws are generally considered acceptable. Those opposing the law suggested the *Sherbert* test. "Under the *Sherbert* test, governmental actions that substantially burden a religious practice must be justified by a compelling governmental interest" (494 U.S. 872: 883). Scalia declined to use the *Sherbert* test in challenges to generally applicable laws, thus overruling *Sherbert*. Scalia argued that this test would create "a private right to ignore generally applicable laws" and so was not acceptable (494 U.S. 872: 886). The Court feared "the rule respondents favor would open the prospect of constitutionally required religious exemptions from civic obligations of almost every conceivable kind" (494 U.S. 872: 888). Scalia held that states could create exceptions for peyote use but were not required to do so.

Justice O'Connor concurred in the judgment. Justices Brennan, Marshall, and Blackmun agreed with most of her opinion but did not concur in the judgment. O'Connor argued that the majority was incorrectly reading the precedents. She first held that a "law that prohibits certain conduct—conduct that happens to be an act of worship for someone—manifestly does prohibit that person's free exercise of his religion" (494 U.S. 872: 893). She disagreed with the decision not to use the *Sherbert* test, instead holding that "once it has been shown that a government regulation or criminal prohibition burdens the free exercise of religion, we have consistently asked the government to demonstrate that unbending application of its regulation to the religious objector 'is essential to accomplish an overriding governmental interest,' . . . or represents 'the least restrictive means of achieving some compelling state interest'" (494 U.S. 872: 899). She also stated that the test had been used recently, disagreeing again with Scalia.

O'Connor then went on to use that test. She first noted that religious conduct was significantly affected by the ban on peyote and that the state of Oregon had a "significant" interest in banning the use, and thus the *Sherbert* test allowed Oregon's practices. After looking at the dangers of peyote and the reasons for the ban, O'Connor held that "I believe that granting a selective exemption in this case would seriously impair Oregon's compelling interest in prohibiting possession of peyote by its citizens. Under such circumstances, the Free Exercise Clause does not require the State to accommodate respondents' religiously motivated conduct" (494 U.S. 872: 906). She also held that just because other states had granted exemptions did not mean Oregon had to do so.

Justices Blackmun, Brennan, and Marshall dissented. They first argued against the elimination of the compelling interest test, holding that "this distorted view of our precedents [by the majority] leads the majority to conclude that strict scrutiny of a state law burdening the free exercise of religion is a 'luxury' that a well-ordered society cannot afford, . . . and that the repression of minority religions is an 'unavoidable consequence of democratic government.' . . . I do not believe the Founders thought their dearly bought freedom from religious persecution a 'luxury,' but an essential element of liberty—and they could not have thought religious intolerance 'unavoidable,' for they drafted the Religion Clauses precisely in order to avoid that intolerance" (494 U.S. 872: 908–909). They then went on to apply the compelling interest test. They argued that what must be weighed is not the state's right to ban peyote versus the religious rights of the Native Americans, but the state's right to refuse to make an exception to the ban versus the religious rights. The dissenters held that no adequate justification for the refusal, using the compelling interest standard, had been made. The dissenters argued that

religious use had not been proven to be harmful and noted that the federal government allows a religious exemption. The dissenters also explained that the Native American religious authorities had regulated the use of peyote and noted some of the positive effects of the use of peyote in religious ceremonies. They also stated there was very little illegal traffic in peyote, as the "total amount of peyote seized and analyzed by federal authorities between 1980 and 1987 was 19.4 pounds; in contrast, total amount of marijuana seized during that period was over 15 million pounds" (494 U.S. 872: 916). The dissenters finally argued against the majority's claim that allowing an exemption for this would create a request for exemptions to every law by noting that the other states (and the federal government), which had allowed religious exemptions, had not been similarly flooded.

The Supreme Court upheld Oregon's ban on peyote and the denial of unemployment benefits. The larger implication of this case was that for generally applicable laws outside the area of unemployment (note that the law ultimately challenged here was outside the unemployment area even though unemployment compensation was still banned), the compelling interest test, which required the government to prove a compelling interest before affecting religious freedom, is no longer in effect. The government must only prove a rational basis for its laws. Thus, religious freedom no longer had the protection, deserved or not, that it arguably had before when generally applicable laws are concerned. Congress tried to restore the compelling interest test in 1993 when it passed the Religious Freedom Restoration Act, which basically told the Supreme Court to use the *Sherbert* standard, but the Supreme Court disagreed. In *Boerne* v. *Flores,* it struck down the Religious Freedom Restoration Act, and the issue of exactly what standard (and test) to use continues to be debated in the courts and legislatures.

See also *Boerne* v. *Flores; Braunfeld* v. *Brown; Cheema* v. *Thompson; Gonzales* v. *O Centro Es-*

pirita Beneficiente Uniao Do Vegetal; Religious Freedom Restoration Act of 1993; *Sherbert* v. *Verner*

For further reading

Brown, Joseph Epes. 2001. *Teaching Spirits: Understanding Native American Religious Traditions.* New York: Oxford University Press.

Epps, Garrett. 2001. *To an Unknown God: Religious Freedom on Trial.* New York: St. Martin's Press.

La Barre, Weston. 1989. *The Peyote Cult.* Norman: University of Oklahoma Press.

Long, Carolyn Nestor. 2000. *Religious Freedom and Indian Rights: The Case of Oregon v. Smith.* Lawrence: University Press of Kansas.

Martin, Joel W. 2001. *The Land Looks after Us: A History of Native American Religion.* New York: Oxford University Press.

Kifaru Prod. 1993. *The Traditional Use of Peyote* [presented] by members of the Native American Church of North America. San Francisco: Kifaru Productions.

Washburn, Wilcomb E. 1975. *The Assault on Indian Tribalism: The General Allotment Law (Dawes Act) of 1887.* Philadelphia: Lippincott.

Engel v. *Vitale*

370 U.S. 421 (1962)

Most of the original colonies had governmentally sanctioned churches and discriminated willingly against certain religious minorities. Most canceled their official churches when they became states or relatively soon after that. This did not mean, however, that they ceased to promote religion or belief in a Western God. In the twentieth century, one of the original colonies, New York, had a state-created prayer that was mandated in all public schools; pupils who wished could opt out, and the prayer was relatively neutral in relationship to specific religions. In 1962 the Supreme Court determined this prayer was not constitutional.

Justice Black wrote the opinion for the Court. He noted that the prayer said "Almighty God, we acknowledge our dependence upon Thee, and we beg Thy blessings upon us, our parents, our teachers and our Country" (370 U.S. 421: 422). After surveying the course of the legislation, Black moved

quickly to the Court's decision holding "we think that by using its public school system to encourage recitation of the Regents' prayer, the State of New York has adopted a practice wholly inconsistent with the Establishment Clause" (370 U.S. 421: 424). He held that it was not the place of government to create prayers.

Black then turned and considered the history of America. He noted that controversies over a type of prayer drove many from England and that colonists nonetheless tried to establish a state prayer. By the time the Constitution was written, however, in Black's view, America's citizens had learned the error of their ways and so passed the First Amendment. He said, "The First Amendment was added to the Constitution to stand as a guarantee that neither the power nor the prestige of the Federal Government would be used to control, support or influence the kinds of prayer the American people can say" (370 U.S. 421: 429). Black noted that as the prayer was neutral and voluntary, it might be acceptable under the free exercise clause, but it still created an establishment of religion, which was prohibited. He believed the First Amendment removed religion from the purview of government. "The Establishment Clause thus stands as an expression of principle on the part of the Founders of our Constitution that religion is too personal, too sacred, too holy, to permit its 'unhallowed perversion' by a civil magistrate" (370 U.S. 421: 431–432). He held that "the New York laws officially prescribing the Regents' prayer are inconsistent both with the purposes of the Establishment Clause and with the Establishment Clause itself" (370 U.S. 421: 433).

Black then turned to the arguments of those opposed to this decision who supported the prayer. He first dealt with the argument that banning school prayer represented an opposition to religion and stated "nothing, of course, could be more wrong" (370 U.S. 421: 434). He believed banning the prayer preserved each individual student's right to the freedom of religion. He surveyed the reason that religious men of the past had written the First Amendment and fled from prosecution, and concluded "it is neither sacrilegious nor antireligious to say that each separate government in this country should stay out of the business of writing or sanctioning official prayers and leave that purely religious function to the people themselves and to those the people choose to look to for religious guidance" (370 U.S. 421: 435). For these reasons, Black felt quite justified in overturning the state prayer as a violation of the establishment clause of the First Amendment.

Douglas concurred with the decision. He argued that any government financing of religion is unconstitutional, going further than Black, who limited his ruling to school prayer. As any financing was unconstitutional, the school prayer was unconstitutional too, even though it took only a small amount of time and was voluntary. Douglas perhaps here uttered one of the better defenses of the absolutist philosophy in the area of freedom of religion, something his fellow justice Black would often do in the area of freedom of speech.

Justice Stewart dissented. He argued that "with all respect, I think the Court has misapplied a great constitutional principle. I cannot see how an 'official religion' is established by letting those who want to say a prayer say it. On the contrary, I think that to deny the wish of these school children to join in reciting this prayer is to deny them the opportunity of sharing in the spiritual heritage of our Nation" (370 U.S. 421: 445). Stewart thought that the history of England and the early history of America was irrelevant, and that "the history of the religious traditions of our people, reflected in countless practices of the institutions and officials of our government" was the most important thing to consider (370 U.S. 421: 446). He reviewed a few of those practices and closed by saying, "Countless similar examples could be listed, but there is no need to belabor the obvious. It was all summed up by this Court just ten

years ago in a single sentence: 'We are a religious people whose institutions presuppose a Supreme Being.' . . . I do not believe that this Court, or the Congress, or the President has by the actions and practices I have mentioned established an 'official religion' in violation of the Constitution. And I do not believe the State of New York has done so in this case. What each has done has been to recognize and to follow the deeply entrenched and highly cherished spiritual traditions of our Nation—traditions which come down to us from those who almost two hundred years ago avowed their 'firm Reliance on the Protection of divine Providence' when they proclaimed the freedom and independence of this brave new world" (370 U.S. 421: 450). Stewart made the opposing argument to the school prayer case that has been made ever since, that America is a religious nation, and a prayer, when voluntary, merely recognizes this. However, his argument was not enough to carry the day. He did not address the apparent contradiction of his accepting the founders' reliance upon divine Providence with his rejection of their motives behind creating the establishment clause.

The Supreme Court has never seriously reconsidered a school prayer case since *Engel*. In other words, decisions since *Engel* have allowed or disallowed prayers in certain situations, but the overall ban on prayers to start each day has stayed put. That does not mean that it has been without controversy, however. Many politicians have campaigned against the "Godless" Supreme Court who took prayer (and God) out of the classroom and started America down the road to wrack, ruin, and the end of Western civilization. A decision in 1963 removing Bible reading from the classroom further increased the ire of these groups. One note to be made here: even though New York claimed that the prayer did not put God into the classroom (as that would have been an establishment of religion), many of those who have opposed the decision have based their opposition on an argument that it took God *out* of the classroom. Interesting how the decision removed something that supposedly was not there. Congress also made itself heard on the whole issue of school prayer, offering amendments on the issue in nearly every single (if not every single) session since 1962. Most have not reached the floor for a vote, and those that did fell short of passage, with the closest one falling nine votes short in the Senate (or about 10 percent) in the 1960s.

The battle moved from a mandated prayer (with an option for exceptions) to a moment of silence in the 1980s. The idea was that a moment of silence was not the same as prayer and so would be constitutional. Justice Brennan, in a concurrence to a 1963 Bible reading case, *School District of Abington Township* v. *Schempp,* noted that there were many ways that schools could secularly do some of the things that prayer was supposed to do including increasing discipline, and one of the ways he suggested was a "moment of reverent silence" (374 U.S. 203: 281). Some of the moment of silence legislation has come closer to promoting prayer, in many people's eyes, than others, and it was one of these cases that made it to the Supreme Court in 1985 in *Wallace* v. *Jaffree.* That case challenged legislation written in 1978 and amended in 1982 to change it from being legislation just allowing a moment of silence to one allowing that moment for "silence or prayer." The Supreme Court struck this amended law down as an endorsement of religion. Another issue of prayer is prayer at individual events, such as football games and graduations. Courts have divided on whether a prayer at a football game is constitutional, but in 1992 the Supreme Court struck down a prayer at a graduation. Thus, in general, the Court continues to follow the line of thought begun in *Engel,* that prayer at school functions and in the school day is generally unacceptable, but this has not ended criticism of that decision, nor has it ended attempts by politicians to allow prayer in schools. Nor will the *Engel* decision end the continuation of all three of these trends for the foreseeable future.

See also ACLU *of Kentucky* v. *McCreary County;* Lee v. *Weisman;* McCreary County v. *ACLU;* Santa Fe Independent School District v. *Doe;* School District of Abington Township v. *Schempp;* Wallace v. *Jaffree*
For further reading
DelFattore, Joan. 2004. *The Fourth R: Conflicts over Religion in America's Public Schools.* New Haven: Yale University Press.
Fraser, James W. 1999. *Between Church and State: Religion and Public Education in a Multicultural America.* New York: St. Martin's Press.
Greenawalt, Kent. 2005. *Does God Belong in Public Schools?* Princeton, NJ: Princeton University Press.
Haas, Carol. 1994. *Engel v. Vitale: Separation of Church and State.* Hillside, NJ: Enslow.
Sears, James T., with James C. Carper, eds. 1998. *Curriculum, Religion, and Public Education: Conversations for an Enlarging Public Square.* New York: Teachers College Press.

Epperson v. *Arkansas*
393 U.S. 97 (1968)

The battle over teaching evolution in public schools first received national prominence with the 1925 Scopes Monkey Trial. It is often thought that, even though the state of Tennessee upheld its law against teaching evolution, the forces of progressivism won that trial and answered the question over whether to teach evolution with a yes for all time. That, however, is misleading in that although the larger public saw Scopes and his allies winning, many in the South and in the areas favoring the ban on the teaching of evolution saw the trial as an attempt by outside forces to control their destiny. Generally, those seeking to restrict evolution sought to control local school boards and write policies that effectively eliminated evolution in actuality, even if they did not do so in their specific verbiage. However, some of the statewide bans created in the *Scopes* era remained in actual policy, and it was one of these bans that was challenged in *Epperson* v. *Arkansas.*

The Arkansas ban was passed in 1928, three years after the Scopes Trial. It made it "unlawful

Susan Epperson, plaintiff in Epperson *v.* Arkansas *(1968), challenged the state's ban on teaching evolution in schools. (Library of Congress)*

Book of Genesis by a particular religious group" (393 U.S. 97: 103).

Justice Fortas then turned and reviewed the legal doctrine of the First Amendment. He noted that the government was supposed to be neutral in the area of religion, and that the Court generally was wary of intervening in religion. However, he held this to be an easy case, as here the state was clearly shaping the curriculum to fit the ideas of one religion. The Court held, "It is clear that fundamentalist sectarian conviction was and is the law's reason for existence" (393 U.S. 97: 107–108). Fortas closed by saying that "Arkansas' law cannot be defended as an act of religious neutrality. Arkansas did not seek to excise from the curricula of its schools and universities all discussion of the origin of man. The law's effort was confined to an attempt to blot out a particular theory because of its supposed conflict with the Biblical account, literally read" (393 U.S. 97: 109).

Justice Black concurred. He first doubted that this case should even be in front of the Supreme Court, stating that the law had never been enforced, among other things. Black noted that the statute was very vague, so vague that he thought it impossible to define it enough to decide whether it violated the First Amendment. Black wanted to strike it down on the basis of vagueness. He stated that Arkansas should have the right to remove evolution from the curriculum but not on the basis of religion, and he felt the law was too vague to stand. Justice Harlan also concurred. He thought it was clear that the statute created an establishment of religion, but he felt the majority opinion delved too far into free speech in its logic.

Justice Stewart also concurred. He focused more on the potential criminal penalty for the teacher demanded by the law, not the ban on evolution. He stated that the ban on the mention of evolution infringed upon the teacher's right of free speech, if the ban was in fact cre-

for a teacher in any state-supported school or university 'to teach the theory or doctrine that mankind ascended or descended from a lower order of animals,' or 'to adopt or use in any such institution a textbook that teaches' this theory" (393 U.S. 97: 98–99). The Supreme Court, in an opinion by Justice Fortas, noted that only Mississippi and Arkansas had similar statutes remaining in force and that there were no prosecutions, as best can be told, under their act. The Court, after reviewing the litigation, held that "the law must be stricken because of its conflict with the constitutional prohibition of state laws respecting an establishment of religion or prohibiting the free exercise thereof. The overriding fact is that Arkansas' law selects from the body of knowledge a particular segment which it proscribes for the sole reason that it is deemed to conflict with a particular religious doctrine; that is, with a particular interpretation of the

ated by the statute. (The Arkansas Supreme Court had upheld the statute, but refused to give it any concrete meaning, thus leaving a great deal of vagueness in the statute.) As the law was so vague, Stewart voted to overturn it on this basis.

The Arkansas statute was struck down by the Supreme Court here and Arkansas made no direct effort to resurrect it. The days of directly banning evolution were past. Those forces opposing evolution turned their efforts into three different avenues. One was to require teachers to spend equal time on evolution and on ideas that were in accordance with fundamentalist Christianity, whether those be creation science or intelligent design. Creation science argues that science supports the first chapter of Genesis and an earth that is only 6,000 (or so) years old. Intelligent design argues that the universe is too complex to not have some higher intelligence designing it, without delving into God's edicts and beliefs. One type of this law was struck down in *Edwards* (1987), but that did not stop other attempts. A second strategy, noted before, is to control school boards. The third is to rewrite the state standards (which mandate what students will learn, and, more recently, what they will be tested on) to eliminate the issue of evolution, or to require "equal time" between evolution and other theories. Thus, clearly, the idea that the Scopes Trial ended the debate over evolution is a false one.

> **See also** Avoidance of the issue of evolution in many teaching standards; *Crowley* v. *Smithsonian Institution; Edwards* v. *Aguillard; Paloza* v. *Capistrano Unified School District; Scopes* v. *Tennessee/Scopes Monkey Trial*

For further reading

Irons, Peter H. 1988. *The Courage of Their Convictions.* New York: Free Press.

Larson, Edward J. 1997. *Summer for the Gods: The Scopes Trial and America's Continuing Debate over Science and Religion.* New York: Basic Books.

Moore, Randy. 2002. *Evolution in the Courtroom: A Reference Guide.* Santa Barbara, CA: ABC-CLIO.

Equal Access Act of 1984

The Equal Access Act of 1984 aimed to force schools to grant equal access to their facilities to religious student groups. Instead of trying to overturn a Supreme Court case, like much federal legislation recently has done, it instead aimed to reinforce a Supreme Court case. In 1981, the court, ruled in *Widmar* v. *Vincent* that a university, in this case the University of Missouri at Kansas City, could not deny a religious group use of its facilities as the facilities were considered public, and it allowed groups not involved with religion to use those facilities. The grounds were two: first, that the university violated the students' First Amendment rights by interfering with their freedom of religion, and second, that the university would become overly entangled with religion by having this exclusion. Congress decided to reinforce this Supreme Court ruling with legislation, and that legislation became the Equal Access Act of 1984.

The Equal Access Act had several portions and provisions. In its portion most directly relevant to the act's purpose, it held, "it shall be unlawful for any public secondary school which receives Federal financial assistance and which has a limited open forum to deny equal access or a fair opportunity to, or discriminate against, any students who wish to conduct a meeting within that limited open forum on the basis of the religious, political, philosophical, or other content of the speech at such meetings." The act stated "a public secondary school has a limited open forum whenever such school grants an offering to or opportunity for one or more noncurriculum related student groups to meet on school premises during noninstructional time." These groups, however, could be restricted if the school chose to ban all such groups. If all groups were banned, the school would have created a nonpublic forum, not a limited open forum. The groups also had to be "voluntary and student-initiated," and school personnel could not lead the groups, but could be present, and "non-school persons" could not "regularly" participate in the activities. There were also a couple of overriding educational concerns inserted. First, the act held that meetings of these groups should "not materially and substantially interfere with the orderly conduct of educational activities within the school," and second, the act held that "nothing in this subchapter shall be construed to limit the authority of the school, its agents or employees, to maintain order and discipline on school premises, to protect the well-being of students and faculty, and to assure that attendance of students at meetings is voluntary."

The Equal Access Act of 1984 was prompted by a number of concerns. First, many conservative and religious groups felt that religious groups had, in some communities, been forbidden to use school facilities, and some of these groups felt that the decision to forbid them had been based on the religious nature of their activities. They desired equal access to those facilities, and they felt that this act helped them gain that. Second, many school boards were in somewhat of a quandary. If they allowed religious groups, those who were atheists or of faiths that did not have groups at that school might feel slighted and sue, accusing the board of promoting religion. If they did not allow religious groups, then the religious groups might *all* sue. Of course, there was also the question of what religious groups to allow, and there were no guidelines on any of these matters in general federal law. A related question was what level of involvement a teacher or other employee might have. Some school districts took a cue from the *Engel* v. *Vitale* case that banned school prayer and assumed that all religion was banned. Conservative groups wanted to end these concerns of school boards and encourage the boards to allow religious groups. A third issue prompting the act was, of course, the Supreme Court's statement of approval in *Widmar* v. *Vincent,* a decision Congress wanted to reinforce. A final concern prompting the act was the general in-

crease in religious fervor of the early 1980s as the Moral Majority gained in power, and these groups felt morally compelled bring religion into schools. A school prayer constitutional amendment did not gain enough votes in the U.S. Senate to be passed along to the states, and religious groups thought that the Equal Access Act would be a good first step. President George W. Bush has taken a second step with his support for faith-based initiatives designed to support monetarily faith-based and community-based organizations helping those in need. As a direct response, when a government agency like the Environmental Protection Agency (EPA) awards a contract, it must now, in addition to stating whether it considered an African American, woman-owned, or other minority business, state whether it considered a faith- or community-based organization for the contract.

This act has not always had the overall effect that the religious groups wanted, however. Some school districts have decided to simply ban all noncurriculum-related clubs, allowing curriculum-related activities, like band or athletic competitions, but banning noncurriculum-related clubs such as Scout groups and Bible studies. Thus, even though the act was passed, in some schools, student activities actually decreased rather than increased, and religious groups were still not allowed to meet. Additionally, some groups that the religious right might not have anticipated used this act to their advantage. As the act went beyond religion and also forbade discrimination on the "political, philosophical, or other content of the speech" used by the group wishing to meet, some underrepresented groups, including gay and lesbian, atheist, and Goth groups, have also sued to meet, using the Equal Access Act as justification.

One case, *Colin* v. *Orange Unified School District* (83 F. Supp. 2d 1135 Central District of California, 2000), upheld the right of the Gay-Straight Alliance Club to meet. Thus, many different groups, not just religious ones, have benefited from this legislation. Whether the school district as a whole benefited from the legislation might depend on your view of the school board and the view of the group.

The overall effect on religious and other groups is statistically difficult to measure. Some high schools allowed groups such as Youth for Christ and the Fellowship of Christian Athletes to meet even before passage of the Equal Access Act, and this act may have had little effect in those schools, other than encouraging the retention of these groups. Other high schools may have been affected in their facility use policies by factors unrelated to religion, such as the availability of transportation for distant students to and from after-school activities. Few schools have acted to ban all activities as a solution, and so there has been little negative effect in that way. Some have, however, as mentioned, banned all noncurriculum-related clubs.

One Supreme Court case testing the Equal Access Act was *Board of Education of the Westside Community Schools* v. *Mergens.* In that case, a Nebraska high school prohibited the establishment of a religious club even while allowing other clubs. The Supreme Court held that the Equal Access Act was constitutional and did not violate the establishment clause by forcing the allowing of religious clubs, if other clubs were allowed. Six justices held that the school did allow noncurriculum-related clubs, and so had to allow the religious club. The justices differed on whether school officials had to follow the Equal Access Act in terms of how much they should dissociate themselves from the religious groups in question. Only one justice dissented, and he (Justice Stevens) thought that the Court was giving a broader effect to the Equal Access Act than it admitted. He argued, "Can Congress really have intended to issue an order to every public high school in the nation stating, in substance, that if you sponsor a chess club, a scuba diving club, or a French club—without having formal classes in those subjects—you must also open your doors to every religious, political, or social organization, no matter how controversial or distasteful its views may be? I

think not" (496 U.S. 226: 271). Stevens felt that the high school had created a much more limited forum than the Court had intended, and that "an extracurricular student organization is "noncurriculum-related" if it has as its purpose (or as part of its purpose) the advocacy of partisan theological, political, or ethical views" (496 U.S. 226: 271). As the religious group did those things, Stevens felt it could be banned if the high school allowed no other such clubs, and he felt that Westside had not. The majority found that clubs such as service clubs and chess clubs were noncurriculum-related, and Stevens disagreed. The Supreme Court in *Mergens,* therefore, upheld the Equal Access Act and ordered the school in question to allow the religious club, with only one dissenting justice.

The Equal Access Act does not answer all questions of religion, nor, by any stretch, does it argue that religion must always enter the schools. For instance, it does not allow school prayer on a daily basis, and, even after this act's passage, the Supreme Court ruled unconstitutional prayer at graduation in *Lee* v. *Weisman.* The Supreme Court has upheld the Equal Access Act, and Congress, by all signs, appears to be continuing its support of that legislation. However, there are few, if any, wide-scale studies on the act's effect on the level of student involvement as a whole or the general treatment of religious groups, never mind more curriculum-related issues such as student performance or retention. (One might argue, of course, that since religious clubs are noncurriculum-related clubs, by definition, curriculum issues such as these do not matter.) More religious speech as a whole occurs in high schools, especially after hours, due to this act, but the exact effect is difficult to measure.

See also Board of Regents of the University of Wisconsin System v. Southworth et al.; Good News Club v. Milford Central School; Good News/Good Sports Club v. School District of the City of Ladue; Lamb's Chapel v. Center Moriches School District; Lee v. Weisman; Rosenberger v. Rector and Visitors of the University of Virginia; Widmar v. Vincent

For further reading

DelFattore, Joan. 2004. *The Fourth R: Conflicts over Religion in America's Public Schools.* New Haven: Yale University Press.

Detwiler, Fritz. 1999. *Standing on the Premises of God: The Christian Right's Fight to Redefine America's Public Schools.* New York: New York University Press.

Equal Access Act. http://assembler.law.cornell .edu/uscode/html/uscode20/usc_sec_20_ 00004071——000-.html.

Gaddy, Barbara B., T. William Hall, and Robert J. Marzano. 1996. *School Wars: Resolving Our Conflicts over Religion and Values.* San Francisco: Jossey-Bass.

Hubbard, Benjamin Jerome, John T. Hatfield, and James A. Santucci. 1997. *America's Religions: An Educator's Guide to Beliefs and Practices.* Englewood, CO: Teacher Ideas Press.

Mangrum, Richard Collin. "Centennial Symposium: Reconciling the Free Exercise and Establishment Clauses: Shall We Sing? Shall We Sing Religious Music in Public Schools?" *Creighton Law Review* 38: 815–870.

Mawdsley, Ralph D. 2004. "Access to Public School Facilities for Religious Expression by Students, Student Groups and Community Organizations: Extending the Reach of the Free Speech Clause." *B.Y.U. Education & Law Journal,* 269–299.

Nord, Warren A. 1995. *Religion and American Education: Rethinking a National Dilemma.* Chapel Hill: University of North Carolina Press.

Sears, James T., with James C. Carper, eds. 1998. *Curriculum, Religion, and Public Education: Conversations for an Enlarging Public Square.* New York: Teachers College Press.

Equal time laws

Equal time laws are one of the multitudinous twists in state laws dealing with the controversial topic of evolution. Equal time laws are of two kinds: they can either require that something else be taught alongside evolution and that both be given equal time, or they can require that *if* evolution is taught, other explanations, the nature of which are usually specified, be given equal time (but the laws of the second type do not require that both be taught). Very often in both incarnations, evolution's critics or intelligent design programs are used alongside evolution in the classroom.

Equal time laws have two very different purposes. The first is their stated purpose, which is to allow students to access a plurality of viewpoints in the classroom in order to decide for themselves. The second, unstated purpose for many people who sponsored these laws is to get Christianity and, for some, especially fundamentalist Christianity, into the classroom.

Creation science used to be the favored theory to teach alongside evolution, and, although this has dwindled even as equal time laws gained in popularity, it still remains in place in some schools. Creation science holds that there is scientific proof that backs up the idea of a quick creation resembling the seven-day account in Genesis. Many groups behind creationism and creation science require belief in God and belief in the literal truth of Genesis before allowing membership. One example of this is the Creation Research Society. A good example of one of the more famous equal time laws is the one challenged in *Edwards* v. *Aguillard,* a case that reached the Supreme Court in 1987. Indeed, the Supreme Court struck down the act, as it felt its requirement that creation science be given equal time if evolution was taught promoted religion, in spite of the enacting legislature's protests to the contrary.

More recently, intelligent design has been the favored theory to teach alongside evolution. Intelligent design argues that humanity and nature are too complex to have come about by chance and that they must have an intelligent creator. It is, in many ways, simply the same argument as the one behind creation science, but wearing new clothing. Equal time acts attempt very often to use science, often dubious science, to defeat evolution. Groups supporting them rarely acknowledge the possibility that evolution may not preclude Christian theories of creation. The acts are created in retaliation against the perceived threat evolution represents to biblical discussions of nature. Their arguments focus on an insistence of scientific proof behind the creation science and intelligent design theories and that therefore they should be included in science classes on the origins of the world and humanity. They hope to protect students' original religious viewpoints by providing them scientific justification for their creation beliefs. However, on paper, they argue that equal treatment through equal classroom time will expose students to multiple views and allow students to choose for themselves. They use the basic scientific principles of hypothesis testing to support their arguments in favor of equal time. Whether high school assessment tests look for students who decide for themselves is, of course, another matter.

It is important to keep the lawmakers' motives in mind when discussing these laws. Their goal very often is to defeat evolution teaching, and the equal time laws do this, regardless of how they are implemented. Requiring science teachers to teach another theory alongside evolution, as if that theory exists in opposition to evolution, muddles the debate, decreasing the amount students actually learn about evolution theory. It also decreases the amount of class time spent on evolution. If the law allows it, many schools simply exclude evolution from science classes in order to avoid teaching another theory along with it. Evolution is thereby removed from the curriculum, preserving the original intent of the equal time laws. Those in the legislature then claim they simply wanted all sides to be presented, but their motives are often questionable.

The effects of the equal time laws, where they are passed, are generally at least two, in addition to the inevitable court challenge. One effect is that many teachers, not having the time or inclination to teach multiple ideas in this area, where allowed, will just teach none. This means that rather than increasing the number of students with the resources to decide for themselves, the laws actually decrease this number. Another effect is that teachers who are required to teach both become embroiled in religion. This is particularly true

when they have to explain the origins of creation science or intelligent design.

Direct attacks on evolution failed in the Scopes Trial, even though the particular law at challenge there was upheld. As those opposed to evolution have been consistently unable to directly prevent its teaching in the schools, they have switched to new tactics to minimize what they perceive as its negative impact, with equal time laws playing a significant role in their activities. Some proponents of these laws sincerely believe that all ideas need to be challenged, but far more seek to ban evolution by only allowing it to be taught in conjunction with another theory. Those in the second camp rise up in apparent defense of academic freedom (as they, in theory, allow more ideas to be taught) while actually reducing that freedom by effectively limiting the teaching of evolution or simply having it written out of state standards.

> ***See also*** Avoidance of the issue of evolution in many teaching standards; Creation Research Society; *Edwards* v. *Aguillard;* Institute for Creation Research; National Center for Science Education; *Scopes* v. *Tennessee*/Scopes Monkey Trial

For further reading

Behe, Michael J. 1996. *Darwin's Black Box: The Biochemical Challenge to Evolution.* New York: Free Press.

Gould, Stephen Jay. 1993. *Eight Little Piggies: Reflections in Natural History.* New York: Norton.

Larson, Edward J. 2004. *Evolution: The Remarkable History of a Scientific Theory.* New York: Modern Library.

Lindberg, David C., and Ronald L. Numbers, eds. 2003. *When Science and Christianity Meet.* Chicago: University of Chicago Press.

Established churches in colonial America

Most of the early colonies had established churches. Some of them were Anglican; others were Congregational. A few colonies did have freedom of religion, but most had an established church and taxes to support that church.

John Winthrop was one of the most powerful political leaders of the Massachusetts Bay Colony during its critical formative years. (Library of Congress)

The churches varied in type and power, as a survey will show.

The Anglican Church was the established church of several American colonies, including the first established colony, Virginia. In Virginia, most of the early settlers had been Anglican, and thus they supported the king and had an established Anglican Church. The established church in Virginia was run by the local rich, and the leaders were initially appointed by church officials in England and then created a continuing body. In Virginia, even though it was the church of the mother country, the church did not have as much influence as in other places as people were more spread out. Virginia was a farming society, with many large farms and plantations, so people lived farther from churches, and their ability to attend weekly services was limited. Virginia also had more of an early emphasis on wealth production. The original intent of the Virginia Bay Company had been to make money, and

the colony's early settlers had been sent there with that goal rather than the aim of forming a stable society. From this and other factors, an increased emphasis on wealth evolved. Therefore, Virginians were more likely to display their wealth, unlike the settlers in Massachusetts, to use a different example.

In Massachusetts, the early settlers had been Puritans and they moved to keep the church Puritan. The Puritans were Anglicans who aimed to make their church pure and so shame the Anglican Church in England into reformation. The Massachusetts colony required people to pay taxes to support the church, a practice that continued until the American Revolution. After the Revolution, Massachusetts' new constitution in 1780 allowed more religious freedom, allowing alternatives to the Puritan church, but it still argued for a strong level of social control from religion. Taxes were still required to support churches, but now people could choose from several established, recognized churches. In 1833 Massachusetts ceased the practice of requiring state support for churches, one of the last states to do so.

Massachusetts also exercised more social control in general. A large part of John Winthrop's whole "City on a Hill" idea was to create a moral society, at both the individual and collective levels, and the only way to achieve this was by strict social control. There are many examples of these attempts at social control. One of the better-known ones was an early court case in which a man was hauled into court for overcharging for basic supplies. The court had forbidden any merchant from selling supplies for more than 5 percent over cost, and this particular merchant was arrested after he was caught charging at least 25 percent (or five times the allowable amount). He claimed he could not do business at only 5 percent because of risks such as Native American attacks and shipping losses, but the court disbelieved him and fined him. In keeping with the ideas of the time, the merchant also had to apologize in court and thus to the entire community. In many ways, Massachusetts believed in the whole idea of the commonwealth, or the wealth of the collective whole; the state is still officially called a commonwealth today. With this heritage, it is not surprising that even Massachusetts' wealthy were more reserved in their displays than were those in Virginia. Also, New England ruled through the town meeting, where all could be heard, whereas Virginia ruled through elected officials. Thus, both government, and, as will be shown, faith, were public events in Massachusetts.

The Anglican Church as a church of all people did not survive long in Massachusetts, even though the church retained more power there than elsewhere. In Massachusetts, a voter had to be a saint, meaning a full male member of the church. To accomplish that, members had to describe their conversion experiences in church. Not all were willing to do so, limiting the number of saints. Even so, a larger percentage of citizens voted in Massachusetts than in England, which had both religious and property qualifications. Baptism was available only to saints and their children. The question then became what to do about all those who were not saints, particularly those who were the young children of non-saints, but were the grandchildren of saints. In 1662, Massachusetts Puritans adopted the Half-Way Covenant, which held that children of the baptized, and thus children of those who were baptized as infants and who never became saints, were allowed to be baptized, but they had to become saints themselves in order to be full members of the church.

Churches were very much supported by local taxes. Both Massachusetts and Virginia had colonial taxes to support the church, and these taxes remained on the books until the American Revolution. After the Revolution, Virginia tried to reimpose its tax. This effort was led by Patrick Henry, who, in a twist characteristic of the complex thinking of early Americans, believed in liberty from central government, liberty from England, but state

support of the church. His effort failed, largely because of a drive led by Thomas Jefferson (who believed in freedom from the church but not for African Americans) and James Madison. Massachusetts reimposed its tax in its constitution of 1780, and some other states joined it, including Connecticut.

The other colonies mostly mirrored Massachusetts and Virginia, based largely on physical location, proximity of one village to another, and the variety of faiths inside their borders. All of New England, with the exception of Rhode Island, established churches with state support soon after their founding. Rhode Island, founded by Roger Williams, believed in freedom of religion, but was more concerned about protecting the religion from the corruption of the state than protecting the state from the church's influence. In some of the middle colonies, there was state support of religion: New York, for instance, had state-supported churches, but the supported church was chosen on a town-by-town basis. Pennsylvania, on the other hand, was tolerant, as was Maryland to some extent. The southern colonies of North and South Carolina and Georgia had more religious diversity and a greater focus on the economy; for example, colonial South Carolina had an established church for only about twenty years, and in colonial Georgia, there was religious toleration of all Protestants (Catholics were not allowed to live there) but state support of the Church of England.

Early churches in America showed great religious diversity. Toleration of other religions generally did not exist except in rare places such as Pennsylvania, where the wide variety of faiths combined with the Quaker tradition to coerce some level of forced accommodation, even if the attitudes would not be what today would be called tolerant. In Maryland, Catholics were tolerated. In most other places, however, Catholics were treated quite badly. They were kept out of Georgia generally after the American Revolution, even though there was no established church there. Thus, lack of an established church did not equate to widespread toleration, even though an established church did correlate with increased dislike of religious minorities. That was the state of church-state relations, religious toleration, and forced accommodation (or lack thereof) in the first two centuries or so of colonial history. Most of the colonies had some level of a state-established and state-supported church, and most provided little incentive, let alone encouragement or toleration, for other churches.

> *See also* American revolution's effect on religion; Bible controversy and riots; *Braunfeld* v. *Brown;* Establishment of Pennsylvania as religious colony for Quakers; Religious freedom in Rhode Island in colonial times; *Torcaso* v. *Watkins;* Treatment of Jews, both in colonial times and after the American Revolution

For further reading

Adams, Arlin M., and Charles J. Emmerich. 1990. *A Nation Dedicated to Religious Liberty: The Constitutional Heritage of the Religion Clauses.* Philadelphia: University of Pennsylvania Press.

Buckley, Thomas E. 1977. *Church and State in Revolutionary Virginia, 1776–1787.* Charlottesville: University Press of Virginia.

Curry, Thomas J. 1986. *The First Freedoms: Church and State in America to the Passage of the First Amendment.* New York: Oxford University Press.

McGarvie, Mark D. 2004. *One Nation under Law: America's Early National Struggles to Separate Church and State.* DeKalb: Northern Illinois University Press.

Noll, Mark A., ed. 1990. *Religion and American Politics: From the Colonial Period to the 1980s.* New York: Oxford University Press.

Upton, Dell. 1997. *Holy Things and Profane: Anglican Parish Churches in Colonial Virginia.* New Haven: Yale University Press.

Establishment of Pennsylvania as religious colony for Quakers

Quakers were treated as a fringe group in the American colonies and persecuted in England, and they needed a safe place to practice their religion. William Penn and his followers therefore founded their own colony where they would not be ostracized for their beliefs. Indeed, this was the reason many of the original colonies were founded. However, in Pennsylvania, unlike most of the others, a plurality of religions was tolerated, making it one of the first places in the world where the freedom of religion was truly practiced. For this reason, Pennsylvania is often looked at by some as a model for America. However, its founding was not as simple as some believe, and the circumstances surrounding it serve as a lens on early America.

The Quaker religion came in large part from a man named George Fox. He traveled to England in the early 1600s and thought that religion was much too formal and complicated. He believed that religion applied directly to people's acts and that people did not need intermediaries between themselves and God. This belief negated the need for clergy or churches. According to Fox's religion, all could have salvation, and no one needed to work for salvation, as grace was granted by God. Also, and even more controversial, men and women were equal in Fox's religion, even though most churches in that era forbade women from taking any leadership roles, let alone becoming equals with men or ministers. Quakers were not allowed to own slaves, again differentiating this religion from the mainstream. The Quakers were marked by plain speech and lifestyle, and all who wished to speak were heard in Quaker meetings. Finally, the Quakers were pacifists.

Much of this ran counter to the ideas of the time, and many of the early Quakers were jailed as their beliefs ran counter to the general ideology of the time. Among the early jailed Quakers was William Penn, who had been arrested for speaking in front of a Quaker meeting, which was illegal at the time. Penn, though, had valuable assets, as the Crown had borrowed money from his father to finance its wars, and Penn had inherited his father's debt from England. The king also wished to move the religious minorities, including the Quakers, out of England, if possible, and he wished to populate his American colonies without a large expense. Penn's idea of a religious colony for Quakers allowed the king to meet all his goals and to pay off the Crown's debt easily. The king did not give up all power over the colony, as Penn still had to submit all laws to the royal council for review (and indeed Penn remained in England and tried to run the colony from there).

The colony was tolerant of the religions of others. In its setup, equality was given to Native Americans and freedom of religion was granted, with few exceptions. There was no religious qualification to vote or to be a lower-level officeholder, and the only religious qualification for being a provincial officeholder was that one had to be a Christian. Jews and Muslims were also allowed into the province and were treated generally fairly. The religious laws in the colony were also less severe than in other provinces. For instance, one convicted of blasphemy in Pennsylvania was given ten days at hard labor. In contrast, in some colonies, such as Connecticut, blasphemers could be punished by death. The colony was not able to impose, if such a term be used, all of its Quaker ideas on those who lived there. There was still some slavery, and some landowners imported and used indentured servants as well, although both practices went against Quakerism. There was also some poor treatment of Native Americans, in spite of the colony's laws, but this does not appear to have been related to religious issues. The colony had a sizable number of different religions. Besides those that might be expected, the Huguenots, Mennonites, and Presbyterians were all present in the colony. Religion played a part in one of the last acts taken by the colony, as Pennsylvania was slow to go to war in the American Revolution, probably in part because of the pacifist nature of Quakers.

Pennsylvania, once it became a state, remained the mixed society that it was as a colony. In 1790, there was no dominant ethnic group, with about one-third being German, one-third English, and the rest being mostly Scots or Scots-Irish. The societies' cultures did not assimilate into one whole, even though there was a fair amount of mixing. Many who came to Pennsylvania, contrary to what some think of America's founding, did not like the low emphasis on religion and tried to change the society, or they moved on. Attempts to change the religious tenor, though, were not generally successful. Most Pennsylvanians seemed to ignore the differences between themselves and others.

After the end of the Revolution, freedom of religion was generally reaffirmed in the state constitution, but some state officeholders were still required to profess a belief in Christianity. In addition to freedom of religion, the right to *not* bear arms was also reaffirmed in the state constitution. Pennsylvania is seen as an area of compromise, and this is in large part due to the multitude of religions and ethnicities in the area. Thus, diversity brought compromise and toleration, not the other way around.

Pennsylvania was, in many ways, a unique colony. It was founded as a place for the Quakers as they were religious dissenters, but Pennsylvania never had a permanent majority of those believers, unlike other colonies. It also practiced religious toleration from its inception, unlike most other colonies. The diversity of the colony forced colonists into compromise and moderation. Thus, while Pennsylvania is a model for what many want in America today, both design and circumstances encouraged this development as an actuality rather than just an idea.

See also American Revolution's effect on religion; Punishment and religion; Religious freedom in Rhode Island in colonial times

For further reading

Dunn, Richard S., and Mary Maples Dunn, eds. 1986. *The World of William Penn.* Philadelphia: University of Pennsylvania Press.

Geiter, Mary K. 2000. *William Penn.* New York: Longman.

Pencak, William A., and Daniel K. Richter, eds. 2004. *Friends and Enemies in Penn's Woods: Indians, Colonists, and the Racial Construction of Pennsylvania.* University Park: Pennsylvania State University Press.

Rossbacher, Richard Irwin. 1987. *Now Remembered: Living Pennsylvania History through 1900.* Lanham, MD: University Press of America.

Schwartz, Sally. 1987. *"A Mixed Multitude": The Struggle for Toleration in Colonial Pennsylvania.* New York: New York University Press.

Estate of Thornton v. Caldor

472 U.S. 703 (1985)

Part of the largest debate over the First Amendment deals with the level of required accommodation that must be given someone because of the person's religion. For those who refuse to work on their Sabbath, should employers be forced to make exceptions? *Thornton* v. *Caldor* turned on this issue.

This was an 8–1 decision, with Rehnquist dissenting. O'Connor filed a concurrence and was joined by Marshall. Chief Justice Burger wrote the opinion for the Court. He first noted the facts of the case, including that Thornton, when he began working, did not have to work Sundays as the store was closed by a Connecticut closing law. Two years later the business began opening on Sundays, and Thornton worked on some Sundays but complained about having to do so a year later. Thornton claimed protection under a Connecticut law that read "no person who states that a particular day of the week is observed as his Sabbath may be required by his employer to work on such day. An employee's refusal to work on his Sabbath shall not constitute grounds for his dismissal" (472 U.S. 703: 706). Thornton was then transferred to a lesser position when he refused either to work on Sundays or to be transferred to a store that was closed Sundays, or to move to a lower (both in salary and rank) position that did not require Sunday work. After being demoted, he sued. Burger then cited the *Lemon* test, which he summarized thus: "To pass constitutional muster under *Lemon* a statute must not only have a secular purpose and not foster excessive entanglement of government with religion, its primary effect must not advance or inhibit religion" (472 U.S. 703: 708).

The Court saw the statute in question as preferring religion in general, summarizing the statute as follows: "The State thus commands that Sabbath religious concerns automatically control over all secular interests at the workplace; the statute takes no account of the convenience or interests of the employer or those of other employees who do not observe a Sabbath" (472 U.S. 703: 709). For this reason, the Court concluded that "the statute has a primary effect that impermissibly advances a particular religious practice" and so overruled the statute and thus, as far as Thornton was concerned (or actually his heirs, as he had died in the interim), he did not have a right to protest his demotion (472 U.S. 703: 710).

Justice Rehnquist dissented without opinion. Justices O'Connor and Marshall concurred, in an opinion written by Justice O'Connor. They noted a second reason, or in their mind a different primary reason, for rejecting the statute. They held that "the Connecticut Sabbath law has an impermissible effect because it conveys a message of endorsement of the Sabbath observance" (472 U.S. 703: 711). O'Connor agreed with the Court that "the statute singles out Sabbath observers for special and, as the Court concludes, absolute protection without according similar accommodation to ethical and religious beliefs and practices of other private employees. There can be little doubt that an objective observer or the public at large would perceive this statutory scheme precisely as the Court does today. . . . The message conveyed is one of endorsement of a particular religious belief, to the detriment of those who do not share it" (472 U.S. 703: 711). However, O'Connor also wanted to note her opinion that this decision did not hold "that the religious accommodation provisions of Title VII of the Civil Rights Act of 1964 are similarly invalid" (472 U.S. 703: 711). These provisions forbade discrimination on the basis of religion. The reason for the difference was the different purpose of Title VII. It was not aimed at protecting only those who worshiped on the Sabbath, as the Connecticut statute was, but instead protected all. O'Connor concluded that "since Title VII calls for reasonable rather than absolute accommodation and extends that requirement to all religious beliefs and practices rather than protecting only the Sabbath observance, I believe an objective observer would perceive it as an antidiscrimination law rather than an endorsement of religion or a particular religious practice" (472 U.S. 703: 712). Thus, this law (Title VII) was valid while the Connecticut law was not.

States cannot force employers to be unable to fire people who insist on taking their Sabbath off. It is unclear how this case differs from that in *Sherbert,* where a state was prohibited from denying unemployment compensation for one who was fired for not working Saturdays, and the majority opinion does not even mention the *Sherbert* decision. In 1990, the Supreme Court reversed *Sherbert* as a general rule in *Employment Division* v. *Smith.*

> **See also** *Boerne* v. *Flores; Braunfeld* v. *Brown; Employment Division* v. *Smith;* Religious Freedom Restoration Act of 1993; *Sherbert* v. *Verner*
>
> **For further reading**
> Cowan, Horace G. 1948. *The Sabbath in Scripture and History.* Kansas City, MO: Beacon Hill Press.
> Heylyn, Peter. 1969. *The History of the Sabbath.* Amsterdam: Theatrum Orbis Terrarum.
> Laband, David N. 1987. *Blue Laws: The History, Economics, and Politics of Sunday-Closing Laws.* Lexington, MA: Lexington Books.
> Schwartz, Gary. 1970. *Sect Ideologies and Social Status.* Chicago: University of Chicago Press.

Everson v. *Board of Education*

330 U.S. 1 (1947)

A state ban on private education, and especially a state ban on religious groups, in most everyone's mind violates the First Amendment. Thus, private religious schools clearly have the right to exist. However, the level of aid allowable to those schools by the state, and the level of aid required from the state for their upkeep is a much less clear question. The first time that the U.S. Supreme Court dealt with this issue was in 1947 in *Everson,* when the

Court ruled it constitutional for the state to reimburse parents for their children's transportation to school when the state reimbursed all parents for transportation, even when the school in question was a Catholic one.

Justice Black wrote the Court's opinion. He first noted the complaint—that the local public school provided "reimbursement to parents of money expended by them for the bus transportation of their children on regular busses operated by the public transportation system" (330 U.S. 1: 3). He then looked at the constitutional objections to this policy, moving quickly to the First Amendment issue, that the statute created an establishment of religion.

Black briefly reviewed the history of the United States before adoption of the Constitution, noting that there was prosecution against religion, both in Europe and in the early colonies, and that the writers of the Bill of Rights wanted to end this. He noted also that the government was not supposed to burden those believing in religion, even while it was not supposed to tax people to support any religion. Black concluded, "We cannot say that the First Amendment prohibits New Jersey from spending tax raised funds to pay the bus fares of parochial school pupils as a part of a general program under which it pays the fares of pupils attending public and other schools" (330 U.S. 1: 17). Black saw that the system, as a whole, "does no more than provide a general program to help parents get their children, regardless of their religion, safely and expeditiously to and from accredited schools" (330 U.S. 1: 18). This decision did not mean that Black thought that the "wall of separation" between church and state should be struck down. "The First Amendment has erected a wall between church and state. That wall must be kept high and impregnable. We could not approve the slightest breach. New Jersey has not breached it here" (330 U.S. 1: 18).

Justice Jackson dissented. "The Court's opinion marshals every argument in favor of state aid and puts the case in its most favorable light, but much of its reasoning confirms my conclusions that there are no good grounds upon which to support the present legislation" (330 U.S. 1: 19). Jackson first noted that students who went to private, nonreligious schools were not reimbursed and that this exclusion created problems, even though it was ignored by the Court. He also noted that the system of transportation was not being changed, as students attending religious schools were not carried on public busses. Their parents were merely reimbursed for their transportation. The justice then reviewed the Catholic school system and held that "Catholic education is the rock on which the whole structure rests, and to render tax aid to its Church school is indistinguishable to me from rendering the same aid to the Church itself" (330 U.S. 1: 24). Jackson said here that, essentially, being Catholic was what gave parents the right to reimbursement and that this created problems. "Neither the fireman nor the policeman has to ask before he renders aid 'Is this man or building identified with the Catholic Church?' But before these school authorities draw a check to reimburse for a student's fare they must ask just that question, and if the school is a Catholic one they may render aid because it is such, while if it is of any other faith or is run for profit, the help must be withheld" (330 U.S. 1: 25).

Justice Rutledge also dissented, joined by Frankfurter, Jackson, and Burton. Rutledge saw the purpose of the First Amendment as being "to create a complete and permanent separation of the spheres of religious activity and civil authority by comprehensively forbidding every form of public aid or support for religion" (330 U.S. 1: 31–32). Any amount was an unlawful contribution, Rutledge suggested. He also saw transportation as being an essential element of education rather than being an incidental one, as suggested by the majority. He concluded, "For me, therefore, the feat is impossible to select so indispensable an item from the composite of total costs, and characterize it as not aiding, contributing to, promoting or sustaining the propagation of beliefs which it is the very end of all to bring about. Unless this can be maintained, and the Court does not maintain it, the aid thus given is outlawed" (330 U.S. 1: 48).

Thus, reimbursement for transportation to Catholic schools, whether given directly or indirectly, was allowed by this opinion. This decision did not make things as simple as desired by those who wanted a policy of no aid, such as Justice Rutledge. Numerous cases since have dealt with what types of aid were allowed, and the ways in which the aid could be provided. The general principle determined now, even though it is still being challenged, is that aid is allowed as long as the purpose is secular, the main effect of the aid is neither to advance nor retard religion, and that there is no "excessive entanglement." Sometimes general programs of aid are allowed as well as aid that is funneled to the schools through the choice of a parent. Quite a tangled web to come out of a few trips to school.

See also Agostini v. Felton; Bob Jones University v. United States; Flast v. Cohen; Lemon v. Kurtzman; McCollum v. Board of Education

For further reading

Formicola, Jo Renée, and Hubert Morken, eds. 1997. *Everson Revisited: Religion, Education, and Law at the Crossroads.* Lanham, MD: Rowman & Littlefield.

Monsma, Stephen V., ed. 2002. *Church-State Relations in Crisis: Debating Neutrality.* Lanham, MD: Rowman & Littlefield.

Yarnold, Barbara M. 2000. *Religious Wars in the Courts.* Huntington, NY: Nova Science.

F

Failure to treat due to religious beliefs

The legal right to refuse medical treatment depends in large part on an individual's age and mental capacity. Of course, the level of care being refused also makes a difference. The refusal of a simple procedure is of far less concern to the medical community than refusal of lifesaving care. Generally those under the age of eighteen are deemed to be under a parent or guardian's care for issues of medical attention. This becomes more controversial when the issue of divorce is added. The danger faced by the child if treatment is withheld also plays a factor.

Religion and the law enter the picture when a person wants to refuse medical care because of religious beliefs. One example of this would be a blood transfusion. Some faiths (including Jehovah's Witnesses) feel that a blood transfusion violates their religion as it puts artificial items into the human body. Most times, when the Court has become involved, it has allowed adults to refuse medical treatment for themselves in this area. However, the record is much more mixed when children are involved. Parents are generally allowed to impose their beliefs on their children in areas that are not life threatening. An example of this would be compulsory schooling. The Amish believe that high school is a threat to their way of life, so they are permitted to remove their children from school after the eighth grade. The state of Wisconsin opposed this, but the Supreme Court allowed it in *Wisconsin* v. *Yoder* (1972). However, one of the reasons the Court cited in holding for the Amish is that the state was not able to show that any definite harm would probably come to the children by withdrawing from school after the eighth grade. "The record strongly indicates that accommodating the religious objections of the Amish . . . will not impair the physical or mental health of the child, or result in an inability to be self-supporting or to discharge the duties and responsibilities of citizenship, or in any other way materially detract from the welfare of society" (406 U.S. 205: 234). Such would not necessarily be the case in the instance of a refused blood transfusion for either adults or children.

One leading case in this area is *Norwood Hospital* v. *Munoz* (1991), decided by the supreme judicial court of Massachusetts, in which an adult wanted to refuse a blood transfusion as she was a Jehovah's Witness. To complicate this case, the woman was the primary caregiver of a young child, and the hospital argued that the government should have the right to protect the young child from losing a parent. The court allowed the woman to refuse treatment as the boy would still have his father in addition to other relatives and so would not be totally orphaned. Thus adults were held to be able to refuse blood transfusions.

However, when a blood transfusion is needed for a child, nearly all courts have held that the child's rights outweigh the parents' religious beliefs, allowing the state to intervene and force the transfusion. The supreme judicial court of Massachusetts concluded, "When a child's life is at issue, 'it is not the rights of the parents that are chiefly to be considered. The first and paramount duty is to consult the welfare of the child'" (565 N.E. 2d 411: 413). Another issue is faith healing. Some religions believe prayer cures illnesses and precludes the need for medication. Treatment obviously could be forced, but when the state does not intervene or when the issue is not as clear as the obvious matter of a blood transfusion, the question often becomes one of responsibility after the child has already died. Again in Massachusetts, one couple relied on faith healing as Christian Scientists, and their two-year-old child died. Medical evidence suggested that the child would have been kept alive with a safe surgical procedure. The parents had consulted their local church and read a pamphlet that suggested faith healing could be relied on without criminal penalty. While this was not an accurate legal summary, it did cause the parents to have their guilty conviction on the charge of involuntary manslaughter overturned and a new trial granted. The court ruled that the parents should have been able to advance the defense that they relied on their understanding of the pamphlet, and it was not their fault that the pamphlet was wrong.

Civil suits are a different matter, as noncustodial parents have won wrongful death suits, and these verdicts have been upheld on appeal as not violating the First Amendment. This is obviously a complex issue balancing the parents' right to religious freedom against the child's right to live. When parents divide on the issue of treatment it becomes even more complicated. However, whatever religious issues are involved, parents are generally not allowed to deny lifesaving treatment to their children, and when the children are young, their very presence factors into whether the parents are allowed to deny themselves medical care, such as transfusions. When the care is medically necessary to save a life, the state can intervene in the case of a child, but the issue becomes less clear when the medical necessity is less certain. Adults can generally decide their own care and take responsibility for it. However, when children are involved, the issue becomes more complex, and the state sometimes has the right to compel care.

See also Banning of suicide in law and its interaction with religion; *Nally v. Grace Community Church of the Valley;* Right to die and religion

For further reading

Holder, Angela Roddey. 1985. *Legal Issues in Pediatrics and Adolescent Medicine.* New Haven: Yale University Press.

McConnell, Terrance C. 2000. *Inalienable Rights: The Limits of Consent in Medicine and the Law.* New York: Oxford University Press.

Rozovsky, F. A. 1990. *Consent to Treatment: A Practical Guide.* Boston: Little, Brown.

Fairfax Covenant Church v. Fairfax City School Board
17 F.3d 703 (4th Cir. 1994)

A number of Supreme Court cases, along with the Equal Access Act of 1984, have held that schools cannot discriminate against religious groups in terms of access to their buildings. One question here, of course, is what type of regulations are allowable.

The *Fairfax Covenant Church* case dealt with the Fairfax City School Board's rental policy for school buildings. The Fairfax City School Board allowed local churches and other groups to rent space before and after school but raised its rates based on how long a church had used the facility. Their goal here was to encourage short-term use, and the legal justification was that long-term use created an establishment of religion, which of course the First Amendment would have banned. It allowed "the church to pay the noncommercial rate for the first five years but, thereafter, require[d] the church to pay a rate which escalate[d] to the commercial rate over the next four years" (17 F.3d 703: 705). The court examined the rental policy and held that this case was controlled by *Widmar* and that the regulation therefore discriminated "against religious speech in violation of the Free Speech Clause" (17 F.3d 703: 707). The school board stated that it wanted to avoid domination of the school's use by religious institutions, but the court found that the actual use showed (by percentage) relatively little utilization by religious groups. Thus, the facts did not justify the school board's concern (at that time, the court left open that justification if usage changed). The court weighed the free exercise rights of those wanting to rent the school for religious reasons versus the school's establishment clause concerns, holding that the school board needed to consider both issues. It held, based on the facts of the case, that the increase in rent after five years was not justified. The court also held that the church could recover those fees that it had overpaid because it should have been charged the same rate as all other nonprofit institutions. Thus, the school board was not allowed to charge churches more than other renters; the court found that although the school board's concern about its rental policy violating the establishment clause might sometimes be justified, it was not in this case. More important, it stated that the school board must balance the free exercise and establishment portions of the First Amendment in its rental policies.

Another concern centers on use of school facilities just before and just after school, and whether use of these facilities by religious groups at those times creates "the perception of endorsement by the schools of religious instruction," an issue decided at the district court level in *Ford* v. *Manuel* (629 F. Supp. 771: 774). The court first noted that the *Lemon* test applied here. The district court reviewed past Supreme Court rulings and found that this policy did indeed create the impression that the school board wanted students to attend these events, and because students' presence was required just before or just after school gave a boost to this perception. The court held that a school was not a traditional public forum at these times and so could restrict access more than at other times.

A third concern is whether a school board can discriminate among groups based on the nature of their speech, which indirectly implicates religion. The KKK wanted to use a school building for a meeting, and a school board first granted and then denied the use. The KKK sued in *Knights of the Ku Klux Klan* v. *East Baton Rouge Parish School Board*. The Fifth Circuit Court of Appeals first considered the historic use of the school and concluded that it had been a forum open to the public, which

meant that content-based restrictions were not allowed. The school board contended that the policies of the KKK distinguished them from other groups, making restrictions allowable. However, the court held that the marketplace of ideas should include unpopular ideas, including those of the KKK. While the school board argued that this policy would be seen as the school board's endorsement of these ideas, the court held that the school board had always allowed equal access and endorsed none of the groups' views. Thus, the school board was forced to allow the meetings. The school board had the opportunity to try to prove that the KKK aimed to exclude people from its meetings. If the school board could have proved this, they could have prevented the KKK, theoretically, from meeting, as the traditional use of the school facilities had been to hold completely public meetings. However, the KKK members would have simply permitted any person to attend their meetings held in school buildings, and they were counting on the distastefulness to outsiders of the organization's views to keep nonmembers from coming. If they had ever forbidden anybody access, they could have been banned from using the building. The case has bearing on the relationship between religion and the law because a by-product of the ruling is that school boards cannot ban a religious group from using their facilities merely because the school board disagrees with that religion's perspective.

Therefore, groups cannot, in general, be banned from facilities that are traditionally kept open to the public. Concerns over the establishment of religion need to be balanced by school boards against the rights of those who wish to worship freely. In general, and this goes beyond the issue of religion, content cannot be used as a reason to deny renting or use access to any group.

See also *Bronx Household of Faith* v. *Community School District No. 10; Chapman* v. *Thomas; Good News Club* v. *Milford Central School; Widmar* v. *Vincent*

For further reading

Flinchbaugh, Robert W. 1993. *The 21st Century Board of Education: Planning, Leading, Transforming.* Lancaster, PA: Technomic.

Marty, Martin E. 2000. *Education, Religion, and the Common Good: Advancing a Distinctly American Conversation about Religion's role in Our Shared Life.* San Francisco: Jossey-Bass.

Parker, Richard A., ed. 2003. *Free Speech on Trial: Communication Perspectives on Landmark Supreme Court Decisions.* Tuscaloosa: University of Alabama Press.

Farrington v. *Tokushige*

273 U.S. 284 (1926)

The *Pierce* case held that states cannot ban private schools from existing. Once that was resolved, the next issue was to decide how much a state could regulate a private school's content. *Farrington,* and a variety of related cases, address that question.

In *Farrington,* the legislature of Hawaii passed a sweeping bill regulating the content taught in Hawaii schools, aiming mostly at private Japanese schools. The legislation, among other things, required proficiency in the English language, control of textbooks, proof that nothing anti-American was being taught, and the payment of fees. The Supreme Court concluded that "the School Act and the measures adopted thereunder go far beyond mere regulation of privately supported schools, where children obtain instruction deemed valuable by their parents and which is not obviously in conflict with any public interest. . . . The Japanese parent has the right to direct the education of his own child without unreasonable restrictions; the Constitution protects him as well as those who speak another tongue" (273 U.S. 284: 298). The Fifth Amendment was used to strike down this act as a deprivation of property against the owners of the schools, and the rights of the parents to control their children's education. These limits on state regulation of school content increase the protection of religious schools, even though the case itself does not directly relate to religion.

However, certain regulations have been found allowable. Nebraska, in order to regulate its schools, passed a variety of requirements. In addition to requiring student attendance, the regulations included a requirement that teachers have certain qualifications, including holding a bachelor's degree, and that the school have an approved curriculum. This case came before the supreme court of Nebraska in *Nebraska v. Faith Baptist Church* in 1981. A private religious school claimed that it had the freedom of religion to operate without interference. However, the court found that the state had a critical interest in educating its youth, and that "although parents have a right to send their children to schools other than public institutions, they do not have the right to be completely unfettered by reasonable government regulations as to the quality of the education furnished" (301 N.W. 2d 571: 579). The court concluded that "the refusal of the defendants to comply with the compulsory education laws of the State of Nebraska as applied in this case is an arbitrary and unreasonable attempt to thwart the legitimate, reasonable, and compelling interests of the State in carrying out its educational obligations, under a claim of religious freedom" (301 N.W. 2d 571: 580). Thus, minimal requirements were allowed as long as they were reasonable and not hostile to religion.

One of the more commonly challenged laws is the compulsory attendance law. Many religious schools that do not meet state certification run afoul of this law, as students are not attending a certified school. North Dakota's attendance law was challenged in the case of *North Dakota v. Shaver* on the basis of the First Amendment. Those in the church school stated that they had "religious convictions against obtaining state approval" (294 N.W. 2d 883: 887). The court held that "the burden on the parents' free exercise of religion in the present case is minimal, and is far outweighed by the state's interest in providing an education for its people" (294 N.W. 2d 883: 897). Thus, the court ruled that the church's justification for refusing to seek state approval was not acceptable. The church held that God was the ultimate authority about everything, but the court determined this was not enough to void the state's compulsory attendance laws.

Regulations, however, cannot so restrict private schools as to eliminate the opportunity for religious instruction. Even restrictions not aimed at eliminating religious instruction might have this effect and can be stricken. That was the holding of the Ohio Supreme Court in *State* v. *Whisner*. There, the court found that "in our view, these standards are so pervasive and all-encompassing that total compliance with each and every standard by a non-public school would effectively eradicate the distinction between public and non-public education, and thereby deprive these appellants of their traditional interest as parents to direct the upbringing and education of their children" (351 N.E. 2d 750: 769). The requirements in this case were much more detailed and complex than the certification requirements and attendance laws challenged in the other cases discussed here.

Some have argued that standardized testing should substitute for the compulsory attendance requirements. Most courts have not agreed, however. The First Circuit Court of Appeals in *New Life Baptist Church Academy* v. *Town of East Long Meadow* reached this same conclusion, that compulsory attendance may be required. It first held that religious objections to the certification process that all schools must go through were not enough to overturn the procedure. It then held that the voluntary testing system preferred by the academy was not enough to replace the compulsory attendance system.

The state has the right to impose reasonable restrictions on private schools, but all of these cases served to identify some of the boundaries of such regulations. The state cannot wipe out the whole system of private schools, nor can it eliminate a private school's religious functions, but it can impose certification, minimum at-tendance, and curriculum review requirements. All of these, of course, must be imposed without religious tests or antireligious bias, either in the requirements as stated or in the way that they are applied.

See also *Agostini* v. *Felton; EEOC* v. *Kamehameha Schools/Bishop's Estate; New Jersey* v. *Massa; Ohio Civil Rights Commission* v. *Dayton Schools; Pierce* v. *Society of Sisters; Synder* v. *Charlotte Public Schools*

For further reading

Klicka, Christopher J. 2002. *The Right to Home School: A Guide to the Law on Parents' Rights in Education.* Durham, NC: Carolina Academic Press.

Kotin, Lawrence, and William F. Aikman. 1980. *Legal Foundations of Compulsory School Attendance Education.* Port Washington, NY: Kennikat Press.

Nord, Warren A. 1995. *Religion and American Education: Rethinking a National Dilemma.* Chapel Hill: University of North Carolina Press.

Pulliam, John D., and James Van Patten. 1995. *History of Education in America.* Englewood Cliffs, NJ: Merrill.

Wiley, Dinah. 1984. *Public and Nonpublic School Relationships: Lighthouse Approaches for State Policymakers.* Alexandria, VA: National Association of State Boards of Education.

Federal income tax and religion

Taxes are one of the two things Founding Father Benjamin Franklin felt were certain in life. As his other certainty was death, it is easy to tell that he did not look forward to paying his taxes each year. The income tax, in particular, has been a necessary force to fund the country's government for a little under a hundred years. The federal government was originally funded largely through import duties, as relatively high taxes were imposed on incoming goods, both to raise revenue and to protect American industry. American industry found this very helpful, but American farmers were endangered by the program, as it both raised the cost of industrial goods and reduced their ability to sell abroad. The latter effect came from the retaliatory high import taxes other

Reverend Greg Dixon prays on his knees along with other supporters and members of the Indianapolis Baptist Temple on November 14, 2000, as they await the arrival of federal marshals. In September, a U. S. district judge ordered the surrender of the church by noon on November 14 to satisfy a $6 million debt to the Internal Revenue Service. (AP Photo/Michael Conroy)

countries placed on goods coming in from the United States. The government's other main tax source was land. There were many protests against the high import duties and also against very rich people, who could make huge sums of money and pay little or nothing in taxes. To equalize this situation for the poor, an income tax was passed in the late 1800s. Though the Supreme Court initially struck it down, a 1913 constitutional amendment allowing federal income taxes formally authorized the program.

Such has been the state of our taxation for the past ninety years. In that time, several challenges have been mounted on the income tax as it applies to religion. The tax as a whole is

difficult to attack on First Amendment grounds, as it was allowed by a constitutional amendment. However, religious groups and individuals have been seeking to avoid paying it on the grounds of religion ever since the amendment was ratified.

One group challenged tax deductions and exemptions. In *Hernandez* v. *Commissioner,* 490 U.S. 680 (1989), a group of Scientologists protested the government's denial of a tax deduction for their payments to the Church of Scientology. The deductions had been denied by the Internal Revenue Service (IRS) because, to qualify for a deduction, a gift must be made to a religion (or other charity) without anything being received in return. If something is received in return, only the amount of the donation above the value of the item received by the donor is deductible. Here, the Scientologists were given training, which the IRS considered a tangible receipt of benefits. The Supreme Court upheld the IRS, as the regulations did not allow deductions for payments that granted access to religious services. The Court here found that the regulation had a secular purpose, that it did not primarily retard religion as it primarily made the tax code more manageable, and that it decreased entanglement between government and religion, because it saved the IRS from having to oversee religious services and evaluate their level of religiosity. Thus, payment for access to the church is not considered a gift. The regulations also were not, either at their creation or now, aimed primarily at Scientology and so were neutral.

However, in 1993, the IRS reached a private agreement with the Church of Scientology allowing its members an income tax deduction for the fees paid to attend services. A Jewish couple, the Sklars, believed that under that agreement, a portion of the tuition used to pay for religious instruction at their children's Jewish school was tax deductible. In fact, the IRS had mistakenly believed the family was deducting Scientology-related expenses and had allowed the deductions for 1991–1993, when the family filed amended returns for those years after the Scientology Church reached its agreement with the IRS. However, the family immediately corrected the IRS's misunderstanding, and, though it went ahead and allowed the deductions for 1991–1993, the IRS denied the deductions in 1994 and again in 1995. The couple sued and repeatedly lost in court. The most recent decision in the case came in 2005, when the tax court, in *Sklar et ux*. v. *Commissioner,* 125 T.C. No. 14, declared that precedents have repeatedly shown that no part of tuition to a religious school is tax deductible.

In the 1990s, members of the Quaker faith argued that the use of their federal income taxes to fund warlike activities violated their religious beliefs. They therefore withheld the portion of their federal income taxes that would have been given to the defense department. The Second Circuit Court of Appeals, though, held in *Browne* v. *United States* (176 F.3d 25 [1999]) that a religious belief does not allow avoidance of an otherwise valid law, particularly when that law is neutral with regard to religion. A similar case was *Adams* v. *Commissioner* (170 F.3d 173) decided by the Third Circuit Court of Appeal in 1999. There, the case was slightly different as the person was a Quaker and also worked for the Quaker religion. Adams volunteered to pay all of her federal income tax if she could be assured that none of it would go to fund any war activities. She used the Religious Freedom Restoration Act as grounds for her argument that the tax system was illegal as it burdened her religion by making her pay for activities odious to her beliefs. The court stated that this act merely restored the state of the law prior to 1990 and required a compelling government interest to be present to justify burdens on religion. The court found that the administration of a tax system was such an interest. The court found further that the government was able, legally, to provide Adams with an exemption, but was not required to do so.

One rare method of challenge, utilized in *Indianapolis Baptist Temple* v. *United States* [224 F.3d 627 (Seventh Circuit Court of Appeals 2000)], is a wholesale attack on the tax. The Indianapolis Baptist Temple claimed the income tax violated some people's religious beliefs. Members of the temple believed that all their possessions belonged to God and that giving any of those possessions to the state violated their religious principles. The court, however, found in 2000, that there was a strong enough interest to allow the government to apply a generally neutral law, even though it had an effect on a religion.

Thus, income taxes have been held to be constitutional, both for those deeply involved in religion and for those less so. Religion may cause dislike for income taxes, either in application or in the use of the funds, but it does not allow anyone to escape paying the IRS.

See also *Bob Jones University* v. *United States; Hibbs* v. *Winn; Swaggart Ministries* v. *California Board of Equalization; Walz* v. *Tax Commission of the City of New York*

For further reading
Brownlee, W. Elliot, ed. 1996. *Funding the Modern American State, 1941–1995: The Rise and Fall of the Era of Easy Finance.* New York: Cambridge University Press.
Leff, Mark Hugh. 1984. *The Limits of Symbolic Reform: The New Deal and Taxation, 1933–1939.* New York: Cambridge University Press.
Steuerle, C. Eugene. 2004. *Contemporary U.S. Tax Policy.* Washington, DC: Urban Institute Press.
Weisman, Steven R. 2002. *The Great Tax Wars.* New York: Simon and Schuster.
Zelizer, Julian E. 1998. *Taxing America: Wilbur D. Mills, Congress, and the State, 1945–1975.* New York: Cambridge University Press.

Fike v. *United Methodist Children's Home of Virginia, Inc.*

709 F.2d 284 (4th Cir. 1983)

Religious groups and companies owned by a religion are sometimes, under certain circumstances, allowed to discriminate under Title VII of the 1964 Civil Rights Act. Under what circumstances one is allowed to discriminate is, of course, a valid question. Another question, of course, is what makes one either a religion or a company owned by a religion, or, to put it more broadly, what makes one an entity allowed to discriminate under those circumstances in Title VII? Three cases, including *EEOC* v. *Townley,* address that second question.

In *EEOC* v. *Townley,* the Townley Engineering and Manufacturing Company was founded by people who had told God their business "would be a Christian, faith-operated business" (859 F.2d 610: 612). They had a mandatory religious service once a week at a Florida plant, and "failure to attend was regarded as equivalent to not attending work" (859 F.2d 610: 612). The

company passed out a handbook requiring attendance at the services, and then began holding the services; eventually an employee was discharged, perhaps due to his opposition to the services. The court first held that Title VII did reach church services and that the company had a duty to accommodate the employee's religious beliefs; in this case the employee was an atheist, so accommodation would mean allowing him not to attend the services. Townley, however, argued that "any attempt at accommodation would have caused it 'undue hardship,'" which was not required (859 F.2d 610: 614). The court stated that those corporations whose spiritual costs Congress had wanted considered were specifically exempted, and the Townley company did not fall into this group and would not have suffered an "undue hardship" by exempting the atheist employee.

The court next considered whether Townley was a "religious corporation," which would have exempted them from having to release the employee from required attendance. The court held that an entity did not have to be a church to be exempted, but "all [in Congress] assumed that only those institutions with extremely close ties to organized religions would be covered" (859 F.2d 610: 618). The court, after considering Townley's situation, stated that "we merely hold that the beliefs of the owners and operators of a corporation are simply not enough in themselves to make the corporation 'religious' within the meaning of section 702" (859 F.2d 610: 619). The Townleys also argued that their free exercise rights required them to proselytize, and the court noted that it must weigh the Townleys' rights versus those of the employee to be left alone in religion. The court held that "where the practices of employer and employee conflict, as in this case, it is not inappropriate to require the employer, who structures the workplace to a substantial degree, to travel the extra mile in adjusting its free exercise rights, if any, to accommodate the employee's Title VII rights" (859 F.2d 610: 621). The Circuit Court of Appeals held that services could continue, as long as those who wished to be excluded were exempted. Thus, mere desire and the belief of the owners that they should serve God through their corporation were not enough to make a corporation religious. Though they were permitted to continue holding the religious services, they were required to exempt employees who did not hold with the Townleys' beliefs.

Another case, that of *EEOC v. Pacific Press* (1983), also considered whether a company could discriminate on religious grounds. The Ninth Circuit Court of Appeals noted that the company was "affiliated with the Seventh-Day Adventist Church and engages in the business of publishing, printing, advertising and selling religiously oriented material. All Press employees are required to be members of the church in good standing" (676 F.2d 1272: 1274). The company had discriminated against a female employee, due to her gender, and was charged with violating Title VII. Its defense was that it was a religious corporation and was following the dictates of its religion. However, the court first found that "every court that has considered Title VII's applicability to religious employers has concluded that Congress intended to prohibit religious organizations from discriminating among their employees on the basis of race, sex or national origin" (676 F.2d 1272: 1277). The court then turned to Title VII and the Civil Rights Act in general and held that these could apply to religious corporations as a whole and that religious beliefs are not implicated as the religion, here the Seventh-Day Adventist Church, did not believe in discrimination against women, by their own admission. The church also had a doctrine of not allowing its members to sue itself, but the court held that this did not mean that Title VII could not be enforced. Additionally, the court held that this was not similar to other cases in which church doctrine was being challenged. Thus, the press was not allowed to discriminate against women. The court therefore determined the EEOC was right to intervene and challenge the company's action, as Title VII still applies against religious

corporations in the area of sex discrimination, and intervention was the only way to enforce Title VII. Whatever small damage occurred to doctrine was outweighed by the nation's purpose in Title VII.

A third case, *Fike v. United Methodist Children's Home of Virginia, Inc.* (1983), dealt with whether a children's home was a religion. A Methodist who was not a minister had served as director, and he was dismissed so that the home could hire a Methodist minister as director. The dismissed director sued, claiming that the children's home had religiously discriminated against him. The children's home claimed it was a religious organization and so was exempt from Title VII. The court examined the facts here and held that the home did not have religious services, nor did it mandate the owning of Bibles by the children, nor did it even have a chaplain who was that interested in increasing Christianity, never mind activity in the Methodist Church. For these reasons, the home was held to not be a religious organization and so was guilty under Title VII. However, there was no religious discrimination, the court found, as discriminating on the basis of whether one is a minister does not constitute religious discrimination, as long as the person disadvantaged was a member of the same religion as the minister. The children's home, even though it received money from the state, was not closely enough connected with the state to be legally considered the state, so any discrimination it practiced was not state action; therefore, Fike could not sue.

All of these cases acted to limit the number and types of corporations and organizations that qualified as "religious organizations" for the purpose of Title VII. Unless an entity is owned or substantially controlled by a church, it probably will not qualify. Also, even if a company qualifies as a religious organization, it still has other burdens to meet before a challenged action is exempted from Title VII.

See also *Corporation of Presiding Bishop v. Amos;*
EEOC v. Kamehameha Schools/Bishop's Estate;

Farrington v. Tokushige; Lemon v. Kurtzman; Ohio Civil Rights Commission v. Dayton Schools
For further reading
EEOC. 1998. *Facts about Religious Discrimination.* Washington, DC: U.S. Equal Employment Opportunity Commission.
Maikovich, Andrew J., and Michele D. Brown. 1989. *Employment Discrimination: A Claims Manual for Employees and Managers.* Jefferson, NC: McFarland.
Noonan, John Thomas. 1998. *The Lustre of Our Country: The American Experience of Religious Freedom.* Berkeley: University of California Press.
U.S. Equal Employment Opportunity Commission. 2000. *The Story of the United States Equal Employment Opportunity Commission: Ensuring the Promise of Opportunity for 35 Years, 1965–2000.* Washington, DC: U.S. Equal Employment Opportunity Commission.

Original copy of the Bill of Rights. (National Archives)

First Amendment

The idea that America was founded for religious liberty is ingrained into schoolchildren's minds from their first social studies and history classes. However, the legal basis of our current freedom, the First Amendment to the Constitution, is generally less studied in schools and is often forgotten once studied. The First Amendment goes beyond religion and actually protects four of our most basic freedoms: assembly, press, religion, and speech (listed alphabetically). However, the current reach of the First Amendment is much larger, especially in the area of religion, than it has been in the past. To further understand this, and the First Amendment in general, a survey of its history is in order.

In the original structure of the colonial system, regulations affecting all colonies were made in England and then passed down to the colonies. However, because of the distance and slow communications of the time, most colonies were allowed to run nearly all of their affairs, except in the area of trade. Trade was regulated by England, as economic prosperity and increased trade had been one of the main reasons, if not the main reason, that England founded the colonies in the first place. England eventually tightened many trade regulations, leading in part to the American Revolution. To avoid having another controlling central government, the Articles of Confederation set up a very weak central government, which failed. To develop a successful system, the Constitutional Convention created a new government, with many more powers. However, many colonists feared this might create another tyrannical government like the one they had just escaped in England. Thus, when the Constitution came around for ratification, many pressed for the addition of a bill of rights to limit the powers of the federal government.

James Madison took charge in the first Congress of writing up a bill of rights. The Congress eventually proposed twelve amendments to the Constitution, and all but the first two were passed and adopted in 1791, becoming what Americans today know as the Bill of Rights. The Third Amendment in the numbering used by Congress, which became our First Amendment, reads "Congress shall make no law respecting an establishment of religion, or prohibiting the free exercise thereof; or abridging the freedom of speech, or of the press; or the right of the people peaceably to assemble, and to petition the government for a redress of grievances." While many might think that our forefathers held the freedoms in the First Amendment to be paramount and therefore put them first, their placement in the First Amendment is, in fact, coincidental.

The First Amendment, once adopted, was put to little use for the first century of its existence. The entire Bill of Rights was held to limit only Congress in 1833, and Congress passed few laws directly impacting religion. The first real test came in 1879, dealing with a federal law banning polygamy in the territories. The Supreme Court upheld this law against a religious challenge, holding that religion does not give a person freedom to do something that is otherwise illegal.

For almost another fifty years after 1879, the First Amendment in the area of religion was discussed little in the courts. However, in 1925, things began to change. In that year, the Supreme Court in *Gitlow* v. *New York* greatly increased the amount of protection given by the U.S. Constitution to Americans' freedoms. It held that parts of the Bill of Rights limited both the federal and state governments. The reason stated was that the Fourteenth Amendment prohibited the states from infringing on the liberty of any person, and the Supreme Court held that parts of the Bill of Rights were included in the liberties that the states could not limit. Thus, if some part of the Bill of Rights, in the eyes of the Supreme Court, was a fundamental freedom, then the states could not infringe on it, just as the federal government could not. The Court did not specifically list freedom of religion as one of those fundamental freedoms in 1925, but they also did not make the list a limited one in that year.

In 1940, the Supreme Court took the next step in protecting religious freedom. In that year, the Court specifically extended the First Amendment's religion clauses against the states. There are two clauses in the religion section of the First Amendment, one protecting the free exercise of religion, generally called the free exercise clause, and another protecting from government establishment of religion, generally called the establishment clause. The 1940 case dealt with the issue of the free exercise of religion, and in 1947 the Supreme Court struck down a law as creating an establishment of religion, thus clearly demonstrating that the establishment clause also applied against the states. The establishment cause protects what people consider the freedom from religion. By 1950, then, in only twenty-five years, the Supreme Court had both informed the states that they could not infringe upon Americans' fundamental freedoms, just as the federal government was limited, and told the states that the religious freedom embodied in the First Amendment was included in those fundamental freedoms.

Since 1950, many Supreme Court cases have dealt with the freedom of religion, both in its area of the individual's free exercise of religion and in its area of the prohibition of a government establishment of religion. While these decisions often caused much controversy, the fact that states are not allowed to infringe upon religious freedom and not allowed to establish a religion has been generally left alone. The application of the First Amendment to the states through the Fourteenth Amendment's protection of liberty remains one of the most significant constitutional decisions in Supreme Court history and has allowed federal jurisdiction over cases regarding everything from prayers in public schools to newspapers' rights to publish controversial stories.

See also Cantwell v. *Connecticut; Gitlow* v. *New York;* Incorporation; Saluting the flag

For further reading

Farish, Leah. 1998. *The First Amendment: Freedom of Speech, Religion, and the Press.* Springfield, NJ: Enslow.

Noonan, John Thomas. 1998. *The Lustre of Our Country: The American Experience of Religious Freedom.* Berkeley: University of California Press.

Urofsky, Melvin I. 2002. *Religious Freedom: Rights and Liberties under the Law.* Santa Barbara, CA: ABC-CLIO.

Willis, Clyde E. 2002. *Student's Guide to Landmark Congressional Laws on the First Amendment.* Westport, CT: Greenwood Press.

Flast v. *Cohen*

392 U.S. 83 (1968)

In this case a federal taxpayer sued because he thought that funds were being spent for an unconstitutional purpose. This is different from the *Doremus* case, in which a local taxpayer sued over alleged misuse of local funds. The cause of the suit was the Elementary and Secondary Education Act of 1965, and the taxpayer claimed that funds under this act were being spent to fund and provide materials for religious schools. The main issue decided here was that of standing, or whether the individual suing had the right to bring the action.

The decision was written by Chief Justice Warren. In general, taxpayers had been held to lack standing, and so taxpayers generally cannot sue. The question here was whether a claimed infringement of the First Amendment allowed a suit. The opinion then surveyed the background of the suit and explained how the monies under the act were funneled to the local authorities, who could then use them to support public or private schools. The suit claimed that some funds had gone to private schools, which was illegal, as those funds represented "compulsory taxation for religious purposes" (392 U.S. 83: 87).

The Court examined the history of similar lawsuits. Warren reviewed the 1923 case, which had held that taxpayers lacked standing to sue the federal government and that the case's holding was one based in policy considerations and not in the Constitution. The Court stated that a real case or controversy must exist, as the federal courts would not give opinions for the sake of advice; it then stated that a federal taxpayer did sometimes have a right to sue, and that the issue of improperly

spent taxes was not one for the Congress and the president to decide, as the government had suggested in this case, but was one for the courts to become involved in.

The real question then was whether the person suing had standing. In determining standing, the issues involved played a large role, and Warren noted that "our decisions establish that, in ruling on standing, it is both appropriate and necessary to look to the substantive issues for another purpose, namely, to determine whether there is a logical nexus between the status asserted and the claim sought to be adjudicated" (392 U.S. 83: 101–102). Warren held that for federal taxpayers to sue, two requirements must be satisfied: "First, the taxpayer must establish a logical link between that status and the type of legislative enactment attacked," and "secondly, the taxpayer must establish a nexus between that status and the precise nature of the constitutional infringement alleged" (392 U.S. 83: 102). Both these requirements were fulfilled here, and so the suit was allowed. General disagreement with how tax monies were spent was not allowed to become a federal case, but if the tax was alleged to violate another part of the Constitution, in this case the establishment clause of the First Amendment, suits were allowed, and thus this suit was an allowable one. The case was then returned to the lower courts for adjudication on the issue of whether the expenditure was unconstitutional.

Justice Douglas wrote a concurrence, arguing for the abandonment of the 1923 standing rule and an overturning of the 1923 case, holding that when the Constitution was affected, taxpayers should be allowed to bring suits and that this would not, unlike what the dissent suggested, result in a flood of lawsuits. Douglas saw the proper role of the Court as being to right wrongs, and that "where wrongs to individuals are done by violation of specific guarantees, it is abdication for courts to close their doors" (392 U.S. 83: 111). Douglas did not think the First Amendment should give one more standing to sue than any other amendment, holding "I would be as liberal in allowing taxpayers standing to object to these violations of the First Amendment as I would in granting standing to people to complain of any invasion of their rights under the Fourth Amendment or the Fourteenth or under any other guarantee in the Constitution itself or in the Bill of Rights" (392 U.S. 83: 113).

Stewart and Fortas wrote short concurrences, arguing that this case only established the rule that a taxpayer's claims under the First Amendment could be brought into courts, basically limiting the holding and not expanding it as Douglas wanted to.

Harlan dissented, holding that one could sue if prosecuted for failure to pay a tax when that failure occurred because of dislike of a government expenditure and that this was the proper way for such an issue to enter the Court system. He suggested that the Court had made the wrong decision on whether taxpayers in cases like this one had standing. His basic disagreement was with the increased power given the First Amendment in terms of what suits were allowed, arguing that the purpose of the First Amendment's establishment clause was not clear, and because it was not clear, it could not serve as the basis for allowing standing. Harlan would allow suits against funds being spent to support religion directly, but that is where he would draw the line. He pointed to the Congress and the president, not the courts, as the proper place to gain relief from what abuses occurred, and that the remedy given in this case would result in too many cases flooding the courts.

However, Harlan did not carry the day, and this lawsuit and similar lawsuits were allowed. In similar cases against state laws, the suits have been somewhat limited due to aggressive use of the Taxpayer Injunction Act, which does not allow one to escape payment of taxes just because of legal opposition to what the taxes are being spent on. One must pay the taxes and then sue, and in general this act, especially re-

cently, has limited access, especially to the federal courts, to those wishing to sue in opposition to a tax.

> ***See also*** *Doremus* v. *Board of Education; Hibbs* v. *Winn; Lemon* v. *Kurtzman; Mueller* v. *Allen;* Paying for tests and other aid for private schools; *Valley Forge College* v. *Americans United*

For further reading

Brownlee, W. Elliot. 2004. *Federal Taxation in America: A Short History.* New York: Cambridge University Press.

Pollack, Sheldon David. 1996. *The Failure of U.S. Tax Policy: Revenue and Politics.* University Park: Pennsylvania State University Press.

Steuerle, C. Eugene. 2004. *Contemporary U.S. Tax Policy.* Washington, DC: Urban Institute Press.

U.S. Office of Non-Public Education. 2000. *Benefits for Private School Students and Teachers from Federal Education Programs.* Washington, DC: U.S. Department of Education, Office of Non-Public Education, Office of Educational Research and Improvement, Educational Resources Information Center.

Footnote Four of *United States v. Carolene Products Company*
304 U.S. 144 (1938)

Seldom do footnotes in a Supreme Court decision seem remarkable, and very often they are overlooked by all but the most ardent scholars or interested attorneys. In a couple of relatively recent instances, however, footnotes have proven to be important and informative in Supreme Court decisions. One of those was in the *Brown* v. *Board of Education* case in 1954. In footnote 11 of that decision, the Supreme Court quoted several academics about segregation's sociological effects. This was condemned by *Brown's* opponents, and segregationists stated that the Supreme Court was not engaged in the law, but in sociology. Footnote 4 of the *Carolene Products* decision was no less important, although it did not produce much controversy at the time.

The overall decision in *United States v. Carolene Products Company* dealt with whether Congress could regulate "filled" (or skim) milk.

Justice Harlan F. Stone's decision held that it could, but the decision itself, unlike *Brown,* is not that remarkable. While discussing Congress's power, Stone noted that Congress only needed a rational basis for legislation. In an attached footnote, Stone added, "There may be narrower scope for operation of the presumption of constitutionality when legislation appears on its face to be within a specific prohibition of the Constitution, such as those of the first ten Amendments, which are deemed equally specific when held to be embraced within the Fourteenth. . . . It is unnecessary to consider now whether legislation which restricts those political processes which can ordinarily be expected to bring about repeal of undesirable legislation, is to be subjected to more exacting judicial scrutiny under the general prohibitions of the Fourteenth Amendment than are most other types of legislation. . . . Nor need we enquire whether similar considerations enter into the review of statutes directed at particular religious, . . . or racial minorities; whether prejudice against discrete and insular minorities may be a special condition, which tends seriously to curtail the operation of those political processes ordinarily to be relied upon to protect minorities, and which may call for a correspondingly more searching judicial inquiry" (304 U.S. 144: 152). This footnote means that while Congress is presumed to act constitutionally when it has a rational reason to pass legislation, it may not be (and Stone, by adding the footnote, hints that it is not) presumed to be acting constitutionally when legislation affects certain minorities, whether racial, religious or other "discrete and insular" minorities. Thus, Congress is given the power to regulate the economy generally, but there is a higher standard of proof required if the legislation is aimed at certain minorities or if it affects the rights given by the Bill of Rights, which is also somewhat applied to the states.

This footnote has come to be much more significant to the American public than the decision from which it came. In it, the Supreme Court placed a greater burden on Congress when dealing with legislation affecting racial, religious, and other minorities. The footnote has been used to justify Court decisions in several subsequent cases. For example, in *West Virginia State Board of Education* v. *Barnette,* in the 1940s, the Supreme Court used the *Carolene Products* footnote to say that people did not have to salute the flag if their religious beliefs prohibited them from doing so. However, in *Employment Division* v. *Smith,* in the 1990s, in which an Oregon employee claimed his workplace could not fire him for religious use of peyote, the Supreme Court limited the effect of the footnote by saying that laws are permitted to limit religion in their effect, so long as those laws are not directed at religion specifically and are broad ranging in their intent.

> **See also** *Employment Division* v. *Smith; Gitlow* v. *New York;* Incorporation; *Palko* v. *Connecticut;* Saluting the flag
>
> **For further reading**
> Coleman, Jules L., and Anthony Sebok, eds. 1994. *Constitutional Law and Its Interpretation.* New York: Garland.
> Perry, Michael J. 1999. *We the People: The Fourteenth Amendment and the Supreme Court.* New York: Oxford University Press.

Felix Frankfurter

Supreme Court Justice
Born: 1882
Died: 1965
Education: City College of New York, 1902; Harvard Law, 1906
Sworn In: January 30, 1939
Retired: August 28, 1962

Unlike many Supreme Court justices, Felix Frankfurter did not practice law as his primary occupation for any significant period of time. He was born in 1882 in Austria and immigrated to the United States at the age of twelve. He graduated from college at the age of twenty and then attended Harvard Law School, receiving the highest academic average in the school's history to that point. For one year in New York

City he practiced law then joined the U.S. attorney's office in that city. He also served in the U.S. Department of War (something like today's Department of Defense). In 1914, Frankfurter joined the faculty of Harvard Law School and largely remained there until 1938, with a hiatus to serve as assistant to the secretary of labor during World War I.

Frankfurter, although clearly at home at Harvard, remained active in legal issues. He was at the forefront of the defense in the Sacco and Vanzetti murder trial. Although not formally a part of the government during the 1930s, he advised President Franklin Delano Roosevelt (FDR) on many issues and helped to find Harvard graduates who were interested in working in Washington. He provided law clerks for Supreme Court Justices Oliver Wendell Holmes and Louis Brandeis, who numbered among his friends. He was chosen to replace Benjamin Cardozo on the Supreme Court when Cardozo died in 1938 because he (Frankfurter) was an advisor, an expert on constitutional law, and quite possibly because he was, like Cardozo, Jewish. Frankfurter's religion is noteworthy because in the twentieth century, beginning in 1916 when Louis Brandeis was appointed (except for a twenty-three-year gap from 1970 to Ruth Bader Ginsburg's 1993 appointment), there was always a Jewish Supreme Court justice. This led to the perception that there is a Jewish seat on the Court.

However, Frankfurter believed strongly that religion should play no role in his judgments. In addition to his Court activities, he also kept up with correspondence and advised FDR. Frankfurter wrote in a clear and witty style, making his opinions engaging reading, even when the reader did not agree with them.

Frankfurter believed in a limited role for the judiciary. He believed acts should be struck down only if they were in clear conflict with the Constitution, and other than that, the legislature should be given the benefit of the doubt and allowed wide latitude of action. Hand in hand with this view came the idea

Felix Frankfurter was an associate justice of the U.S. Supreme Court from 1939 to 1962. He advocated the exercise of judicial restraint by the Court. (Library of Congress)

that the legislature reflected the views of the people who elected it, and judges should not supplant the people's desires, except in clear cases of constitutional conflict. Among constitutional scholars, this view is known as judicial restraint, and judges who practice it generally restrain from striking down legislation. Unlike some advocates of judicial restraint, Frankfurter tried to follow this view in all areas of the law, not just those in which he agreed with what the legislature was doing.

Throughout the 1940s, Frankfurter was considered a leader among those justices who believed in judicial restraint and limited reading of the Constitution and the Bill of Rights. On the other wing were those believing in judicial activism and a broader reading of the Constitution and the Bill of Rights. This wing, led by Hugo Black, held that judges should not be afraid to strike down unconstitutional legislation. Black and Frankfurter notoriously disagreed on most cases, and both wanted someone from his own wing to become chief justice. Frankfurter was disappointed when Truman went outside the court to select Fred Vinson and then when Eisenhower selected Earl Warren. When Vinson was selected, Justice Jackson thought that he had been promised the job by FDR, and Jackson made his thoughts public. (Black and Douglas had threatened to resign if Jackson was named chief justice, and Frankfurter and Jackson may have threatened to resign if Black was chosen.) Relations between Frankfurter and Black, never good, were worse after this. Frankfurter and Black would eventually come to terms, but, oddly enough, as theirs was the less publicized quarrel, Frankfurter and Douglas never did. (Jackson died in 1954 without coming to terms with Black either.)

Frankfurter made immense contributions to the law in his legal opinions. One of his first notable opinions came only a year after joining the Court. In 1940, he wrote the Court's opinion in *Minersville School District* v. *Gobitis,* which held that school districts could force Jehovah's Witnesses to salute the flag. He considered the flag salute to be justified in the promotion of patriotism, and he deferred to the wisdom of the legislature, writing, "The wisdom of training children in patriotic impulses by those compulsions which necessarily pervade so much of the educational process is not for our independent judgment. Even were we convinced of the folly of such a measure, such belief would be no proof of its unconstitutionality" (310 U.S. 586: 598). Just three years later, though, the court reversed itself in *West Virginia* v. *Barnette.* Furious as he found himself on the short end of a 6–3 decision, Frankfurter believed that Black and Douglas, among others, had reversed themselves for political reasons, which is not permitted for Supreme Court justices. Frankfurter's famous dissent in *Barnette* noted his own religion. He wrote "one who belongs to the most vilified and persecuted minority in history is not likely to be insensible to the freedoms guaranteed by our Constitution. Were my purely personal attitude relevant I should whole-heartedly associate myself with the general libertarian views in the Court's opinion, representing as they do the thought and action of a lifetime. But as judges we are neither Jew nor Gentile, neither Catholic nor agnostic" (319 U.S. 624: 646–657). This is perhaps his best single statement of his view on the Supreme Court justice's role in American life and the significance he attributed to his job.

In 1962, Frankfurter resigned at the age of eighty because of bad health and lived for a few more years in Washington; however, he engaged in little activity after leaving the Court.

See also Hugo Black; Saluting the flag

For further reading

Frankfurter, Felix. 1960. *Felix Frankfurter Reminisces.* New York: Reynal.

Frankfurter, Felix, and Joseph P. Lash. 1975. *From the Diaries of Felix Frankfurter.* New York: Norton.

Hockett, Jeffrey D. 1996. *New Deal Justice: The Constitutional Jurisprudence of Hugo L. Black, Felix Frankfurter, and Robert H. Jackson.* Lanham, MD: Rowman & Littlefield.

Murphy, Bruce Allen. 1982. *The Brandeis/Frankfurter Connection.* New York: Oxford University Press.

Simon James F. 1989. *The Antagonists: Hugo Black, Felix Frankfurter and Civil Liberties in Modern America.* New York: Simon and Schuster.

G

Gay marriage

While marriage is technically a state-based institution, it is one with unquestionable religious ties. Repressive social and religious mores forced gays and lesbians into the closet for most of America's history, and it was not until the late twentieth century that same-sex partners could have public relationships. Fundamentalist Christians, particularly, express their opposition to gay marriages (and gay rights legislation in general), and very few states support same-sex marriages.

In the nineteenth century, many women lived together in what were frequently called Boston marriages. At least some of these relationships were homosexual ones. However, this was also the only way women could live acceptably outside of a family situation. Single women living alone were assumed to be prostitutes, so in order to move to a new city or leave her parents' home without moving in with another relative, a woman had to find a roommate. Finances also contributed to such living arrangements, as most women did not make enough money to be able to live alone. Research into these arrangements has shown that some, but not all, were romantic in nature. Same-sex couples never thought publicly about marriage as their sexual preference was generally ranked a crime and therefore needed to be hidden.

With the twentieth century, more and more people who were homosexual came to accept their sexual orientation and sometimes even publicly proclaim it. In the 1940s, two important developments promoted homosexual awareness. The first was World War II, when many gays and lesbians moved from small towns into the larger cities and/or served in the armed forces, situations in which they could come into contact with other gays and lesbians and realize that they were not alone. The 1940s also saw the publication of the first Kinsey report, which focused on male sexual behavior and argued that homosexuality was not deviant, and a fair number of men were exclusively homosexual. The second Kinsey report focused on female sexual behavior and was released in the early 1950s, and its findings were similar. The studies stated that roughly 4 percent of men and 2 percent of women were exclusively homosexual.

Both of these studies offered support to gays and lesbians in the form of scientific documentation suggesting that their sexual orientation was not an immoral aberration. This encouraged them to begin to fight for their own rights at a time when gay and lesbian groups were leading increasingly closeted lives, thanks to the homosexual paranoia fostered by the Red Scare, the fear of communist infiltration of the U.S. government following World War II. The growing civil rights movement also encouraged gays and lesbians to begin to believe that they deserved rights. Indeed, both the gay and lesbian movements and the women's rights movements learned tactics from the civil rights movement.

In the 1950s, the first gay and lesbian organizations were founded. The Mattachine Society and the Daughters of Bilitis formed to provide gays and lesbians with political outlets and meeting places. The groups hoped science would ultimately prove to the mainstream populace that homosexuals were not a threat. However, they were fairly conservative and so were frequently derided by the much more radical gay and lesbian movement of the late 1960s and beyond.

By the 1960s, many gays and lesbians were becoming more open about their sexuality, and they even persuaded the ACLU to take a stand supporting the position that a person's sexual activities in private should not be criminalized. All this set the stage for the radical gay rights movement, which began at the Stonewall Inn.

On June 27, 1969, the New York Police raided the Stonewall Bar, a gay bar in Greenwich Village, New York. The raid turned into a riot, and this is widely seen as the start of the gay and lesbian rights movement that became prominent in the 1970s. Paralleling this movement came the public iteration that gays and lesbians wanted to marry. In 1975, Jack Baker and Michael McConnell applied for a marriage license in Minneapolis to protest Minnesota's refusal to allow same-sex marriages. They were refused, and McConnell lost a job offer because of his open sexuality.

Backlash against the movement, spearheaded by the right-wing religious right, was strong. However, gays and lesbians did make significant advances in this period. In 1979, the first adoption of a child by an openly gay man was legalized. However, gays and lesbians who wanted to adopt children as couples still faced significant barriers—and in many states they continue to confront these barriers today. Indeed, until the 1990s, gay and lesbian marriages remained unheard of, and same-sex partners wishing to publicize and formalize their commitment to one another usually held private ceremonies that offered no legal status.

In Hawaii, one group of plaintiffs had some success in the 1990s. In the case of *Baehr* v. *Lewin* (later *Baehr* v. *Miike*), Hawaii's Judge Levinson found that Hawaii's constitution made it illegal to discriminate against gays and lesbians in the area of marriage and so ordered that three gay couples be allowed to have marriage licenses. This decision was upheld by the Hawaii Supreme Court. However, it created a firestorm of controversy. Meanwhile, at the national level, Congress got involved, primarily because of the full faith and credit clause of the Constitution, which generally has been held to require one state to respect the rulings of another state in certain areas. Marriage and divorce are two of these areas. If one state considers a couple to be married, it generally has been held that other states are required to consider the couple married as well. This practice used to create huge controversies, as many heterosexual couples who were too young to be married in one state went to another and got married. Divorce was generally seen in the same way, as some couples would obtain a divorce in another state with easier divorce laws, at which point the question became whether the first state had to respect the ruling of the second. In the twentieth century, the answer generally was that, yes, the first state would have to respect the second state's ruling, and this did not cause a large controversy until the issue of gay marriages surfaced. Thus, if Hawaii allowed gay marriages, all of the other states might have to respect those marriages.

Gays and lesbians and supporters of gay and lesbian rights everywhere celebrated a triumph in Hawaii's ruling, but it was relatively short-lived. Those opposed to the measure rallied support in Congress and passed the Defense of Marriage Act (or DOMA) in 1996. DOMA held that states had to respect marriages in other states only when these unions were between one man and one woman. Hawaii itself soon acted to make the point moot, passing a constitutional amendment banning same-sex marriages in 1999.

Other states, though, were not as wholly hostile to gay rights. Vermont passed a law creating civil unions in 2000, marriages in everything but name on the state level and carrying the same benefits statewide as marriages. Civil unions, however, did not have to be respected in other states. In 2004, New Jersey passed a similar measure, and in 2005 Massachusetts broke new ground in the United States, becoming the first state to legalize gay marriage. Meanwhile, in 2003, Canada legalized gay marriages on a province-by-province basis, and, as the country has no residency requirement, same-sex couples have been crossing the border to wed ever since. The law was made national in 2005, forcing all provinces to allow same-gender unions. In September 2004, President George W. Bush's proposed constitutional amendment banning gay marriage was defeated in the Senate.

However, other states were not required to follow the leads of their progressive neighbors, health institutions do not have to honor a civil union partner as next of kin, and no federal benefits in taxes or other areas came from these civil unions and marriages. California has passed legislation giving spousal benefits to same-sex partners, and a number of universities and private organizations do the same. As recently as 2005, California's supreme court ruled that a law banning same-sex marriages was unconstitutional, forcing the issue of a constitutional amendment to a likely statewide vote. While most states have currently ratified constitutional amendments banning same-sex marriage, the U.S. Supreme Court has not made any rulings about this on the national level.

Canadian churches opposed to same-sex marriage feared they would be forced to perform such weddings, but a Canadian supreme court ruling guaranteed that they would not be required to marry same-sex couples. However, an increasing number of churches and religious organizations are accepting of gay and lesbian couples, and some encourage gay and lesbian marriages.

The battle over same-gender marriages was in no way completed by the Defense of Marriage Act in 1996 or Vermont's actions in 2000. George W. Bush's proposed constitutional amendment was based in the argument that DOMA was only an act and it could be struck down by the courts, whereas an amendment would provide permanent status to the issue. Similarly, gay rights advocates would like to see a federal constitutional amendment guaranteeing gay and lesbian couples the right to marry for exactly the same reason. Thus, in all likelihood the issue will continue to be politically and personally hot for some time to come.

See also Baehr v. Lewin; Bowers v. Hardwick; Divorce, marriage, and religion; Loving v. United States; Religion and attitudes toward marriage historically in the United States

For further reading

Baird, Robert M. 1997. *Same-Sex Marriage: The Moral and Legal Debate.* Amherst, NY: Prometheus Books.

Bourassa, Kevin, and Joe Varnell. 2002. *Just Married: Gay Marriage and the Expansion of Human Rights.* Madison: University of Wisconsin Press.

Moats, David. 2004. *Civil Wars: A Battle for Gay Marriage.* Orlando: Harcourt.

Robinson, Bruce A. 1995. Homosexual (Same Sex) Marriages in Canada: Ontario Court Case pt. 1. Toronto: Ontario Consultants on Religious Tolerance. http://www.religious tolerance.org/hom_marb2.htm.

Stychin, Carl, and Didi Herman, eds. 2001. *Law and Sexuality: The Global Arena.* Minneapolis: University of Minnesota Press.

Wolfson, Evan. 2004. *Why Marriage Matters: America, Equality, and Gay People's Right to Marry.* New York: Simon and Schuster.

General legal treatment of Mormons

The law has generally treated Mormons with some disdain, especially in the church's first century, and the public, especially in the early years, went far beyond the law to force the Mormons west and then to scorn their church. The Mormon religion, also known as the Church of Latter-day Saints, was founded in 1827 by Joseph Smith, who claimed personal revelations as the foundation of his belief. He believed an angel had shown him a new version of the Bible, the Book of Mormon. Among its revelations were claims that many contemporaries considered blasphemous, including the belief that America had been founded by ancient Hebrews and that Native Americans were the descendants of this group, but that they had forsaken Jesus, who had also appeared in America, and were turned dark for their error.

Smith gathered a following, in part for a number of reasons not directly connected to his revelations. To begin with, the mid-1800s was a period of religious revival and renewal in the United States, known as the Second Great Awakening. Many people were leaving their old religions and finding new ones, and Mormonism was just one of several to grow up in the atmosphere (the Shaker faith, which has died out, and Unitarianism, which still exists today, are two others). Smith claimed that America had been the site of the new revelation, and the country was special to God. American exceptionalism has always played well, and it certainly had success in this religious context. Smith also believed that human beings could be made perfect and that God had once been man and man could become God. The Mormons drew from those disenfranchised by the period's economic changes, and Mormonism provided order and answers, which people craved. However, many outside the religion thought that the Bible and the Constitution were what had made America great, and they felt that the Book of Mormon was a blasphemous text that sought to disrupt both church and state alike.

The Mormon religion also drew more negativity at its outset because it was more direct than most new sects or denominations in claiming to be the only true religion. Smith and his followers believed Mormonism would ultimately replace all other forms of Christianity. The Mormons, as a whole, were subject to persecution to the point that in 1838, the governor of Missouri, Lilburn Briggs, ordered the group to leave the state, saying that they should be killed if they failed to go.

The Mormons then settled in Illinois, where they again met with discrimination and public anger. In 1843, Smith stated that God had spoken to him again, telling him men were allowed to have multiple wives and instituting polygamy as an acceptable church practice. This, combined with Smith's desire to be president of the United States, caused him to be jailed on a charge of treason. The charge stemmed from Smith's supposed attempts to negotiate with Mexico for Mexico's allowance of a new settlement for Mormons to the Southwest (what was then northern Mexico and what is now the United States). The people, though, did not want to wait for the law to do its work. A mob forcibly removed Smith from jail and lynched him in 1844.

After Smith's lynching, Brigham Young led the Mormons, moving the group on a 2,000 mile trek west to what would become Utah. There the Mormons established their own colony, in a territory that was pretty much deserted and unwanted. Utah was, at the time, part of Mexico, and it would remain so until 1848 and the Mexican-American War, just after the Mormon migration. The area seemed largely uninhabitable, and the Mormons survived by irrigating the desert, founding Salt Lake City.

The U.S. government did not leave the Mormons alone, largely because of the practice of polygamy by the church leaders. For instance, long-term leader Brigham Young had at least nineteen wives. The United States passed a series of acts regulating the territories (as the Utah territory, like all other territories, fell under federal law) between 1862 and 1887 and outlawed polygamy very quickly. The first polygamy case came in front of the U.S. Supreme Court in 1879, and the Court upheld the law, ruling that behavior based in religion was not necessarily protected by the First Amendment. The battle culminated in the Mormon Church being stripped of its charter and possessions in 1890. The church then reversed its position on polygamy in the early 1890s, banning it. The U.S. government returned to the church what was left of its assets a few years later.

Some groups continued to push for stronger laws against polygamy or a federal amendment banning the practice, but the federal government did not act. The U.S. government has generally left the question of polygamy alone since the 1890s, even though polygamy is discussed along with the gay marriage controversy today. The argument made by gay marriage opponents is that if gay marriage is legalized, then polygamy will also have to be legalized. Polygamy has also declined correspondingly, with the cessation of formal Mormon recognition. After 1890, polygamists generally stayed out of the limelight, and the Utah constitution was required to have a provision banning polygamy or plural marriage. The Supreme Court has occasionally gotten into the polygamy debate since 1890, as some cases involving the practice have been appealed to that body. The Court upheld a conviction of a Mormon man under the White Slave Act, as he had taken his wives across state lines and fallen afoul of that act. The Supreme Court also refused to review a Utah decision removing custody from parents who supported polygamy. In that case, the parents did not practice polygamy but merely had advocated the idea of polygamy to their families. The practice still lives on, primarily in Utah, as splinter Mormon sects not recognized by the main church still support the practice. Close to 100,000 people may be living in polygamous marriages, with no regular campaign of prosecution against them. Besides being illegal as polygamous marriages, the unions have been a source of sexual abuse and underage marriages, also illegal, in which unwilling girls are forced to marry much older men. Thus, it is not outside the realm of possibility that polygamy prosecutions will resume at some point in the future. However, few, if any, of the practice's adherents will be members of the mainstream Mormon Church, and it is highly unlikely that any successful religious defense can be mounted for polygamy.

Outside of polygamy, Mormons have generally been treated better by the law than other groups who also evangelize. Mormon men are generally required to take a two-year mission, usually around the age of eighteen, and travel around spreading their faith. Few prosecutions of Mormons have been reported for these efforts, however. This is quite a contrast from other well-known groups of evangelizers including the Hare Krishnas and the Jehovah's Witnesses. The Hare Krishnas have repeatedly come before the Supreme Court for their efforts in public places to sell their literature, solicit donations, and inform people about their faith. The Jehovah's Witnesses require each active Witness to distribute literature and spread his or her ideas, often in a door-to-door style of evangelizing. The Jehovah's Witnesses, ever since the 1930s, have been repeatedly arrested for their activities, and it has been estimated that this group has appeared in front of the Supreme Court at least seventy times on the issue of door-to-door canvassing, refusing to salute the flag, refusing to receive blood transfusions, and refusing to serve in the army, among other issues. The Mormons have not been prosecuted so heavily, but this should not suggest that they are always well received by those to whom they evangelize, just that they suffer less government intrusion.

Several possibilities to rationalize this anomaly exist, though none can be defined as the certain reason for it. The first reason is political. Mormons are allowed by their beliefs to be active in politics, while the Jehovah's Witnesses must refrain from doing so. Thus, across the nation there are elected and appointed officials who are Mormons. This presence in politics may explain why some arrests never turn into prosecutions, as the elected and appointed officials can intervene with the arresting officials and convince them not to prosecute. This is not to say that the Mormons are above the law, but just that those with friends in higher office can convince officials to drop the charges in many cases. The second is the stance of the Mormon Church on prosecutions, as the church, especially recently, works with municipalities to educate them about the Mormons' right to evangelize, while other faiths may not develop such a close relationship with local legal entities. A third possibility is the nature and frequency of the evangelization. Mormons are required to go on only a two-year mission and then only if young and male (women do go on a mission sometimes, but less frequently). In contrast, all Jehovah's Witnesses and all Hare Krishnas, in most interpretations of their faiths, are told to witness. Thus, there is a smaller percentage of Mormon Church members proselytizing at any given time. The public may be more accepting, or at least more understanding, of an individual on a short-term one-time mission than of one on a repeating mission and less likely to push for prosecution. All of these reasons (and possibly others) probably contribute to the fewer prosecutions, but no good study has been done on the matter.

Thus, although not well received by the public in the early years of its existence, the Mormon Church has recently been less subject to prosecutions than other evangelizing churches. And those offshoots of the Mormon Church that are not under its control and still practice polygamy are also not regularly subjected to waves of prosecution. The non-Mormon public may not view the group as favorably as other religions, but the law has had fewer encounters with the Mormons in general and for evangelizing than with other churches who contact the public directly and personally in order to spread their message. While subject to intense hatred by the public in its early years, the Mormon Church has now become, more or less, part of the American landscape.

See also *Baehr* v. *Lewin; Employment Division* v. *Smith; International Society for Krishna Consciousness* v. *Lee; Loving* v. *United States; Reynolds* v. *United States; Watchtower Bible and Tract Society of New York* v. *Village of Stratton*

For further reading

Alexander, Thomas G., ed. 1980. *The Mormon People, Their Character and Traditions.* Provo, UT: Brigham Young University Press.

Alexander, Thomas G. 1986. *Mormonism in Transition: A History of the Latter-Day Saints, 1890–1930.* Urbana: University of Illinois Press.

Bushman, Claudia Lauper, and Richard Lyman Bushman. 2001. *Building the Kingdom: A History of Mormons in America.* New York: Oxford University Press.

Foster, Lawrence. 1984. *Religion and Sexuality: The Shakers, the Mormons, and the Oneida Community.* Urbana: University of Illinois Press.

Gordon, Sarah Barringer. 2002. *The Mormon Question: Polygamy and Constitutional Conflict in Nineteenth-Century America.* Chapel Hill: University of North Carolina Press.

Peters, Shawn Francis. 2000. *Judging Jehovah's Witnesses: Religious Persecution and the Dawn of the Rights Revolution.* Lawrence: University Press of Kansas.

Ghost Dance Massacre

In the mid-1800s, the U.S. government attempted to relocate Native Americans onto reservations. Very often these moves were accompanied by promises of supplies that were later broken. Fixed settlement on the reservations differed greatly from the many traditional Native American lifestyles in the West, which often had been very mobile, following the buffalo and moving often from season to season.

After moving the Native Americans onto the reservations and extinguishing the last of the concerted Native American military campaigns, the U.S. government passed the Dawes Severalty Act in 1887. Bluntly stated, the Dawes Act aimed to eliminate Native American culture and religion, which were inextricably intertwined, and replace them with white culture and religion. The act was designed to convert the Native Americans into white farmers by dealing with them on a family rather than a tribal basis, which was at variance with how most tribes governed their affairs. It gave each family 160 acres of land and granted them ownership of the land after a certain period. In addition to its total lack of respect for tribal culture, the act granted land that was generally not fit for farming. This was the backdrop for the Ghost Dance Massacre, also known as the Massacre at Wounded Knee. Whites originally called it the Battle at Wounded Knee, but Native Americans have consistently contested the term's accuracy, as the white soldiers outnumbered the Native Americans by a huge number.

In 1890, the Native Americans were desperate for a revival of their culture. A Piute prophet, Wovoka, believed the world would soon end and be reborn, inherited by the Native Americans if they could live harmoniously and keep themselves free from the pollution of white culture. Wovoka did not believe in mourning, as the dead were among those he believed would inherit the earth. He told people to dance so that they might die briefly and thereby catch glimpses of the foretold paradise. These dances, called Ghost Dances, produced visions. The dances spread out from the Piute and included the Sioux in South Dakota. The visions they produced included a return of the buffalo. The buffalo had originally numbered in the tens of millions, but by the 1890s very few were left on the plains. By the end of the 1870s the herd was estimated at about 1,000, with even fewer remaining by the 1890s.

The white population greatly feared the Ghost Dances, particularly after two Native American mystics, Kicking Bear and Short Bull, began to focus on the elimination of the whites that the visions promised. Native Americans were routinely mistreated by the white people who ran the reservations. Some reduced the amount of food given out to the Native Americans, others tried to profit from their positions, and still others were simply inept.

It has been estimated that only about 4,000–5,000 Native Americans (mostly Sioux) were participating in these dances, and many of these were women and children. The dances were banned on Lakota reservations, and the U.S. Army brought in 6,000–7,000 soldiers to subdue the Ghost Dancers. The reasons for the massive show of force were multiple, but one was that the army hoped to frighten the Native Americans into surrender with a show of force. The army, headed by General Miles, also hoped to show the need for a continued western military presence so they would not have

Aftermath of the Wounded Knee Massacre at the Pine Ridge Agency in South Dakota in 1890. Reacting to the fervor created by the Ghost Dance, the U.S. Army mobilized a large force to control the Native Americans. Tensions at the Pine Ridge Agency led to violence on December 29, 1890, near Wounded Knee Creek, as between 150 and 300 Sioux were killed and 50 wounded in what would mark the end of 400 years of organized Native American resistance to white culture. (Library of Congress)

to modernize. Without the need for the military to guard the reservations, the army might have had to modernize and prepare to fight forces outside the United States, and some in the army, including Miles, did not want this. Miles and others also wanted the army, not the Indian office, to be given control over Native Americans.

However, the large show of force backfired in many ways and was one of the factors leading directly to the massacres. First, along with the alarmist reports that were circulated, the presence of so many soldiers caused the white people of the region to panic. Past activities of the troops also caused problems. Earlier, even Native Americans not participating in anti-white activities had had their horses taken and their homes raided by the soldiers, and the sheer number of troops caused them to worry as well. Kicking Bear invited Chief Sitting Bull, a remaining chief from the Battle of Little Bighorn, to join in the dances, and Sitting Bull allowed them to be taught at Standing Rock until Kicking Bear and Short Bull were removed by the army.

The Lakota who were participating in the Ghost Dances invited Sitting Bull to join them, but before he could set out, his arrest was ordered. On December 15, 1890, in the process of arresting him, and claiming he resisted arrest, government officials killed him. The remnants of his band went to join Kicking Bear and Short Bull at Wounded Knee. The army, on December 28, decided to disarm the Native Americans. There were 500 soldiers at Wounded Knee, but only around 350 Native Americans. The soldiers segregated the Native Americans, separating men from women. Four large Hotchkiss cannons, which could fire fifty heavy shells per minute, were trained on the groups. As the soldiers attempted to disarm the Native Americans, violence erupted. Though only about 150 of their bodies could be located for interment in a mass grave, around 300 Native Americans were murdered, and about two-thirds of that number were women and children. Only a small number of U.S. Army soldiers died, and most of them were killed by friendly fire. A fair percentage of the Native Americans who died were killed in execution-style incidents. Twenty-three of the soldiers participating in the massacre were given Medals of Honor.

The movement and the massacre have remained controversial and a source of tension. Government policy continued to focus on eliminating Native American culture and religion until the 1930s, and until recently, the foregone conclusion about the massacre was that a Native American fired first and that all were killed in the initial exchange. More recent research has put heavy doubt on the first conclusion, suggesting instead that when soldiers tried to disarm a deaf Native American, his gun discharged harmlessly. This research has also demonstrated clearly that people were killed after having fled the initial firing and were executed despite proving no danger to anyone. In the 1970s, the Wounded Knee site, where the massacre occurred, was the location of protests. Congress, eventually, in 1990 expressed regret, but paid no monies in reparation.

> ***See also*** American Indian Religious Freedom Act; Dawes Severalty Act and the banning of Native American religions; *Employment Division* v. *Smith; Lyng* v. *Northwest Indian CPA;* Native American combination of religion and law

For further reading

Kehoe, Alice Beck. 1989. *The Ghost Dance: Ethnohistory and Revitalization.* New York: Holt, Rinehart and Winston.

Ostler, Jeffrey. 2004. *The Plains Sioux and U.S. Colonialism from Lewis and Clark to Wounded Knee.* New York: Cambridge University Press.

Smith, Paul Chaat, and Robert Allen Warrior. 1996. *Like a Hurricane: The Indian Movement from Alcatraz to Wounded Knee.* New York: New Press.

Gitlow v. *New York*
268 U.S. 652 (1925)

A prosecution of a socialist for speaking against New York might seem like an odd place to increase the freedom of religion, but that was exactly what happened in the case of *Gitlow* v. *New York.* In the early twentieth century, America was quite concerned about the spread of socialism and anarchism, and many states passed laws forbidding anyone to speak against the government. A leader of the Socialist Party in New York, Benjamin Gitlow, was arrested in 1919 for criminal anarchy. His case eventually made it to the U.S. Supreme Court as *Gitlow* v. *New York.* Though his conviction was upheld, the Court's decision determined that the First Amendment did, in fact, apply to the states, because of the due process clause of the Fourteenth Amendment.

Criminal anarchy is defined as the belief that "the doctrine that organized government should be overthrown by force or violence, or by assassination of the executive head or of any of the executive officials of government, or by any unlawful means" (268 U.S. 652: 654). The main evidence against Gitlow was two pamphlets he helped write and print. Gitlow, at trial, claimed that the statute he was accused of violating itself violated the due process clause of the Fourteenth Amendment, which held "nor shall any State deprive any person of life, liberty, or property, without due process of law." He argued that the liberty referred to in the due process clause included the freedom of speech. The Court held, first, that New York's statute did "not penalize the utterance or publication of abstract 'doctrine' or academic discussion," but aimed at those things actually overthrowing the government (268 U.S. 652: 664). However, the Court did grant "for present purposes we may and do assume that freedom of speech and of the press—which are protected by the First Amendment from abridgment by Congress—are among the fundamental personal rights and 'liberties' protected by the due process clause of the Fourteenth Amendment from impairment by the States" (268 U.S. 652: 666). This was the first time that the U.S. Supreme Court had held that parts of the First Amendment applied against the states. The Court went on to say that even though those freedoms were protected, they were not absolute. Thus, the punishment of Gitlow was justified, as he, in the eyes of his convicting jury, represented a threat to overthrow the state, and in the eyes of the Court, the statute was written narrowly enough to punish only real threats and not abstract doctrine.

Justices Holmes and Brandeis dissented, arguing that Gitlow did not represent a true danger to the state. Holmes wrote, "It is said that this manifesto was more than a theory, that it was an incitement. Every idea is an incitement" (268 U.S. 652: 673). Holmes did not think that it had been demonstrated that Gitlow was enough of a danger to be suppressed.

It is important to understand what *Gitlow* held, and did not hold, as far as the First

Benjamin Gitlow in 1928. Gitlow had been convicted of violating New York's Criminal Anarchy Law, and the Supreme Court upheld the conviction in Gitlow v. New York *(1925). However, the Court also, for the first time, held that the First Amendment's freedom of speech applied to the states as well as the federal government. (UPI-Bettmann/Corbis)*

Amendment went. Gitlow's conviction was still upheld, as was New York's basic law of criminal anarchy. Indeed, even though parts of the First Amendment were applied against the states, the Court also stated that the First Amendment had its limits, as threats to the state, either written or spoken, could still be suppressed. Thus, First Amendment freedoms, now protected against interference by both the federal and state governments, were by far not without their limits. It would take several decades for the freedom of speech and of the press to be expanded to the limits we know today. It was a much narrower definition of those freedoms that was applied against the states through the *Gitlow* decision. This holding, which occurred almost in passing and without any citation by the Court, was applied in other free speech cases throughout the 1920s and 1930s.

In 1934, three justices of the Supreme Court, but not a majority, held that the freedom of religion is applied by the Fourteenth Amendment against the states. After that, in 1938, the Supreme Court stated that there was a higher level of scrutiny for those liberties protected by the Bill of Rights and the Fourteenth Amendment. The first time the freedom of religion section of the First Amendment was held against a state was in 1940, when it was used to strike down a state prosecution for "breach of the peace." In fifteen years, the protection of the freedom of religion against state intrusion moved from an abstract idea to enough of a concrete proposition to be used to overturn a conviction.

Since 1940, this idea that the freedom of religion is protected against state intrusion has not been seriously challenged. In 1943, the Supreme Court went so far as to argue that the First Amendment, including the freedom of religion, had a preferred position versus other rights, even other fundamental rights. Some concurrences and dissents by a few members of the Supreme Court have very recently suggested that the establishment clause should not be applied against the states, but as of this writing, such a view has not commanded a majority of the Court. Also, even within that argument, the idea that the First Amendment as a whole should be applied against the states is not challenged, but was instead granted, with the argument that the free exercise part of it applies but not the establishment clause. Thus, the ideas started officially in the *Gitlow* case have created a great deal more freedom in general, including religious freedom, by application of the First Amendment to the Constitution against state governments as well as the federal government.

See also Cantwell v. Connecticut; Employment Division v. Smith; Palko v. Connecticut; Pierce v. Society of Sisters; Saluting the flag

For further reading

Eastland, Terry, ed. 1995. *Benchmarks: Great Constitutional Controversies in the Supreme Court.* Washington, DC: Ethics and Public Policy Center.

Fourteenth Amendment. http://www .archives.gov/national-archives-experience/ charters/constitution_amendments_11–27 .html.

Miller, William Lee. 1986. *The First Liberty: Religion and the American Republic.* New York: Knopf.

Noonan, John Thomas. 1998. *The Lustre of Our Country: The American Experience of Religious Freedom.* Berkeley: University of California Press.

Urofsky, Melvin I. 2002. *Religious Freedom: Rights and Liberties under the Law.* Santa Barbara, CA: ABC-CLIO.

Goldman v. Weinberger
475 U.S. 503 (1986)

The question here was whether the armed forces could order a soldier to remove an item of clothing that was required by his religion. In this case, a U.S. Air Force member brought a lawsuit against the secretary of defense, as a defense regulation required that he not wear his yarmulke while in the armed forces. Goldman sued because he thought the regulation infringed on his First Amendment rights. In a 5–4 decision, the Supreme Court upheld the regulation, with the majority opinion written by Justice Rehnquist. Goldman had served in the armed forces for five years as a clinical psychologist without incident and had worn his yarmulke the whole time, wearing his service hat over the yarmulke while outside. The Supreme Court first looked at the facts and held that the military was different from civilian life, holding "the military is, by necessity, a specialized society separate from civilian society" (475 U.S. 503: 506).

The Supreme Court then noted that it gave the military more deference than other groups in the area of the First Amendment, even while not granting total deference. The justification of the air force for the regulation was that it "encourages the subordination of personal preferences and identities in favor of the overall group mission. Uniforms encourage a sense of hierarchical unity by tending to eliminate outward individual distinctions except for those of rank" (475 U.S. 503: 508). Goldman argued that an exception should be made, but the Court held that "desirability of dress regulations in the military is decided by the appropriate military officials, and they are under no constitutional mandate to abandon their considered professional judgment" (475 U.S. 503: 509–510). Thus, the regulations were upheld.

Justices Stevens, White, and Powell concurred, in an opinion by Stevens. They noted that enforcement of the regulation on Goldman may have been personally based, rather than objective, and that the exception perhaps should have been allowed. However, the concurrence concluded, "The rule that is challenged in this case is based on a neutral, completely objective standard—visibility" and that an exception for yarmulkes would favor one religion over another, and so the rule should be upheld (475 U.S. 503: 513).

Justices Brennan and Marshall dissented, in an opinion by Brennan, arguing that the Court overlooked the fact that the regulation destroys Goldman's religion and focused instead on the right of the military to make regulations. They agreed that the military has more power than most areas, but did not believe that the power is needed in this case. They sarcastically described the majority's argument as that "Jewish personnel will perceive the wearing of a yarmulke by an Orthodox Jew as an unauthorized departure from the rules and will begin to question the principle of unswerving obedience. Thus shall our fighting forces slip down the treacherous slope toward unkempt appearance, anarchy, and, ultimately, defeat at the hands of our enemies" (475 U.S. 503: 516–517). They also noted that the air force never explained why an exception for yarmulkes would destroy the desired "discipline and uniformity," citing other exceptions, such as those

Prior to becoming Ronald Reagan's secretary of defense and orchestrating an unprecedented peacetime military buildup, Caspar Weinberger, defendent in this case, had earned a reputation as a budget slasher at both the state and federal government levels. (AP/Wide World Photos)

for rings, that were allowed. They concluded that "the Court and the military services have presented patriotic Orthodox Jews with a painful dilemma—the choice between fulfilling a religious obligation and serving their country" (475 U.S. 503: 524). Justice Blackmun dissented, arguing that the costs of allowing the yarmulke should be weighed against the religious burden, but since no costs had ever been shown, the yarmulke should be allowed.

O'Connor also dissented, joined by Marshall, noting that the government should have to show that an "important" interest is at issue and that this interest would suffer harm before the First Amendment is restricted and that the government, and the majority, had failed to do so. While the armed forces are different,

O'Connor stated, that finding does not end the debate, which is what the majority believes. She also noted that the dress regulations, in their very own description, admit that they are not uniform and that Goldman served for years wearing a yarmulke without incident; therefore, the regulations in general cannot be upheld if the military has not "consistently or plausibly justified its asserted need for rigidity of enforcement" (475 U.S. 503: 532).

Thus, this regulation was narrowly upheld by the Supreme Court. The ruling, though, did not end the issue. Two years later, Congress approved a regulation allowing any armed forces member to wear clothing from his or her religion unless the clothing was found to obstruct the person's duties or if it was not "neat and conservative" (Lee, 2002: 188). Thus, even though the Supreme Court ruled that a yarmulke was not allowed to be worn, Congress acted to allow its wearing.

> **See also** *Employment Division* v. *Smith; Sherbert* v. *Verner; Trans World Airlines* v. *Hardison;* Treatment of Jews, both in colonial times and after the American Revolution

For further reading

Boyne, Walter J. 1997. *Beyond the Wild Blue: A History of the United States Air Force, 1947–1997.* New York: St. Martin's Press.

Lee, Francis Graham. 2002. *Church-State Relations.* Westport, CT: Greenport Press.

Patrick, John J., and Gerald P. Long. 1999. *Constitutional Debates on Freedom of Religion: A Documentary History.* Westport, CT: Greenwood Press.

Weinberger, Caspar W. 1990. *Fighting for Peace: Seven Critical Years in the Pentagon.* New York: Warner Books.

Gonzales v. O Centro Espirita Beneficiente Uniao Do Vegetal

126 S. Ct. 1211 (2006)

This case reexamined the issue of whether the federal government can ban the use of a controlled substance in a religious ceremony. *Employment Division* v. *Smith* (1990) dealt with a state's right to prohibit the use of a controlled

substance, holding that a state could have such a ban. The Religious Freedom Restoration Act (RFRA), passed in 1993, aimed to reverse *Employment Division* and held that the states and federal government could not ban such substances or otherwise substantially burden religion without proving a compelling interest. The RFRA was struck down as it applied to the states in *Boerne,* but not as it applied to limiting the federal government. This case directly asked the question of whether the RFRA prohibits the federal government from banning the use of a controlled substance.

The church in question here was the O Centro Espirita Beneficiente Uniao Do Vegetal (UDV Church). The religion originated in Brazil, combining elements of Catholicism and native Brazilian religions, and its members are given communion through the use of a tea brewed from hoasca, which contains a hallucinogen banned by the federal government. The UDV Church brought the lawsuit after the federal government seized a shipment of its hoasca. The federal government claimed three compelling interests: preventing health risks to the church's members, preventing the risk of the hallucinogen's distribution from the church's stock to others, and fulfilling U.S. treaty obligations under a current treaty banning the drug. The Supreme Court ruled for the church.

The government advanced a number of different arguments in favor of keeping the ban. The first argument was that all of the drugs in the same class as this hallucinogen are very dangerous and that no exceptions should be given to any group. The Court, however, ruled that the RFRA prohibits the use of wide classes and that, instead, both the church and the context of the usage needed to be considered. The government also argued that the ban of the substance did meet this criterion, but the act in question, which set up the general drug classification, itself allowed exceptions to be made by the Department of Justice, and this undercut the broad rejection of all exceptions. The Court here cited the fact that the U.S.

Congress (at the federal level) has created an exception for peyote, used by many Native Americans in religious ceremonies, as another reason to reject the government's argument.

The government's final argument lay in an international treaty. It argued that the United States needed to uphold its treaty obligations, specifically those under the 1971 United Nations Convention on Psychotropic Substances, and granting an exception for hoasca, banned by the treaty, would undermine the war on drugs. The Court granted that the government had proven the need to fight the war on drugs but also held that the government had never proven the impact of granting this exception on that war. Failure to enforce one part of a treaty, the Court held, does not demonstrate that the war on drugs will be lost or other nations will stop cooperating. The Court did not address the question of whether peyote was also covered by the 1971 treaty.

The government urged the Court to defer to Congress and let the desire of Congress to ban illegal substances overrule the religious freedom that was being balanced against it. However, the Court pointed out a difficulty here in deferring to Congress. The Court asked which of two congressional acts should have preference, noting that Congress had enacted both the Religious Freedom Restoration Act and the ban on hallucinogens. As this question did not produce an easy answer, the Court followed the desires of Congress in the RFRA and balanced the rights of the church against the government interests demonstrated, holding that the government had not yet advanced a compelling state interest to justify the restriction. It should be noted that under the RFRA, even after the government advances a compelling state interest, it must also prove—and the Court pointed out that the government had not done this—that the action being challenged (here the ban on the hallucinogen) "is the least restrictive means of furthering that compelling governmental interest" (126 S. Ct. 1211, 1217). Thus, the gov-

ernment must prove either that the universal ban is the only way to restrict recreational use of the drug or that all other ways to advance the government's compelling interests would burden the UDV's religious liberty even more.

Government restrictions on liberty are never something to be taken lightly, but many people also feel that the war on drugs is one worth fighting. In both this case and in *Employment Division* v. *Smith,* the question of a government ban on a controlled substance used in a religious ceremony was considered. Here, the government did not prove a sufficiently compelling interest, as of the time of the case, to ban the UDV from using hoasca. In *Employment Division,* the Court held that Congress could not restrain the states, and that states could, but were not required to, grant religious exceptions to their drug policy. Thus, the permissibility of a universal ban on a drug depends both on what groups are restricting its religious use and what interests are demonstrated to be at stake.

See also Boerne v. Flores; Braunfeld v. Brown; Cheema v. Thompson; Cutter v. Wilkinson; Employment Division v. Smith; Religious Freedom Restoration Act of 1993; Sherbert v. Verner

For further reading
Epps, Garrett. 2001. *To an Unknown God: Religious Freedom on Trial.* New York: St. Martin's Press.
Long, Carolyn Nestor. 2000. *Religious Freedom and Indian Rights: The Case of Oregon v. Smith.* Lawrence: University Press of Kansas.
Norgren, Jill, and Serena Nanda. 1996. *American Cultural Pluralism and Law.* 2nd ed. Westport, CT: Praeger.
Urofsky, Melvin I. 2002. *Religious Freedom: Rights and Liberties under the Law.* Santa Barbara, CA: ABC-CLIO.

Good News Club v. Milford Central School
533 U.S. 98 (2001)

This case dealt with whether a school district could ban the meetings of a private religious group if it allowed meetings of nonreligious groups. In New York, a school district allowed

Reverend Stephen Fournier sits in the Milford Community Bible Church on June 11, 2001, the same day that his Christian Good News Club was awarded the right to hold meetings in the local public school by the U.S. Supreme Court. (AP/ Wide World Photos)

district residents to use the school after hours for purposes including "instruction in any branch of education, learning or the arts, social, civic and recreational meetings and entertainment events, and other uses pertaining to the welfare of the community, provided that such uses shall be nonexclusive and shall be opened to the general public" (533 U.S. 98: 102). However, the Good News Club was not allowed to use it for "a fun time of singing songs, hearing a Bible lesson and memorizing scripture," as this purpose was the same as worship in the eyes of the school board, and the policy forbade use "by any individual or organization for religious purposes" (533 U.S. 98: 103). This policy prompted a lawsuit, resulting in the Supreme Court case.

Justice Thomas wrote the majority opinion and ruled that the Good News Club had a right to use the space. He first considered "the nature of the forum," allowing that Milford had created "a limited public forum" (as both sides had agreed to this designation) (533 U.S. 98: 106). With this type of forum, the governing body could deny use as long as "the restriction must not discriminate against speech on the basis of viewpoint, . . . and the restriction must be 'reasonable in light of the purpose served by the forum'" (533 U.S. 98: 106–107). The Court held that viewpoint discrimination occurred here as the school allowed "morals and character development" by other groups, but not by the Good News Club (533 U.S. 98: 108). Even though this club was religiously oriented, this difference did not allow the viewpoint discrimination. The Court also held that no reasonable person would see the school as endorsing religion, and so the school could not claim a desire to avoid violating the establishment clause as a reason to ban the club's meetings.

Besides Thomas's opinion there were also two concurrences and two dissents. Justice Scalia concurred, noting that there was no pressure here and so virtually no endorsement of religion and that the club should be allowed to give reasons for its good news without moving into being a religious group rather than one teaching morals. This was important, as the claim that the club was a religious group was what had touched off the action, and if the Good News Club could be viewed as a group teaching morals, then it would clearly be beyond regulation. Justice Breyer also concurred, noting that because this case overturned the motion for summary judgment for Milford (the decision at the district court level) did not mean that summary judgment was given for Good News—that is, just because Milford clearly lost does not mean that the Good News Club wholly won.

Justice Stevens dissented, categorizing the nature of the Good News Club's discussion as amounting to worship, which moved it away from just morals and character development; Stevens did not believe that allowing some discussion of morals meant that a school had to allow worship and that this regulation could be upheld in a viewpoint-neutral way. Justice Souter dissented, holding that "it is beyond question that Good News intends to use the public school premises not for the mere discussion of a subject from a particular, Christian point of view, but for an evangelical service of worship calling children to commit themselves in an act of Christian conversion" (533 U.S. 98: 138); this thus created worship, which was banned by the policy, and the reasonableness of the policy had never been in question before this case. Souter also thought that the record

was too scarce to allow the sweeping nature of the majority's conclusion.

This decision continues the trend set by other decisions of the Rehnquist Court, including *Lamb's Chapel,* and these hold, essentially, that a school board cannot discriminate on the basis of a group's views as to whether the group will be allowed to use the building. One can forbid all groups who are non-school related to use the building and could, theoretically, ban all student clubs; but if clubs are allowed, religious clubs must be allowed as well (although school personnel can restrict their involvement), and if outside groups can use the facility, then use by religious groups can be permitted if nonreligious groups who also deal with moral issues are allowed to meet in the building.

> **See also** Chapman v. *Thomas; Employment Division* v. *Smith;* Equal Access Act of 1984; *Good News/ Good Sports Club* v. *School District of the City of Ladue; Lamb's Chapel* v. *Center Moriches School District; McCollum* v. *Board of Education; Rosenberger* v. *Rector and Visitors of the University of Virginia; Tipton* v. *University of Hawaii; Widmar* v. *Vincent*

For further reading

Gerber, Scott Douglas. 1999. *First Principles: The Jurisprudence of Clarence Thomas.* New York: New York University Press.

Greenawalt, Kent. 2005. *Does God Belong in Public Schools?* Princeton, NJ: Princeton University Press.

Patrick, John J., and Gerald P. Long, eds. 1999. *Constitutional Debates on Freedom of Religion: A Documentary History.* Westport, CT: Greenwood Press.

Schwendiman, Jed, and Jennifer Fager. 1999. *After-School Programs: Good for Kids, Good for Communities.* Portland, OR: Northwest Regional Educational Laboratory.

Good News/Good Sports Club v. School District of the City of Ladue
28 F.3d 1501 (8th Cir. 1994)

Many of the most strongly fought legal battles in this country involve the use of public school facilities by religious groups after school hours. Those backing the religious groups feel they should have the same right to use the facilities as any nonreligious group. They feel that limiting the access of religious groups to these public locations inhibits their participants' free exercise of religion. However, those opposing the use feel that the school district may be giving a benefit to a specific religion by allowing it to use school buildings. They also feel such permission encourages the participation of schoolchildren, since having the activities at school might imply school approval of the religion. Several cases have examined school district bans on religious groups.

The *Good News/Good Sports* decision dealt with this issue. The school board had established a policy of allowing only certain groups to use school facilities, those being athletic and Scout groups. The Good News/Good Sports Club was a "community-based, non-affiliated group that seeks to foster the moral development of junior high school students from the perspective of Christian religious values," and it was described as "religious, but non-denominational" (28 F.3d 1501: 1502). The Eighth Circuit Court of Appeals held that the ban constituted unconstitutional viewpoint discrimination. It reiterated past decisions that "control over access to a non-public forum can be based on subject matter and speaker identity so long as the distinctions drawn are reasonable in light of the purpose served by the forum and are viewpoint neutral" (28 F.3d 1501: 1505). Scouts were allowed to discuss issues "relating to moral character and youth development," but, the court held, as the Good News/Good Sports Club was denied this opportunity, the denial constituted viewpoint discrimination. It then turned to the issue of whether a compelling government interest justified the discrimination. The school board had argued that use of the facilities would create establishment of religion. Part of its argument was that the club met immediately after school. However, the court disagreed, holding that since students were not compelled to at-

tend and because the club did not constitute a large percentage of the overall meetings held in the school after hours, no establishment issue existed.

One judge strongly dissented. He held "no court to date has determined that a parent-sponsored religious club has a constitutional right to meet on school property before school children have had the opportunity to depart school premises following mandatory instruction, merely because Scout and community athletic groups are permitted to do so" (28 F.3d 1501: 1515). The dissent argued that the school board had legitimate reasons to try to prevent the club from meeting and that Scouting was quite different from the club. "Scouting is a secular, skills-oriented activity analogous to and supplementary to learning which takes place in the public school classroom. The Club is a sectarian, worship-oriented activity which seems more analogous to a church-operated Sunday school for junior high youngsters" (28 F.3d 1501: 1518). The dissent also pointed out that the Scouts and athletic groups were the likely ones to suffer, as the easiest way for the school board to change their policy was simply to ban all non-school groups until after 6 P.M., which was the original starting point for religious groups.

Other school districts have used a standard of the best interests of the school district. In Colorado, one school district banned a meeting of the Million Man March, which wanted to hold an "Attitude and Consciousness Youth Forum." The meeting was banned in part because a large number of students had walked out the day before to protest, and the school board did not want a repeat of this action. However, the district court, in *Local Organizing Committee, Million Man March v. Cook,* held that the people who were going to speak at the forum were not connected closely enough to the walkout to justify the ban.

A final issue to consider is what makes a public school after hours a public forum. This was the issue before the Third Circuit in *Gre-*

goire v. *Centennial School District.* The school district wished to ban a group from worshiping and presenting a religious program even though the district had previously allowed a wide range of groups. The court held that when the school district "permits potentially divisive or conversion-oriented speech by outsiders to a student audience in school facilities in the afternoon and determines that this speech is consistent with the function and mission of the school system, it cannot, on maturity or 'mission' grounds, exclude the same type of speech directed to the same audience from its facilities in the evening. Where it identifies student-directed conversion speech as its criterion for exclusion, it cannot reasonably allow some members of some groups to meet with each other and deny access to others whose speech does not implicate this conversion element" (907 F.2d 1366: 1379). Thus, the regulations needed to be consistent, and denial of only a few groups did not create a nonpublic forum.

Several different questions need to be asked by school boards before deciding policy and by courts before deciding whether an exclusion is acceptable. Those include the nature of the forum created for discussion, the rules on that forum, the consistency in following the rules, and whether exclusions are based on viewpoints. Once a forum is opened for one type of discussion, such as that of morals, most courts have held that all people discussing morals, including religious groups, must be allowed. Viewpoint discrimination, including that based on religion, thus has been generally banned.

See also *Airport Commissioners* v. *Jews for Jesus; Bronx Household of Faith* v. *Community School District No. 10; Good News Club* v. *Milford Central School; International Society for Krishna Consciousness* v. *Lee; Widmar* v. *Vincent*

For further reading

Greenawalt, Kent. 2005. *Does God Belong in Public Schools?* Princeton, NJ: Princeton University Press.

Haynes, Charles C., et al. 2003. *The First Amendment in Schools: A Guide from the First Amendment Center.* Alexandria, VA: Association for Supervision and Curriculum Development.

Patrick, John J., and Gerald P. Long, eds. 1999. *Constitutional Debates on Freedom of Religion: A Documentary History.* Westport, CT: Greenwood Press.

BIBLIOGRAPHY

ABC News Productions. 2003. *Why the Hate? America, from a Muslim Point of View.* Princeton, NJ: Films for the Humanities & Sciences.

Adams, Arlin M., and Charles J. Emmerich. 1990. *A Nation Dedicated to Religious Liberty: The Constitutional Heritage of the Religion Clauses.* Philadelphia: University of Pennsylvania Press.

Ahdar, Rex J., ed. 2000. *Law and Religion.* Burlington, VT: Ashgate/Dartmouth.

Alexander, Kern, and M. David Alexander. 2001. *American Public School Law.* Belmont, CA: West/Thomson Learning.

Allen, Paula Gunn. 1991. *Grandmothers of the Light.* Boston: Beacon Press.

Alley, Robert S., ed. 1999. *The Constitution and Religion: Leading Supreme Court Cases on Church and State.* Amherst, NY: Prometheus Books.

Alley, Robert S., ed. 1985. *James Madison on Religious Liberty.* Buffalo, NY: Prometheus Books.

Alley, Robert S., ed. 1988. *The Supreme Court on Church and State.* New York: Oxford University Press.

Arden, Harvey, Steve Wall, and White Deer of Autumn. 1990. *Wisdomkeepers.* Hillsboro, OR: Beyond Words.

Atkinson, Clarissa W., Constance H. Buchanan, and Margaret R. Miles, eds. 1987. *Shaping New Vision: Gender and Values in American Culture.* Ann Arbor, MI: UMI Research Press.

Atwell, Mary Welek. 2002. *Equal Protection of the Law? Gender and Justice in the United States.* New York: P. Lang.

Aveni, Anthony F. 2003. *The Book of the Year: A Brief History of Our Seasonal Holidays.* New York: Oxford University Press.

Ayorinde, Christine. 2004. *Afro-Cuban Religiosity, Revolution, and National Identity.* Gainesville: University Press of Florida.

Baer, John W. 1992. *"Under God" and Other Pledge of Allegiance Questions and Answers (Q&A).* http://pledgeqanda.com/ (accessed June 25, 2006).

Baker, Leonard. 1984. *Brandeis and Frankfurter: A Dual Biography.* New York: Harper & Row.

Ball, Howard. 1996. *Hugo L. Black: Cold Steel Warrior.* New York: Oxford University Press.

Ball, Howard. 2002. *The Supreme Court in the Intimate Lives of Americans: Birth, Sex, Marriage, Childbearing, and Death.* New York: New York University Press.

Ball, Howard, and Phillip J. Cooper. 1992. *Of Power and Right: Hugo Black, William O. Douglas, and America's Constitutional Revolution.* New York: Oxford University Press.

Banner, Stuart. 2002. *The Death Penalty: An American History.* Cambridge, MA: Harvard University Press.

Barlow, Connie, ed. 1994. *Evolution Extended: Biological Debates on the Meaning of Life.* Cambridge, MA: MIT Press.

Barr, Margaret J., and Associates. 1988. *Student Services and the Law: A Handbook for Practitioners.* San Francisco: Jossey-Bass.

Bauman, Kurt. 2001. *Home Schooling in the United States: Trends and Characteristics.* Washington, DC: U.S. Census Bureau.

Bayer, Linda N. 2000. *Ruth Bader Ginsburg.* Philadelphia: Chelsea House.

Benedict, Michael Les. 1987. *Civil Rights and Civil Liberties.* Washington, DC: American Historical Association.

Berger, Raoul. 1989. *The Fourteenth Amendment and the Bill of Rights.* Norman: University of Oklahoma Press.

Bisson, Julie. 1997. *Celebrate! An Anti-Bias Guide to Enjoying Holidays in Early Childhood Programs.* St. Paul, MN: Redleaf Press.

Black, Edwin. 2001. *IBM and the Holocaust: The Strategic Alliance between Nazi Germany and America's Most Powerful Corporation.* New York: Crown.

Blakely, William A. 1970. *American State Papers Bearing on Sunday Legislation: Legislative, Executive, Judicial.* Compiled and annotated by William Addison Blakely. Rev. ed. Edited by Willard Allen Colcord. Foreword by Thomas M. Cooley. New York: Da Capo Press.

Blasi, Vincent, ed. 1983. *The Burger Court: The Counter-Revolution That Wasn't.* New Haven: Yale University Press.

Bolt, Christine, and Seymour Drescher, eds. 1980. *Anti-Slavery, Religion, and Reform: Essays in Memory of Roger Anstey.* Folkestone, UK: W. Dawson.

Bosmajian, Haig A. 1999. *The Freedom Not to Speak.* New York: New York University Press.

Bosmajian, Haig A. 1987. *Freedom of Religion*. New York: Neal-Schuman.

Boston, Rob. 1997. "Watchdog on the Wall: The Americans United Story." *Church and State* 50 (November): 7–12.

Bourassa, Kevin, and Joe Varnell. 2002. *Just Married: Gay Marriage and the Expansion of Human Rights*. Madison: University of Wisconsin Press.

Bower, Tom. 1997. *Nazi Gold: The Full Story of the Fifty-Year Swiss-Nazi Conspiracy to Steal Billions from Europe's Jews and Holocaust Survivors*. New York: HarperCollins.

Bradley, Gerard V. 1987. *Church-State Relationships in America*. New York: Greenwood Press.

Breneman, David W. 1994. *Liberal Arts Colleges: Thriving, Surviving, or Endangered?* Washington, DC: Brookings Institution Press.

Breneman, David W., and and Susan C. Nelson. 1981. *Financing Community Colleges: An Economic Perspective*. Washington, DC: Brookings Institution Press.

Bridenbaugh, Carl. 1974. *Fat Mutton and Liberty of Conscience: Society in Rhode Island, 1636–1690*. Providence: Brown University Press.

Brisbin, Richard A. 1997. *Justice Antonin Scalia and the Conservative Revival*. Baltimore: Johns Hopkins University Press.

Brownlee, W. Elliot. 2004. *Federal Taxation in America: A Short History*. New York: Cambridge University Press.

Brugger, E. Christian. 2003. *Capital Punishment and Roman Catholic Moral Tradition*. Notre Dame, IN: University of Notre Dame Press.

Brumberg, Stephen F. 1986. *Going to America, Going to School: The Jewish Immigrant Public School Encounter in Turn-of-the-Century New York City*. New York: Praeger.

Bryant, Edwin F., and Maria L. Ekstrand. 2004. *The Hare Krishna Movement: The Postcharismatic Fate of a Religious Transplant*. New York: Columbia University Press.

Bryson, Joseph E. 1990. *The Supreme Court and Public Funds for Religious Schools: The Burger Years, 1969–1986*. Jefferson, NC: McFarland.

Buchanan, Robert. 1999. *Illusions of Equality: Deaf Americans in School and Factory, 1850–1950*. Washington, DC: Gallaudet University Press.

Buckley, Thomas E. 1977. *Church and State in Revolutionary Virginia, 1776–1787*. Charlottesville: University Press of Virginia.

Bukhari Zahid H., et al. 2004. *Muslims' Place in the American Public Square: Hope, Fears, and Aspirations*. Walnut Creek, CA: AltaMira Press.

Burkett, Elinor. 1998. *The Right Women: A Journey through the Heart of Conservative America*. New York: Scribner's.

Burns, Eric. 2004. *The Spirits of America: A Social History of Alcohol*. Philadelphia: Temple University Press.

Burstein, Abraham. 1980. *Religion, Cults, and the Law*. Dobbs Ferry, NY: Oceana.

Burstein, Paul. 1985. *Discrimination, Jobs, and Politics: The Struggle for Equal Employment Opportunity in the United States since the New Deal*. Chicago: University of Chicago Press.

Burt, Robert. 1988. *Two Jewish Justices: Outcasts in the Promised Land*. Berkeley: University of California Press.

Burton, David Henry. 1998. *Taft, Holmes, and the 1920s Court: An Appraisal*. Madison, NJ: Fairleigh Dickinson University Press.

Burton, John. 1993. *Whither Sunday Trading? The Case for Deregulation*. London: Institute of Economic Affairs.

Button, James W., Barbara A. Rienzo, and Kenneth D. Wald. 1997. *Private Lives, Public Conflicts: Battles over Gay Rights in American Communities*. Washington, DC: CQ Press.

Buzzard, Lynn Robert, and Susan Edwards. 1995. *Risky Business: Church Hiring and Volunteer Selection: A Legal and Policy Guide*. Buies Creek, NC: Church-State Resource Center.

Campbell, John Angus, and Stephen C. Meyer, eds. 2003. *Darwinism, Design, and Public Education*. East Lansing: Michigan State University Press.

Canipe, Lee. 2003. "Under God and Anti-Communist: How the Pledge of Allegiance Got Religion in Cold War America." *A Journal of Church and State* 45 (No. 2): 305+.

Carleton, David. 2002. *Landmark Congressional Laws on Education*. Westport, CT: Greenwood Press.

Carty, Thomas. 2004. *A Catholic in the White House: Religion, Politics, and John F. Kennedy's Presidential Campaign*. New York: Palgrave Macmillan.

Casebeer, Kenneth M. 2005. *Work Law in American Society*. Durham, NC: Carolina Academic Press.

Chambers, John Whiteclay. 1987. *To Raise an Army: The Draft Comes to Modern America*. New York: Free Press.

Chesebrough, David B. 1996. *Clergy Dissent in the Old South, 1830–1865*. Carbondale: Southern Illinois University Press.

Chesnoff, Richard Z. 1999. *Pack of Thieves: How Hitler and Europe Plundered the Jews and Committed the Greatest Theft in History*. New York: Doubleday.

Chidester, David. 1998. *Patterns of Power: Religion and Politics in American Culture.* Englewood Cliffs, NJ: Prentice-Hall.

Clifford, J. Garry, and Samuel R. Spencer, Jr. 1986. *The First Peacetime Draft.* Lawrence: University Press of Kansas.

Connelly, Mark. 1999. *Christmas: A Social History.* New York: I. B. Tauris.

Coontz, Stephanie. 2005. *Marriage, a History: From Obedience to Intimacy, or How Love Conquered Marriage.* New York: Viking.

Cottrell, Robert C. 2000. *Roger Nash Baldwin and the American Civil Liberties Union.* New York: Columbia University Press.

Coughtry, Jay. 1981. *The Notorious Triangle: Rhode Island and the African Slave Trade, 1700–1807.* Philadelphia: Temple University Press.

Cousineau, Phil, ed. 2006. *A Seat at the Table: Huston Smith in Conversation with Native Americans on Religious Freedom.* Berkeley: University of California Press.

Covey, Denise Troll. 2002. *Usage and Usability Assessment: Library Practices and Concerns.* Washington, DC: Digital Library Federation.

Cowan, Horace G. 1948. *The Sabbath in Scripture and History.* Kansas City, MO: Beacon Hill Press.

Cretser, Gary A., and Joseph J. Leon, eds. 1982. *Intermarriage in the United States.* New York: Haworth Press.

Cromartie, Michael. 2005. *Religion and Politics in America: A Conversation.* Lanham, MD: Rowman & Littlefield.

Cross, Christopher T. 2004. *Political Education: National Policy Comes of Age.* New York: Teachers College Press.

Curry, Thomas J. 1986. *The First Freedoms: Church and State in America to the Passage of the First Amendment.* New York: Oxford University Press.

Curtis, Michael Kent, ed. 1993. *The Constitution and the Flag.* New York: Garland.

Daniels, Bruce Colin. 1983. *Dissent and Conformity on Narragansett Bay: The Colonial Rhode Island Town.* Middletown, CT: Wesleyan University Press.

Davis, Derek. 1991. *Original Intent: Chief Justice Rehnquist and the Course of American Church-State Relations.* Buffalo, NY: Prometheus Books.

Davis, P. William, and Dean H. Kenyon. 1989. *Of Pandas and People: The Central Questions of Biological Origins.* Dallas, TX: Haughton.

Davis, Sue. 1989. *Justice Rehnquist and the Constitution.* Princeton, NJ: Princeton University Press.

Dawidowicz, Lucy S. 1986. *The War against the Jews, 1933–1945.* New York: Bantam Books.

Dawson, Nelson L., ed. 1989. *Brandeis and America.* Lexington: University Press of Kentucky.

De La Torre, Miguel A. 2004. *Santería: The Beliefs and Rituals of a Growing Religion in America.* Grand Rapids, MI: William B. Eerdmans.

DelFattore, Joan. 2004. *The Fourth R: Conflicts over Religion in America's Public Schools.* New Haven: Yale University Press.

Deloria, Vine, and David E. Wilkins. 1999. *Tribes, Treaties, and Constitutional Tribulations.* Austin: University of Texas Press.

Dembski, William A., and Michael Ruse, eds. 2004. *Debating Design: From Darwin to DNA.* New York: Cambridge University Press.

Dennis, Everette E., and Donald M. Gillmor. 1978. *Justice Hugo Black and the First Amendment: "'No Law' Means No Law."* Ames: Iowa State University Press.

Dennis, Matthew. 2002. *Red, White, and Blue Letter Days: An American Calendar.* Ithaca, NY: Cornell University Press.

Detwiler, Fritz. 1999. *Standing on the Premises of God: The Christian Right's Fight to Redefine America's Public Schools.* New York: New York University Press.

Devins, Neal E., ed. 1989. *Public Values, Private Schools.* London: Falmer Press.

Doerr, Ed, and Albert J. Menendez. 1993. *Religious Liberty and State Constitutions.* Buffalo, NY: Prometheus Books.

Douglas, Gillian. 2001. *An Introduction to Family Law.* New York: Oxford University Press.

Dreisbach, Daniel L. 2002. *Thomas Jefferson and the Wall of Separation between Church and State.* New York: New York University Press.

Dwyer, James G. 1998. *Religious Schools v. Children's Rights.* Ithaca, NY: Cornell University Press.

Eastland, Terry. 1993. *Religious Liberty in the Supreme Court: The Cases That Define the Debate over Church and State.* Washington, DC: Ethics and Public Policy Center.

Eastland, Terry, ed. 1995. *Benchmarks: Great Constitutional Controversies in the Supreme Court.* Washington, DC: Ethics and Public Policy Center.

Eastland, Terry, ed. 2000. *Freedom of Expression in the Supreme Court: The Defining Cases.* Lanham, MD: Rowman & Littlefield.

Ellis, Richard. 2005. *To the Flag: The Unlikely History of the Pledge of Allegiance.* Lawrence: University Press of Kansas.

Epstein, Noel, ed. 2004. *Who's in Charge Here? The Tangled Web of School Governance and Policy.* Denver, CO: Education Commission of the States.

Epstein, Richard Allen. 1992. *Forbidden Grounds: The Case against Employment Discrimination Laws.* Cambridge, MA: Harvard University Press.

Ericson, David F. 2000. *Debate over Slavery: Antislavery and Proslavery Liberalism in Antebellum America.* New York: New York University Press.

Eskridge, William N. 2002. *Equality Practice: Civil Unions and the Future of Gay Rights.* New York: Routledge.

Evans, Dennis L., ed. 2005. *Taking Sides: Clashing Views on Controversial Issues in Teaching and Educational Practice.* Dubuque, IA: McGraw-Hill/Dushkin.

Farish, Leah. 2000. *Lemon v. Kurtzman: The Religion and Public Funds Case.* Berkeley Heights, NJ: Enslow.

Fassett, John D. 1994. *New Deal Justice: The Life of Stanley Reed of Kentucky.* New York: Vantage Press.

Feldberg, Michael. 1980. *The Turbulent Era: Riot and Disorder in Jacksonian America.* New York: Oxford University Press.

Feldman, Stephen M., ed. 2000. *Law and Religion: A Critical Anthology.* New York: New York University Press.

Finkelman, Paul ed. 1989. *Religion and Slavery.* New York: Garland.

Fisher, Leonard Everett. 1993. *Stars and Stripes: Our National Flag.* New York: Holiday House.

Fisher, Louis. 2002. *Religious Liberty in America.* Lawrence: University Press of Kansas.

Fiss, Owen M. 1978. *The Civil Rights Injunction.* Bloomington: Indiana University Press.

Flinchbaugh, Robert W. 1993. *The 21st Century Board of Education: Planning, Leading, Transforming.* Lancaster, PA: Technomic.

Flynn, George Q. 1993. *The Draft, 1940–1973.* Lawrence: University Press of Kansas.

Formicola, Jo Renée, and Hubert Morken, eds. 1997. *Everson Revisited: Religion, Education, and Law at the Crossroads.* Lanham, MD: Rowman & Littlefield.

Foster, Lawrence. 1984. *Religion and Sexuality: The Shakers, the Mormons, and the Oneida Community.* Urbana: University of Illinois Press.

Franciosi, Robert J. 2004. *The Rise and Fall of American Public Schools: The Political Economy of Public Education in the Twentieth Century.* Westport, CT: Praeger.

Frankfurter, Felix. 1960. *Felix Frankfurter Reminisces.* New York: Reynal.

Fraser, James W. 1999. *Between Church and State: Religion and Public Education in a Multicultural America.* New York: St. Martin's Press.

Friedman, Ian C. 2004. *Education Reform.* New York: Facts on File.

Friedman, Leon, and Fred L. Israel, eds. 1997. *The Justices of the United States Supreme Court: Their Lives and Major Opinions.* New York: Chelsea House.

Fuller, Wayne E. 2003. *Morality and the Mail in Nineteenth-Century America.* Urbana: University of Illinois Press.

Garcia, Alfredo. 2002. *The Fifth Amendment: A Comprehensive Approach.* Westport, CT: Greenwood Press.

Garrow, David J. 1994. *Liberty and Sexuality: The Right to Privacy and the Making of Roe v. Wade.* New York: Macmillan.

Gaustad, Edwin S. 2003. *Proclaim Liberty throughout All the Land: A History of Church and State in America.* New York: Oxford University Press.

Gaylin, Willard. 1970. *In the Service of Their Country: War Resisters in Prison.* New York: Viking Press.

Gerber, Scott Douglas. 1999. *First Principles: The Jurisprudence of Clarence Thomas.* New York: New York University Press.

Gibbs, Annette. 1992. *Reconciling Rights and Responsibilities of Colleges and Students: Offensive Speech, Assembly, Drug Testing, and Safety.* Washington, DC: School of Education and Human Development, George Washington University.

Gibson, James L., and Richard D. Bingham. 1985. *Civil Liberties and Nazis: The Skokie Free-Speech Controversy.* Urbana, IL: Praeger.

Gilbert, James Burkhart. 1997. *Redeeming Culture: American Religion in an Age of Science.* Chicago: University of Chicago Press.

Gilbert, Janice Dee. 1982. *United States Selective Service: The Aftermath of Vietnam.* Monticello, IL: Vance Bibliographies.

Goggin, Malcolm L., ed. 1993. *Understanding the New Politics of Abortion.* Newbury Park, CA: Sage.

Goldberg-Hiller, Jonathan. 2002. *The Limits to Union: Same-Sex Marriage and the Politics of Civil Rights.* Ann Arbor: University of Michigan Press.

Goonen, Norma M., and Rachel S. Blechman. 1999. *Higher Education Administration: A Guide to Legal, Ethical, and Practical Issues.* Westport, CT: Greenwood Press.

Gordon, Sarah Barringer. 2002. *The Mormon Question: Polygamy and Constitutional Conflict in Nineteenth-Century America.* Chapel Hill: University of North Carolina Press.

Gordon-Reed, Annette, ed. 2002. *Race on Trial: Law and Justice in American History.* New York: Oxford University Press.

Gould, Stephen Jay. 1995. *Dinosaur in a Haystack: Reflections in Natural History.* New York: Harmony Books.

Gray, Tony. 1972. *Psalms and Slaughter: A Study in Bigotry.* London: Heinemann.

Greenawalt, Kent. 2005. *Does God Belong in Public Schools?* Princeton, NJ: Princeton University Press.

Gregory, John DeWitt, Peter N. Swisher, and Sheryl L. Wolf. 2001. *Understanding Family Law.* Newark, NJ: LexisNexis.

Guterson, David. 1992. *Family Matters: Why Home-Schooling Makes Sense.* New York: Harcourt Brace Jovanovich.

Haas, Carol. 1994. *Engel v. Vitale: Separation of Church and State.* Hillside, NJ: Enslow.

Haddad, Yvonne Yazbeck. 2004. *Not Quite American?: The Shaping of Arab and Muslim Identity in the United States.* Waco, TX: Baylor University Press.

Haddad, Yvonne Yazbeck, and Ellison Banks Findly, eds. 1985. *Women, Religion, and Social Change.* Albany: State University of New York Press.

Haiman, Franklyn Saul. 2003. *Religious Expression and the American Constitution.* East Lansing: Michigan State University Press.

Hamilton, Marci. 2005. *God vs. the Gavel: Religion and the Rule of Law.* New York: Cambridge University Press.

Hamm, Richard F. 1995. *Shaping the Eighteenth Amendment: Temperance Reform, Legal Culture, and the Polity, 1880–1920.* Chapel Hill: University of North Carolina Press.

Hansen, W. Lee, and James F. Byers, with the assistance of Jan Levine Thal. 1990. *Unemployment Insurance: The Second Half-Century.* Madison: University of Wisconsin Press.

Harris, George E. 1980. *A Treatise on Sunday Laws: The Sabbath—The Lord's Day, Its History and Observance, Civil and Criminal.* Littleton, CO: Fred B. Rothman.

Hauck, Vern E. 1997. *Arbitrating Race, Religion, and National Origin Discrimination Grievances.* Westport, CT: Quorum Books.

Hayes, William. 2001. *So You Want to Be a School Board Member?* Lanham, MD: Scarecrow Education.

Haynes, Charles C., et al. 2003. *The First Amendment in Schools: A Guide from the First Amendment Center.* Alexandria, VA: Association for Supervision and Curriculum Development.

Heylyn, Peter. 1969. *The History of the Sabbath.* Amsterdam: Theatrum Orbis Terrarum.

Higgens-Evenson, R. Rudy. 2003. *The Price of Progress: Public Services, Taxation, and the American Corporate State, 1877 to 1929.* Baltimore: Johns Hopkins University Press.

Hockett, Jeffrey D. 1996. *New Deal Justice: The Constitutional Jurisprudence of Hugo L. Black, Felix Frankfurter, and Robert H. Jackson.* Lanham, MD: Rowman & Littlefield.

Holder, Angela Roddey. 1985. *Legal Issues in Pediatrics and Adolescent Medicine.* New Haven: Yale University Press.

Hopkins, Bruce R. 2003. *The Law of Tax-Exempt Organizations.* Hoboken, NJ: John Wiley.

Hostetler, John Andrew. 1993. *Amish Society.* Baltimore: Johns Hopkins University Press.

Hoxby, Caroline M, ed. 2003. *The Economics of School Choice.* Chicago: University of Chicago Press.

Hull, N. E. H., and Peter Charles Hoffer. 2001. *Roe v. Wade: The Abortion Rights Controversy in American History.* Lawrence: University Press of Kansas.

Hunt, Thomas C., and James C. Carper. 1997. *Religion and Schooling in Contemporary America: Confronting Our Cultural Pluralism.* New York: Garland.

Hunter, Nan D., Courtney G. Joslin, and Sharon M. McGowan. 2004. *The Rights of Lesbians, Gay Men, Bisexuals, and Transgender People: The Authoritative ACLU Guide to a Lesbian, Gay, Bisexual, or Transgender Person's Rights.* Carbondale: Southern Illinois University Press.

Hutchinson, Earl Ofari. 1996. *Beyond O.J.: Race, Sex, and Class Lessons for America.* Los Angeles: Middle Passage Press.

Irons, Peter, ed. 2000. *May It Please the Court: Courts, Kids, and the Constitution.* New York: New Press.

Irons, Peter, ed. 1997. *May It Please the Court: The First Amendment: Transcripts of the Oral Arguments Made before the Supreme Court in Sixteen Key First Amendment Cases.* New York: New Press.

Irons, Peter H. 1988. *The Courage of Their Convictions.* New York: Free Press.

Isaacs, Stephen D. 1974. *Jews and American Politics.* Garden City, NY: Doubleday.

Israel, Charles A. 2004. *Before Scopes: Evangelicalism, Education, and Evolution in Tennessee, 1870–1925.* Athens: University of Georgia Press.

Ivers, Gregg. 1991. *Lowering the Wall: Religion and the Supreme Court in the 1980s.* New York: Anti-Defamation League.

Jakobsen, Janet R., and Ann Pellegrini. 2003. *Love the Sin: Sexual Regulation and the Limits of Religious Tolerance.* New York: New York University Press.

James, Sydney V. 1975. *Colonial Rhode Island: A History.* New York: Scribner's.

James, Thomas, and Henry M. Levin, eds. 1983. *Public Dollars for Private Schools: The Case of Tuition Tax Credits.* Philadelphia: Temple University Press.

Johansen, Bruce E., ed. 2004. *Enduring Legacies: Native American Treaties and Contemporary Controversies.* Westport, CT: Praeger.

Johns, Warren L. 1967. *Dateline Sunday, U.S.A.: The Story of Three and a Half Centuries of Sunday-Law Battles in America.* Mountain View, CA: Pacific Press Publishing Association.

Johnson, Donald Oscar. 1963. *The Challenge to American Freedoms: World War I and the Rise of the American Civil Liberties Union.* Lexington: University of Kentucky Press.

Johnson, Phillip E. 1991. *Darwin on Trial.* Lanham, MD: National Book Network.

Johnston, Aaron Montgomery. 1979. *School Celebrations: Teaching Practices Related to Celebration of Special Events, Grades K–6, in the United States.* Knoxville: Bureau of Educational Research and Service, College of Education, University of Tennessee.

Jordan, David William. 1987. *Foundations of Representative Government in Maryland, 1632–1715.* New York: Cambridge University Press.

Jurinski, James. 1998. *Religion in the Schools: A Reference Handbook.* Santa Barbara, CA: ABC-CLIO.

Kaplan, William. 1989. *State and Salvation: The Jehovah's Witnesses and Their Fight for Civil Rights.* Toronto: University of Toronto Press.

Karfunkel, Thomas, and Thomas W. Ryley. 1978. *The Jewish Seat: Anti-Semitism and the Appointment of Jews to the Supreme Court.* Hicksville, NY: Exposition Press.

Kehoe, Alice Beck. 1989. *The Ghost Dance: Ethnohistory and Revitalization.* New York: Holt, Rinehart, and Winston.

Kersch, Kenneth Ira. 2004. *Constructing Civil Liberties: Discontinuities in the Development of American Constitutional Law.* New York: Cambridge University Press.

Keynes, Edward, with Randall K. Miller. 1989. *The Court vs. Congress: Prayer, Busing, and Abortion.* Durham, NC: Duke University Press.

Kirkpatrick, David W. 1990. *Choice in Schooling: A Case for Tuition Vouchers.* Chicago: Loyola University Press.

Klaits, Joseph. 1985. *Servants of Satan: The Age of the Witch Hunts.* Bloomington: Indiana University Press.

Klicka, Christopher J. 2002. *The Right to Home School: A Guide to the Law on Parents' Rights in Education.* Durham, NC: Carolina Academic Press.

Kohn, Stephen M. 1994. *American Political Prisoners: Prosecutions under the Espionage and Sedition Acts.* Westport, CT: Praeger.

Kohn, Stephen M. 1986. *Jailed for Peace: The History of American Draft Law Violators, 1658–1985.* Westport, CT: Greenwood Press.

Kohut, Andrew, et al. 2000. *The Diminishing Divide: Religion's Changing Role in American Politics.* Washington DC: Brookings Institution Press.

Kosters, Marvin H., ed. 1999. *Financing College Tuition: Government Policies and Educational Priorities.* Washington, DC: AEI Press.

Kraushaar, Otto F. 1972. *American Nonpublic Schools: Patterns of Diversity.* Baltimore: Johns Hopkins University Press.

Kraybill, Donald B. 2001. *The Riddle of Amish Culture.* Baltimore: Johns Hopkins University Press.

Krugler, John D. 2004. *English and Catholic: The Lords Baltimore in the Seventeenth Century.* Baltimore: Johns Hopkins University Press.

Kusch, Frank. 2001. *All American Boys: Draft Dodgers in Canada from the Vietnam War.* Westport, CT: Praeger.

La Morte, Michael W. 2001. *School Law: Cases and Concepts.* Boston: Allyn and Bacon.

Laband, David N., and Deborah Hendry Heinbuch. 1987. *Blue Laws: The History, Economics, and Politics of Sunday-Closing Laws.* Lexington, MA: Lexington Books.

LaPlante, Eve. 2004. *American Jezebel: The Uncommon Life of Anne Hutchinson, the Woman Who Defied the Puritans.* San Francisco: HarperSanFrancisco.

Larson, Edward J. 1997. *Summer for the Gods: The Scopes Trial and America's Continuing Debate over Science and Religion.* New York: Basic Books.

Larson, Edward J. 2003. *Trial and Error: The American Controversy over Creation and Evolution.* New York: Oxford University Press.

Laurie, Bruce. 1980. *Working People of Philadelphia, 1800–1850.* Philadelphia: Temple University Press.

Lee, Francis Graham. 2002. *Church-State Relations.* Major Issues in American History series. Westport, CT: Greenwood Press.

Levinson, Nan. 2003. *Outspoken: Free Speech Stories.* Berkeley: University of California Press.

Levy, Leonard Williams. 1999. *Origins of the Bill of Rights.* New Haven: Yale University Press.

Lewis, James R. 1998. *Cults in America: A Reference Handbook.* Santa Barbara, CA: ABC-CLIO.

Livingstone, David N. 1987. *Darwin's Forgotten Defenders: The Encounter between Evangelical Theology and Evolutionary Thought.* Grand Rapids, MI: William B. Eerdmans.

Long, Carolyn Nestor. 2000. *Religious Freedom and Indian Rights: The Case of Oregon v. Smith.* Lawrence: University Press of Kansas.

MacLean, Nancy. 2006. *Freedom Is Not Enough: The Opening of the American Workplace.* Cambridge, MA: Harvard University Press.

Maddex, Robert L. 1998. *State Constitutions of the United States.* Washington, DC: Congressional Quarterly.

Mallak, D. Neven, and Joel D. Joseph. 1989. *The Pledge: The Pledge of Allegiance, Schools, and the Supreme Court.* Bethesda, MD: National Press.

Maltz. Earl M., ed. 2003. *Rehnquist Justice: Understanding the Court Dynamic.* Lawrence: University Press of Kansas.

Marion, David E. 1997. *The Jurisprudence of Justice William J. Brennan, Jr.: The Law and Politics of "Libertarian Dignity."* Lanham, MD: Rowman & Littlefield.

Marsden, George M. 1994. *The Soul of the American University: From Protestant Establishment to Established Nonbelief.* New York: Oxford University Press.

Marsel, Robert S. Fall. 1987. "Mr. Justice Potter Stewart: The Constitutional Jurisprudence of Justice Potter Stewart: Reflections on a Life of Public Service." *Tennessee Law Review* 55 (No. 1): 1–39.

Martin, William C. 1991. *A Prophet with Honor: The Billy Graham Story.* New York: Morrow.

Marty, Martin E. 2000. *Education, Religion, and the Common Good: Advancing a Distinctly American Conversation about Religion's Role in our Shared Life.* San Francisco: Jossey-Bass.

McCarthy, Martha M. 1983. *A Delicate Balance: Church, State, and the Schools.* Bloomington, IN: Phi Delta Kappan Educational Foundation.

McConnell, Terrance C. 2000. *Inalienable Rights: The Limits of Consent in Medicine and the Law.* New York: Oxford University Press.

McCormick, Richard L. 1986. *The Party Period and Public Policy: American Politics from the Age of Jackson to the Progressive Era.* New York: Oxford University Press.

McCoy, Alfred W. 2006. *A Question of Torture: CIA Interrogation, from the Cold War to the War on Terror.* New York: Metropolitan Books/Henry Holt.

McGarvie, Mark D. 2004. *One Nation under Law: America's Early National Struggles to Separate Church and State.* DeKalb: Northern Illinois University Press.

McKenna, George, and Stanley Feingold, eds. 1997. *Taking Sides: Clashing Views on Controversial Political Issues.* Guilford, CT: Dushkin.

McKivigan, John R. 1999. *Abolitionism and American Religion.* New York: Garland.

McKivigan, John R., and Mitchell Snay, eds. 1998. *Religion and the Antebellum Debate over Slavery.* Athens: University of Georgia Press.

McMillan, Richard C. 1984. *Religion in the Public Schools: An Introduction.* Macon, GA: Mercer University Press.

Mello, Michael. 2004. *Legalizing Gay Marriage.* Philadelphia: Temple University Press.

Melton, J. Gordon. 1992. *Encyclopedic Handbook of Cults in America.* New York: Garland.

Meltzer, Milton. 1985. *Ain't Gonna Study War No More: The Story of America's Peace Seekers.* New York: Harper & Row.

Mendus, Susan, ed. 1988. *Justifying Toleration: Conceptual and Historical Perspectives.* Cambridge: Cambridge University Press.

Miller, Robert Thomas, and Ronald B. Flowers. 1996. *Toward Benevolent Neutrality: Church, State, and the Supreme Court.* Waco, TX: Markham Press Fund of Baylor University Press.

Miller, William Lee. 1996. *Arguing about Slavery: The Great Battle in the United States Congress.* New York: Knopf.

Miller, William Lee. 1986. *The First Liberty: Religion and the American Republic.* New York: Knopf.

Minneman, Charles E., ed. 1970. *Students, Religion, and the Contemporary University.* Ypsilanti: Eastern Michigan University Press.

Moats, David. 2004. *Civil Wars: A Battle for Gay Marriage.* Orlando, FL: Harcourt.

Mohler, J. David, and Edward C. Bolmeier. 1968. *Law of Extracurricular Activities in Secondary Schools.* Cincinnati, OH: W. H. Anderson.

Mohr, Richard D. 2005. *The Long Arc of Justice: Lesbian and Gay Marriage, Equality, and Rights.* New York: Columbia University Press.

Monsma, Stephen V., ed. 2002. *Church-State Relations in Crisis: Debating Neutrality.* Lanham, MD: Rowman & Littlefield.

Montagu, Ashley, ed. 1984. *Science and Creationism.* New York: Oxford University Press.

Mooney, Christopher F. 1990. *Boundaries Dimly Perceived: Law, Religion, Education, and the Common Good.* Notre Dame, IN: University of Notre Dame Press.

Moore, Randy. 2002. *Evolution in the Courtroom: A Reference Guide.* Santa Barbara, CA: ABC-CLIO.

Moran, Rachel F. 2001. *Interracial Intimacy: The Regulation of Race and Romance.* Chicago: University of Chicago Press.

Muller, Eric L. 2001. *Free to Die for Their Country: The Story of the Japanese American Draft Resisters in World War II.* Chicago: University of Chicago Press.

Murphy, Bruce Allen. 1982. *The Brandeis/Frankfurter Connection.* New York: Oxford University Press.

Murphy, Paul L., ed. 1990. *The Bill of Rights and American Legal History.* New York: Garland.

Murphy, Teresa Anne. 1992. *Ten Hours' Labor: Religion, Reform, and Gender in Early New England.* Ithaca, NY: Cornell University Press.

National Academy of Sciences. 1999. *Science and Creationism: A View from the National Academy of Sciences.* Washington, DC: National Academy Press.

National Academy of Sciences. 1998. *Teaching about Evolution and the Nature of Science.* Washington, DC: National Academy Press.

National Indian Law Library. 2002. *Landmark Indian Law Cases.* Buffalo, NY: William S. Hein.

Newbeck, Phyl. 2004. *Virginia Hasn't Always Been for Lovers: Interracial Marriage Bans and the Case of Richard and Mildred Loving.* Carbondale: Southern Illinois University Press.

Newton, Merlin Owen. 1995. *Armed with the Constitution: Jehovah's Witnesses in Alabama and the U.S. Supreme Court, 1939–1946.* Tuscaloosa: University of Alabama Press.

Noll, Mark A., ed. 1990. *Religion and American Politics: From the Colonial Period to the 1980s.* New York: Oxford University Press.

Noonan, John Thomas. 1998. *The Lustre of Our Country: The American Experience of Religious Freedom.* Berkeley: University of California Press.

Nord, Warren A. 1995. *Religion and American Education: Rethinking a National Dilemma.* Chapel Hill: University of North Carolina Press.

Numbers, Ronald L. 1992. *The Creationists.* New York: Knopf.

O'Brien, David M. 2004. *Animal Sacrifice and Religious Freedom: Church of the Lukumi Babalu Aye v. City of Hialeah.* Lawrence: University Press of Kansas.

Olyan, Saul M., and Martha C. Nussbaum, eds. 1998. *Sexual Orientation and Human Rights in American Religious Discourse.* New York: Oxford University Press.

Ostler, Jeffrey. 2004. *The Plains Sioux and U.S. Colonialism from Lewis and Clark to Wounded Knee.* New York: Cambridge University Press.

Outhwaite, R. B., ed. 1982. *Marriage and Society: Studies in the Social History of Marriage.* New York: St. Martin's Press.

Owen, J. Judd. 2001. *Religion and the Demise of Liberal Rationalism: The Foundational Crisis of the Separation of Church and State.* Chicago: University of Chicago Press.

Parfitt, Tudor, and Yulia Egorova, eds. 2004. *Jews, Muslims, and Mass Media: Mediating the "Other."* New York: RoutledgeCurzon.

Patrick, John J., and Gerald P. Long, eds. 1999. *Constitutional Debates on Freedom of Religion: A Documentary History.* Westport, CT: Greenwood Press.

Pegram, Thomas R. 1998. *Battling Demon Rum: The Struggle for a Dry America, 1800–1933.* Chicago: Ivan R. Dee.

Pennock, Robert T., ed. 2001. *Intelligent Design Creationism and Its Critics: Philosophical, Theological, and Scientific Perspectives.* Cambridge, MA: MIT Press.

Perry, Michael J. 1999. *We the People: The Fourteenth Amendment and the Supreme Court.* New York: Oxford University Press.

Peters, Edward. 1978. *The Magician, the Witch, and the Law.* Philadelphia: University of Pennsylvania Press.

Peters, Shawn Francis. 2000. *Judging Jehovah's Witnesses: Religious Persecution and the Dawn of the Rights Revolution.* Lawrence: University Press of Kansas.

Peters, Shawn Francis. 2003. *The Yoder Case: Religious Freedom, Education, and Parental Rights.* Lawrence: University Press of Kansas.

Peterson, Carl L. 1998. *Avoidance and Evasion of Military Service: An American History, 1626–1973.* San Francisco: International Scholars.

Peterson, H. C., and Gilbert Fite. 1957. *Opponents of War.* Madison: University of Wisconsin Press.

Peterson, Merrill D., and Robert C. Vaughan. 1988. *The Virginia Statute for Religious Freedom: Its Evolution and Consequences in American History.* Cambridge: Cambridge University Press.

Peterson, Paul E., and David E. Campbell, eds. 2001. *Charters, Vouchers, and Public Education.* Washington, DC: Brookings Institution Press.

Poindexter, Beverly M., ed. 1969. *Selective Service: The Attorney's View.* Ann Arbor, MI: Institute of Continuing Legal Education.

Pollack, Sheldon David. 1996. *The Failure of U.S. Tax Policy: Revenue and Politics.* University Park: Pennsylvania State University Press.

Powell, Arthur G., Eleanor Farrar, and David K. Cohen. 1985. *The Shopping Mall High School: Winners and Losers in the Educational Marketplace.* Boston: Houghton Mifflin.

Prejean, Helen. 1994. *Dead Man Walking: An Eyewitness Account of the Death Penalty in the United States.* New York: Vintage Books.

Prejean, Helen. 2005. *The Death of Innocents: An Eyewitness Account of Wrongful Executions.* New York: Random House.

Pulliam, John D., and James Van Patten. 1995. *History of Education in America.* Englewood Cliffs, NJ: Merrill.

Purkiss, Diane. 1996. *The Witch in History: Early Modern and Twentieth-Century Representations.* New York: Routledge.

Radan, Peter, Denise Meyerson, and Rosalind F. Croucher. 2005. *Law and Religion: God, the State and the Common Law.* New York: Routledge.

Ramsey, Claire L. 1997. *Deaf Children in Public Schools: Placement, Context, and Consequences.* Washington, DC: Gallaudet University Press.

Randall, E.Vance. 1994. *Private Schools and Public Power: A Case for Pluralism.* New York: Teachers College Press, Teachers College, Columbia University.

Raskin, Jamin B. 2003. *We the Students: Supreme Court Decisions for and about Students.* Washington, DC: CQ Press.

Ravitch, Frank S.1999. *School Prayer and Discrimination: The Civil Rights of Religious Minorities and Dissenters.* Boston: Northeastern University Press.

Reagan, Leslie J. 1997. *When Abortion Was a Crime: Women, Medicine, and Law in the United States, 1867–1973.* Berkeley: University of California Press.

Reed, Betsy. 2002. *Nothing Sacred: Women Respond to Religious Fundamentalism and Terror.* New York: Thunder's Mouth Press.

Reis, Elizabeth, ed.1998. *Spellbound: Women and Witchcraft in America.* Wilmington, DE: Scholarly Resources.

Rhode, Deborah L. 1989. *Justice and Gender: Sex Discrimination and the Law.* Cambridge, MA: Harvard University Press.

Rich, Andrew. 2004. *Think Tanks, Public Policy, and the Politics of Expertise.* New York: Cambridge University Press.

Richardson, Darcy G. 2004. *Others: Third Party Politics from the Nation's Founding to the Rise and Fall of the Greenback-Labor Party.* New York: IUniverse.

Robbins, Thomas, and Susan J. Palmer, eds. 1997. *Millennium, Messiahs, and Mayhem: Contemporary Apocalyptic Movements.* New York: Routledge.

Rochford, E. Burke. 1985. *Hare Krishna in America.* New Brunswick, NJ: Rutgers University Press.

Rogers, Nicholas. 2002. *Halloween: From Pagan Ritual to Party Night.* New York: Oxford University Press.

Rose, Kenneth D. 1996. *American Women and the Repeal of Prohibition.* New York: New York University Press.

Roth, Andrew R. 2001. *Saving for College and the Tax Code: A New Spin on the "Who Pays for Higher Education?" Debate.* New York: Garland.

Rubenstein, Michael C. 1998. *Title I Services for Private School Students under the Reauthorization of*

ESEA: A Snapshot of Federal Assistance in Transition. Washington, DC: U.S. Department of Education, Office of the Under Secretary, Office of Educational Research and Improvement, Educational Resources Information Center.

Russo, Charles J. 2003. *"The Pledge of Allegiance:* Patriotic Duty or Unconstitutional Establishment of Religion." *School Business Affairs* (July/August 2003): 22–27.

Rutherglen, George. 1996. *Major Issues in the Federal Law of Employment Discrimination.* Washington, DC: Federal Judicial Center.

Ryden, David K., ed. 2000. *The U.S. Supreme Court and the Electoral Process.* Washington, DC: Georgetown University Press.

Sandin, Robert T. 1990. *Autonomy and Faith: Religious Preference in Employment Decisions in Religiously Affiliated Higher Education.* Atlanta: Omega.

Sarna, Jonathan D. 2004. *American Judaism: A History.* New Haven: Yale University Press.

Schneider, Gregory L., ed. 2003. *Conservatism in America since 1930: A Reader.* New York: New York University Press.

Schuh, John H., ed. 2003. *Contemporary Financial Issues in Student Affairs.* San Francisco: Jossey-Bass.

Schultz, David A., and Christopher E. Smith. 1996. *The Jurisprudential Vision of Justice Antonin Scalia.* Lanham, MD: Rowman & Littlefield.

Schwartz, Bernard. 1990. *The Ascent of Pragmatism: The Burger Court in Action.* Reading, MA: Addison-Wesley.

Schwartz, Bernard. 1992. *The Great Rights of Mankind: A History of the American Bill of Rights.* Madison, WI: Madison House.

Schwartz, Bernard. 1983. *Super Chief, Earl Warren and His Supreme Court: A Judicial Biography.* New York: New York University Press.

Schwartz, Gary. 1970. *Sect Ideologies and Social Status.* Chicago: University of Chicago Press.

Schwendiman, Jed, and Jennifer Fager. 1999. *After-School Programs: Good for Kids, Good for Communities.* Portland, OR: Northwest Regional Educational Laboratory.

Sears, James T., with James C. Carper, eds. 1998. *Curriculum, Religion, and Public Education: Conversations for an Enlarging Public Square.* New York: Teachers College Press.

Segers, Mary C., and Ted G. Jelen. 1998. *A Wall of Separation? Debating the Public Role of Religion.* Lanham, MD: Rowman & Littlefield.

Selective Service System. 1984. *A Short History of the Selective Service System.* Washington, DC: Office of

Public Affairs, National Headquarters, Selective Service System.

Shulman, Carol Herrnstadt. 1974. *Private Colleges: Present Conditions and Future Prospects.* Washington, DC: American Association for Higher Education.

Sickels, Robert Judd. 1988. *John Paul Stevens and the Constitution: The Search for Balance.* University Park: Pennsylvania State University Press.

Sikorski, Robert, ed. 1993. *Prayer in Public Schools and the Constitution, 1961–1992.* New York: Garland.

Simon, James F. 1989. *The Antagonists: Hugo Black, Felix Frankfurter and Civil Liberties in Modern America.* New York: Simon and Schuster.

Sistare, Christine T., ed. 2004. *Civility and Its Discontents: Essays on Civic Virtue, Toleration, and Cultural Fragmentation.* Lawrence: University Press of Kansas.

Smith, Paul Chaat, and Robert Allen Warrior. 1996. *Like a Hurricane: The Indian Movement from Alcatraz to Wounded Knee.* New York: New Press.

Smith, Rodney K. 1987. *Public Prayer and the Constitution: A Case Study in Constitutional Interpretation.* Wilmington, DE: Scholarly Resources.

Snay, Mitchell. 1993. *Gospel of Disunion: Religion and Separatism in the Antebellum South.* New York: Cambridge University Press.

Sollors, Werner. 2000. *Interracialism: Black-White Intermarriage in American History, Literature, and Law.* New York: Oxford University Press.

Spann, Girardeau A. 1993. *Race against the Court: The Supreme Court and Minorities in Contemporary America.* New York: New York University Press.

Spring, Joel H. 1989. *The Sorting Machine Revisited: National Educational Policy since 1945.* New York: Longman.

St. John, Edward P., and Michael D. Parsons. 2004. *Public Funding of Higher Education: Changing Contexts and New Rationales.* Baltimore: Johns Hopkins University Press.

Steinmetz, Paul B. 1998. *Pipe, Bible, and Peyote among the Oglala Lakota: A Study in Religious Identity.* Syracuse, NY: Syracuse University Press.

Stevens, Mitchell L. 2001. *Kingdom of Children: Culture and Controversy in the Homeschooling Movement.* Princeton, NJ: Princeton University Press.

Stychin, Carl, and Didi Herman, eds. 2001. *Law and Sexuality: The Global Arena.* Minneapolis: University of Minnesota Press.

Sullivan, A. 2004. "Kerry and Religion: A Baptist Gives the Catholic Candidate Political Advice." *Commonweal* 131, Part 11 (June 4): 13–14.

Summers, Mark W. 2000. *Rum, Romanism, and Rebellion: The Making of a President, 1884.* Chapel Hill, NC: University of North Carolina Press.

Swanson, Wayne R. 1990. *The Christ Child Goes to Court.* Philadelphia: Temple University Press.

Szafran, Robert F. 1984. *Universities and Women Faculty: Why Some Organizations Discriminate More Than Others.* New York: Praeger.

Tabor, James D. 1995. *Why Waco? Cults and the Battle for Religious Freedom in America.* Berkeley: University of California Press.

Thelin, John R. 2004. *A History of American Higher Education.* Baltimore: Johns Hopkins University Press.

Theoharis, Jeanne, and Athan Theoharis. 2003. *These Yet to Be United States: Civil Rights and Civil Liberties in America since 1945.* Belmont, CA: Wadsworth/Thomson Learning.

Thomas, R. Murray. 2006. *Religion in Schools: Controversies around the World.* Westport, CT: Praeger.

Treat, James. 2003. *Around the Sacred Fire.* New York: Palgrave Macmillan.

Tribe, Laurence H. 1990. *Abortion: The Clash of Absolutes.* New York: Norton.

Tushnet, Mark V. 2005. *A Court Divided: The Rehnquist Court and the Future of Constitutional Law.* New York: Norton.

Tushnet, Mark V. 1997. *Making Constitutional Law: Thurgood Marshall and the Supreme Court, 1961–1991.* New York: Oxford University Press.

Tweed, Thomas A., ed. 1997. *Retelling U.S. Religious History.* Berkeley: University of California Press.

Twomley, Dale E. 1979. *Parochiaid and the Courts.* Berrien Springs, MI: Andrews University Press.

Urofsky, Melvin I. 2002. *Religious Freedom: Rights and Liberties under the Law.* Santa Barbara, CA: ABC-CLIO.

U.S. Department of Education. 2000. *Benefits for Private School Students and Teachers from Federal Education Programs.* Washington, DC: U.S. Department of Education, Office of Non-Public Education: Office of Educational Research and Improvement, Educational Resources Information Center.

U.S. Department of Education. 1998. *Religious Expression in Public Schools: A Statement of Principles.* Washington, DC: U.S. Department of Education.

U.S. Department of Justice. 2002. *Protecting the Religious Freedom of All Americans: Federal Laws against Religious Discrimination.* Washington, DC: U.S. Department of Justice, Civil Rights Division.

U.S. Equal Employment Opportunity Commission. 2000. *The Story of the United States Equal Employment Opportunity Commission: Ensuring the Promise of Opportunity for 35 Years, 1965–2000.* Washington, DC: U.S. Equal Employment Opportunity Commission.

Van Galen, Jane, and Mary Anne Pitman. 1991. *Home Schooling: Political, Historical, and Pedagogical Perspectives.* Norwood, NJ: Ablex.

Van Sickel, Robert W. 1998. *Not a Particularly Different Voice: The Jurisprudence of Sandra Day O'Connor.* New York: P. Lang.

Volokh, Eugene. 2004. "First Myths: Some on the Right Are Getting the First Amendment Wrong." *The National Review* (January 5). http://national review.com/comment/volokh200401050906.asp (accessed June 25, 2006).

Wald, Kenneth D. 1987. *Religion and Politics in the United States.* New York: St. Martin's Press.

Walker, Samuel. 1990. *In Defense of American Liberties: A History of the ACLU.* New York: Oxford University Press.

Wallenstein, Peter. 2002. *Tell the Court I Love My Wife: Race, Marriage, and Law: An American History.* New York: Palgrave Macmillan.

Wallis, Jim. 2005. *God's Politics: Why the Right Gets It Wrong and the Left Doesn't Get It.* San Francisco: HarperSanFrancisco.

Wardle, Lynn D., ed. 2003. *Marriage and Same-Sex Unions: A Debate.* Westport, CT: Praeger.

Wasby, Stephen L., ed. 1990. *"He Shall Not Pass This Way Again": The Legacy of Justice William O. Douglas.* Pittsburgh, PA: University of Pittsburgh Press for the William O. Douglas Institute.

Washington, Joseph R.1970. *Marriage in Black and White.* Boston: Beacon Press.

Weil, Danny K. 2002. *School Vouchers and Privatization: A Reference Handbook.* Santa Barbara, CA: ABC-CLIO.

Weitz, Mark A. 2001. *Clergy Malpractice in America: Nally v. Grace Community Church of the Valley.* Lawrence: University Press of Kansas.

White House Historical Association. 2005, July 5. "President and Public Pressure." http://www.whitehousehistory.org/04/subs/04_a03_d01.html (accessed June 25, 2006).

Whitehead, John W. 1993. *Home Education: Rights and Reasons.* Wheaton, IL: Crossway Books.

Wildenthal, Bryan H. 2003. *Native American Sovereignty on Trial: A Handbook with Cases, Laws, and Documents.* Santa Barbara, CA: ABC-CLIO.

Wiley, Dinah. 1984. *Public and Nonpublic School Relationships: Lighthouse Approaches for State Policymakers.* Alexandria, VA: National Association of State Boards of Education.

Williams, Mary, ed. 2005. *Education: Opposing Viewpoints.* Detroit: Greenhaven Press.

Witmer, Linda F. 2002. *The Indian Industrial School.* Carlisle, PA: Cumberland County Historical Society.

Witte, John. 2000. *Religion and the American Constitutional Experiment: Essential Rights and Liberties.* Boulder, CO: Westview Press.

Wolfson, Evan. 2004. *Why Marriage Matters: America, Equality, and Gay People's Right to Marry.* New York: Simon and Schuster.

Wood, Jr., James E. 1984. *Religion, the State, and Education.* Waco, TX: Baylor University Press.

Wunder, John R., ed. 1996. *Native American Cultural and Religious Freedoms.* New York: Garland.

Wuthnow, Robert. 2004. *Saving America? Faith-Based Services and the Future of Civil Society.* Princeton, NJ: Princeton University Press.

Yarbrough, Tinsley E. 2000. *The Burger Court: Justices, Rulings, and Legacy.* Santa Barbara, CA: ABC-CLIO.

Yarbrough, Tinsley E. 1988. *Mr. Justice Black and His Critics.* Durham, NC: Duke University Press.

Yarnold, Barbara M. 2000. *Religious Wars in the Courts.* Huntington, NY: Nova Science Publishers.

Zahn, Gordon Charles. 1979. *Another Part of the War: The Camp Simon Story.* Amherst: University of Massachusetts Press.

Zanca, Kenneth J., ed. 1994. *American Catholics and Slavery, 1789–1866: An Anthology of Primary Documents.* Lanham, MD: University Press of America.

Ziegler, Jean. 1998. *The Swiss, the Gold, and the Dead.* New York: Harcourt Brace.

INDEX

ABOUT THE AUTHOR

Dr. Scott A. Merriman teaches history at the University of Kentucky and online for the University of Maryland University College. He received his Ph.D. from the University of Kentucky in 2003. Scott has served as an associate editor of *History Reviews On-Line* and the *Journal of the Association for History and Computing.* His current research interests include the Espionage and Sedition Acts during World War I and the interaction of technology and teaching.

His books include *The History Highway: A 21st Century Guide to Internet Resources, History .edu: Essays on Teaching with Technology,* and *The History Highway 3.0: A Guide to Internet Resources.* He has contributed to the *Register of the Kentucky Historical Society, Historical Encyclopedia of World Slavery, American National Biography, Choice,* and *American Decades Primary Sources,* among numerous other publications.